A FRAMEWORK FOR MARKETING MANAGEMENT

Fifth Edition

International Edition

Philip Kotler

Northwestern University

Kevin Lane Keller

Dartmouth College

Boston   Columbus   Indianapolis   New York   San Francisco   Upper Saddle River
Amsterdam   Cape Town   Dubai   London   Madrid   Milan   Munich   Paris   Montreal   Toronto
Delhi   Mexico City   Sao Paulo   Sydney   Hong Kong   Seoul   Singapore   Taipei   Tokyo

Editorial Director: Sally Yagan
Editor-in-Chief: Eric Svendsen
Executive Editor: Melissa Sabella
Senior Acquisitions Editor, Global Edition:
  Steven Jackson
Director of Editorial Services: Ashley Santora
Editorial Project Manager: Kierra Bloom
Editorial Assistant: Elizabeth Scarpa
Director of Marketing: Patrice Lumumba Jones
Senior Marketing Manager: Anne Fahlgren
Marketing Manager, International: Dean Erasmus

Managing Editor: Judy Leale
Production Project Manager: Ann Pulido
Senior Operations Supervisor: Arnold Vila
Manufacturing Buyer: Cathleen Petersen
Creative Director: John Christiano
Senior Art Director: Blair Brown
Text Design: Blair Brown
Cover Design: Blair Brown and Jodi Notowitz
Full-Service Project Management: Sharon
  Anderson/BookMasters, Inc.
Cover Printer: Lehigh-Phoenix Color/Hagerstown

Pearson Education Limited
Edinburgh Gate
Harlow
Essex CM20 2JE
England

and Associated Companies throughout the world

Visit us on the World Wide Web at:
www.pearsoned.co.uk

© Pearson Education Limited 2012

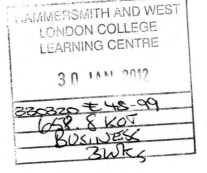

The rights of Philip Kotler and Kevin Lane Keller to be identified as authors of this work have been asserted by them in accordance with the Copyright, Designs and Patents Act 1988.

Authorised adaptation from the United States edition, entitled A Framework for Marketing Management, 5th Edition, ISBN: 978-0-13-253930-2 by Philip Kotler and Kevin Lane Keller, published by Pearson Education, publishing as Prentice Hall © 2012.

Credits and acknowledgments borrowed from other sources and reproduced, with permission, in this textbook appear on the appropriate page within text.

ISBN 13: 978-0-273-75251-6
ISBN 10: 0-273-75251-0

British Library Cataloguing-in-Publication Data
A catalogue record for this book is available from the British Library

10 9 8 7 6 5 4 3 2 1
15 14 13 12 11

Typeset in 10/12 Minion by Integra
Printed and bound by Edward Brothers in The United States of America

The publisher's policy is to use paper manufactured from sustainable forests.

A FRAMEWORK FOR MARKETING MANAGEMENT

International Edition

Brief Contents

Contents

Preface

The fifth edition of *A Framework for Marketing Management* is a concise paperback adapted from Philip Kotler and Kevin Lane Keller's fourteenth edition of *Marketing Management*. Its streamlined approach will appeal to those who want an authoritative account of current marketing management practices and theory plus a text that is short enough to allow the incorporation of outside cases, simulations, and projects. Like previous editions, the fifth edition of *A Framework for Marketing Management* is dedicated to helping companies, groups, and individuals adapt their marketing strategies and management to the marketplace of the twenty-first century.

WHAT'S NEW IN THE FIFTH EDITION

- New coverage of the changing social media landscape and the communications environment, including Facebook, Twitter, YouTube, mobile marketing, and other key trends and issues.
- New coverage of recent, dramatic changes in the marketing environment, including the rise of sustainability and "green" marketing, the challenges of marketing during difficult economic periods, and the effect of rapid technological advances on marketing management.
- New opening vignettes for each chapter show marketing management in action at real-world companies and provide great classroom discussion starters for chapter concepts. Companies featured in the fifth edition include Yahoo!, Kimberly-Clark, LEGO, Club Med, and lululemon.
- New "Marketing Insight" boxes cover a variety of cutting-edge topics and marketing situations, showcasing the latest marketing thinking and techniques. Topics include price increase strategies, channel marketing, account management, and the marketing of organic products.
- New coverage of contemporary theories and approaches such as behavioral decision theory, brand equity models, brand mantras, multichannel marketing, buzz marketing, e-commerce, and m-commerce.
- Updated supplements.

FEATURES OF THE FIFTH EDITION
Major Themes

Building on the broad theme of holistic marketing, this new edition explores the vital role of creativity and innovation in successful marketing. Other major themes include customer value creation, marketing ethics and social responsibility, and marketing accountability. Another key theme is the impact of technology on contemporary marketing, driving developments as diverse as podcasts and marketing dashboards. And in updating every chapter, we have incorporated the latest concepts and ideas drawn from recent academic research studies.

STUDENT SUPPLEMENTS
Marketing Management Cases

Through Pearson Education Custom Business, instructors can create Custom Coursepacks or CustomCaseBooks for each course. Resources include top-tier cases from Darden, Harvard, Ivey, NACRA, and Thunderbird, plus full access to a database of articles. For details on how to order these value-priced packages, contact your local rep. To aid in your case selection, we have provided the following list of cases from our custom business Web site:

9-583-151	National Chemical Corp.: Tiger-Tread	Richard N. Cardozo	General Marketing	Harvard Business School Publishing
9-396-264	Virtual Vineyards	Jeffrey F. Rayport, Alvin J. Silk, Thomas A. Gerace, Lisa R. Klein	Marketing Strategy	Harvard Business School Publishing
9-593-064	Colgate-Palmolive Co.: The Precision Toothbrush	John A. Quelch, Nathalie Laidler	Marketing Strategy	Harvard Business School Publishing
9-504-009	XM Satellite Radio (A)	David B. Godes, Elie Ofek	Marketing Strategy	Harvard Business School Publishing
9-501-021	Freeport Studio	Rajiv Lal, James B. Weber	Market Research	Harvard Business School Publishing
9-501-002	Omnitel Pronto Italia	Rajiv Lal, Carin-Isabel Knoop, Suma Raju	Market Research	Harvard Business School Publishing
9-593-082	Bayerische Motoren Werke AG (BMW)	Robert J. Dolan	Market Research	Harvard Business School Publishing
9-703-516	Ice-Fili	Michael G. Rukstad, Sasha Mattu, Asya Petinova	Market Research	Harvard Business School Publishing
9-599-113	The Coop: Market Research	Ruth Bolton, Youngme Moon	Market Research	Harvard Business School Publishing
9-500-024	The Brita Products Co	John Deighton	Customer Retention	Harvard Business School Publishing
9-501-050	Customer Value Measurement at Nortel Networks—Optical Networks Division	Das Narayandas	Customer Retention	Harvard Business School Publishing
9-582-026	CIBA-GEIGY Agricultural Division	Benson P. Shapiro, Anne T. Pigneri, Roy H. Schoeman	Consumer Marketing	Harvard Business School Publishing
9-595-035	Nestle Refrigerated Foods: Contadina Pasta & Pizza (A)	V. Kasturi Rangan, Marie Bell	Consumer Marketing	Harvard Business School Publishing
9-500-052	Webvan: Groceries on the Internet	John Deighton, Kayla Bakshi	Consumer Marketing	Harvard Business School Publishing
9A99A009	Augat Electronics, Inc.	Adrian Ryans	Business-to-Business Marketing	Ivey
9-500-041	VerticalNet (www.verticalnet.com)	Das Narayandas	Business-to-Business Marketing	Harvard Business School Publishing
9-598-056	L'Oréal of Paris: Bringing "Class to Mass" with Plenitude	Robert J. Dolan	Market Segmentation	Harvard Business School Publishing
9-594-001	American Airlines' Value Pricing (A)	Alvin J. Silk, Steven C. Michael	Market Segmentation	Harvard Business School Publishing
9-596-036	Land Rover North America, Inc.	Susan Fournier	Brands	Harvard Business School Publishing
9-591-133	Barco Projection Systems (A): Worldwide Niche Marketing	Rowland T. Moriarty Jr., Krista McQuade	Product Lines	Harvard Business School Publishing
9-594-074	Planet Reebok (A)	John A. Quelch, Jamie Harper	Advertising	Harvard Business School Publishing
2069	Mountain Man Brewing Company: Bringing the Brand to Light	Heide Abelli	Marketing Strategy	Harvard Business School Publishing

9-500-024	The Brita Products Co.	John Deighton	Marketing Strategy	Harvard Business School Publishing
9-582-103	Sealed Air Corp.	Robert J. Dolan	Market Positioning	Harvard Business School Publishing
9-594-023	Mary Kay Cosmetics: Asian Market Entry	John A. Quelch, Nathalie Laidler	Market Positioning	Harvard Business School Publishing
9-596-076	Dewar's (A): Brand Repositioning in the 1990s	Alvin J. Silk, Lisa R. Klein	Brands	Harvard Business School Publishing
2086	Saxonville Sausage	Kate Moore	Product Positioning	Harvard Business School Publishing
9-593-064	Colgate-Palmolive Co.: The Precision Toothbrush	John A. Quelch, Nathalie Laidler	Product Positioning	Harvard Business School Publishing
9-500-070	Priceline.com: Name Your Own Price	Robert J. Dolan	Marketing Strategy	Harvard Business School Publishing
SAW007	TiVo: Changing the Face of Television	Mohanbir Sawhney	Product Positioning	Kellogg
9-592-035	Calyx and Corolla	Walter J. Salmon, David Wylie	Services Management	Harvard Business School Publishing
9-388-064	ServiceMaster Industries, Inc.	James L. Heskett	Services Management	Harvard Business School Publishing
9-597-063	Computron, Inc.—1996	John A. Quelch	Pricing Strategy	Harvard Business School Publishing
M284A	Value Pricing at Procter & Gamble	Rajiv Lal, Mitchell Kristofferson	Pricing Strategy	Harvard Business School Publishing
9-598-109	FreeMarkets Online	V. Kasturi Rangan	Pricing Strategy	Harvard Business School Publishing
9-575-060	Southwest Airlines (A)	Christopher H. Lovelock	Pricing Strategy	Harvard Business School Publishing
9-595-001	RCI Master Distributor: The Evolution of Supplier Relationships	V. Kasturi Rangan	Distribution Channels	Harvard Business School Publishing
9-500-015	Autobytel.com	Youngme Moon	Distribution Channels	Harvard Business School Publishing
9-800-305	Staples.com	Joanna Jacobson, Thomas Eisenmann, Gillian Morris	Distribution Channels	Harvard Business School Publishing
9-503-004	GolfLogix: Measuring the Game of Golf	John T. Gourville, Jerry N. Conover	Strategic Planning	Harvard Business School Publishing
9-799-158	Matching Dell	Jan W. Rivkin, Michael E. Porter	Strategic Planning	Harvard Business School Publishing
9-593-094	MathSoft, Inc. (A)	V. Kasturi Rangan, Gordon Swartz	Strategic Planning	Harvard Business School Publishing
9-585-019	Suave (C)	Mark S. Albion	Marketing Communications	Harvard Business School Publishing
2066	MedNet.com Confronts 'Click-Through' Competition	Allegra Young	Marketing Communications	Harvard Business School Publishing
9-594-051	Northern Telecom (A): Greenwich Investment Proposal (Condensed)	Robert J. Dolan	Marketing Strategy	Harvard Business School Publishing
9-593-104	Northern Telecom (B): The Norstar Launch	Robert J. Dolan	Marketing Strategy	Harvard Business School Publishing
UVA-M-0340	Reagan-Bush '84 (A)	John Norton	Marketing Strategy	Darden
9-584-012	Milford Industries (A)	Benson P. Shapiro, Robert J. Dolan	Marketing Communications	Harvard Business School Publishing
9-584-013	Milford Industries (B)	Benson P. Shapiro, Robert J. Dolan	Marketing Communications	Harvard Business School Publishing
9-504-009	XM Satellite Radio (A)	David B. Godes, Elie Ofek	International Markets	Harvard Business School Publishing
9-598-150	Biopure Corp.	John T. Gourville	International Markets	Harvard Business School Publishing
9-595-026	Citibank: Launching the Credit Card in Asia-Pacific (A)	V. Kasturi Rangan	International Markets	Harvard Business School Publishing
9A99A016	Rougemont Fruit Nectar: Distributing in China	Tom Gleave, Paul Beamish	International Markets	Ivey
9-505-056	Unilever in India: Hindustan Lever's Project Shakti—Marketing FMCG to the Rural Consumer	V. Kasturi Rangan, Rohithari Rajan	International Markets	Harvard Business School Publishing

Framework of Marketing Management Video Library

Take your students on location and behind closed doors with the Marketing Management Video Library. Each video clip profiles a well-known company leading the way in its industry. Highlighting various companies, the issue-focused footage includes interviews with top executives, industry research analysts, and marketing and advertising experts. A video guide, including synopses and discussion questions, is available. The video library is available on DVD.

**Marketing
PlanPro**

The Marketing Plan Handbook, *Fourth Edition with Marketing Plan Pro*

The new edition of *The Marketing Plan Handbook*, by Marian Burk Wood, supplements the in-text marketing plan material with an in-depth guide to what student marketers really need to know. A structured learning process leads to a complete and actionable marketing plan. Also included are timely, real-world examples that illustrate key points, sample marketing plans, and Internet resources. Marketing Plan Pro is a highly rated commercial software program that guides students through the entire marketing plan process. The software is totally interactive and features 10 sample marketing plans, step-by-step guides, and customizable charts. Customize your marketing plan to fit your marketing needs by following easy-to-use plan wizards. Follow the clearly outlined steps from strategy to implementation. Click to print, and your text, spreadsheet, and charts come together to create a powerful marketing plan. The *Handbook* and Marketing Plan Pro software are available as value-pack items at a discounted price. Contact your local Pearson Education representative for more information.

INTERPRETIVE SIMULATIONS AT-A-GLANCE

When you adopt a Pearson Education textbook packaged *with* an Interpretive simulation, each new textbook purchased will contain an access code that will give you immediate access to your simulation online from Interpretive.

To ensure your students receive textbooks that contain access codes, make sure your bookstore orders the appropriate value-package ISBN. Your local Pearson Education representative will be happy to assist you.

PharmaSim

Predominantly used in: Marketing Management, Brand Management, and Marketing Strategy.

Take the role of a brand manager in the over-the-counter cold medicine market.

This leading marketing management online simulation drives home the four Ps of marketing: pricing, promotion, product, and place (distribution), while introducing students to the concepts of brand equity and marketing planning for multiple product lines.

In PharmaSim, students take the role of a brand manager in the over-the-counter pharmaceutical industry and manage Allround, the leading multisymptom cold medicine. Over the course of up to 10 simulated periods, students may reformulate their brand, introduce a line extension, and launch a new product. PharmaSim is modeled from a brand management perspective, but the issues raised apply to marketers in any industry.

StratSim

Predominantly used in: Marketing Strategy, Marketing Management, and other advanced marketing courses.

Use a market-oriented strategy to navigate the fast-paced automobile industry.

This competitive marketing strategy simulation allows teams to target consumer segments and B2B opportunities based on market attractiveness and core competencies. Students have the opportunity to utilize advanced marketing research techniques such as conjoint analysis, perceptual mapping, and concept testing to enhance their understanding of the environment and consumers.

StratSim also highlights the importance of integrated decision making by demonstrating the impact of marketing decisions on other functional areas of the business such as operations and finance.

ACKNOWLEDGMENTS

This edition of *A Framework for Marketing Management* bears the imprint of many people who have contributed to the previous edition of this text and to the fourteenth edition of *Marketing Management*. We reserve special thanks to Marian Burk Wood for her extensive development and editorial work on this edition. Many thanks also to the professional editorial and production teams at Pearson Education. We gratefully acknowledge the many reviewers who helped shape this book over the years.

John H. Antil, University of Delaware

Bill Archer, Northern Arizona University

Timothy W. Aurand, Northern Illinois University

Ruth Clottey, Barry University

Jeff Conant, Texas A&M University

Mike Dailey, University of Texas, Arlington

Brian Engelland, Mississippi State University

Brian Gibbs, Vanderbilt University

Thomas Gruca, University of Iowa

Mark Houston, University of Missouri, Columbia

Nicole Howatt, University of Central Florida

Gopal Iyer, Florida Atlantic University

Jack Kasulis, University of Oklahoma

Susan Keaveney, University of Colorado, Denver

Bob Kent, University of Delaware

Robert Kuchta, Lehigh University

Jack K. H. Lee, City University of New York Baruch College

Ning Li, University of Delaware

Steven Lysonski, Marquette University

Naomi Mandel, Arizona State University

Ajay K. Manrai, University of Delaware

Denny McCorkle, Southwest Missouri State University

James McCullough, Washington State University

Ron Michaels, University of Central Florida

George R. Milne, University of Massachusetts, Amherst

Marian Chapman Moore, Duke University

Steve Nowlis, Arizona State University

Louis Nzegwu, University of Wisconsin, Platteville

K. Padmanabhan, University of Michigan, Dearborn

Mary Anne Raymond, Clemson University

William Robinson, Purdue University

Carol A. Scott, University of California at Los Angeles

Stanley F. Slater, Colorado State University

Robert Spekman, University of Virginia

Edwin Stafford, Utah State University

Vernon Stauble, California State Polytechnic

Mike Swenson, Brigham Young University

Kimberly A. Taylor, Florida International University

Bronis J. Verhage, Georgia State University

Philip Kotler
S. C. Johnson & Son Distinguished Professor
   of International Marketing
Kellogg School of Management
Northwestern University
Evanston, Illinois

Kevin Lane Keller
E.B. Osborn Professor of Marketing
Tuck School of Business
Dartmouth College
Hanover, New Hampshire

A FRAMEWORK FOR MARKETING MANAGEMENT

International Edition

Defining Marketing for the 21st Century

In this chapter, we will address the following questions:

1. Why is marketing important?
2. What is the scope of marketing?
3. What are some fundamental marketing concepts and new marketing realities?
4. What are the tasks necessary for successful marketing management?

Marketing Management at "Obama for President"

The "Obama for America" presidential campaign combined a charismatic politician, a powerful message of hope, and a thoroughly integrated marketing program. The marketing plan aimed to expand the electorate via broader messages while targeting very specific audiences using both online and offline media, free and paid. When research showed that the more voters learned about Barack Obama, the more they identified with him, the campaign added long-form videos to traditional print, broadcast, and outdoor ads.

The Obama team—aided by its agency GMMB—also put the Internet at the heart of the 50-state campaign, seeking to "build online tools to help people self-organize and then get out of their way." Although social media like Facebook, Meetup, YouTube, and Twitter were crucial, perhaps Obama's most powerful digital tool was a massive 13.5 million–name e-mail list. The results: About $500 million (most in sums of less than $100) was raised online from 3 million donors; 35,000 groups were organized through the My.BarackObama.com site; 1,800 videos were posted to YouTube; and, of course, Obama was elected president.[1]

Good marketing is no accident, but a result of careful planning and execution using state-of-the-art tools and techniques. It becomes both an art and a science as marketers strive to find creative new solutions to often-complex challenges amid profound changes in the 21st century marketing environment. In this book, we describe how top marketers balance discipline and imagination to address these new marketing realities. In the first chapter, we lay the foundation by reviewing important marketing concepts, tools, frameworks, and issues.

The Importance of Marketing

The first decade of the 21st century challenged firms to prosper financially and even survive in the face of an unforgiving economic environment. Marketing is playing a key role in addressing those challenges. Finance, operations, accounting, and other business functions won't really matter without sufficient demand for products and services so the firm can make a profit. In other words, there must be a top line for there to be a bottom line. Thus financial success often depends on marketing ability.

Marketing's broader importance extends to society as a whole. Marketing has helped introduce and gain acceptance of new products that have eased or enriched people's lives. It can inspire enhancements in existing products as marketers innovate to improve their marketplace position. Successful marketing builds demand for goods and services, which, in turn, creates jobs. By contributing to the bottom line, successful marketing also allows firms to more fully engage in socially responsible activities.[2]

Many organizations now have a chief marketing officer (CMO), to put marketing on a more equal footing with other C-level executives such as the chief financial officer (CFO) or chief information officer (CIO).[3] However, making the right marketing decisions isn't always easy. Marketers must decide what features to design into a new product or service, what prices to set, where to sell offerings, and how much to spend on advertising, sales, Internet marketing, or mobile marketing. They must make those decisions in an Internet-fueled environment where consumers, competition, technology, and economic forces change rapidly, and the consequences of the marketer's words and actions can quickly multiply.

At greatest risk are firms that fail to carefully monitor their customers and competitors, continuously improve their value offerings and marketing strategies, or satisfy their employees, stockholders, suppliers, and channel partners in the process. Good marketers are always seeking new ways to satisfy their customers and beat the competition.[4]

The Scope of Marketing

To prepare to be a marketer, you need to understand what marketing is, how it works, who does it, and what is marketed.

What Is Marketing?

Marketing is about identifying and meeting human and social needs. One of the shortest good definitions of marketing is "meeting needs profitably." When eBay recognized that people were unable to locate some of the items they desired most, it created an online auction clearinghouse. When IKEA noticed that people wanted good furnishings at substantially lower prices, it created knockdown furniture. These two firms demonstrated marketing savvy and turned a private or social need into a profitable business opportunity.

The American Marketing Association offers the following formal definition: *Marketing is the activity, set of institutions, and processes for creating, communicating, delivering, and exchanging offerings that have value for customers, clients, partners, and society at large.*[5] We see **marketing management** as *the art and science of choosing target markets and getting, keeping, and growing customers through creating, delivering, and communicating superior customer value.*

Note that selling is *not* the most important part of marketing. Peter Drucker, a leading management theorist, says that "the aim of marketing is to make selling superfluous. The aim of marketing is to know and understand the customer so well that the product or service fits him and sells itself. Ideally, marketing should result in a customer who is ready to buy. All that should be needed then is to make the product or service available."[6] When Apple designed its iPhone and when Toyota introduced its Prius hybrid automobile, these companies were swamped with orders because they designed the right product based on careful marketing homework.

What Is Marketed?

Marketers market 10 main types of entities: goods, services, events, experiences, persons, places, properties, organizations, information, and ideas.

Goods   Physical goods constitute the bulk of most countries' production and marketing efforts. Each year, U.S. companies market billions of fresh, canned, bagged, and frozen food products and other tangible items.

Services   As economies advance, a growing proportion of their activities focuses on the production of services. The U.S. economy today produces a 70–30 services-to-goods mix. Services include the work of airlines, hotels, car rental firms, barbers and beauticians, maintenance and repair people, and accountants, bankers, lawyers, engineers, doctors, and software programmers. Many market offerings mix goods and services, such as restaurants offering both food and service.

Events   Marketers promote time-based events, such as major trade shows, artistic performances, and company anniversaries. Global sporting events such as the Olympics and the World Cup are promoted aggressively to both companies and fans.

Experiences   By orchestrating services and goods, a firm can create, stage, and market experiences. At Walt Disney World's Magic Kingdom, for example, customers can visit a fairy kingdom or a pirate ship. There is also a market for customized experiences, such as attending baseball camp with retired major league stars.[7]

Persons   Artists, musicians, CEOs, high-profile physicians, and other professionals all get help from celebrity marketers.[8] Management consultant Tom Peters, a master at self-branding, has advised each person to become a "brand."

Places   Cities, states, regions, and nations compete to attract tourists, residents, factories, and company headquarters.[9] Place marketers include economic development specialists, real estate agents, commercial banks, local business groups, and advertising and public relations agencies.

Properties   Properties are intangible rights of ownership to either real property (real estate) or financial property (stocks and bonds), which can be bought and sold through the marketing efforts of real estate agents, investment companies, and banks.

Organizations   Organizations work to build a strong, favorable, and unique image in the minds of their target publics. Tesco's "Every Little Helps" marketing program, for instance, has vaulted it to the top of the UK supermarket industry. Universities, museums, performing arts organizations, and nonprofits also use marketing to shape their images and compete for audiences and funds.

Information   Schools and universities essentially produce, market, and distribute information at a price to parents, students, and communities. The former CEO of Siemens Medical Solutions USA once observed that his firm's product "is not necessarily an X-ray or an MRI, but information. Our business is really health care information technology, and our end product is really an electronic patient record: information on lab tests, pathology, and drugs as well as voice dictation."[10]

Ideas   Every market offering includes a basic idea. For instance, social marketers are promoting such ideas as "Friends Don't Let Friends Drive Drunk" and "Don't Drive and Text."

Who Markets?

A **marketer** is someone who seeks a response—attention, a purchase, a vote, a donation—from another party, called the **prospect**. If two parties are seeking to sell something to each other, both are marketers. Marketers must have quantitative and qualitative skills, entrepreneurial attitudes, and a keen understanding of how marketing creates value within the organization.[11]

Increasingly, however, marketing is *not* done only by the marketing department. Marketers must infuse a customer perspective and orientation in business decisions affecting any customer *touch point* (where a customer directly or indirectly interacts with the company in some form)—store layouts, package designs, product functions, employee training, and shipping and logistics. They should also be involved in key management activities such as product innovation and new-business development. To create a strong marketing organization, marketers must think like executives in other departments, and executives in other departments must think more like marketers.[12]

What Is a Market?

Traditionally, a market was a physical place where buyers and sellers gathered to buy and sell goods. Economists describe a *market* as a collection of buyers and sellers who transact over a particular product or product class (such as the housing market). Marketers use the term **market** to cover groupings of customers. They view sellers as constituting the industry and buyers as constituting the market. They talk about need markets (the diet-seeking market), product markets (the shoe market), demographic markets (the youth market), and geographic markets (the Chinese market); or they extend the concept to cover voter markets, labor markets, and donor markets, for instance. Marketers may serve consumer markets, business markets, global markets, and non-profit markets, or a combination of these.

Figure 1.1 shows the relationship between the industry and the market. Sellers send goods, services, and communications (such as ads and direct mail) to the market; in return they receive money and information (customer attitudes, sales data). The inner loop shows an exchange of money for goods and services; the outer loop shows an exchange of information.

The *marketplace* is physical, such as a store you shop in; the *marketspace* is digital, as when you shop on the Internet.[13] Northwestern University's Mohan Sawhney has proposed the concept

FIGURE 1.1 A Simple Marketing System

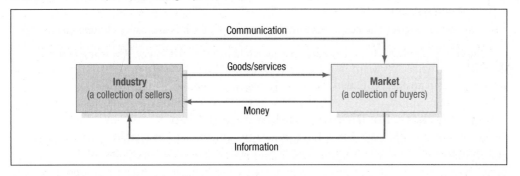

of a *metamarket* to describe a cluster of complementary products and services closely related in the minds of consumers, but spread across a diverse set of industries. The automobile metamarket consists of automobile manufacturers, new and used car dealers, financing companies, insurance companies, mechanics, spare parts dealers, service shops, auto magazines, classified auto ads in newspapers, and auto sites on the Internet.

A car buyer will engage many parts of this metamarket, creating an opportunity for *metamediaries* to assist him or her in moving seamlessly through them. Edmunds (www.edmunds.com) lets a car buyer find the features and prices of different vehicles and search for the lowest-price dealer for financing, accessories, and used cars. Metamediaries also serve other metamarkets, such as the home ownership market and the wedding market.[14]

Core Marketing Concepts

To understand the marketing function, we need to understand the following core set of concepts.

Needs, Wants, and Demands

Needs are the basic human requirements for air, food, water, clothing, and shelter. Humans also have strong needs for recreation, education, and entertainment. These needs become *wants* when they are directed to specific objects that might satisfy the need. A U.S. consumer needs food but may want a Philly cheesesteak and an iced tea. A person in Afghanistan needs food but may want rice, lamb, and carrots. Wants are shaped by our society. *Demands* are wants for specific products backed by an ability to pay. Many people want a Mercedes; only a few are able to buy one. Companies must measure not only how many people want their product, but also how many are willing and able to buy it.

These distinctions shed light on the frequent criticism that "marketers create needs" or "marketers get people to buy things they don't want." Marketers do not create needs: Needs preexist marketers. Marketers, along with other societal factors, influence wants. They might promote the idea that a Mercedes would satisfy a person's need for social status. They do not, however, create the need for social status.

Some customers have needs of which they are not fully conscious or that they cannot articulate. Consider the customer who asks for an "inexpensive car." Marketers may distinguish among five types of needs in this case:

1. Stated needs (The customer wants an inexpensive car.)
2. Real needs (The customer wants a car whose operating cost, not initial price, is low.)
3. Unstated needs (The customer expects good service from the dealer.)

4. Delight needs (The customer would like the dealer to include an onboard GPS navigation system.)
5. Secret needs (The customer wants to be seen by friends as a savvy consumer.)

Responding only to the stated need may shortchange the customer.[15] Consumers sometimes do not know what they want in a product, especially breakthrough products such as e-book readers. To gain an edge, companies must help customers learn what they want.

Target Markets, Positioning, and Segmentation

Not everyone likes the same cereal, restaurant, college, or movie. Therefore, marketers identify and profile distinct groups of buyers who might prefer or require varying product and service mixes by examining demographic, psychographic, and behavioral differences among buyers. Then the marketer decides which groups present the greatest opportunities—which are its *target markets*. For each, the firm develops a *market offering* that it *positions* in the minds of the target buyers as delivering some central benefit(s). Volvo, for example, positions its car as the safest that drivers can buy, developed for buyers concerned about automobile safety.

Offerings and Brands

Companies address customer needs by putting forth a **value proposition**, a set of benefits that satisfy those needs. The intangible value proposition is made physical by an *offering,* which can be a combination of products, services, information, and experiences. A *brand* is an offering from a known source. A brand such as McDonald's carries many associations in people's minds that make up the image: hamburgers, cleanliness, convenience, courteous service, and golden arches. All companies strive to build a strong, favorable, and unique brand image.

Value and Satisfaction

The offering will be successful if it is perceived to deliver the most *value,* the sum of the tangible and intangible benefits and costs to customers. Value, a central marketing concept, is primarily a combination of quality, service, and price, called the *customer value triad*. Value perceptions increase with quality and service but decrease with price. Marketing can be seen as the identification, creation, communication, delivery, and monitoring of customer value.

Satisfaction reflects a person's judgment of a product's perceived performance in relationship to expectations. If the performance falls short of expectations, the customer is disappointed. If it matches expectations, the customer is satisfied. If it exceeds them, the customer is delighted.

Marketing Channels

To reach a target market, the marketer uses three kinds of marketing channels. *Communication channels* deliver and receive messages from target buyers. These include newspapers, magazines, radio, television, mail, telephone, billboards, posters, and the Internet. Marketers also communicate through the look of their retail stores, their Web sites, and other media. More and more marketers are adding dialogue channels such as e-mail, blogs, and toll-free numbers to supplement monologue channels such as advertising.

The marketer uses *distribution channels* to display, sell, or deliver the physical product or service to the buyer or user. Channels may be direct to the buyer or indirect, with distributors, wholesalers, retailers, and agents serving as intermediaries. The marketer also carries out transactions with buyers using *service channels* such as warehouses, transportation companies, banks, and insurance companies. Marketers clearly face a design challenge in choosing the best mix of communication, distribution, and service channels for their offerings.

Supply Chain

The supply chain is a longer channel stretching from raw materials to components to finished products carried to final buyers. The supply chain for coffee may start with farmers who plant, tend, and pick the coffee beans. After farmers sell their harvest to wholesalers or perhaps a Fair Trade cooperative, the beans are washed, dried, and packaged for shipment, and then transported to marketers who sell directly to buyers or through wholesale and retail channels. Each company captures only a certain percentage of the total value generated by the supply chain's value delivery system. When a company acquires competitors or expands upstream or downstream, its aim is to capture a higher percentage of supply chain value.

Competition

Competition includes all the actual and potential rival offerings and substitutes a buyer might consider. An automobile manufacturer can buy steel from U.S. Steel, or from a firm based in Japan or Korea, or from mini-mills. Other alternatives are to buy aluminum for certain parts to reduce the car's weight, or to choose engineered plastics instead of steel for bumpers. Clearly, U.S. Steel would be thinking too narrowly about its competition if it thought only of other integrated steel companies. In the long run, U.S. Steel is more likely to be hurt by substitute products than by other steel companies.

Marketing Environment

The marketing environment consists of the task environment and the broad environment. The *task environment* includes the actors engaged in producing, distributing, and promoting the offering, such as the company, suppliers, distributors, dealers, and target customers. In the supplier group are material suppliers and service suppliers (such as marketing research agencies, advertising agencies, banking and insurance firms, transportation firms, and telecommunications firms). Distributors and dealers include agents, brokers, manufacturer representatives, and others who facilitate finding and selling to customers.

The *broad environment* consists of six components: demographic environment, economic environment, sociocultural environment, natural environment, technological environment, and political-legal environment. Marketers must pay close attention to the trends and developments in these environments and adjust their marketing strategies as needed.

The New Marketing Realities

Today's marketplace is dramatically different from what it was even 10 years ago. The new marketing realities are being shaped by major societal forces, new consumer capabilities, and new company capabilities.

Major Societal Forces

Major and sometimes interlinking societal forces are now creating new marketing behaviors, opportunities, and challenges. Network information technology promises to lead to more accurate levels of production, more targeted communications, and more relevant pricing. Globalization—particularly advances in transportation, shipping, and communication—makes it easier for companies to market in, and consumers to buy from, almost any country in the world. Deregulation has created greater competition and growth opportunities in many areas. In some countries, privatization is putting public firms into private hands as a way to increase efficiency.

Intense competition among domestic and foreign brands is raising marketing costs and shrinking profit margins. Many strong brands have become megabrands and have extended into other product categories, presenting a significant competitive threat. Industry convergence is increasing as companies recognize new opportunities at the intersection of two or more industries (such as the computing and consumer electronics industries converging).

Retailing is being transformed, with store-based retailers competing against nonstore retailers. For their part, consumers are seeking out new shopping "experiences." Amazon.com and others created *disintermediation* in the delivery of products and services by intervening in the traditional flow of goods through distribution channels when the Internet was young. Since then, traditional companies have engaged in *reintermediation*, becoming "brick-and-click" retailers by adding online services.

New Consumer Capabilities

Disintermediation is one reason that consumers have substantially increased buying power. They can also go online to collect information about practically any offering. Personal connections and user-generated content are thriving on social media such as Facebook, Flickr (photos), Wikipedia (encyclopedia articles), and YouTube (video).[16] Given these new consumer capabilities, some marketers are strengthening relationships by inviting customers to help design and market offerings. Nonetheless, some customers perceive few real product differences these days, and many have become less brand-loyal and more resistant to marketing efforts.

New Company Capabilities

Companies also have new capabilities. They can use the Internet as a powerful information and sales channel to augment their geographical reach. Also, they can collect fuller and richer information about markets, customers, prospects, and competitors, as well as being able to provide information to consumers and encourage purchases through online and social-media activities. Dell, for example, has generated more than $6 million in sales from its various Twitter accounts during the past three years.[17]

In addition, companies are benefiting from online and offline "buzz" through brand advocates and user communities. Thanks to special-interest TV channels and magazines, plus Internet technology, marketers can more efficiently micro-target audiences to deliver ads, coupons, and personalized messages. They are also using mobile marketing to reach consumers on the move. With advances in factory customization, computer technology, and database marketing software, manufacturers can now make and sell individually differentiated goods. Also, companies are using the Internet to improve purchasing, recruit and train employees, and facilitate internal communications. Finally, corporate buyers are increasing cost efficiency and improving service quality through skillful use of online technology.

"Marketing Insight: Marketing in an Age of Turbulence" offers some recommendations as companies adjust to the new marketing realities.

Company Orientation Toward the Marketplace

Given these new marketing realities, what philosophy should guide a company's marketing efforts? Increasingly, marketers operate consistent with the holistic marketing concept. Let's first review the evolution of earlier marketing ideas.

MARKETING IN AN AGE OF TURBULENCE

Philip Kotler and John Caslione see management entering a new Age of Turbulence in which chaos, risk, and uncertainty characterize many industries, markets, and companies. They say turbulence is the new normal, punctuated by periodic and intermittent spurts of prosperity and downturns. They see many new challenges in the foreseeable future, and unlike past recessions, there may be no assurance that a return to past management practices would ever be successful again. Therefore, marketers should keep the following eight factors in mind as they create strategies to deal with turbulence:

1. Secure your core customer segments against competitive moves.
2. Push aggressively to take market share from weakened competitors.
3. Conduct more research while customers' needs and wants are in flux.
4. Rather than cutting the marketing budget, maintain or even increase it.
5. Emphasize core values and the safety and security of your firm and your offerings.
6. Act quickly to drop programs that aren't working.
7. Don't discount your best brands.
8. Save the strongest brands and products; lose the weakest.

Source: Based on Philip Kotler and John A. Caslione, *Chaotics: The Business and Marketing in the Age of Turbulence* (New York: AMACOM, 2009), pp. 151–53.

The Production Concept

The **production concepts**, one of the oldest concepts in business, holds that consumers prefer products that are widely available and inexpensive. Managers of production-oriented businesses concentrate on achieving high production efficiency, low costs, and mass distribution. This orientation makes sense in developing countries such as China, where the largest PC manufacturer, Lenovo, takes advantage of the country's huge and inexpensive labor pool to dominate the market.[18] Marketers also apply the production concept when they want to expand the market.

The Product Concept

The **product concept** proposes that consumers favor products offering the most quality, performance, or innovative features. However, managers are sometimes caught in a love affair with their products. They might commit the "better-mousetrap" fallacy, believing a better product will by itself lead people to beat a path to their door. A new or improved product will not necessarily be successful unless it's priced, distributed, advertised, and sold properly.

The Selling Concept

The **selling concept** holds that consumers and businesses, if left alone, won't buy enough of the organization's products, so the organization must undertake an aggressive selling effort. It is practiced most aggressively with unsought goods—goods buyers don't normally think of buying, such as insurance and cemetery plots—and when firms with overcapacity aim to sell what they make, rather than make what the market wants. Marketing based on hard selling is risky. It assumes customers coaxed into buying a product not only won't return or bad-mouth it or complain to consumer organizations but might even buy it again.

The Marketing Concept

The **marketing concept** emerged in the mid-1950s[19] as a customer-centered, sense-and-respond philosophy. The job is to find not the right customers for your products, but the right products for your customers. The marketing concept holds that the key to achieving organizational goals is being more effective than competitors in creating, delivering, and communicating superior customer value to your target markets.

Harvard's Theodore Levitt drew a perceptive contrast between the selling and marketing concepts:

> Selling focuses on the needs of the seller; marketing on the needs of the buyer. Selling is preoccupied with the seller's need to convert his product into cash; marketing with the idea of satisfying the needs of the customer by means of the product and the whole cluster of things associated with creating, delivering, and finally consuming it.[20]

Several scholars found that companies embracing the marketing concept at that time achieved superior performance.[21]

The Holistic Marketing Concept

The **holistic marketing concept** is based on the development, design, and implementation of marketing programs, processes, and activities that recognize their breadth and interdependencies. Holistic marketing acknowledges that everything matters in marketing—and that a broad, integrated perspective is often necessary. Thus, holistic marketing recognizes and reconciles the scope and complexities of marketing activities. Figure 1.2 is an overview of four broad components characterizing holistic

FIGURE 1.2 Holistic Marketing Dimensions

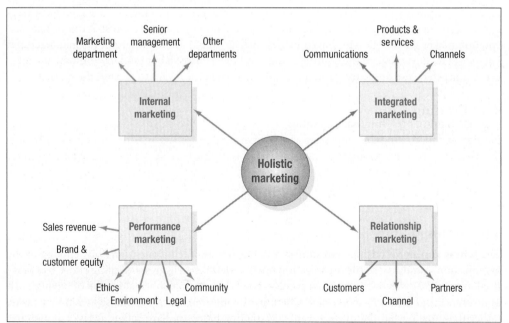

marketing, themes that will appear throughout this book: relationship marketing, integrated marketing, internal marketing, and performance marketing. Successful companies apply holistic marketing to keep their programs and activities changing with the changes in their marketplace and marketspace.

Relationship Marketing   **Relationship marketing** aims to build mutually satisfying long-term relationships with key constituents in order to earn and retain their business.[22] Four key constituents for relationship marketing are customers, employees, marketing partners (channels, suppliers, distributors, dealers, agencies), and members of the financial community (shareholders, investors, analysts).

The ultimate outcome of relationship marketing is a unique company asset called a **marketing network**, consisting of the company and its supporting stakeholders—customers, employees, suppliers, distributors, retailers, and others—with whom it has built mutually profitable business relationships. The operating principle is simple: build an effective network of relationships with key stakeholders, and profits will follow.[23]

Companies are also shaping separate offers, services, and messages to individual customers, based on information about past transactions, demographics, psychographics, and media and distribution preferences. By focusing on their most profitable customers, products, and channels, these firms hope to achieve profitable growth, capturing a larger share of each customer's expenditures by building high customer loyalty. They estimate individual customer lifetime value and design their market offerings and prices to make a profit over the customer's lifetime. Marketing must skillfully conduct not only customer relationship management, but also partner relationship management, so that partners such as suppliers and distributors will benefit, as well.

Integrated Marketing   Integrated marketing occurs when the marketer devises marketing activities and assembles marketing programs to create, communicate, and deliver value for consumers such that "the whole is greater than the sum of its parts." Two key themes are that (1) many different marketing activities can create, communicate, and deliver value and (2) marketers should design and implement any one marketing activity with all other activities in mind. When a hospital buys an MRI from General Electric's Medical Systems division, for instance, it expects good installation, maintenance, and training services along with the purchase.

Using an integrated communication strategy means choosing communication options and messages that reinforce and complement each other. The company must also develop an integrated channel strategy, weighing the trade-off between too many channels (leading to conflict among channel members and/or a lack of support) and too few (resulting in market opportunities being overlooked).

Internal Marketing   **Internal marketing**, an element of holistic marketing, is the task of hiring, training, and motivating able employees who want to serve customers well. It ensures that everyone in the organization embraces appropriate marketing principles, especially senior management. Smart marketers recognize that marketing activities *within* the company can be as important—or even more important—than those directed outside the company. It makes no sense to promise excellent service before the company's staff is ready to provide it (see "Marketing Skills: Internal Marketing").

Marketing is no longer the responsibility of a single department—it is a company-wide undertaking[25] that drives the company's vision, mission, and strategic planning. It succeeds only when all departments work together to achieve customer goals: when engineering designs the right products, finance furnishes the right amount of funding, purchasing buys the right materials, production makes the right products in the right time horizon, and accounting measures profitability in the right ways. Such interdepartmental harmony can only truly coalesce, however, when management clearly communicates a vision of how the company's marketing orientation and philosophy serve customers.

INTERNAL MARKETING

One of the most valuable skills marketers can have is the ability to select, educate, and rally people inside the organization to build mutually satisfying, long-term relationships with stakeholders. Internal marketing starts with the selection of managers and employees who have positive attitudes toward the company, its products, and its customers. The next step is to train, motivate, and empower the entire staff so that they have the knowledge, tools, and authority to provide value to customers. After establishing standards for employee performance, the final step is to monitor employee actions, then reward and reinforce good performance.

Internal marketing is a priority at the Snowshoe Mountain ski resort in Snowshoe, West Virginia. Snowshoe recently rebranded itself with a promise of an "authentic, rustic, and engaging wilderness experience" for skiers. In launching this marketing initiative, the resort's marketers started inside. They incorporated the new brand promise in a 40-page book about the resort's history and included a list of seven attitude words characterizing how employees should interact with guests. On-mountain messaging and signs also reminded employees to deliver on the brand promise. Finally, new hires attended a special marketing presentation to help them better understand the brand and become effective advocates.[24]

Performance Marketing   **Performance marketing** requires understanding the financial and nonfinancial returns to business and society from marketing activities and programs. Top marketers are increasingly going beyond sales revenue to examine the marketing scorecard and interpret what is happening to market share, customer loss rate, customer satisfaction, product quality, and other measures.

- Financial accountability. Marketers are increasingly asked to justify their investments in financial and profitability terms, as well as in terms of building the brand and growing the customer base.[26] They're employing a broader variety of financial measures and metrics to assess the direct and indirect value their marketing efforts create. They're also recognizing that much of their firms' market value comes from intangible assets, particularly brands, customer base, employees, distributor and supplier relations, and intellectual capital.

- Social responsibility marketing. Marketers must consider the ethical, environmental, legal, and social context of their role and activities.[27] The organization's task is to determine the needs, wants, and interests of target markets and satisfy them more effectively and efficiently than competitors while preserving or enhancing consumers' and society's long-term well-being. As goods become more commoditized, and consumers grow more socially conscious, some companies—including Timberland and Patagonia—incorporate social responsibility as a way to differentiate themselves from competitors, build consumer preference, and increase sales and profits. Table 1.1 displays some different types of corporate social initiatives, illustrated by McDonald's.[28]

Updating the Four Ps

McCarthy classified various marketing activities into *marketing-mix* tools of four broad kinds, which he called *the four Ps* of marketing: product, price, place, and promotion (see Figure 1.3).[29]

TABLE 1.1	Corporate Social Initiatives	
Type	**Description**	**Example**
Corporate social marketing	Supporting behavior change campaigns	McDonald's promotion of a statewide childhood immunization campaign in Oklahoma
Cause marketing	Promoting social issues through efforts such as sponsorships, licensing agreements, and advertising	McDonald's sponsorship of Forest (a gorilla) at Sydney's Zoo—a 10-year sponsorship commitment, aimed at preserving this endangered species
Cause-related marketing	Donating a percentage of revenues to a specific cause based on the revenue occurring during the announced period of support	McDonald's earmarking of $1 for Ronald McDonald Children's Charities from the sale of every Big Mac and pizza sold on McHappy Day
Corporate philanthropy	Making gifts of money, goods, or time to help nonprofit organizations, groups, or individuals	McDonald's contributions to Ronald McDonald House Charities
Corporate community involvement	Providing in-kind or volunteer services in the community	McDonald's catering meals for firefighters in the December 1997 bushfires in Australia
Socially responsible business practices	Adapting and conducting business practices that protect the environment and human and animal rights	McDonald's requirement that suppliers increase the amount of living space for laying hens on factory farms

Source: Philip Kotler and Nancy Lee, *Corporate Social Responsibility: Doing the Most Good for Your Company and Your Cause* (Hoboken, NJ: Wiley, 2004). Copyright © 2005 by Philip Kotler and Nancy Lee. Used by permission of John Wiley & Sons, Inc.

   Given the breadth, complexity, and richness of marketing, clearly these four Ps are not the whole story anymore. Table 1.2 shows an updated, more representative set that encompasses the modern realities of the holistic marketing concept: people, processes, programs, and performance. These new four Ps apply to all disciplines within the company; by thinking this way, managers grow more closely aligned with the rest of the company.

FIGURE 1.3 The Four P Components of the Marketing Mix

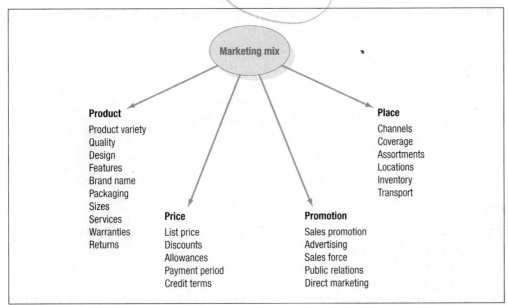

TABLE 1.2	The Evolution of Marketing Management	
Marketing Mix Four Ps		**Modern Marketing Management Four Ps**
Product	→	People
Place	→	Processes
Promotion	→	Programs
Price	→	Performance

People, employees and internal marketing, are critical to marketing success. Also, as part of the new four Ps, marketers must view consumers as people to understand their lives more broadly, and not just as they shop for and consume market offerings.

Processes are all the creativity, discipline, and structure brought to marketing management. Only by instituting the right set of processes to guide activities and programs can a firm engage in mutually beneficial long-term relationships, generate insights, and create breakthrough products, services, and marketing activities.

Programs are all the firm's consumer-directed activities, online and offline. These encompass the old four Ps as well as other marketing activities that might not fit as neatly into the old view of marketing but must be integrated to accomplish multiple objectives for the firm.

Performance reflects, as in holistic marketing, the range of possible outcomes that have financial and nonfinancial implications (profitability as well as brand and customer equity), and implications beyond the company itself (social responsibility, legal, ethical, and community related).

Marketing Management Tasks

With holistic marketing as a backdrop, we can identify a specific set of tasks that make up successful marketing management and marketing leadership.

- **Developing marketing strategies and plans.** The first task is to identify the organization's long-run opportunities, given its market experience and core competencies. Chapter 2 discusses this process in some detail.
- **Capturing marketing insights.** Marketers must closely monitor the marketing environment to continually assess market potential and forecast demand. Chapter 3 looks at marketing information and research, market demand, and the marketing environment.
- **Connecting with customers.** The firm must determine how to best create value for its chosen target markets and develop strong, profitable, long-term relationships with customers, as discussed in Chapter 4. Chapters 5 and 6 explore the analysis of consumer and business markets. Next, marketers must divide the market into major market segments, evaluate each one, and target those it can best serve, as explained in Chapter 7.
- **Building strong brands.** Marketers need to understand how customers perceive their brands' strengths and weaknesses, the subject of Chapter 8. In addition, they must develop a positioning strategy and plan ways of dealing with the competition, as discussed in Chapter 9.
- **Shaping the market offerings.** At the heart of the marketing program is the product—the firm's tangible offering to the market, which includes the product quality, design, features, and packaging, all explored in Chapter 10. Chapter 11 explains how firms can market services, and Chapter 12 examines critical marketing decisions related to pricing.

- Delivering value. How can the firm deliver value to its target market? Chapter 13 discusses channel activities needed to make the product offering accessible and available to customers. Chapter 14 explores the various types of retailers, wholesalers, and physical-distribution firms and how they make their decisions.

- Communicating value. Marketers must adequately communicate to the target market the value embodied by their products and services. They will need an integrated marketing communications program that maximizes the individual and collective contribution of all communication activities, as discussed in Chapter 15. Chapter 16 examines the use of mass communications such as advertising and public relations. Chapter 17 looks at personal communications such as direct and interactive marketing.

- Creating successful long-term growth. The marketing strategy should take into account changing global opportunities and challenges. Management must also put in place a marketing organization capable of implementing the marketing plan. See Chapter 18 for more detail.

EXECUTIVE SUMMARY

Marketing is the activity, set of institutions, and processes for creating, communicating, delivering, and exchanging offerings that have value for customers, clients, partners, and society at large. Marketing management is the art and science of choosing target markets and getting, keeping, and growing customers through creating, delivering, and communicating superior customer value. Marketers can market goods, services, events, experiences, persons, places, properties, organizations, information, and ideas. They operate in four different marketplaces: consumer, business, global, and nonprofit.

Today's marketplace is fundamentally different as a result of major societal forces that have resulted in many new consumer and company capabilities. Organizations can choose to conduct their business under five competing concepts: the production concept, the product concept, the selling concept, the marketing concept, or the holistic marketing concept. The holistic marketing concept is based on the development, design, and implementation of marketing programs, processes, and activities that recognize their breadth and interdependencies. Holistic marketing recognizes that everything matters in marketing and that a broad, integrated perspective is often necessary. Four components of holistic marketing are relationship marketing, integrated marketing, internal marketing, and performance marketing.

Successful marketing management includes developing marketing strategies and plans, capturing marketing insights, connecting with customers, building strong brands, shaping the market offerings, delivering and communicating value, and creating long-term growth. These are accomplished through a new set of four Ps based on the holistic marketing concept: people, processes, programs, and performance.

NOTES

1. "Social Electioneering: How the U.S. Created the 'Social Election,'" *Marketing*, April 8, 2010, p. 18; Michael Learmonth, "Social Media Paves Way to White House," *Advertising Age*, March 30, 2009, p. 16; Noreen O'Leary, "GMBB," *AdweekMedia*, June 15, 2009, p. 2; John Quelch, "The Marketing of a President," *Harvard Business School Working Knowledge*, November 12, 2008.

2. Philip Kotler, "Marketing: The Underappreciated Workhorse," *Market Leader*, Quarter 2 (2009), pp. 8–10.

3. Peter C. Verhoef and Peter S. H. Leeflang, "Understanding the Marketing Department's Influence within the Firm," *Journal of Marketing* 73 (March 2009), pp. 14–37.

4. Jon Fine, "Marketing's Drift Away from Media," *BusinessWeek*, August 17, 2009, p. 64.

5. American Marketing Association, "Definition of Marketing," www.marketingpower.com/AboutAMA/Pages/DefinitionofMarketing.aspx, 2007; Lisa Keefe,

"Marketing Defined," *Marketing News*, January 15, 2008, pp. 28–29.

6. Peter Drucker, *Management: Tasks, Responsibilities, Practices* (New York: Harper and Row, 1973), pp. 64–65.

7. B. Joseph Pine II and James Gilmore, *The Experience Economy* (Boston: Harvard Business School Press, 1999); Bernd Schmitt, *Experience Marketing* (New York: Free Press, 1999); Philip Kotler, "Dream Vacations: The Booming Market for Designed Experiences," *The Futurist*, October 1984, pp. 7–13.

8. Irving J. Rein, Philip Kotler, Michael Hamlin, and Martin Stoller, *High Visibility*, 3rd ed. (New York: McGraw-Hill, 2006).

9. Philip Kotler, Christer Asplund, Irving Rein, and Donald H. Haider, *Marketing Places in Europe: Attracting Investments, Industries, Residents, and Visitors to European Cities, Communities, Regions, and Nations* (London: Financial Times Prentice Hall, 1999); Philip Kotler, Irving J. Rein, and Donald Haider, *Marketing Places: Attracting Investment, Industry, and Tourism to Cities, States, and Nations* (New York: Free Press, 1993).

10. John R. Brandt, "Dare to Be Different," *Chief Executive*, May 2003, pp. 34–38.

11. Richard Rawlinson, "Beyond Brand Management," *Strategy+Business*, Summer 2006.

12. Constantine von Hoffman, "Armed with Intelligence," *Brandweek*, May 29, 2006, pp. 17–20.

13. Jeffrey Rayport and John Sviokla, "Exploring the Virtual Value Chain," *Harvard Business Review*, November–December 1995, pp. 75–85; Jeffrey Rayport and John Sviokla, "Managing in the Marketspace," *Harvard Business Review*, November–December 1994, pp. 141–50.

14. Mohan Sawhney, *Seven Steps to Nirvana* (New York: McGraw-Hill, 2001).

15. Nikolaus Franke, Peter Keinz, and Christoph J. Steger, "Testing the Value of Customization: When Do Customers Really Prefer Products Tailored to Their Preferences?" *Journal of Marketing* 73, no. 5 (September 2009), pp. 103–21.

16. Anya Kamenetz, "The Network Unbound," *Fast Company*, June 2006, pp. 69–73.

17. Christopher Calnan, "Dell, Others, Don't Pigeonhole Social Media," *Austin Business Journal*, June 19, 2010, www.bizjournals.com; Antonio Gonsalves, "Dell Makes $3 Million from Twitter-Related Sales," *InformationWeek*, June 12, 2009.

18. Michael Schuman, "Lenovo's Legend Returns," *Time*, June 10, 2010, www.time.com/time/magazine/article/0,9171,1986004,00.html.

19. Robert J. Keith, "The Marketing Revolution," *Journal of Marketing* (January 1960), pp. 35–38; John B. McKitterick,

"What Is the Marketing Management Concept?" Frank M. Bass, ed., *The Frontiers of Marketing Thought and Action* (Chicago: American Marketing Association, 1957), pp. 71–82; Fred J. Borch, "The Marketing Philosophy as a Way of Business Life," *The Marketing Concept: Its Meaning to Management* (Marketing series, no. 99; New York: American Management Association, 1957), pp. 3–5.

20. Theodore Levitt, "Marketing Myopia," *Harvard Business Review*, July–August 1960, p. 50.

21. Rohit Deshpande and John U. Farley, "Measuring Market Orientation: Generalization and Synthesis," *Journal of Market-Focused Management* 2 (1998), pp. 213–32; Ajay K. Kohli and Bernard J. Jaworski, "Market Orientation: The Construct, Research Propositions, and Managerial Implications," *Journal of Marketing* (April 1990), pp. 1–18; John C. Narver and Stanley F. Slater, "The Effect of a Market Orientation on Business Profitability," *Journal of Marketing* (October 1990), pp. 20–35.

22. Evert Gummesson, *Total Relationship Marketing* (Boston: Butterworth-Heinemann, 1999); Regis McKenna, *Relationship Marketing* (Reading, MA: Addison-Wesley, 1991); Martin Christopher, Adrian Payne, and David Ballantyne, *Relationship Marketing: Bringing Quality, Customer Service, and Marketing Together* (Oxford, UK: Butterworth-Heinemann, 1991).

23. James C. Anderson, Hakan Hakansson, and Jan Johanson, "Dyadic Business Relationships within a Business Network Context," *Journal of Marketing* (October 15, 1994), pp. 1–15.

24. Paula Andruss, "Employee Ambassadors," *Marketing News*, December 15, 2008, pp. 26–27; www.snowshoemtn.com.

25. Christian Homburg, John P. Workman Jr., and Harley Krohmen, "Marketing's Influence within the Firm," *Journal of Marketing* (January 1999), pp. 1–15.

26. Robert Shaw and David Merrick, *Marketing Payback: Is Your Marketing Profitable?* (London, UK: Pearson Education, 2005).

27. Rajendra Sisodia, David Wolfe, and Jagdish Sheth, *Firms of Endearment: How World-Class Companies Profit from Passion* (Upper Saddle River, NJ: Wharton School Publishing, 2007).

28. If choosing to develop a strategic corporate social responsibility program, see Michael E. Porter and Mark R. Kramer, "Strategy and Society: The Link between Competitive Advantage and Corporate Social Responsibility," *Harvard Business Review*, December 2006, pp. 78–92.

29. E. Jerome McCarthy and William D. Perreault, *Basic Marketing: A Global-Managerial Approach*, 14th ed. (Homewood, IL: McGraw-Hill/Irwin, 2002).

chapter 2

Developing Marketing Strategies and Plans

In this chapter, we will address the following questions:

1. How does marketing affect customer value?
2. How is strategic planning carried out at different levels of the organization?
3. What does a marketing plan include?
4. How can management assess marketing performance?

Marketing Management at Yahoo!

Founded in 1994 by Web-surfing Stanford University grad students, Yahoo! grew from a tiny upstart to a powerful force in Internet media. Yahoo! has worked hard to be more than just a search engine. The company proudly proclaims itself as "the only place anyone needs to go to find anything, communicate with anyone, or buy anything," offering e-mail, news, weather, music, photos, games, shopping, auctions, and travel services. A large percentage of revenues comes from advertising, but the company also profits from online personal ads, premium e-mail, small business services, and other services.

Although Yahoo! strives to achieve a competitive advantage over rival Google with its vast array of original content, Google's ascension to the runaway leader in search, e-mail, and related services has made it a darling with advertisers. Yahoo!'s acquisition of photo-sharing service Flickr, social bookmark manager Del.icio.us, and online video editing site Jumpcut strengthened its capabilities. It has a 10-year deal to use Microsoft's Bing search engine for searches on the Yahoo! site and share in the ad revenue. Yahoo! has also continued to grow in Europe and Asia. Looking ahead, what should Yahoo! be doing to plan for long-term marketing success?[1]

Key ingredients of the marketing management process are insightful, creative strategies and plans that can guide marketing activities. As Yahoo! knows, developing the right marketing strategy over time requires a blend of discipline and flexibility. Firms must stick to a strategy but also constantly improve it. They must also develop strategies for a range of products and services within the organization and determine how to measure marketing performance, as we discuss in this chapter.

Marketing and Customer Value

The task of any business is to deliver customer value at a profit. In a hypercompetitive economy, with increasingly informed buyers faced with abundant choices, a company can win only by fine-tuning the value delivery process and choosing, providing, and communicating superior value. Great marketing companies succeed because their marketers know how to thoughtfully and creatively devise marketing plans for delivering value and then bring them to life (see Table 2.1).

The Value Delivery Process

The traditional view of marketing is that the firm makes something and then sells it, with marketing taking place in the selling process. Companies that subscribe to this view have the best chance of succeeding in economies marked by goods shortages where consumers are not fussy about quality, features, or style—for example, basic staple goods in developing markets.

This traditional view will not work, however, in economies with many different types of people, each with individual wants, perceptions, preferences, and buying criteria. The smart competitor must design and deliver offerings for well-defined target markets. This realization inspired a new view of business processes that places marketing at the *beginning* of planning. Instead of emphasizing making and selling, companies now see themselves as part of a value delivery process.

The value creation and delivery sequence consists of three phases.[2] In the first phase, *choosing the value,* marketers segment the market, select the appropriate target, and develop the offering's value positioning. The formula "segmentation, targeting, positioning (STP)" is the essence of strategic marketing. The second phase is *providing the value* through specific product features, prices, and distribution. The third phase is *communicating the value* through the sales

---

TABLE 2.1	Characteristics of a Great Marketing Company

- The company selects target markets in which it enjoys superior advantages and exits or avoids markets where it is intrinsically weak.

- Virtually all the company's employees and departments are customer- and market-minded.

- There is a good working relationship between marketing, R&D, manufacturing, sales, and customer service.

- The company has incentives designed to lead to the right behaviors.

- The company continuously builds and tracks customer satisfaction and loyalty.

- The company manages a value delivery system in partnership with strong suppliers and distributors.

- The company is skilled in building its brand name(s) and image.

- The company is flexible in meeting customers' varying requirements.

force, Internet, advertising, and other communication tools to announce and promote the product. The value delivery process begins before there is a product and continues through development and after launch.

The Value Chain

Harvard's Michael Porter has proposed the **value chain** as a tool for identifying ways to create more customer value.[3] According to this model, every firm is a synthesis of activities performed to design, produce, market, deliver, and support its product. The value chain identifies nine strategically relevant activities—five primary and four support activities—that create value and cost in a specific business.

The *primary activities* are (1) inbound logistics, or bringing materials into the business; (2) operations, or converting materials into final products; (3) outbound logistics, or shipping out final products; (4) marketing, which includes sales; and (5) service. Specialized departments handle the *support activities*—(1) procurement, (2) technology development, (3) human resource management, and (4) firm infrastructure. (Infrastructure covers the costs of general management, planning, finance, accounting, legal, and government affairs.)

The firm's task is to examine its costs and performance in each value-creating activity and look for ways to improve it. Managers should estimate competitors' costs and performances as *benchmarks* against which to compare their own. And they should go further and study the "best of class" practices of the world's best companies. The firm's success depends not only on how well each department performs its work, but also on how well the company coordinates departmental activities to conduct these five *core business processes*.[4]

- The market-sensing process. All the activities in gathering and acting upon market information
- The new-offering realization process. All the activities in researching, developing, and launching new high-quality offerings quickly and within budget
- The customer acquisition process. All the activities in defining target markets and prospecting for new customers
- The customer relationship management process. All the activities in building deeper understanding of, relationships with, and offerings for individual customers
- The fulfillment management process. All the activities in receiving and approving orders, shipping the goods on time, and collecting payment

To be successful, a firm also needs to look for competitive advantages beyond its own operations, into the value chains of suppliers, distributors, and customers. Many companies today have partnered with specific suppliers and distributors to create a superior **value delivery network**, also called a **supply chain**.

Core Competencies

Traditionally, companies owned and controlled most of the resources that entered their businesses—labor power, materials, machines, information, and energy—but many today outsource less-critical resources if they can obtain better quality or lower cost. The key, then, is to own and nurture the resources and competencies that make up the *essence* of the business. Many textile, chemical, and computer/electronic product firms do not manufacture their own products because offshore manufacturers are more competent in this task. Instead, they focus on product design and development and marketing, their core competencies.

A **core competency** has three characteristics: (1) It is a source of competitive advantage and makes a significant contribution to perceived customer benefits; (2) it has applications in a wide variety of markets; and (3) it is difficult for competitors to imitate.[5] Competitive advantage also accrues to companies that possess *distinctive capabilities* or excellence in broader business processes.

Wharton's George Day sees market-driven organizations as excelling in three distinctive capabilities: market sensing, customer linking, and channel bonding.[6] Day says tremendous opportunities and threats often begin as "weak signals" from the "periphery" of a business.[7] He offers a systematic process for building "vigilant organizations" attuned to changes in the environment by learning from the past, evaluating the present, and envisioning the future. Competitive advantage ultimately derives from how well the company has fitted its core competencies and distinctive capabilities into tightly interlocking "activity systems." Competitors find it hard to imitate Southwest Airlines, Walmart, and IKEA because they are unable to copy their activity systems.

A Holistic Marketing Orientation and Customer Value

Holistic marketers succeed by managing a superior value chain that delivers a high level of product quality, service, and speed. They achieve profitable growth by expanding customer share, building customer loyalty, and capturing customer lifetime value through customer focus, core competencies, and a collaborative network.[8] Holistic marketers address three key management questions to create, maintain, and renew customer value:

1. *Value exploration*—How a company identifies new value opportunities
2. *Value creation*—How a company efficiently creates more promising new value offerings
3. *Value delivery*—How a company uses its capabilities and infrastructure to deliver the new value offerings more efficiently

The Central Role of Strategic Planning

Successful marketing thus requires capabilities such as understanding, creating, delivering, capturing, and sustaining customer value. To ensure they select and execute the right activities, marketers must give priority to strategic planning in three key areas: (1) managing a company's businesses as an investment portfolio, (2) assessing each business's strength by considering the market's growth rate and the company's position and fit in that market, and (3) establishing a strategy. The company must develop a game plan for achieving each business's long-run objectives.

Most large companies consist of four organizational levels: corporate, division, business unit, and product. Corporate headquarters is responsible for designing a corporate strategic plan to guide the whole enterprise; it makes decisions on the resources to allocate to each division, as well as on which businesses to start or eliminate. Each division establishes a plan covering the allocation of funds to each business unit within the division. Each business unit develops a strategic plan to carry that unit into a profitable future. Finally, each product level (product line, brand) develops a marketing plan for achieving its objectives.

The **marketing plan** is the central instrument for directing and coordinating the marketing effort, operating at both the strategic and the tactical levels. The **strategic marketing plan** lays out the target markets and the firm's value proposition, based on an analysis of the best market opportunities. The **tactical marketing plan** specifies the marketing tactics, including product features, promotion, merchandising, pricing, sales channels, and service. The complete planning, implementation, and control cycle of strategic planning is shown in Figure 2.1.

FIGURE 2.1 Strategic Planning, Implementation, and Control

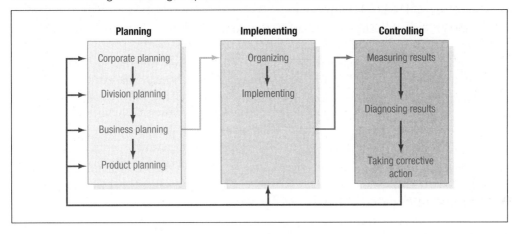

Corporate and Division Strategic Planning

All corporate headquarters undertake four planning activities: (1) defining the corporate mission, (2) establishing strategic business units, (3) assigning resources to each unit, and (4) assessing growth opportunities. These activities are discussed next.

Defining the Corporate Mission

An organization exists to accomplish something: to make cars, lend money, provide a night's lodging. Over time, the mission may change, to take advantage of new opportunities or respond to new market conditions. For example, Amazon.com changed its mission from being the world's largest online bookstore to becoming the world's largest online store.

To define its mission, a company should address Peter Drucker's classic questions:[9] What is our business? Who is the customer? What is of value to the customer? What will our business be? What should our business be? Successful companies continuously raise and answer these simple-sounding questions, which are among the most difficult that management will ever have to answer.

A clear, thoughtful **mission statement** of what the organization exists to accomplish provides employees with a shared sense of purpose, direction, and opportunity. Good mission statements focus on a limited number of goals, stress the company's major policies and values, and define the company's major competitive spheres. They also take a long-term view and are as short, memorable, and meaningful as possible.

Some key competitive dimensions for mission statements include:

- Industry. Some companies operate in only one industry; some only in a set of related industries; some only in industrial goods, consumer goods, or services; and some in any industry. For example, Caterpillar focuses on the industrial market; John Deere operates in the industrial and consumer markets.
- Products and applications. Firms define the range of products and applications they will supply. St. Jude Medical is "dedicated to developing medical technology and services that put more control in the hands of physicians, and that advance the practice of medicine and contribute to successful outcomes for every patient."
- Competence. The firm identifies the range of technological and other core competencies it will master and leverage. Japan's NEC has built its core competencies in computing,

communications, and components to support production of laptop computers, television receivers, and handheld telephones.

- Market segment. The type of market or customers a company will serve is the market segment. To illustrate, Gerber serves primarily the baby market.
- Vertical. The vertical sphere is the number of channel levels, from raw material to final product and distribution, in which a company will participate. At one extreme are companies with a large vertical scope. At the other extreme are "hollow corporations," which outsource the production of nearly all goods and services to suppliers.
- Geographical. The range of regions, countries, or country groups in which a company will operate defines its geographical sphere. Some companies operate in a specific city or state. Others are multinationals like Royal Dutch/Shell, which operates in more than 100 countries.

Establishing Strategic Business Units

Companies often define themselves in terms of products: They are in the "auto business" or the "clothing business." *Market definitions* of a business, however, describe the business as a customer-satisfying process. Products are transient; basic needs and customer groups endure forever. Transportation is a need: the horse and carriage, automobile, railroad, airline, ship, and truck are products that meet that need.

Viewing businesses in terms of customer needs can suggest additional growth opportunities. A *target market definition* tends to focus on selling a product or service to a current market. Pepsi could define its target market as everyone who drinks carbonated soft drinks, and competitors would therefore be other carbonated soft drink companies. A *strategic market definition,* however, also focuses on the potential market. If Pepsi considered everyone who might drink something to quench their thirst, its competition would include noncarbonated soft drinks, bottled water, fruit juices, tea, and coffee. To better compete, Pepsi might decide to sell additional beverages with promising growth rates.

A business can define itself in terms of three dimensions: customer groups, customer needs, and technology.[10] Consider a small company that defines its business as designing incandescent lighting systems for television studios. Its customer group is television studios; the customer need is lighting; the technology is incandescent lighting. The company might want to expand to make lighting for homes and offices, or it could supply other services television studios need, such as heating or ventilation. It could design other lighting technologies for television studios, such as environmentally friendly "green" fluorescent bulbs.

Large companies normally manage quite different businesses, each requiring its own strategy. A **strategic business unit (SBU)** has three characteristics: (1) It is a single business, or a collection of related businesses, that can be planned separately from the rest of the company; (2) it has its own set of competitors; and (3) it has a manager responsible for strategic planning and profit performance who controls most of the factors affecting profit. The purpose of identifying the company's strategic business units is to develop separate strategies and assign appropriate funding. Senior management knows its portfolio of businesses usually includes a number of "yesterday's has-beens" as well as "tomorrow's breadwinners."[11]

Assigning Resources to Each SBU[12]

Once SBUs have been defined, management must decide how to allocate corporate resources to each. Newer methods of making decisions about SBU investment rely on shareholder value analysis, and on whether a company's market value is greater with an SBU or without it (whether it is sold or spun off). These value calculations assess the potential of a business based on growth opportunities from global expansion, repositioning or retargeting, and strategic outsourcing.

Assessing Growth Opportunities

Assessing growth opportunities includes planning new businesses, downsizing, and terminating older businesses. If there is a gap between future desired sales and projected sales, corporate management will need to develop or acquire new businesses to fill it. Three options for increasing sales and profits are intensive growth opportunities, integrative growth opportunities, and diversification growth opportunities.

- Intensive growth. One useful framework for detecting new intensive-growth opportunities is a "product–market expansion grid."[13] The company first considers whether it could gain more market share with its current products in their current markets, using a *market-penetration strategy*. Next it considers whether it can find or develop new markets for its current products, in a *market-development strategy*. Then it considers whether it can develop new products of potential interest to its current markets with a *product-development strategy*. Later the firm will also review opportunities to develop new products for new markets in a *diversification strategy*.
- Integrative growth. A business can increase sales and profits through backward integration (acquiring a supplier), forward integration (acquiring a distributor), or horizontal integration (acquiring a competitor). Horizontal mergers and alliances don't always work out. In that case, the company must consider diversification.
- Diversification growth. This makes sense when good opportunities exist outside the present businesses—the industry is highly attractive and the company has the right mix of business strengths to succeed. The company could seek new products that have technological or marketing synergies with existing product lines, though appealing to a different group of customers. Or it might use a horizontal strategy to search for unrelated new products that appeal to current customers. Finally, it might seek new businesses that have no relationship to its current technology, products, or markets, adopting a conglomerate strategy to diversification.

To release needed resources for other uses, and to reduce costs, companies must carefully prune, harvest, or divest tired old businesses. As an example, to focus on its travel and credit card operations, American Express spun off American Express Financial Advisors, which provided insurance, mutual funds, investment advice, and brokerage and asset management services (it was renamed Ameriprise Financial).

Organization, Organizational Culture, and Innovation

Strategic planning happens within the context of the organization. A company's *organization* consists of its structures, policies, and corporate culture, all of which can become dysfunctional in a rapidly changing business environment. **Corporate culture** has been defined as "the shared experiences, stories, beliefs, and norms that characterize an organization." A customer-centric culture can affect all aspects of an organization.

Sometimes corporate culture develops organically and is transmitted directly from the CEO's personality and habits to the company employees. Mike Lazaridis, president and co-CEO of BlackBerry producer Research In Motion, hosts a weekly, innovation-centered "Vision Series" meeting focusing on new research and company goals. As he states, "I think we have a culture of innovation here, and [engineers] have absolute access to me. I live a life that tries to promote innovation."[14]

CREATING INNOVATIVE MARKETING

When IBM surveyed top CEOs and government leaders about their priorities, business-model innovation and coming up with unique ways of doing things scored high. IBM's own drive for business-model innovation led to much collaboration, both within IBM itself and externally with companies, governments, and educational institutions. Procter & Gamble (P&G) similarly has made it a goal for 50 percent of new products to come from outside P&G's labs—from inventors, scientists, and suppliers whose new-product ideas can be developed in-house, as well as from international partners such as the Tesco supermarket chain.

Finally, to find breakthrough ideas, some companies immerse a range of employees in solving marketing problems. Samsung's Value Innovation Program isolates product development teams of engineers, designers, and planners with a timetable and end date in the company's center just south of Seoul, Korea, while 50 specialists help guide their activities. To help make tough trade-offs, team members draw "value curves" that rank attributes such as a product's sound or picture quality on a scale from 1 to 5.

Sources: Lucy Handley, "Brands and Retailers Take a Collaborative Approach," *Marketing Week,* June 24, 2010, www.marketingweek.co.uk; Steve Hamm, "Innovation: The View from the Top," *BusinessWeek,* April 3, 2006, pp. 52–53; Jena McGregor, "The World's Most Innovative Companies," *BusinessWeek,* April 24, 2006, pp. 63–74; Rich Karlgard, "Digital Rules," *Forbes,* March 13, 2006, p. 31; Moon Ihlwan, "Camp Samsung," *BusinessWeek,* July 3, 2006, pp. 46–47.

Innovation in marketing is critical. Imaginative ideas on strategy exist in many places within a company.[15] Senior management should identify and encourage fresh ideas from three underrepresented groups: employees with youthful or diverse perspectives, employees far removed from company headquarters, and employees new to the industry. "Marketing Insight: Creating Innovative Marketing" (above) describes how some leading companies approach innovation.

Firms develop strategy by identifying and selecting among different views of the future. The Royal Dutch/Shell Group has pioneered **scenario analysis**, which develops plausible representations of a firm's possible future using assumptions about forces driving the market and different uncertainties. Managers think through each scenario with the question, "What will we do if it happens?" They then adopt one scenario as the most probable, and watch for signposts that might confirm or disconfirm it.[16]

Business Unit Strategic Planning

The business unit strategic-planning process consists of the steps shown in Figure 2.2. We examine each step in the sections that follow.

The Business Mission

Each business unit needs to define its specific mission within the broader company mission. Thus, a television-studio-lighting-equipment company might define its mission as, "To target major television studios and become their vendor of choice for lighting technologies that represent the most advanced and reliable studio lighting arrangements."

FIGURE 2.2 The Business Unit Strategic-Planning Process

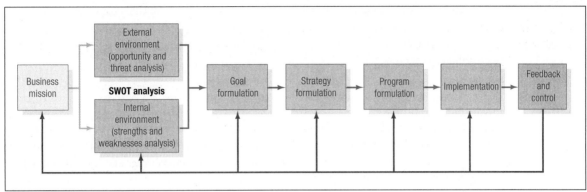

SWOT Analysis

The overall evaluation of a company's strengths, weaknesses, opportunities, and threats is called *SWOT analysis*. It's a way of monitoring the external and internal marketing environment.

External Environment (Opportunity and Threat) Analysis A business unit must monitor key *macroenvironment forces* and significant *microenvironment factors* that affect its ability to earn profits. It should track trends and important developments and any related opportunities and threats.

A **marketing opportunity** is an area of buyer need and interest that a company has a high probability of profitably satisfying. There are three main sources of market opportunities.[17] The first is to offer something that is in short supply. The second is to supply an existing product or service in a new or superior way. How? The *problem detection method* asks consumers for their suggestions, the *ideal method* has them imagine an ideal version of the product or service, and the *consumption chain method* asks them to chart their steps in acquiring, using, and disposing of a product. This last method often leads to a totally new product or service.

Marketers need to be good at spotting opportunities. Consider the following:

- A company may benefit from converging industry trends and introduce hybrid products or services that are new to the market. Major cell manufacturers have released phones with digital photo and video capabilities, and Global Positioning Systems (GPS).
- A company may make a buying process more convenient or efficient. Consumers can use the Internet to find more books than ever and search for the lowest price with a few clicks.
- A company can meet the need for more information and advice. Angie's List connects individuals with local home improvement contractors and doctors that have been reviewed by others.
- A company can customize a product or service. Timberland allows customers to choose colors for different sections of their boots, add initials or numbers to their boots, and choose different stitching and embroidery.
- A company can introduce a new capability. Consumers can create and edit digital "iMovies" with the iMac and upload them to an Apple Web server or Web site such as YouTube to share with friends around the world.

- A company may be able to deliver a product or service faster. FedEx discovered a way to deliver mail and packages much more quickly than the U.S. Post Office.
- A company may be able to offer a product at a much lower price. Pharmaceutical firms have created generic versions of brand-name drugs, and mail-order drug companies often sell for less.

The company applies *market opportunity analysis (MOA)* to evaluate opportunities by asking questions like:

1. Can we articulate the benefits convincingly to a defined target market?
2. Can we locate the target market(s) and reach them with cost-effective media and trade channels?
3. Does our company possess or have access to the critical capabilities and resources we need to deliver the customer benefits?
4. Can we deliver the benefits better than any actual or potential competitors?
5. Will the financial rate of return meet or exceed our required threshold for investment?

An **environmental threat** is a challenge posed by an unfavorable trend or development that, in the absence of defensive marketing action, would lead to lower sales or profit. Minor threats can be ignored, although somewhat more serious threats must be carefully monitored. Major threats, which have a high probability of occurrence and can seriously hurt the company, require the development of contingency plans.

Internal Environment (Strengths and Weaknesses) Analysis   It's one thing to find attractive opportunities, and another to be able to take advantage of them. Each business needs to evaluate its internal strengths and weaknesses. Clearly, the business doesn't have to correct *all* its weaknesses, nor should it gloat about all its strengths. The big question is whether it should limit itself to those opportunities for which it possesses the required strengths, or consider those that might require it to find or develop new strengths.

Goal Formulation

Once the company has performed a SWOT analysis, it can proceed to *goal formulation*, developing specific goals for the planning period. Goals are objectives that are specific with respect to magnitude and time. Most business units pursue a mix of objectives, including profitability, sales growth, market share improvement, risk containment, innovation, and reputation. The business unit sets these objectives and then manages by objectives (MBO). For an MBO system to work, the unit's objectives must be (1) arranged hierarchically, from most to least important; (2) quantitative whenever possible; (3) realistic; and (4) consistent. Other important trade-offs include short-term profit versus long-term growth, deep penetration of existing markets versus development of new markets, profit goals versus nonprofit goals, and high growth versus low risk. Each choice calls for a different marketing strategy.[18]

Strategy Formulation

Goals indicate what a business unit wants to achieve; **strategy** is a game plan for getting there. Every business must design a strategy for achieving its goals, consisting of a *marketing strategy* and a compatible *technology strategy* and *sourcing strategy*. Michael Porter has proposed three generic strategies that provide a good starting point for strategic thinking: overall cost leadership, differentiation, and focus.[19]

- Overall cost leadership. Firms work to achieve the lowest production and distribution costs so they can underprice competitors and win market share. They need less skill in marketing. The problem is that other firms will usually compete with still-lower costs and hurt the firm that rested its whole future on cost.
- Differentiation. The business concentrates on achieving superior performance in an important customer benefit area valued by a large part of the market.
- Focus. The business focuses on one or more narrow market segments, gets to know them intimately, and pursues either cost leadership or differentiation within the target segment.

Firms directing the same strategy to the same target market constitute a *strategic group*.[20] The firm that carries out that strategy best will make the most profits. Circuit City went out of business because it did not stand out in the consumer electronics industry as lowest in cost, highest in perceived value, or best in serving some market segment.

Porter draws a distinction between operational effectiveness and strategy. Competitors can quickly copy the operationally effective company using benchmarking and other tools, thus diminishing the advantage of operational effectiveness. Porter defines strategy as "the creation of a unique and valuable position involving a different set of activities." A company has a strategy when it "performs different activities from rivals or performs similar activities in different ways."[21]

Even giant companies such as AT&T and Philips often cannot achieve leadership, either nationally or globally, without forming alliances with domestic or multinational companies that complement or leverage their capabilities and resources. Marketing alliances may involve products or services (licensing or jointly marketing an offering), promotions (one company carrying a promotion for another), logistics (delivering or distributing another company's product), or pricing (offering mutual price discounts). To keep their strategic alliances thriving, corporations have begun to develop organizational structures to support them, and many have come to view the ability to form and manage mutually satisfying long-term partnerships as core skills called **partner relationship management (PRM)**.

Program Formulation and Implementation

Great marketing strategies can be sabotaged by poor implementation. For example, if the business has decided to attain technological leadership, it must strengthen its R&D department, gather technological intelligence, develop leading-edge products, train its technical sales force, and communicate its technological leadership. Management must also estimate each marketing program's costs and returns. Activity-based cost accounting (ABC) can help determine whether each marketing program is likely to produce sufficient results to justify its cost.[22]

Today's businesses recognize that unless they nurture other stakeholders—customers, employees, suppliers, distributors—they may never earn sufficient profits for the stockholders. A company might aim to delight its customers, perform well for its employees, and deliver a threshold level of satisfaction to its suppliers. In setting these levels, it must not violate any stakeholder group's sense of fairness about the treatment it is receiving relative to the others.[23]

According to McKinsey & Company, strategy is only one of seven elements—all of which start with the letter S—in successful business practice.[24] The first three—strategy, structure, and systems—are considered the "hardware" of success. The next four—style (how employees think and behave), skills (to carry out the strategy), staff (able people who are properly trained), and shared values (values that guide employees' actions)—are the "software." When these elements are present, companies are usually more successful at strategy implementation.[25] See "Marketing Skills: Managing Implementation" for more about effective implementation.

MANAGING IMPLEMENTATION

Careful implementation can translate a good marketing strategy into great profits. First, marketers must break every program down into its component activities, identify the needed resources and their associated costs, estimate how long each activity should last and who should handle it, and set up measures to monitor results. Second, they should enlist the support of other departments to enhance creativity and prepare for potential problems. Third, marketers should be flexible enough to find workable options when dealing with unexpected twists such as late delivery of materials. Finally, they need a sense of urgency about implementing every phase of every strategy and program.

For example, ESPN's strategy is to be wherever sports fans watch, read, and discuss sports. Creatively implementing this strategy, its marketers have expanded the brand into multiple cable channels and Web sites, a magazine, the ESPN Zone restaurant chain, more than 750 radio affiliates, movies, book publishing, a sports merchandise catalog and online store, video games, and mobile services. ESPN's marketers plan and monitor every detail of every marketing initiative and work closely with partners in advance of major sporting events such as the World Cup. Now owned by Walt Disney, ESPN is active in 197 countries and earns more than $5 billion a year in revenue.[26]

Feedback and Control

A company's strategic fit with the environment will inevitably erode, because the market environment changes faster than the company's seven Ss. Thus, a company might remain efficient yet lose effectiveness. Peter Drucker pointed out that it is more important to "do the right thing"—to be effective—than "to do things right"—to be efficient. The most successful companies, however, excel at both. Organizations, especially large ones, are subject to inertia. It's difficult to change one part without adjusting everything else. Yet, organizations can be changed through strong leadership, preferably in advance of a crisis. The key to organizational health is willingness to examine the changing environment and adopt new goals and behaviors.

The Marketing Plan and Marketing Performance

Working within the plans set by the levels above them, product managers come up with a marketing plan for individual products, lines, brands, channels, or customer groups. Each product level, whether product line or brand, must develop a marketing plan for achieving its goals. A *marketing plan* summarizes what the marketer has learned about the marketplace and indicates how the firm plans to reach its marketing objectives.[27] It contains tactical guidelines for the marketing programs and financial allocations over the planning period.[28]

Marketing plans are becoming more customer- and competitor-oriented, better reasoned, and more realistic. Planning is becoming a continuous process to respond to rapidly changing market conditions. The most frequently cited shortcomings of current marketing plans, according to marketing executives, are lack of realism, insufficient competitive analysis, and a short-run focus.

Contents of a Marketing Plan

A marketing plan usually contains the following sections.

- Executive summary and table of contents. The plan should open with a table of contents and brief summary of the main goals and recommendations.
- Situation analysis. This section presents relevant background data on sales, costs, the market, competitors, and the various forces in the macroenvironment. How do we define the market, how big is it, and how fast is it growing? What are the relevant trends and critical issues? Firms will use all this information to carry out a SWOT analysis.
- Marketing strategy. Here the marketing manager defines the mission, marketing and financial objectives, and needs the market offering is intended to satisfy as well as its competitive positioning. All this requires inputs from other areas, such as purchasing, manufacturing, sales, finance, and human resources.
- Financial projections. Financial projections include a sales forecast (by month and product category), an expense forecast (marketing costs broken down into finer categories), and a break-even analysis (how many units the firm must sell to offset its fixed costs and average per-unit variable costs).
- Implementation controls. This section outlines the metrics and controls for monitoring and adjusting implementation of the plan. Typically, it spells out the goals, schedule, and budget for each month or quarter, so management can review each period's results and take corrective action as needed. Some organizations include contingency plans for handling specific developments (such as price wars).

From Marketing Plan to Marketing Action

Most companies create yearly marketing plans, starting well in advance of the implementation date to allow time for marketing research, analysis, management review, and coordination between departments. As each action program begins, they monitor ongoing results, investigate any deviation from plans, and take corrective steps as needed, ready to update and adapt the marketing plan at any time. The plan should also define how progress toward objectives will be measured, so management can assess the results and evaluate the effectiveness and efficiency of the organization's marketing.

Measuring Marketing Performance

Marketers are facing increased pressure to show how the marketing function is helping the firm achieve its goals and objectives. In one survey, 65 percent of marketers indicated that return on marketing investment was a concern.[29] Yet outcomes such as broader brand awareness, enhanced brand image, greater customer loyalty, and improved new product prospects may take months or even years to manifest themselves. Organizations therefore use marketing metrics, marketing dashboards, and various analyses to assess marketing performance over time.

Marketing Metrics   **Marketing metrics** is the set of measures that helps organizations quantify, compare, and interpret their marketing performance. London Business School's Tim Ambler believes managers can split evaluation into two parts: (1) short-term results and (2) changes in brand equity. Short-term results often reflect profit-and-loss concerns as shown by metrics such as sales turnover, shareholder value, or a combination of the two. Brand-equity measures could include customer awareness, attitudes, and behaviors; market share; relative price premium; number of complaints; distribution and availability; total number of customers; perceived quality; and loyalty and retention.[30] Companies can also monitor an extensive set of internal metrics, such as innovation. For example, 3M tracks the proportion of sales resulting from its recent innovations. See Chapter 18 for more about marketing metrics.

Marketing Dashboards   Management can assemble a summary set of relevant internal and external measures in a *marketing dashboard* for synthesis and interpretation. Marketing dashboards are like the instrument panel in a car or plane, visually displaying real-time indicators to ensure proper functioning and improve understanding and analysis. Ideally, the number of metrics presented in the marketing dashboard would be reduced to a handful of key drivers over time.

As input to the marketing dashboard, companies can include two key market-based scorecards that reflect performance and provide possible early warning signals. A *customer-performance scorecard* records how well the company is doing year after year on such customer-based measures as the percentage of customers who say they would repurchase the product. A *stakeholder-performance scorecard* tracks the satisfaction of various constituencies who have a critical interest in and impact on the company's performance: employees, suppliers, banks, distributors, retailers, and stock-holders. Again, management should take action when one or more groups register increased or above-norm levels of dissatisfaction.[31]

Marketing Plan Performance   Four ways to measure key aspects of the marketing plan's performance are sales analysis, market share analysis, marketing expense-to-sales analysis, and financial analysis. *Sales analysis* measures and evaluates actual sales in relationship to goals. With *sales-variance analysis,* management measures the relative contribution of different factors to a gap in sales performance. With *microsales analysis,* management looks at specific products, territories, and other factors that failed to produce expected sales.

Company sales don't reveal how well the company is performing relative to competitors. For this, management needs to track its market share in one of three ways. *Overall market share* expresses the company's sales as a percentage of total market sales. *Served market share* is sales as a percentage of the total sales to the market. The *served market* is all the buyers able and willing to buy the product, and served market share is always larger than overall market share. A company could capture 100 percent of its served market and yet have a relatively small share of the total market. *Relative market share* is market share in relationship to the largest competitor. A relative market share of exactly 100 percent means the company is tied for the lead; over 100 percent indicates a market leader. A rise in relative market share means a company is gaining on its leading competitor.

To be sure the company isn't overspending to achieve sales goals, management must monitor the *marketing expense-to-sales* ratio and investigate fluctuations outside the normal range. They should also analyze the expense-to-sales ratios within the overall financial framework to determine how and where the company is making its money.

In addition, management can use *financial analysis* to identify factors that affect the company's *rate of return on net worth.*[32] The return on net worth is the product of two ratios, the company's *return on assets* and its *financial leverage.* To improve its return on net worth, the company must increase its ratio of net profits to assets, or increase the ratio of assets to net worth.

The company should analyze the composition of its assets (cash, accounts receivable, inventory, and plant and equipment) and see whether it can improve its asset management. The *return on assets* is the product of two ratios, the *profit margin* and the *asset turnover.* The marketing executive can seek to improve performance in two ways: (1) increasing the profit margin by increasing sales or cutting costs, and (2) increasing the asset turnover by increasing sales or reducing assets (inventory, receivables) held against a given level of sales.

Profitability Analysis   Measuring the profitability of products, territories, customer groups, segments, trade channels, and order sizes helps companies determine whether any should be changed or eliminated. To start, managers identify the specific expenses for each marketing function (such as advertising and delivery) and assign these costs to marketing entities (such as type of channel). Next, they prepare a profit-and-loss statement for each marketing entity. Then they can determine whether corrective action is needed to improve the relative profitability of different marketing entities. Many firms now use marketing profitability analysis, or its broader version, activity-based cost accounting (ABC), to quantify the true profitability of different activities.[33] Managers can then reduce the resources required to perform various activities, make the resources more productive, acquire them at lower cost, or raise prices on resource-intensive products.

EXECUTIVE SUMMARY

The value delivery process includes choosing (or identifying), providing (or delivering), and communicating superior value. The value chain is a tool for identifying key activities that create value and costs in a business. Strong companies develop superior capabilities in core business processes such as market sensing, new-product realization, customer acquisition and retention, and fulfillment management. Companies no longer compete—marketing networks do. Through holistic marketing, a firm can integrate value exploration, value creation, and value delivery by managing the relationships between itself, its customers, and its collaborators.

Market-oriented strategic planning is the managerial process of developing and maintaining a viable fit between the organization's objectives, skills, and resources and its changing market opportunities. The corporate strategy establishes the framework within which divisions and business units prepare strategic plans. Setting a corporate strategy means defining the mission, establishing strategic business units (SBUs), assigning resources, and assessing growth opportunities. Planning for SBU strategy includes defining the business mission, analyzing opportunities and threats, analyzing strengths and weaknesses, formulating goals and strategy, formulating and implementing programs, and gathering feedback and exercising control. Each product must have a marketing plan for achieving its goals. Organizations use marketing metrics, marketing dashboards, and various analyses to assess marketing performance.

NOTES

1. Scott Morrison, "Yahoo Chief Defends Her Site, Strategy," *Wall Street Journal,* June 25, 2010, www.wsj.com; Ina Fried, "Microsoft's Mehdi on Yahoo, Bing Cashback, and More," *CNet News,* June 23, 2010, http://news.cnet.com/8301-13860_3-20008604-56.html; Catherine Holahan, "Yahoo!'s Bid to Think Small," *BusinessWeek,* February 26, 2007, p. 94; Ben Elgin, "Yahoo!'s Boulevard of Broken Dreams," *BusinessWeek,* March 13, 2006, pp. 76–77; Justin Hibbard, "How Yahoo! Gave Itself a Face-Lift," *BusinessWeek,* October 9, 2006, pp. 74–77; Kevin J. Delaney, "As Yahoo! Falters, Executive's Memo Calls for Overhaul," *Wall Street Journal,* November 18, 2006; "Yahoo!'s Personality Crisis," *Economist,* August 13, 2005, pp. 49–50; Fred Vogelstein, "Yahoo!'s Brilliant Solution," *Fortune,* August 8, 2005, pp. 42–55.

2. Nirmalya Kumar, *Marketing as Strategy: The CEO's Agenda for Driving Growth and Innovation* (Boston: Harvard Business School Press, 2004); Frederick E. Webster Jr., "The Future Role of Marketing in the Organization," Donald R. Lehmann and Katherine Jocz, eds., *Reflections on the Futures of Marketing* (Cambridge, MA: Marketing Science Institute, 1997), pp. 39–66.

3. Michael E. Porter, *Competitive Advantage: Creating and Sustaining Superior Performance* (New York: Free Press, 1985).

4. Michael Hammer and James Champy, *Reengineering the Corporation: A Manifesto for Business Revolution* (New York: HarperBusiness, 1993).

5. C. K. Prahalad and Gary Hamel, "The Core Competence of the Corporation," *Harvard Business Review,* May–June 1990, pp. 79–91.

6. George S. Day, "The Capabilities of Market-Driven Organizations," *Journal of Marketing* (October 1994), p. 38.

7. George S. Day and Paul J. H. Schoemaker, *Peripheral Vision: Detecting the Weak Signals That Will Make or Break Your Company* (Cambridge, MA: Harvard Business School Press, 2006); Paul J. H. Schoemaker and George S. Day, "How to Make Sense of Weak Signals," *MIT Sloan Management Review* (Spring 2009), pp. 81–89.

8. P. Kotler, D. C. Jain, and S. Maesincee, *Marketing Moves* (Boston: Harvard Business School Press, 2002), p. 29.

9. Peter Drucker, *Management: Tasks, Responsibilities, and Practices* (New York: Harper and Row, 1973), chapter 7.

10. Jeffrey F. Rayport and Bernard J. Jaworski, *e-Commerce* (New York: McGraw-Hill, 2001), p. 116.

11. Tilman Kemmler, Monika Kubicová, Robert Musslewhite, and Rodney Prezeau, "E-Performance II—The Good, the Bad, and the Merely Average," *McKinsey Quarterly* (2001), www.mckinseyquarterly.com.

12. This section is based on Robert M. Grant, *Contemporary Strategy Analysis*, 7th ed. (New York: Wiley, 2009), chapter 17.

13. The same matrix can be expanded into nine cells by adding modified products and modified markets. See S. J. Johnson and Conrad Jones, "How to Organize for New Products," *Harvard Business Review,* May–June 1957, pp. 49–62.

14. Jena McGregor, "The World's Most Innovative Companies," *BusinessWeek*, April 24, 2006, pp. 63–74.

15. E. Jerome McCarthy, *Basic Marketing: A Managerial Approach,* 12th ed. (Homewood, IL: Irwin, 1996).

16. Paul J. H. Shoemaker, "Scenario Planning: A Tool for Strategic Thinking," *Sloan Management Review* (Winter 1995), pp. 25–40.

17. Philip Kotler, *Kotler on Marketing* (New York: Free Press, 1999).

18. Dominic Dodd and Ken Favaro, "Managing the Right Tension," *Harvard Business Review,* December 2006, pp. 62–74.

19. Michael E. Porter, *Competitive Strategy: Techniques for Analyzing Industries and Competitors* (New York: Free Press, 1980), chapter 2.

20. Michael E. Porter, "What Is Strategy?" *Harvard Business Review,* November–December 1996, pp. 61–78.

21. Michael E. Porter, *Competitive Strategy* (New York: Free Press, 1980), chapter 2; Michael E. Porter, "What Is Strategy?" *Harvard Business Review,* November–December 1996, pp. 61–78.

22. Robin Cooper and Robert S. Kaplan, "Profit Priorities from Activity-Based Costing," *Harvard Business Review,* May–June 1991, pp. 130–35.

23. See Robert S. Kaplan and David P. Norton, *The Balanced Scorecard* (Boston: Harvard Business School Press, 1996) as a tool for monitoring stakeholder satisfaction.

24. Thomas J. Peters and Robert H. Waterman Jr., *In Search of Excellence: Lessons from America's Best-Run Companies* (New York: Harper and Row, 1982), pp. 9–12.

25. John P. Kotter and James L. Heskett, *Corporate Culture and Performance* (New York: Free Press, 1992); Stanley M. Davis, *Managing Corporate Culture* (Cambridge, MA: Ballinger, 1984); Terrence E. Deal and Allan A. Kennedy, *Corporate Cultures: The Rites and Rituals of Corporate Life* (Reading, MA: Addison-Wesley, 1982); "Corporate Culture," *BusinessWeek,* October 27, 1980, pp. 148–60.

26. Richard Sandomir, "World Cup Ratings Certify a TV Winner," *New York Times,* June 28, 2010, www.nytimes.com; Tom Lowry, "ESPN's Cell Phone Fumble," *BusinessWeek,* October 30, 2006, p. 26.

27. Marian Burk Wood, *The Marketing Plan Handbook,* 4th ed. (Upper Saddle River, NJ: Prentice Hall, 2011), p. 5.

28. Donald R. Lehmann and Russell S. Winer, *Product Management,* 3rd ed. (Boston: McGraw-Hill/Irwin, 2001).

29. "Report: Marketers Place Priority on Nurturing Existing Customers," http://directmag.com/roi/0301-customer-satisfaction-retention, December 9, 2010.

30. Kusum L. Ailawadi, Donald R. Lehmann, and Scott A. Neslin, "Revenue Premium as an Outcome Measure of Brand Equity," *Journal of Marketing* 67 (October 2003), pp. 1–17.

31. Robert S. Kaplan and David P. Norton, *The Balanced Scorecard* (Boston: Harvard Business School Press, 1996).

32. Alternatively, companies need to focus on factors affecting shareholder value. The goal of marketing planning is to increase shareholder value, which is the present value of the future income stream created by the company's present actions. Rate-of-return analysis usually focuses on only one year's results. See Alfred Rapport, *Creating Shareholder Value*, rev. ed. (New York: Free Press, 1997).

33. Robin Cooper and Robert S. Kaplan, "Profit Priorities from Activity-Based Costing," *Harvard Business Review*, May–June 1991, pp. 130–35; for a recent application to shipping, see Tom Kelley, "What Is the *Real* Cost: How to Use Lifecycle Cost Analysis for an Accurate Comparison," *Beverage World*, January 2010, pp. 50–51.

chapter 3

Collecting Information and Forecasting Demand

In this chapter, we will address the following questions:

1. What are the components of a modern marketing information system?
2. How can companies collect marketing intelligence?
3. What constitutes good marketing research?
4. How can marketers accurately measure and forecast demand?
5. What are some influential developments in the macroenvironment?

Marketing Management at Kimberly-Clark

A series of novel innovations through the years has transformed Kimberly-Clark from a paper mill company to a consumer products powerhouse. A good example is the successful launch of Huggies Supreme Natural Fit disposable diapers, after nearly three years of research and design. Kimberly-Clark's marketers assembled a sample of new mothers from different parts of the country with different income backgrounds and ethnicities, conducted in-home interviews, and placed motion-activated cameras in homes to learn about diaper-changing routines.

Seeing moms struggle to straighten a squirming infant's legs when putting on a diaper led marketers to shape the new diaper for a baby's body curves. They also designed the new diaper to be thinner, with a closer fit and more stretch in the waistband. When research revealed that moms used the cartoon graphics on another diaper to distract the baby during a diaper change, Kimberly-Clark added more active images of Disney-licensed Winnie the Pooh characters. By carefully researching and responding to the needs of this market, and communicating the benefits of its diaper products, the firm has boosted market share and increased its annual sales of diapers beyond $4 billion.[1]

Good marketers need insights to help them analyze the market and customers' needs, interpret past performance and trends, and plan future activities. Discovering a consumer insight and understanding its marketing implications can often lead to a successful product launch or spur the growth of a brand. In this chapter, we consider how firms can gather information about their markets, research specific problems and opportunities, follow important environmental trends, and forecast demand.

The Marketing Information System and Marketing Intelligence

The major responsibility for identifying significant marketplace changes falls to the company's marketers. Marketers have two advantages for the task: disciplined methods for collecting information, and time spent interacting with customers and observing competitors and other outside groups.

Every firm must organize and distribute a continuous flow of information to its marketing managers. A **marketing information system (MIS)** consists of people, equipment, and procedures to gather, sort, analyze, evaluate, and distribute needed, timely, and accurate information to marketing decision makers. This system draws from data based on internal company records, marketing intelligence, and marketing research.

Internal Records and Database Systems

To spot important opportunities and potential problems, marketing managers rely on internal reports and databases of all sorts.

The Order-to-Payment Cycle The heart of the internal records system is the order-to-payment cycle. Sales representatives, dealers, and customers send orders to the firm. The sales department prepares invoices, transmits copies to various departments, and back-orders out-of-stock items. Shipped items generate shipping and billing documents that go to various departments. Because customers favor firms that can promise timely delivery, companies need to perform these steps quickly and accurately.

Sales Information Systems For decision making, marketing managers need timely and accurate reports on current sales. Walmart captures data on the sale of every item, to every customer, in every store, every day, and refreshes the data every hour. Companies must carefully interpret the sales data, however, so as not to draw the wrong conclusions.

Databases, Data Warehousing, and Data Mining Companies often organize their information into customer, product, and salesperson databases, and then create data warehouses. The customer database will contain every customer's name, address, past transactions, and sometimes demographics and psychographics (activities, interests, and opinions). Analysts can "mine" these databases (*data mining*) and garner fresh insights into neglected customer segments, recent customer trends, customer loyalty, and other useful information, as discussed in Chapter 4. Cross-tabulating customer data with product and salesperson data yields still-deeper insights.

Marketing Intelligence

A **marketing intelligence system** is a set of procedures and sources that managers use to obtain everyday information about developments in the marketing environment. The internal records system supplies *results* data, but the marketing intelligence system supplies *happenings* data.

TABLE 3.1	Improving Marketing Intelligence
Action	**Example**
Train and motivate the sales force to spot and report new developments.	Have sales representatives observe how customers use the firm's products in innovative ways, which can lead to new product ideas.
Motivate distributors, retailers, and other intermediaries to pass along important intelligence.	Studying the combination of products bought together can yield insights about effective store displays and seasonal sales.
Hire external experts to collect intelligence.	Use mystery shoppers to uncover problems with quality, services, and facilities.
Network internally and externally.	Buy competitors' products, read competitors' published reports, and collect competitors' ads.
Set up a customer advisory panel.	Invite the largest, most outspoken, most sophisticated, or most representative customers to provide feedback.
Take advantage of government data.	Check U.S. Census Bureau data to learn about population swings, demographic groups, and changing family structure.
Buy information from outside research firms and vendors.	Obtain data from well-known suppliers such as the A.C. Nielsen Company and Information Resources Inc.
Collect marketing intelligence on the Internet.	Check Web sites, blogs, and social media that post customer reviews and complaints, expert opinions, and product or company feedback.

Marketing managers collect marketing intelligence in a variety of different ways, such as by reading books, newspapers, and trade publications; talking to customers, suppliers, and distributors; monitoring social media and Internet sources; and meeting with other company managers. Table 3.1 shows eight ways to improve the quality and quantity of marketing intelligence.

In particular, marketers can use the Internet to gather data about consumers and competitors. For instance, independent review forums such as Bizrate.com collect consumer reviews from members and from store customers who make purchases. Marketers can also read comments on distributor sites, such as on Amazon.com, or check sites such as ZDNet.com, which posts experts' and consumers' opinions of high-tech products. Forums such as PlanetFeedback, where customers voice unfavorable company experiences, are another source. Finally, marketers can analyze comments on social media and blogs to gain insights into consumer sentiment.

Companies that make good use of "cookies," records of Web site usage stored on personal browsers, are smart users of targeted marketing. Many consumers are happy to cooperate: A recent survey showed that 49 percent of individuals agreed cookies are important to them when using the Internet. Not only do they *not* delete cookies, but they also expect customized marketing appeals and deals once they accept them.

The Marketing Research System

Marketing managers often commission formal marketing studies of specific problems and opportunities, such as a market survey, a product-preference test, a sales forecast by region, or an advertising evaluation. *Marketing insights* provide diagnostic information about how and why we observe certain effects in the marketplace, and what that means to marketers.[2] Gillette's Venus razor has become the most successful female shaving line ever—holding more than 50 percent of the global women's shaving market—as a result of insightful research that led to product design, packaging, and advertising cues that better satisfied female shaving needs.[3]

Defining Marketing Research

Marketing research is the systematic design, collection, analysis, and reporting of data and findings relevant to a specific marketing situation facing the company. Most large firms have their own marketing research departments. Procter & Gamble has dedicated Consumer & Market Knowledge (CMK) market research groups working for P&G businesses worldwide to improve brand strategies and marketing execution. It also maintains a centralized corporate CMK group to research big-picture concerns that transcend all lines of business. At much smaller companies, everyone carries out marketing research—including customers, in some cases.

Most companies use a combination of marketing research resources to study their industries, competitors, audiences, and channel strategies, budgeting marketing research at 1 percent to 2 percent of company sales. Much of the budget is spent on the services of outside firms, which fall into three categories. Syndicated-service research firms such as Nielsen gather consumer and trade information, which they sell for a fee. Custom marketing research firms design studies, carry them out, and report the findings. Specialty-line marketing research firms provide specific services such as field interviewing.

The Marketing Research Process

Effective marketing research follows the six steps shown in Figure 3.1. We illustrate these steps with the following situation. Assume that American Airlines is reviewing new ideas for serving customers, especially the businesspeople who buy expensive first-class tickets on long flights. Among these ideas are: (1) an Internet connection for e-mail and limited access to Web pages, (2) 24 channels of satellite cable TV, and (3) a 50-CD audio system that lets each passenger customize an in-flight play list. The marketing research manager is investigating how first-class passengers would rate these services, specifically the Internet connection, and how much extra they would be willing to pay for it. One source estimates revenues of $70 billion from in-flight Internet access over 10 years, if enough first-class passengers paid $25. Making the connection available would cost the airline $90,000 per plane.[4]

Step 1: Define the Problem, Decision Alternatives, and Research Objectives

Marketing managers must be careful not to define the problem too broadly or too narrowly for the marketing researcher. American's marketing manager and marketing researcher define the problem as follows: "Will offering an in-flight Internet service create enough incremental preference and profit for American Airlines to justify its cost against other possible investments in service enhancements American might make?" The objective is to answer these questions: (1) What types of first-class passengers would respond to an in-flight Internet service? (2) How many first-class passengers are likely to use the Internet service at different price levels? (3) How many extra first-class passengers might choose American because of this new service? (4) How much long-term goodwill will this service add to the airline's image? (5) Relative to other services, how important is Internet service to first-class passengers?

FIGURE 3.1 The Marketing Research Process

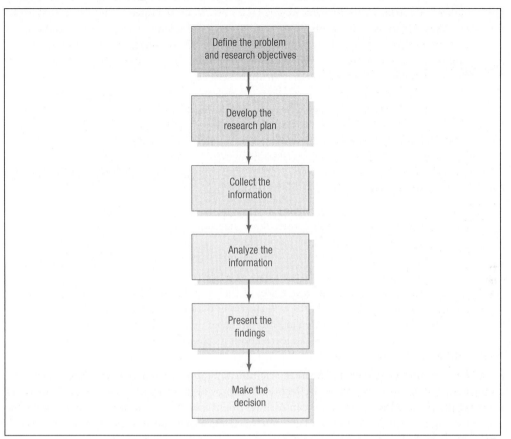

Not all research projects can be this specific. Some research is *exploratory*, to shed light on the nature of the problem and suggest possible solutions or new ideas. Some research is *descriptive,* to quantify demand, such as how many first-class passengers would purchase in-flight Internet service at $25. Some research is *causal,* to test a cause-and-effect relationship.

Step 2: Develop the Research Plan

In the second stage of marketing research, managers develop a plan for gathering the needed information. This involves decisions about data sources, research approaches, research instruments, sampling plan, and contact methods.

Data Sources   The researcher can gather secondary data, primary data, or both. *Secondary data* are data that were collected for another purpose and already exist somewhere. *Primary data* are freshly gathered for a specific purpose or for a specific research project.

Researchers usually start by examining secondary data. If the needed data don't exist or are dated, inaccurate, incomplete, or unreliable, the researcher will need to collect primary data.

Research Approaches   Marketers collect primary data in five main ways: through observation, focus groups, surveys, behavioral data, and experiments.

- Observational research. Researchers can gather fresh data by observing the relevant actors and settings. *Ethnographic research* is an observational research approach that uses concepts and tools from anthropology and other social science disciplines to provide deep cultural understanding of how people live and work.[5] The American Airlines researchers might meander around first-class lounges to hear travelers talk about different carriers or fly on competitors' planes to observe in-flight service.

- Focus group research. A *focus group* is a gathering of 6 to 10 people selected by researchers based on certain demographic, psychographic, or other considerations and brought together to discuss various topics of interest at length, assisted by a professional research moderator. To allow for more in-depth discussion, focus groups are trending smaller in size.[6] In the American Airlines case, the moderator might ask, "How do you feel about first-class air travel?" and later ask how people view different airlines and proposed services, specifically Internet service.

- Survey research. Firms undertake surveys to assess people's knowledge, beliefs, preferences, and satisfaction and to measure these magnitudes in the general population. American Airlines' researchers might prepare their own questions, add questions to a larger survey, survey an ongoing consumer panel, survey people in a shopping mall, or survey people online.

- Behavioral data. Customers leave traces of their purchasing behavior in store scanning data, catalog and online purchases, and customer databases. Actual purchases reflect consumers' preferences and often are more reliable than statements made to market researchers. American Airlines can learn about its passengers by analyzing ticket purchase records and online behavior.

- Experimental research. The most scientifically valid research is *experimental research*, designed to capture cause-and-effect relationships by eliminating competing explanations of the observed findings. American Airlines might introduce Internet service on one of its international flights at a price of $25 one week and $15 the next week. If the plane carried approximately the same number of first-class passengers each week and the particular weeks made no difference, researchers could relate any significant difference in the number of passengers using the service to the different prices charged.

Research Instruments   Marketing researchers have a choice of three main research instruments in collecting primary data: questionnaires, qualitative measures, and technological devices. A *questionnaire* consists of a set of questions presented to respondents. Because of its flexibility, it is the most common instrument used to collect primary data.

Researchers need to carefully develop, test, and debug questionnaires before administering them on a large scale. The form, wording, and sequence of the questions can all influence the responses. *Closed-end questions* specify all the possible answers and provide answers that are easier to interpret and tabulate. *Open-end questions* allow respondents to answer in their own words, revealing more about how people think. They are especially useful in exploratory research, where the researcher is looking for insight into how people think rather than measuring how many people think a certain way.

Some marketers prefer more qualitative methods for gauging consumer opinion, because consumer actions don't always match their answers to survey questions. *Qualitative research techniques* are relatively unstructured measurement approaches that permit a range of possible responses. This can be a useful first step in exploring consumers' brand and product perceptions. It is indirect in nature, so consumers may reveal more about themselves in the process.

There has been much interest in recent years in technological devices for marketing research. Galvanometers can measure the interest or emotions aroused by exposure to a specific marketing message. Marketers sometimes use skin sensors, brain wave scanners, and full body scanners to gauge consumer responses.[7] The term *neuromarketing* describes brain research on the effect of marketing stimuli. By applying neurological techniques, researchers are trying to move toward a more complete picture of what goes on inside consumers' heads.

Sampling Plan After deciding on the research approach and instruments, the marketing researcher must design a sampling plan. This calls for three decisions:

1. *Sampling unit: Whom should we survey?* In the American Airlines survey, should the sampling unit consist of first-class business travelers, first-class vacation travelers, or both? Once they have determined the sampling unit, marketers develop a sampling frame so everyone in the target population has an equal or known chance of being sampled.

2. *Sample size: How many people should we survey?* Large samples give more reliable results than small samples. However, samples of less than 1 percent of a population can be reliable, with a credible sampling procedure.

3. *Sampling procedure: How should we choose the respondents?* Probability sampling allows marketers to calculate confidence limits for sampling error and makes the sample more representative.

Contact Methods Now the marketing researcher must decide how to contact the subjects: by mail, by telephone, in person, or online. The advantages and disadvantages of each method are shown in Table 3.2.

Step 3: Collect the Information

The data collection phase of marketing research is generally the most expensive and the most prone to error. Four major problems arise in surveys: (1) some respondents will be away from home or otherwise inaccessible and must be contacted again or replaced; (2) some respondents will not cooperate; (3) some respondents will give biased or dishonest answers; and (4) some interviewers will be biased or dishonest.

TABLE 3.2	Marketing Research Contact Methods	
Contact Method	**Advantages**	**Disadvantages**
By mail	Good way to reach people who would not give personal interviews or whose responses might be biased or distorted by the interviewer.	Response rate is usually low or slow.
By telephone	Good method for gathering information quickly and clarifying questions if respondents do not understand. Response rate is typically higher than for mailed questionnaires.	Interviews must be brief and not too personal. Telephone contact getting more difficult because of consumers' growing antipathy toward telemarketers.
In person	Most versatile, because researcher can ask more questions and record additional observations about respondents, such as dress and body language.	Most expensive method, subject to interviewer bias, and requires more administrative planning and supervision.
Online	Inexpensive, fast, and versatile. Firms can post questionnaires on their Web sites, place banners on other sites, host a consumer panel or virtual focus group, sponsor a chat room or blog.	Samples can be skewed and small. Online research can suffer from technological problems and inconsistencies. Online panels can suffer from excessive turnover.

Step 4: Analyze the Information

The next step is to extract findings by tabulating the data and developing summary measures. The researchers now compute averages and measures of dispersion for the major variables and apply statistical techniques and decision models in the hope of discovering additional findings. They may test different hypotheses and theories, applying sensitivity analysis to test assumptions and the strength of the conclusions.

Step 5: Present the Findings

As the last step, the researcher presents findings relevant to the major marketing decisions facing management. Researchers increasingly are being asked to play a more proactive, consulting role in translating data and information into insights and recommendations.[8] They're also considering ways to present research findings in ways that are understandable and compelling. In the American Airlines case, findings show about five passengers out of every ten would use the service at $25; about six would use it at $15. Thus, a price of $15 would produce less revenue ($90 = 6 × $15) than $25 ($125 = 5 × $25). Assuming the same flight takes place 365 days a year, American could collect $45,625 ($125 × 365) annually. Given an investment of $90,000, it would take two years to break even.

Step 6: Make the Decision

The American Airlines managers who commissioned the research need to weigh the evidence. If their confidence in the findings is low, they may decide against introducing in-flight Internet service. If they are predisposed to launching the service, the findings support their inclination. Or they may decide to do more research. The decision is theirs, but the research has provided them with insight into the problem.

Forecasting and Demand Measurement

Conducting marketing research and collecting marketing intelligence can help to identify marketing opportunities. The company must then measure and forecast the size, growth, and profit potential of each new opportunity. Sales forecasts prepared by marketing are used by finance to raise cash for investment and operations; by manufacturing to establish capacity and output; by purchasing to acquire the right amount of supplies; and by human resources to hire the needed workers. The first step is to determine which market to measure.

The Measures of Market Demand

There are many productive ways to break down the market when preparing to evaluate opportunities. The **potential market** is the set of consumers with a sufficient level of interest in a market offer. However, interest is not enough to define a market unless they also have sufficient income and access to the product. The **available market** is the set of consumers who have interest, income, *and* access to a particular offer. A subset is the *qualified available market,* consumers who have the interest, income, access, and qualifications for the offer. The **target market** is the part of the qualified available market the company decides to pursue. Finally, the **penetrated market** is the set of consumers who are buying the company's product.

These definitions are a useful tool for market planning. If the company isn't satisfied with current sales, it can try to attract a larger percentage of buyers from its target market, lower the qualifications for potential buyers, expand its available market by adding distribution or lowering its price, or reposition itself in the minds of its customers.

FIGURE 3.2 Market Demand Functions

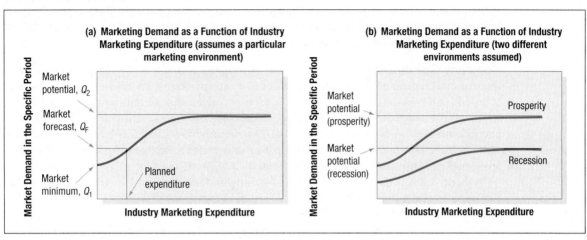

The Market Demand Function

The next step in evaluating new opportunities is to estimate total market demand. **Market demand** for a product is the total volume that would be bought by a defined customer group in a defined geographical area in a defined time period in a defined marketing environment under a defined marketing program. Market demand is not a fixed number, but rather a function of the stated conditions, which is why it is called the *market demand function*.

Figure 3.2(a) shows how market demand depends on underlying conditions. The horizontal axis shows different possible levels of industry marketing expenditure in a given time period. The vertical axis shows the resulting demand level. The curve represents the estimated market demand associated with varying levels of marketing expenditure.

Some base sales (the *market minimum*, labeled Q_1 in the figure) would take place without any demand-stimulating expenditures. Higher marketing expenditures would yield higher levels of demand, first at an increasing rate, then at a decreasing rate. Marketing expenditures beyond a certain level would not stimulate much further demand, suggesting an upper limit called the *market potential* (labeled Q_2).

Markets and Market Potential   Two extreme types of market are the expansible and the nonexpansible. The size of an *expansible market* is greatly affected by industry marketing expenditures; in Figure 3.2(a), the distance between Q_1 and Q_2 is relatively large. The size of a *nonexpansible market* is not much affected by the level of marketing expenditures, so the distance between Q_1 and Q_2 is relatively small. Organizations selling in a nonexpansible market must accept the market's size—the level of *primary demand* for the product class—and try to win a larger **market share**, that is, a higher level of *selective demand* for their product.

Remember, the market demand function is not a picture of market demand over time. Rather, it shows alternative current forecasts of market demand associated with possible levels of industry marketing effort. Only one level of industry marketing expenditure will actually occur; the market demand at this level is the **market forecast**. This forecast shows the expected demand, not the maximum demand.

Market potential is the limit approached by market demand as industry marketing expenditures approach infinity for a given marketing environment. The phrase "for a given market environment" is crucial. The market potential for many products is higher during prosperity than during recession, as illustrated in Figure 3.2(b). Companies can do nothing about the position of the market demand function, which is determined by the marketing environment, but their marketing spending can influence their location on the function.

Company Demand and Sales Forecast   **Company demand** is the company's estimated share of market demand at alternative levels of company marketing effort in a given time period. It depends on how the company's products, services, prices, and communications are perceived relative to the competitors'. Other things equal, the company's market share depends on the scale and effectiveness of its market expenditures. Marketing model builders have developed sales response functions to measure how a company's sales are affected by its marketing expenditure level, marketing mix, and marketing effectiveness.[9]

Once marketers have estimated company demand, they choose a level of marketing effort. The **company sales forecast** is the expected level of company sales based on a chosen marketing plan and an assumed marketing environment. We represent the company sales forecast graphically with sales on the vertical axis and marketing effort on the horizontal axis, as in Figure 3.2 (the sales forecast being the result of an assumed marketing expenditure plan).

A **sales quota** is the sales goal set for a product line, company division, or sales representative. It is primarily a managerial device for defining and stimulating sales effort, often set slightly higher than estimated sales to stretch the sales force's effort. A **sales budget** is a conservative estimate of the expected volume of sales, primarily for making current purchasing, production, and cash flow decisions. It's based on the need to avoid excessive risk and is generally set slightly lower than the sales forecast.

Company sales potential is the sales limit approached by company demand as company marketing effort increases relative to that of competitors. The absolute limit of company demand is, of course, the market potential. The two would be equal if the company got 100 percent of the market. In most cases, company sales potential is less than the market potential, even when company marketing expenditures increase considerably. Each competitor has a hard core of loyal buyers unresponsive to other companies' efforts to woo them.

Estimating Current Demand

In estimating current market demand, marketing executives want to estimate total market potential and area market potential, as well as total industry sales and market shares.

Total Market Potential   *Total market potential* is the maximum sales available to all firms in an industry during a given period, under a given level of industry marketing effort and environmental conditions. One way to estimate total market potential is to multiply the potential number of buyers by the average quantity each purchases, times the price. If 100 million people buy books each year, and the average buyer buys three books a year at an average price of $20 each, the total market potential for books is $6 billion (100 million × 3 × $20). The number of buyers can be difficult to estimate. Marketers often start with the total population, eliminate groups that obviously would not buy the product, and conduct research to eliminate groups without interest or income to buy.

Area Market Potential   Because companies must allocate their marketing budget optimally among their best territories, they need to estimate the market potential of different cities, states, and nations. Two major methods are the market-buildup method, used primarily by business marketers, and the multiple-factor index method, used primarily by consumer marketers.

The *market-buildup method* calls for identifying all the potential buyers in each market and estimating their potential purchases. It produces accurate results if we have a list of all potential buyers and a good estimate of what each will buy, but this information is not always easy to gather. For efficiency, some business marketers use the *North American Industry Classification System (NAICS)*, developed by the U.S. Bureau of the Census in conjunction with the Canadian and Mexican governments.[10]

To use the NAICS, a lathe manufacturer would first determine the six-digit NAICS codes that represent products whose manufacturers are likely to require lathe machines. Then the firm determines an appropriate base for estimating the number of lathes each industry will use, such as customer industry sales. Once the company estimates the rate of lathe ownership relative to the customer industry's sales, it can compute the market potential.

Consumer companies also estimate area market potentials, but since their customers are too numerous to list they commonly use a straightforward index. A drug manufacturer might assume the market potential for drugs is directly related to population size. If the state of Virginia has 2.55 percent of the U.S. population, Virginia might be a market for 2.55 percent of total drugs sold. Yet a single factor is rarely a complete indicator of sales opportunity. Thus, it makes sense to develop a multiple-factor index and assign each factor a specific weight. Suppose Virginia has 2.00 percent of U.S. disposable personal income, 1.96 percent of U.S. retail sales, and 2.28 percent of U.S. population, and the respective weights are 0.5, 0.3, and 0.2. The buying-power index for Virginia is then 2.04 $[0.5(2.00) + 0.3(1.96) + 0.2(2.28)]$.

Industry Sales and Market Shares   A company also needs to know the actual industry sales in its market, which means identifying competitors and estimating their sales. Some information may be available from industry trade associations, although not for individual competitors. With this information, however, each company can evaluate its own performance against the industry's. Because distributors typically will not supply information about how much of competitors' products they are selling, business-to-business marketers operate with less knowledge of their market share results.

Estimating Future Demand

Forecasting is the art of anticipating what buyers are likely to do under a given set of conditions. The few products or services that lend themselves to easy forecasting generally enjoy an absolute level or a fairly constant trend, and competition that is either nonexistent (public utilities) or stable (pure oligopolies). In most markets, in contrast, good forecasting is a key factor in success.

Companies commonly prepare a macroeconomic forecast first, followed by an industry forecast and a company sales forecast. The macroeconomic forecast projects inflation, unemployment, interest rates, consumer spending, business investment, government expenditures, net exports, and other variables. The end result is a forecast of gross domestic product (GDP), which the firm uses, along with other indicators, to forecast industry sales. The company derives its sales forecast by assuming it will win a certain market share. Methods for sales forecasting are shown in Table 3.3 on page 70.

Analyzing the Macroenvironment

Another way marketers find opportunities is by identifying trends in the macroenvironment. A **trend** is a direction or sequence of events with momentum and durability, revealing the shape of the future. In contrast, a **fad** is a craze that is unpredictable, of brief duration, and without long-term significance. A company can cash in on a fad, but getting it right requires luck and good

TABLE 3.3	Sales Forecast Methods	
Forecast Method	**Description**	**Use**
Survey of buyers' intentions	Survey customers about purchase probability, future finances, and expectations about the economy.	To estimate demand for industrial products, consumer durables, purchases requiring advance planning, and new products.
Composite of sales force opinions	Have sales representatives estimate their future sales.	To gather detailed forecast estimates by product, territory, customer, and sales rep.
Expert opinion	Obtain forecasts from experts such as dealers, distributors, suppliers, consultants, and trade associations, or buy from economic-forecasting firms.	To gather estimates from knowledgeable specialists who may offer good insights.
Past-sales analysis	Use time-series analysis, exponential smoothing, statistical demand analysis, or econometric analysis to analyze past sales.	To project future demand on the basis of an analysis of past demand.
Market-test method	Conduct a direct-market test to understand customer response and estimate future sales.	To forecast sales of new products or sales of an established product in a new channel or area.

timing. Marketers should develop their trend-spotting skills so they can distinguish trends from fads and prepare to respond (see "Marketing Skills: Spotting Trends").

Identifying the Major Forces

The end of the new century's first decade brought new challenges: the steep decline of the stock market, which affected savings, investment, and retirement funds; increasing unemployment;

Marketing Skills

SPOTTING TRENDS

Marketers need good trend-spotting skills so they can take action in time to turn a change into a profitable opportunity rather than a profit-sapping threat. Trend-spotting requires "splatter vision," the ability to look at the big picture without becoming too focused on one factor. Marketers can also use their mental models of future expectations—based on sales or industry forecasts—to identify deviations that could affect marketing. In the ever-changing technology industry, experts use a combination of five approaches: seeing the future as an extension of the past, searching for cycles and patterns, analyzing the actions of customers and other stakeholders, monitoring technical and social events as they unfold, and discerning trends from the interaction of these four approaches.

For example, Apple uses a variety of methods to identify emerging trends and respond with timely offerings. Analyzing what, when, and how customers download from its iTunes, App Store, and iBooks sites helps the company dig deeper into media usage, gauge the popularity of individual digital products, and plan for mobile marketing. Apple was also one of the earliest to recognize the trend toward faster adoption of touch-screen technology, which has fueled sales of its iPod, iPhone, iTouch, and, most recently, iPad, which sold 3 million units in the first 80 days. With Apple leading the way, the market for touch-screen gadgets is burgeoning.[11]

TABLE 3.4	A Global Profile of Extremes	
Highest fertility rate	Niger	6.88 children per woman
Highest education expenditure as percent of GDP	Kiribati	17.8% of GDP
Highest number of mobile phone subscribers	China	547,286,000
Largest number of airports	United States	14,951 airports
Highest military expenditure as percent of GDP	Oman	11.4% of GDP
Largest refugee population	Pakistan	21,075,000 people
Highest divorce rate	Aruba	4.4 divorces per 1,000 population
Highest color TV ownership per 100 households	United Arab Emirates	99.7 TVs
Mobile telephone subscribers per capita	Lithuania	138.1 subscribers per 100 people
Highest cinema attendance	India	1,473,400,000 cinema visits
Biggest beer drinkers per capita	Czech Republic	81.9 liters per capita
Biggest wine drinkers per capita	Portugal	33.1 liters per capita
Highest number of smokers per capita	Greece	8.2 cigarettes per person per day
Highest GDP per person	Luxembourg	$87,490
Largest aid donors as % of GDP	Sweden	1.03% of GDP
Most economically dependent on agriculture	Liberia	66% of GDP
Highest population in workforce	Cayman Islands	69.2%
Highest percent of women in workforce	Belarus	53.3%
Most crowded road networks	Qatar	283.6 vehicles per km of road
Most deaths in road accidents	South Africa	31 killed per 100,000 population
Most tourist arrivals	France	79,083,000
Highest life expectancy	Andorra	83.5 years
Highest diabetes rate	United Arab Emirates	19.5% of population aged 20–79

Sources: *CIA World Fact Book*, www.cia.gov/library/publications/the-world-factbook/geos/xx.html, accessed July 24, 2009; *The Economist's Pocket World in Figures, 2009 edition*, www.economist.com.

corporate scandals; stronger indications of global warming and other signs of deterioration in the national environment; and of course, the rise of terrorism. These dramatic events were accompanied by the continuation of many trends that have already profoundly influenced the global landscape (see Table 3.4).[12]

Firms must monitor six major forces in the broad environment: demographic, economic, sociocultural, natural, technological, and political-legal. Although we'll describe them separately, remember that their interactions will lead to new opportunities and threats.

The Demographic Environment

The main demographic force monitored by marketers is *population,* including the size and growth rate of population in cities, regions, and nations; age distribution; diversity; educational levels; and household patterns.

FINDING GOLD AT THE BOTTOM OF THE PYRAMID

Business professor C. K. Prahalad wrote that much innovation can come from developments in emerging markets such as China and India. He estimated there are 5 billion unserved and underserved people at the so-called "bottom of the pyramid." One study showed that 4 billion people live on $2 or less a day. Firms operating in those markets have had to learn how to do more with less.

In Brazil, Eastern Europe, and other markets, Microsoft offers a pay-as-you-go FlexGo program, allowing users to prepay to use a fully loaded PC only for as long as wanted or needed, rather than paying the full price of the PC. When the payment runs out, the PC stops operating and the user prepays again to restart it. Other firms apply "reverse innovation" by developing products for countries like China and India and then distributing them globally. After GE successfully introduced a $1,000 handheld electrocardiogram device for rural India and a portable ultrasound machine for rural China, it began to sell these products in the United States.

Sources: C. K. Prahalad, *The Fortune at the Bottom of the Pyramid* (Upper Saddle River, NJ: Wharton School Publishing, 2010); Bill Breen, "C. K. Prahalad: Pyramid Schemer," *Fast Company*, March 2007, p. 79; Pete Engardio, "Business Prophet: How C. K. Prahalad Is Changing the Way CEOs Think," *BusinessWeek*, January 23, 2006, pp. 68–73; Reena Jane, "Inspiration from Emerging Economies," *BusinessWeek*, March 23 and 30, 2009, pp. 38–41; Jeffrey R. Immelt, Vijay Govindarajan, and Chris Trimble, "How GE Is Disrupting Itself," *Harvard Business Review*, October 2009, pp. 56–65; Peter J. Williamson and Ming Zeng, "Value-for-Money Strategies for Recessionary Times," *Harvard Business Review*, March 2009, pp. 66–74.

Worldwide Population Growth   World population growth is explosive: Earth's population totaled 6.8 billion in 2010 and will exceed 9 billion by 2040.[13] Developing regions of the world currently account for 84 percent of the world population and are growing at 1 percent to 2 percent per year; the population in developed countries is growing at only 0.3 percent.[14] In developing nations, modern medicine is lowering the death rate, but the birthrate remains fairly stable. Sometimes the lessons from developing markets are helping businesses in developed markets. See "Marketing Insight: Finding Gold at the Bottom of the Pyramid (above)."

Population Age Mix   Marketers generally divide the population into six age groups (preschool children, school-age children, teens, young adults age 20 to 40, middle-aged adults 40 to 65, and older adults 65 and older), with a global trend toward an aging population. Some marketers focus on *cohorts*, groups of individuals born during the same time period who travel through life together. The defining moments they experience as they come of age and become adults (roughly ages 17 through 24) can stay with them for a lifetime and influence their values, preferences, and buying behaviors.

Diversity within Markets   Ethnic and racial diversity varies across countries, which affects needs, wants, and buying habits. At one extreme is Japan, where almost everyone is Japanese; at the other is the United States, where nearly 25 million people—more than 9 percent of the population—were born in another country. Major groups within the U.S. population include whites, African Americans, Hispanics (with large subgroups of Mexican, Puerto Rican, and Cuban descent), and Asian Americans (with large subgroups of Chinese, Filipino, Japanese, Asian Indian, and Korean descent). Marketers must not overgeneralize about ethnic groups, however, because within each group are consumers who are quite different from each other.[15] Diversity goes beyond ethnic and racial markets. More than 51 million U.S. consumers have disabilities, and they constitute a market for many goods and services.

Educational Groups   The population in any society falls into five educational groups: illiterates, high school dropouts, high school diplomas, college degrees, and professional degrees. Over two-thirds of the world's 785 million illiterate adults are found in only eight countries (India, China, Bangladesh, Pakistan, Nigeria, Ethiopia, Indonesia, and Egypt); of all illiterate adults in the world, two-thirds are women.[16] The United States has one of the world's highest percentages of college-educated citizens, which drives demand for books, magazines, and travel.

Household Patterns   The traditional household consists of a husband, wife, and children (and sometimes grandparents). Yet only one in five U.S. households consists of a married couple with children under 18. Other households are single live-alones, single-parent families, childless married couples and empty nesters, living with nonrelatives only, and other family structures.[17] More people are divorcing or separating, choosing not to marry, marrying later, or marrying without intending to have children, which affects their needs and buying habits. Nontraditional households are growing more quickly than traditional households. The gay and lesbian population, for example, is estimated to range between 4 percent and 8 percent of the total U.S. population, higher in urban areas.[18]

The Economic Environment

The available purchasing power in an economy depends on current income, prices, savings, debt, and credit availability. As the recent economic downturn vividly demonstrated, trends affecting purchasing power can have a strong impact on business, especially for companies whose products are geared to high-income and price-sensitive consumers.

Consumer Psychology   Did new consumer spending patterns during the recent recession reflect short-term, temporary adjustments or long-term, permanent changes?[19] Identifying the more likely long-term scenario would help marketers decide on marketing investments. For example, after months of research and development in the baby boomer market, Starwood introduced two new hotel chains as affordable yet stylish alternatives to its high-end chains. Targeting consumers seeking both thrift and luxury, its Aloft hotels reflect the urban cool of loft apartments, and its Element hotels feature suites with spa-like bathrooms.[20]

Income Distribution   There are four types of industrial structures: *subsistence economies* with few opportunities for marketers; *raw-material-exporting economies* like Saudi Arabia (oil), a good market for equipment, tools, supplies, and luxury goods for the rich; *industrializing economies* like India and the Philippines, where the rich and middle class demand new types of goods; and *industrial economies* like Western Europe, good markets for all sorts of goods. Marketers often distinguish countries using five income-distribution patterns: very low incomes; mostly low incomes; very low, very high incomes; low, medium, high incomes; and mostly medium incomes.

Income, Savings, Debt, and Credit   Consumer expenditures are affected by income levels, savings rates, debt practices, and credit availability. U.S. consumers have a high debt-to-income ratio, which slows expenditures on housing and large-ticket items. When credit became scarcer in the recession, especially to lower-income borrowers, consumer borrowing dropped. An economic issue of increasing importance is the migration of manufacturers and service jobs offshore, which affects incomes in the United States and in the countries where the jobs have been relocated.

The Sociocultural Environment

From our sociocultural environment we absorb, almost unconsciously, a world view that defines our relationships to ourselves, others, organizations, society, nature, and the universe.

- Views of ourselves. In the United States during the 1960s and 1970s, "pleasure seekers" sought fun and escape while others sought "self-realization." Today, some are adopting more conservative behaviors and ambitions.
- Views of others. People are concerned about the homeless, crime and victims, and other social problems. At the same time, they seek those like themselves for long-lasting relationships, suggesting a growing market for health clubs, cruises, and religious activity as well as for "social surrogates" like video games and social networking sites.
- Views of organizations. After a wave of layoffs and corporate scandals, organizational loyalty has declined.[21] Companies need new ways to win back consumer and employee confidence, ensure that they are good corporate citizens, and show their honesty.[22]
- Views of society. Some people defend society, some run it, some take what they can from it, some want to change it, some are looking for something deeper, and still others want to leave it.[23] Consumption patterns often reflect these social attitudes. For example, those who want to change it may live more frugally and drive smaller cars.
- Views of nature. Business has responded to increased awareness of nature's fragility and finiteness by producing wider varieties of camping, hiking, boating, and fishing gear such as boots, tents, backpacks, and accessories.
- Views of the universe. Most U.S. citizens are monotheistic, although religious conviction and practice have waned through the years or been redirected into an interest in evangelical movements or Eastern religions, mysticism, the occult, and the human potential movement.

High Persistence of Core Cultural Values   *Core beliefs* and values are passed from parents to children and reinforced by social institutions—schools, churches, businesses, and governments. *Secondary beliefs* and values are more open to change. Believing in the institution of marriage is a core belief; believing people should marry early is a secondary belief. Marketers have some chance of changing secondary values, but little chance of changing core values. The nonprofit organization Mothers Against Drunk Drivers (MADD) does not try to stop the sale of alcohol but promotes lower legal blood-alcohol levels for driving and limited operating hours for businesses that sell alcohol.

Existence of Subcultures   Each society contains **subcultures**, groups with shared values, beliefs, preferences, and behaviors emerging from their special life experiences or circumstances. Marketers have always loved teenagers because they are trendsetters in fashion, music, entertainment, and attitudes. Attract someone as a teen, and you will likely keep the person as a customer. Frito-Lay, which draws 15 percent of its sales from teens, has noted a rise in chip snacking by grown-ups. "We think it's because we brought them in as teenagers," said Frito-Lay's marketing director.[24]

The Natural Environment

In Western Europe, "green" parties have pressed for public action to reduce industrial pollution. In the United States, experts have documented ecological deterioration, and watchdog groups such as the Sierra Club carry these concerns into political and social action. Although environmental regulations have hit certain industries hard, opportunities await those who can reconcile prosperity with environmental protection.

Corporate environmentalism recognizes the need to integrate environmental issues into the firm's strategic plans. Trends in the natural environment to be aware of include the shortage of raw materials, especially water; the increased cost of energy; increased pollution levels; and the changing role of governments.[25]

- The earth's raw materials consist of the infinite, the finite renewable, and the finite nonrenewable. Firms whose products require *finite nonrenewable resources*—oil, coal, platinum, zinc, silver—face substantial cost increases as depletion approaches. Firms that can develop substitute materials have an excellent opportunity.
- One finite nonrenewable resource, oil, has created serious problems for the world economy. As oil prices soar, companies search for practical means to harness solar, nuclear, wind, and other alternative energies.
- Some industrial activity will inevitably damage the natural environment, creating a large market for pollution-control solutions such as scrubbers, recycling centers, and landfill systems as well as for alternative ways to produce and package goods.
- Many poor nations are doing little about pollution, lacking the funds or the political will. It is in the richer nations' interest to help them control their pollution, but even richer nations today lack the necessary funds.

In the past, some green marketing programs had difficulty gaining acceptance; consumers may have thought a product was inferior because it was green, or may have believed the product was not really green to begin with. Those green products that have been successful have persuaded consumers that they are acting in their own and society's long-run interest at the same time. For example, Clorox's Green Works line of green cleaning products found the sweet spot of a target market wanting to take smaller steps toward a greener lifestyle. Clorox priced the line at a modest premium to competing products and used grassroots marketing to bring its sustainability message to the target market.[26]

The Technological Environment

Major new technologies stimulate the economy's growth rate; between innovations, an economy can stagnate. Lower-risk, minor innovations may fill the gap, but they can also divert research effort away from major breakthroughs. Innovation's long-run consequences are not always foreseeable, and when established industries fight or ignore new technologies, their businesses decline. To be prepared, marketers should monitor these technology trends:

- Accelerating pace of technological pace. More new ideas than ever are in the works, and the time between idea and implementation is shrinking, as is the time between introduction and peak production.
- Unlimited opportunities for innovation. Some of the most exciting innovations today are taking place in biotechnology, computers, microelectronics, telecommunications, robotics, and designer materials.
- Varying R&D budgets. A growing portion of U.S. R&D expenditures goes to development rather than research, raising concerns about whether the nation can maintain its lead in basic science. Many firms put their money into copying competitors' products and making minor feature and style improvements. Even basic research companies such as

Dow Chemical and Pfizer are proceeding cautiously, and more consortiums than single companies are directing research efforts toward major breakthroughs.

- Increased regulation of technological change. Government has expanded its agencies' powers to investigate and ban potentially unsafe products. Safety and health regulations have increased for food, automobiles, clothing, electrical appliances, and construction.

The Political-Legal Environment

The political and legal environment consists of laws, government agencies, and pressure groups that influence various organizations and individuals. Sometimes these laws create new business opportunities, the way mandatory recycling laws have boosted the recycling industry and encouraged new companies to make new products from recycled materials. Two major trends in this arena are the increase in business legislation and the growth of special-interest groups.

Increase in Business Legislation
Business legislation is intended to protect companies from unfair competition, protect consumers from unfair business practices, protect society from unbridled business behavior, and charge businesses with the social costs of their products or processes. However, each new law may also have the unintended effect of sapping initiative and slowing growth. The United States has many consumer protection laws covering competition, product safety and liability, fair trade and credit practices, and packaging and labeling. The European Commission has laws covering competitive behavior, product standards, product liability, and commercial transactions for members of the European Union.

Growth of Special-Interest Groups
Political action committees (PACs) lobby government officials and pressure business executives to respect the rights of consumers, women, senior citizens, minorities, and gays and lesbians. The *consumerist movement* organized citizens and government to strengthen the rights and powers of buyers in relationship to sellers. Consumerists have won many rights, including the right to know the real cost of a loan and the nutritional content of foods. Privacy issues and identify theft are also public policy hot buttons. Wise companies have consumer affairs departments to formulate policies and resolve complaints.

EXECUTIVE SUMMARY

A marketing information system (MIS) consists of people, equipment, and procedures to gather, sort, analyze, evaluate, and distribute needed, timely, and accurate information to marketing decision makers. It draws from data in internal company records as well as from marketing intelligence and marketing research. The marketing research process has six steps: define the problem and objectives, develop the plan, collect the data, analyze the data, present the findings, and make the decision. The company uses forecasting and demand measurement to evaluate the size, growth, and profit potential of each new opportunity.

Marketers must monitor six major environmental forces: demographic, economic, socio-cultural, natural, technological, and political-legal. In the demographic arena, marketers must be aware of worldwide population growth; mixes of age, diversity, and educational levels; and household patterns. In the economic arena, marketers should focus on income distribution and levels of savings, debt, and credit availability, as well as consumer psychology. In the sociocultural arena, marketers must understand people's views of themselves, others, organizations, society, nature, and the universe; the role of core cultural values; and subcultures. In the natural environment, marketers need to be aware of the public's increased concern about environmental health. In the technological arena, marketers should note the accelerating pace of change, opportunities for innovation, varying R&D budgets, and increased regulation. In the political-legal environment, marketers must work within the many laws regulating business practices and with various special-interest groups.

NOTES

1. Andrew Adam Newman, "Getting Dad to Do Diaper (Buying) Duty," *New York Times,* June 22, 2010, www.nytimes.com; Jia Lynn Yang, "The Bottom Line," *Fortune,* September 1, 2008, pp. 107–12; Jack Neff, "From Mucus to Maxi Pads: Marketing's Dirtiest Jobs," *Advertising Age,* February 16, 2009, p. 9.

2. See Robert Schieffer, *Ten Key Customer Insights: Unlocking the Mind of the Market* (Mason, OH: Thomson, 2005) for a comprehensive discussion of how to generate customer insights to drive business results.

3. Jenn Abelson, "Gillette Sharpens Its Focus on Women," *Boston Globe,* January 4, 2009.

4. For background information on in-flight Internet service, see "In-flight Wireless Internet to Expand to Hundreds of American Airlines Planes," *Los Angeles Times,* March 30, 2009, www.latimes.com; "Boeing In-Flight Internet Plan Goes Airborne," *Associated Press,* April 18, 2004; John Blau, "In-Flight Internet Service Ready for Takeoff," *IDG News Service,* June 14, 2002; "In-Flight Dogfight," *Business2.com,* January 9, 2001, pp. 84–91.

5. For a review of relevant academic work, see Eric J. Arnould and Amber Epp, "Deep Engagement with Consumer Experience," Rajiv Grover and Marco Vriens, eds., *Handbook of Marketing Research* (Thousand Oaks, CA: Sage Publications, 2006). For a range of academic discussion, see the following special issue, "Can Ethnography Uncover Richer Consumer Insights?" *Journal of Advertising Research* 46 (September 2006). For practical tips, see Richard Durante and Michael Feehan, "Leverage Ethnography to Improve Strategic Decision Making," *Marketing Research* (Winter 2005).

6. Piet Levy, "In with the Old, in Spite of the New," *Marketing News,* May 30, 2009, p. 19.

7. Louise Witt, "Inside Intent," *American Demographics,* March 2004, pp. 34–39; Andy Raskin, "A Face Any Business Can Trust," *Business 2.0,* December 2003, pp. 58–60; Laurie Burkitt, "Battle for the Brain," *Forbes,* November 16, 2009, pp. 76–77.

8. Michael Fielding, "Global Insights: Synovate's Chedore Discusses MR Trends," *Marketing News,* May 15, 2006, pp. 41–42.

9. For further discussion, see Gary L. Lilien, Philip Kotler, and K. Sridhar Moorthy, *Marketing Models* (Upper Saddle River, NJ: Prentice Hall, 1992).

10. www.naics.com; www.census.gov/epcd/naics02, December 9, 2010.

11. Adam Satariano, "Apple Studies User Downloads to Fine-Tune Mobile Ads," *BusinessWeek,* July 6, 2010, www.businessweek.com; David Needle, "iPad Raises Fortunes for Touchscreen Makers," *InternetNews,* July 7, 2010, www.internetnews.com/hardware/article.php/3891641; Peter Bisson, Elizabeth Stephenson, and S. Patrick Viguerie, "Global Forces: An Introduction," *McKinsey Quarterly,* June 2010, www.mckinseyquarterly.com; Cynthia G. Wagner, "Top 10 Reasons to Watch Trends," *The Futurist,* March–April 2002, pp. 68+; Wayne Burkan, "Developing Your Wide-Angle Vision," *The Futurist,* March 1998, pp. 35+; Edward Cornish, "How We Can Anticipate Future Events," *The Futurist,* July 2001, pp. 26+; "Techniques for Forecasting," *The Futurist,* March 2001, p. 56.

12. Indata, *IN* (June 2006), p. 27.

13. World POPClock, U.S. Census Bureau, www.census.gov, 2009.

14. "World Development Indicators Database," *World Bank,* http://siteresources.worldbank.org/DATASTATISTICS/Resources/POP.pdf, September 15, 2009; "World Population Growth," www.worldbank.org/depweb/english/beyond/beyondco/beg_03.pdf.

15. Mark R. Forehand and Rohit Deshpandé, "What We See Makes Us Who We Are: Priming Ethnic

Self-Awareness and Advertising Response," *Journal of Marketing Research* (August 2001), pp. 336–48.

16. *The Central Intelligence Agency's World Factbook,* www.cia.gov/library/publications/the-world-factbook, December 9, 2010.

17. "Projections of the Number of Households and Families in the United States: 1995–2010, P25–1129," *U.S. Department of Commerce, Bureau of the Census,* www.census.gov/prod/1/pop/p25-1129.pdf, December 9, 2010.

18. Rebecca Gardyn, "A Market Kept in the Closet," *American Demographics,* November 2001, pp. 37–43.

19. Elisabeth Sullivan, "The Age of Prudence," *Marketing News,* April 15, 2009, pp. 8–11; Steve Hamm, "The New Age of Frugality," *BusinessWeek,* October 20, 2008, pp. 55–60; Jessica Deckler, "Never Pay Retail Again," *CNNMoney.com,* May 30, 2008.

20. David Welch, "The Incredible Shrinking Boomer Economy," *BusinessWeek,* August 3, 2009, pp. 27–30.

21. Pamela Paul, "Corporate Responsibility," *American Demographics,* May 2002, pp. 24–25.

22. Stephen Baker, "Wiser about the Web," *BusinessWeek,* March 27, 2006, pp. 53–57.

23. "Clearing House Suit Chronology," *Associated Press,* January 26, 2001; Paul Wenske, "You Too Could Lose $19,000!" *Kansas City Star,* October 31, 1999.

24. Laura Zinn, "Teens: Here Comes the Biggest Wave Yet," *BusinessWeek,* April 11, 2004, pp. 76–86.

25. Subhabrata Bobby Banerjee, Easwar S. Iyer, and Rajiv K. Kashyap, "Corporate Environmentalism: Antecedents and Influence of Industry Type," *Journal of Marketing* 67 (April 2003), pp. 106–22.

26. Gregory Unruh, "Sustainable Product Strategies for Going Green," *Environmental Leader,* June 21, 2010, www.environmentalleader.com.

Creating Long-term Loyalty Relationships

In this chapter, we will address the following questions:

1. How can companies deliver customer value, satisfaction, and loyalty?
2. What is the lifetime value of customers, and how can marketers maximize it?
3. How can companies attract and retain the right customers and cultivate strong customer relationships?
4. What are the pros and cons of database marketing?

Marketing Management at Harrah's Entertainment

Harrah's Entertainment, based in Las Vegas, has pioneered a loyalty program that pulls all customer data into a centralized data warehouse and provides sophisticated analysis to understand the value of the investments made in its customers. Harrah's has over 10 million active members in its Total Rewards loyalty program, a system it has fine-tuned to achieve near-real-time analysis: As customers interact with slot machines, check into casinos, or buy meals, they receive reward offers—food vouchers or gambling credits, for example—based on the predictive analyses.

The firm has now identified hundreds of highly specific customer segments, and by targeting offers to each of them, it can almost double its share of customers' gaming budgets and generate $6.4 billion annually (80 percent of its gaming revenue). Harrah's dramatically cut back its traditional ad spending, largely replacing it with direct mail and e-mail; a good customer may receive as many as 150 communications in a year. Harrah's is also active in mobile marketing, sending time-based and location-based offers to customers' mobile devices in real time.[1]

As Harrah's knows, the cornerstone of holistic marketing is strong customer relationships. Marketers must win customers by connecting with them—listening and responding to them, informing and engaging them, and maybe even energizing them in the process. This chapter discusses how marketers can beat competitors by connecting with customers to build value, satisfaction, and long-term loyalty.

Building Customer Value, Satisfaction, and Loyalty

Consumers are better educated and informed than ever, and they have the tools to verify companies' claims and seek out superior alternatives.[2] How then do they ultimately make choices? Customers tend to be value maximizers, within the bounds of search costs and limited knowledge, mobility, and income. They estimate which offer they believe will deliver the most perceived value and act on it. Whether the offer lives up to expectation affects customer satisfaction and the probability that the customer will purchase the product again. Effective competition depends largely on the company's ability to do a better job of providing value to customers and meeting or exceeding their expectations.

Customer Perceived Value

Customer-perceived value (CPV) is the difference between the prospective customer's evaluation of all the benefits and all the costs of an offering and the perceived alternatives (see Figure 4.1).

FIGURE 4.1 Determinants of Customer-Perceived Value

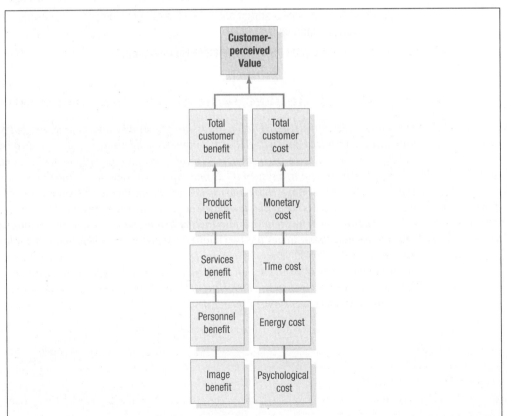

Total customer benefit is the perceived monetary value of the bundle of economic, functional, and psychological benefits customers expect from a given market offering because of the product, service, people, and image. **Total customer cost** is the perceived bundle of costs customers expect to incur in evaluating, obtaining, using, and disposing of the given market offering, including monetary, time, energy, and psychological costs.

Suppose the buyer for a construction company wants to buy a tractor from either Caterpillar or Komatsu. After evaluating the two tractors on the basis of reliability, durability, performance, and resale value, the buyer decides Caterpillar has greater product benefits. He also decides Caterpillar provides better service and has more knowledgeable and responsive staff. Finally, he places higher value on Caterpillar's corporate image and reputation. He adds up all the benefits from product, services, personnel, and image, and perceives Caterpillar as delivering greater customer benefits.

The buyer also examines his total cost of transacting with Caterpillar versus Komatsu, including money plus time, energy, and psychological costs expended in product acquisition, usage, maintenance, ownership, and disposal. Then he considers whether Caterpillar's total customer cost is too high compared to total customer benefits. If it is, he might choose Komatsu. The buyer will buy from whichever source delivers the highest perceived value.

In this situation, Caterpillar can improve its offer in three ways. First, it can increase total customer benefit by improving economic, functional, and psychological benefits. Second, it can reduce the buyer's nonmonetary costs by reducing the time, energy, and psychological investment. Third, it can reduce its product's monetary cost to the buyer.

Some marketers might argue that this process is too rational. Suppose the customer chooses the Komatsu tractor. How can we explain this choice? Here are three possibilities.

1. *The buyer might be under orders to buy at the lowest price.* Caterpillar's task is then to convince the buyer's manager that buying on price alone will result in lower long-term profits and customer value.

2. *The buyer will retire before the company realizes the Komatsu tractor is more expensive to operate.* Caterpillar's task is to convince other people in the customer company that it delivers greater customer value.

3. *The buyer enjoys a long-term friendship with the Komatsu salesperson.* Here, Caterpillar must show the buyer that the Komatsu tractor will draw complaints from the tractor operators when they discover its high fuel cost and need for frequent repairs.

Customer-perceived value is a useful framework that applies to many situations and yields rich insights. It suggests that the seller must assess the total customer benefit and total customer cost associated with each competitor's offer to learn how his or her offer rates in the buyer's mind. It also implies that the seller at a disadvantage has two alternatives: increase total customer benefit or decrease total customer cost.

Consumers have varying degrees of loyalty to specific brands, stores, and companies. Oliver defines **loyalty** as "a deeply held commitment to rebuy or repatronize a preferred product or service in the future despite situational influences and marketing efforts having the potential to cause switching behavior."[3] The *value proposition* consists of the whole cluster of benefits the company promises to deliver. For example, Volvo's core positioning has been "safety," but it also promises other benefits, such as a long-lasting car and good service. The value proposition is thus a promise about the total experience customers can expect and their relationship with the marketer. Whether the promise is kept depends on the company's ability to manage its **value delivery system**, all the experiences the customer will have on the way to obtaining and using the offering.[4]

Total Customer Satisfaction

In general, **satisfaction** is a person's feelings of pleasure or disappointment that result from comparing a product's perceived performance (or outcome) to expectations.[5] If the performance falls short of expectations, the customer is dissatisfied. If it matches expectations, the customer is satisfied. If it exceeds expectations, the customer is highly satisfied or delighted.[6] Customer assessments of product performance depend on many factors, especially the type of loyalty relationship the customer has with the brand.[7]

Buyers form their expectations from past buying experience, friends' and associates' advice, and marketers' and competitors' information and promises. If marketers raise expectations too high, the buyer is likely to be disappointed. If they set expectations too low, they won't attract enough buyers (although they will satisfy those who do buy).[8] Some of today's most successful companies are raising expectations and delivering performances to match. Korean automaker Kia has found success in the United States by launching low-cost, high-quality cars with enough reliability to offer 10-year, 100,000 mile warranties.

However, high customer satisfaction is not the ultimate goal. Increasing customer satisfaction by lowering price or increasing services may result in lower profits. The company might be able to increase its profitability by means other than increased satisfaction (for example, by improving manufacturing processes). Also, the company has many stakeholders, including employees, dealers, suppliers, and stockholders. Spending more to increase customer satisfaction might divert funds from increasing the satisfaction of other "partners." Ultimately, the company must try to deliver a high level of customer satisfaction while also delivering acceptable levels to other stakeholders.[9]

Monitoring Satisfaction

Many companies are systematically measuring how well they treat customers, identifying the factors shaping satisfaction, and changing operations and marketing as a result.[10] A highly satisfied customer generally stays loyal longer, buys more as the company introduces new and upgraded products, talks favorably about the company and its products, pays less attention to competing brands and is less sensitive to price, offers product or service ideas to the company, and costs less to serve than new customers because transactions can become routine.[11] Greater customer satisfaction has also been linked to higher returns and lower risk in the stock market.[12]

The link between customer satisfaction and customer loyalty is not proportional, however. Suppose customer satisfaction is rated on a scale from one to five. At a very low level of satisfaction (level one), customers are likely to abandon the company and even bad-mouth it. At levels two to four, customers are fairly satisfied but find it easy to switch to better offers. At level five, the customer is very likely to repurchase and spread good word of mouth about the company. High satisfaction creates an emotional bond with the brand or firm, not just a rational preference. Xerox found that its "completely satisfied" customers were six times more likely to repurchase Xerox products over the following 18 months than even its "very satisfied" customers.[13]

Yet customers vary in how they define good performance. Good delivery could mean early delivery, on-time delivery, or order completeness, and two customers can report being "highly satisfied" for different reasons. One may be easily satisfied most of the time and the other might be hard to please but was pleased on this occasion. Bain's Frederick Reichheld suggests only one customer question really matters: "How likely is it that you would recommend this product or service to a friend or colleague?" According to Reichheld, a customer's willingness to recommend results from how well the customer is treated by frontline employees, which in turn is determined by all the functional areas that contribute to a customer's experience.[14] For more on monitoring satisfaction, see "Marketing Skills: Gauging Customer Satisfaction."

GAUGING CUSTOMER SATISFACTION

The vital skill of gauging customer satisfaction requires a working knowledge of marketing research coupled with a sensitivity for customer concerns. Marketers start by defining their specific research goals as they relate to customer satisfaction. Next, they build on their knowledge of customer behavior to design the study and encourage participation. After gathering and analyzing data, marketers communicate the findings internally to highlight good news, act on bad news, and plan new ways of satisfying customers. Repeating this research at regular intervals allows marketers to track satisfaction trends and determine the effect of changes.

For example, JD Sports, a British sportswear retailer, monitors satisfaction through feedback from a sample of shoppers at its 450 UK stores. Even when respondents don't make a purchase during a particular visit, the retailer wants them to have a good experience so they will return in the future. JD Sports requires fast turnaround of research results so it can determine immediate customer satisfaction with employee training, promotions, and other efforts. Focusing on satisfaction has helped the chain attract and retain customers, even during difficult economic periods, building annual sales beyond $1 billion.[15]

Product and Service Quality

Satisfaction will also depend on product and service quality. What exactly is quality? Various experts have defined it as "fitness for use," "conformance to requirements," and "freedom from variation." We'll use the American Society for Quality's definition: **Quality** is the totality of features and characteristics of a product or service that bear on its ability to satisfy stated or implied needs.[16] The seller has delivered quality whenever its product or service meets or exceeds the customers' expectations. It's important to distinguish between *conformance* quality and *performance* quality (or grade). A Lexus provides higher performance quality than a Hyundai: The Lexus rides smoother, goes faster, and lasts longer. Yet both a Lexus and a Hyundai deliver the same conformance quality if all the units deliver their respective promised quality.

Studies have shown a high correlation between relative product quality and company profitability.[17] Total quality is everyone's job, just as marketing is everyone's job. Marketers play several roles in helping their companies define and deliver high-quality goods and services to target customers. They must (1) correctly identify customers' needs and requirements; (2) communicate customer expectations properly to product designers; (3) make sure customers' orders are filled correctly and on time; (4) check that customers have received proper instructions, training, and technical assistance in using the product; (5) follow up after the sale to ensure customers are, and remain, satisfied; and (6) gather customer ideas for product and service improvements and communicate them internally. When marketers do all this, they make substantial contributions to total quality management and customer satisfaction, as well as to customer and company profitability.

Maximizing Customer Lifetime Value

Ultimately, marketing is the art of attracting and keeping profitable customers. Yet every company loses money on some of its customers. The well-known 80–20 rule states that 80 percent or more of the company's profits come from the top 20 percent of its customers. Some cases may be more extreme—the most profitable 20 percent of customers (on a per capita basis) may contribute as much as 150 percent to 300 percent of profitability. The least profitable 10 percent to 20 percent, on the other hand, can actually reduce profits between 50 percent to 200 percent per account, with the middle 60 percent to 70 percent breaking even.[18] The implication is that a company could improve its profits by "firing" its worst customers.

The largest customers don't always yield the most profit, because they can demand considerable service and deep discounts. The smallest customers pay full price and receive minimal service, but transaction costs can reduce their profitability. Midsize customers who receive good service and pay nearly full price are often the most profitable.

Customer Profitability

A **profitable customer** is a person, household, or company that over time yields a revenue stream exceeding by an acceptable amount the company's cost stream for attracting, selling, and serving that customer. Note the emphasis is on the *lifetime* stream of revenue and cost, not the profit from a particular transaction.[19] Marketers can assess customer profitability individually, by market segment, or by channel.

Many companies measure customer satisfaction, but few measure individual customer profitability.[20] Banks say this is because each customer uses different banking services and the transactions are logged in different departments. However, the number of unprofitable customers in their customer base has appalled banks that have linked customer transactions. Some report losing money on over 45 percent of their retail customers.

Figure 4.2 shows a useful type of profitability analysis.[21] Customers are arrayed along the columns and products along the rows. Each cell contains a symbol representing the profitability of selling that product to that customer. Customer 1 is very profitable, buying two profit-making products. Customer 2 yields mixed profitability, buying one profitable and one unprofitable product. Customer 3 is a losing customer, buying one profitable product and two unprofitable products. What can the company do about customers 2 and 3? (1) It can raise the

FIGURE 4.2 Customer-Product Profitability Analysis

Products		Customers			
		C_1	C_2	C_3	
	P_1	+	+	+	Highly profitable product
	P_2	+			Profitable product
	P_3		−	−	Unprofitable product
	P_4			−	Highly unprofitable product
		High-profit customer	Mixed-bag customer	Losing customer	

price of less profitable products or eliminate them, or (2) it can try to sell customers 2 and 3 its profit-making products. In fact, the firm should encourage unprofitable customers to switch to competitors.

Customer profitability analysis is best conducted with an accounting technique called *activity-based costing (ABC)*. The company estimates all revenue coming from the customer, less all costs (including the direct and indirect costs associated with serving each customer). Companies that fail to measure their costs correctly are also not measuring their profit correctly and are likely to misallocate their marketing effort.

Measuring Customer Lifetime Value

The case for maximizing long-term customer profitability is captured in the concept of customer lifetime value.[22] **Customer lifetime value (CLV)** describes the net present value of the stream of future profits expected over the customer's lifetime purchases. The company must subtract from its expected revenues the expected costs of attracting, selling, and servicing the account of that customer, applying the appropriate discount rate (say, between 10 percent and 20 percent, depending on cost of capital and risk attitudes). Lifetime value calculations for a product or service can be tens of thousands of dollars or more.[23]

CLV calculations provide a formal quantitative framework for planning customer investment and help marketers adopt a long-term perspective. Many methods exist to measure CLV.[24] Columbia's Don Lehmann and Harvard's Sunil Gupta illustrate their approach by calculating the CLV of 100 customers over a 10-year period (see Table 4.1). In this example, the firm acquires 100 customers with an acquisition cost per customer of $40. Therefore, in year 0, it spends $4,000. Some of these customers defect each year. The present value of the profits from this cohort of customers over 10 years is $13,286.52. The net CLV (after deducting acquisition costs) is $9,286.52, or $92.87 per customer.[25]

TABLE 4.1	A Hypothetical Example to Illustrate CLV Calculations										
	Year 0	Year 1	Year 2	Year 3	Year 4	Year 5	Year 6	Year 7	Year 8	Year 9	Year 10
Number of Customers	100	90	80	72	60	48	34	23	12	6	2
Revenue per Customer		100	110	120	125	130	135	140	142	143	145
Variable Cost per Customer		70	72	75	76	78	79	80	81	82	83
Margin per Customer		30	38	45	49	52	56	60	61	61	62
Acquisition Cost per Customer	40										
Total Cost or Profit	−4,000	2,700	3,040	3,240	2,940	2,496	1,904	1,380	732	366	124
Present Value	−4,000.00	2,454.55	2,512.40	2,434.26	2,008.06	1,549.82	1,074.76	708.16	341.48	155.22	47.81

Source: Sunil Gupta and Donald R. Lehmann, "Models of Customer Value," Berend Wierenga, ed., *Handbook of Marketing Decision Models* (Springer Science Business Media, 2007).

Cultivating Customer Relationships

Once companies understand customer lifetime value, they can use information about customers to enact precision marketing designed to build strong, profitable long-term relationships.[26] **Customer relationship management (CRM)** is the process of carefully managing detailed information about individual customers and all customer touch points to maximize loyalty.[27] A *touch point* is any occasion on which a customer encounters the brand and product—from actual experience to marketing communications to casual observation. For a hotel, the touch points include reservations, check-in and checkout, frequent-stay programs, room service, business services, exercise facilities, and restaurants.

CRM enables companies to provide excellent real-time customer service through the effective use of individual account information. Based on what they know about each valued customer, companies can customize market offerings, services, programs, messages, and media. CRM is important because a major driver of company profitability is the aggregate value of the company's customer base.[28] Don Peppers and Martha Rogers outline a framework for one-to-one marketing that can be adapted to CRM marketing as follows:[29]

1. *Identify your prospects and customers.* Don't go after everyone. Build, maintain, and mine a rich customer database with information from all the channels and customer touch points.

2. *Differentiate customers in terms of (1) their needs and (2) their value to your company.* Spend proportionately more effort on the most valuable customers. Calculate customer lifetime value and estimate net present value of all future profits from purchases, margin levels, and referrals, less customer-specific servicing costs.

3. *Interact with individual customers to improve your knowledge about their individual needs and to build stronger relationships.* Facilitate customer interaction through the company contact center and Web site.

4. *Customize products, services, and messages to each customer.* Formulate customized offerings you can communicate in a personalized way.

Although much has been made of the newly empowered consumer—in charge, setting the direction of the brand, and playing a much bigger role in how it is marketed—it's still true that only *some consumers* want a relationship with *some of the brands* they use and, even then, only *some of the time*. Although the strongest influence on consumer choice remains "recommended by relative/friend," an increasingly important factor is "recommendations from consumers." Thus, online customer ratings and reviews now play an important role for online retailers such as Amazon.com and traditional retailers such as Staples.[30] Marketers are also paying close attention to what bloggers post, because their comments can influence whether some consumers start or continue a relationship.

Attracting and Retaining Customers

Companies seeking to expand their profits and sales must spend considerable time and resources searching for new customers. To generate leads, they use advertising, telemarketing, trade shows, and other methods of reaching new prospects. Different acquisition methods yield customers with varying CLVs. One study showed that the long-term value of customers acquired through the offer of a 35 percent discount was about one-half that of customers acquired without a discount.[31]

It is not enough to attract new customers; the company must also keep them and increase their business.[32] Too many companies suffer from high **customer churn** or defection. Some cellular carriers and cable TV operators lose 25 percent of their subscribers each year, at an estimated cost of $2 billion to $4 billion. To reduce the defection rate, the firm must first define and measure its retention rate, distinguish the causes of customer attrition and identify those that can be managed better, and compare the lost customer's CLV to the costs of cutting the defection rate. If the cost to discourage defection is lower than the lost profit, the firm should spend to retain the customer. Moreover, it's often easier to reattract ex-customers (because the company knows their names and histories) than to find new ones.

Figure 4.3 shows the main steps in attracting and retaining customers in terms of a funnel. The **marketing funnel** identifies the percentage of the potential target market at each stage in the decision process, from merely aware to highly loyal. Some marketers extend the funnel to include loyal customers who are brand advocates or even partners with the firm. By calculating *conversion rates*—the percentage of customers at one stage who move to the next—the funnel allows marketers to identify any bottleneck or barrier to building loyalty. The funnel also emphasizes how important it is not just to attract new customers, but to retain and cultivate existing ones.

Customer profitability analysis and the marketing funnel help marketers decide how to manage groups of customers that vary in loyalty, profitability, and other factors.[33] Winning companies know how to reduce the rate of customer defection; increase the longevity of customer relationships; enhance the growth potential of each customer through "share of wallet," up-selling, and cross-selling; make low-profit customers more profitable or terminate them; and treat high-profit customers in a special way. Even "free" customers who pay little or nothing and are subsidized by paying customers, as in print and online media, may be important to the firm because of their direct and indirect network effects.[34]

FIGURE 4.3 The Marketing Funnel

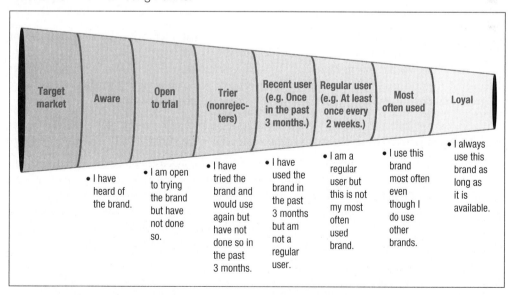

Building Loyalty

Creating a strong, tight connection to customers is the dream of any marketer and often the key to long-term marketing success. One set of researchers sees retention-building activities as adding financial benefits, social benefits, or structural ties.[35] The following sections explain three types of marketing activities companies are using to improve loyalty and retention.

Interacting with Customers   Listening to customers is crucial to customer relationship management. Some firms have an ongoing mechanism that keeps their marketers permanently plugged in to frontline customer feedback. For example, Deere & Company, which makes John Deere tractors and has a superb record of customer loyalty—nearly 98 percent annual retention in some product areas—has used retired employees to interview defectors and customers.[36] Listening is only part of the story. It is also important to be a customer advocate and, as much as possible, take the customers' side and understand their point of view.[37]

Developing Loyalty Programs   **Frequency programs (FPs)** are designed to reward customers who buy frequently and in substantial amounts.[38] They can help build long-term loyalty with high CLV customers, creating cross-selling opportunities in the process. Pioneered by the airlines, hotels, and credit card companies, FPs now exist in many other industries. Typically, the first company to introduce an FP in an industry gains the most benefit. After competitors react, FPs can become a financial burden to all the offering companies, but some marketers are more efficient and creative in managing them. Some FPs generate rewards in a way that locks customers in and creates significant costs to switching. FPs can also produce a feeling of being special and elite that customers value.[39]

Club membership programs can be open to everyone who purchases a product or service, or limited to an affinity group or those willing to pay a small fee. Although open clubs are good for building a database or snagging customers from competitors, limited-membership clubs are more powerful long-term loyalty builders. Fees and membership conditions prevent those with only a fleeting interest in a company's products from joining. These clubs attract and keep those customers responsible for the largest portion of business. Apple, for instance, encourages customers to form local Apple-user groups. Now there are over 700, ranging in size from fewer than 30 members to over 1,000.[40]

Creating Institutional Ties   The company may supply customers with special equipment or services that help them manage orders or inventory. Customers are less inclined to switch to another supplier when it means high capital costs, high search costs, or the loss of loyal-customer discounts. A good example is Milliken & Company, which provides proprietary software programs, marketing research, sales training, and sales leads to loyal customers.

Customer Databases and Database Marketing

Marketers must know their customers.[41] And in order to know customers and market to them, the company must collect information and store it in database form. A *customer database* is an organized collection of comprehensive information about individual customers or prospects that is current, accessible, and actionable for lead generation, lead qualification, sales, or maintenance of customer relationships. **Database marketing** is the process of building, maintaining, and using customer databases and other databases (products, suppliers, resellers) to contact, transact with, and build relationships with customers.

A customer database contains information accumulated through customer transactions, registration information, telephone queries, cookies, and every customer contact. In addition to name, address, and contact information, a customer database should contain the consumer's past purchases, demographics (age, income, family members, birthdays), psychographics (activities, interests, and opinions), mediagraphics (preferred media), and other useful information.

A *business database* should contain business customers' past purchases; past volumes, prices, and profits; buyer team member names (and ages, birthdays, hobbies, etc.); status of current contracts; an estimate of the supplier's share of the customer's business; competitive suppliers; assessment of competitive strengths and weaknesses in selling and servicing the account; and relevant customer buying practices, patterns, and policies.

Data Warehouses and Data Mining

Savvy companies capture information every time a customer comes into contact with any of their departments, whether it is a customer purchase, a customer-requested service call, an online query, or a mail-in rebate card. Information collected by the company is organized into a **data warehouse** where marketers can capture, query, and analyze it to draw inferences about an individual customer's needs and responses. This allows the firm to respond to customer inquiries based on a complete picture of the customer relationship, and to customize marketing activities for individual customers. Through **data mining**, marketing statisticians can extract from the mass of data useful information about individuals, trends, and segments.

In general, companies can use their databases to (1) identify the best prospects by sorting through responses to marketing efforts; (2) match specific offers to specific customers and find a way to sell, up-sell, and cross-sell; (3) deepen customer loyalty by remembering customer preferences and offering relevant incentives and information; (4) reactivate customer purchasing through timely reminders or promotions; and (5) avoid serious mistakes such as sending a customer two offers for the same product but at different prices.

Database marketing is most frequently used by business marketers and service providers that normally and easily collect a lot of customer data, like hotels, banks, airlines, credit card companies, and telecommunications firms. Other types of firms that benefit from such marketing are those that do a lot of cross-selling and up-selling (such as General Electric) or those whose customers have highly differentiated needs and whose customers are of highly differentiated value to the company.

The Downside of Database Marketing and CRM

Five main problems can prevent a firm from effectively using database marketing for CRM. First, some situations are not conducive to database management, such as when the product is a once-in-a-lifetime purchase or when the unit sale is very small. Second, building and maintaining a customer database requires a large investment in computer hardware, database software, analytical programs, communication links, and skilled staff. Third, getting everyone in the company to be customer oriented and to use the available information for CRM can be a challenge.

A fourth problem is that not all customers want a relationship with the company and may resent having their personal data collected and stored. (See "Marketing Insight: The Behavioral Targeting Controversy" for an overview of privacy and security issues.) And fifth, the assumptions behind CRM may not always hold true. High-volume customers often know their value to a company and can leverage it to extract premium service and/or price discounts, so that it may not cost the firm less to serve them. Loyal customers may expect and demand more and resent any attempt to charge full prices.

Thus, the benefits of database marketing do not come without costs and risks, not only in collecting the original customer data, but also in maintaining and mining them. When it works, a data warehouse yields more than it costs, but the data must be in good condition, and the discovered relationships must be valid and acceptable to consumers.

THE BEHAVIORAL TARGETING CONTROVERSY

Behavioral targeting allows firms to track customers' online behavior and find the best match between ads and prospects. Tracking online behavior relies on cookies—data stored on the user's computer hard drive that reveal which sites have been visited, the amount of time spent there, and so on. A customer who signs up with Microsoft for a free Hotmail e-mail account, for example, must provide his or her name, age, gender, and zip code. Microsoft then combines those facts with data, such as observed online behavior and characteristics of the area in which the customer lives, to help advertiser clients better understand when and how to contact that customer. Although Microsoft says it won't purchase an individual's income history, it can still provide advertising clients with behavioral targeting information.

Proponents of behavioral targeting say that consumers see more relevant ads. However, consumers have misgivings about being tracked online by advertisers. In one survey, about two-thirds of respondents objected to the practice. Now government regulators are weighing whether industry self-regulation is sufficient or legislation is needed.

Sources: Laurie Birkett, "The Cookie That Won't Crumble," *Forbes*, January 18, 2010, p. 32; Alden M. Hayashi, "How *Not* to Market on the Web," *MIT Sloan Management Review* (Winter 2010), pp. 14–15; Elisabeth Sullivan, "Behave," *Marketing News*, September 15, 2008, pp. 12–15; Stephanie Clifford, "Two-Thirds of Americans Object to Online Tracking," *New York Times*, September 30, 2009; Jessica Mintz, "Microsoft Adds Behavioral Targeting," *Associated Press*, December 28, 2006; Becky Ebenkamp, "Behavior Issues," *Brandweek*, October 20, 2008, pp. 21–25; Brian Morrissey, "Connect the Thoughts," *Adweek Media*, June 29, 2009, pp. 10–11.

EXECUTIVE SUMMARY

Customers are value maximizers; they will buy from the firm that they perceive to offer the highest customer-delivered value, defined as the difference between total customer benefits and total customer cost. A buyer's satisfaction is a function of the product's perceived performance and the buyer's expectations. Recognizing that high satisfaction leads to high customer loyalty, companies must ensure that they meet and exceed customer expectations.

Customer lifetime value (CLV) is the net present value of the stream of future profits expected over the customer's lifetime purchases. Companies are becoming skilled in customer relationship management (CRM), which focuses on developing programs to attract and retain the right customers and meeting the individual needs of those valued customers. Customer relationship management often requires building a customer database and data mining to detect trends, segments, and individual needs. A number of significant risks also exist, so marketers must proceed thoughtfully.

NOTES

1. Michael Bush, "Why Harrah's Loyalty Effort Is Industry's Gold Standard," *Advertising Age*, October 5, 2009, p. 8; Louis Columbus, "Lessons Learned in Las Vegas: Loyalty Programs Pay," *CRM Buyer*, July 29, 2005; Oskar Garcia, "Harrah's Broadens Customer Loyalty Program; Monitors Customer Behavior," *Associated Press*, September 27, 2008; Dan Butcher, "Harrah's Casino Chain Runs Mobile Coupon Pilot," *Mobile Marketer*, November 19, 2008.

2. Glen L. Urban, "The Emerging Era of Customer Advocacy," *Sloan Management Review* 45, no. 2 (2004), pp. 77–82.

3. Gary Hamel, "Strategy as Revolution," *Harvard Business Review,* July–August 1996, pp. 69–82.

4. Michael J. Lanning, *Delivering Profitable Value* (Oxford, UK: Capstone, 1998).

5. Michael Tsiros, Vikas Mittal, and William T. Ross Jr., "The Role of Attributions in Customer Satisfaction: A Reexamination," *Journal of Consumer Research* 31 (September 2004), pp. 476–83; for a succinct review, see Richard L. Oliver, "Customer Satisfaction Research," Rajiv Grover and Marco Vriens, eds., *Handbook of Marketing Research* (Thousand Oaks, CA: Sage Publications, 2006), pp. 569–87.

6. For some analysis and discussion, see Praveen K. Kopalle and Donald R. Lehmann, "Setting Quality Expectations when Entering a Market: What Should the Promise Be?" *Marketing Science* 25 (January–February 2006), pp. 8–24; Susan Fournier and David Glenmick, "Rediscovering Satisfaction," *Journal of Marketing* (October 1999), pp. 5–23.

7. Jennifer Aaker, Susan Fournier, and S. Adam Brasel, "When Good Brands Do Bad," *Journal of Consumer Research* 31 (June 2004), pp. 1–16; Pankaj Aggrawal, "The Effects of Brand Relationship Norms on Consumer Attitudes and Behavior," *Journal of Consumer Research* 31 (June 2004), pp. 87–101.

8. For an analysis of the effects of different types of expectations, see William Boulding, Ajay Kalra, and Richard Staelin, "The Quality Double Whammy," *Marketing Science* 18, no. 4 (April 1999), pp. 463–84.

9. For more discussion, see Michael D. Johnson and Anders Gustafsson, *Improving Customer Satisfaction, Loyalty, and Profit* (San Francisco: Jossey-Bass, 2000).

10. Neil A. Morgan, Eugene W. Anderson, and Vikas Mittal, "Understanding Firms' Customer Satisfaction Information Usage," *Journal of Marketing* 69 (July 2005), pp. 131–51.

11. See, for example, Christian Homburg, Nicole Koschate, and Wayne D. Hoyer, "Do Satisfied Customers Really Pay More? A Study of the Relationship between Customer Satisfaction and Willingness to Pay," *Journal of Marketing* 69 (April 2005), pp. 84–96.

12. Claes Fornell, Sunil Mithas, Forrest V. Morgeson III, and M. S. Krishnan, "Customer Satisfaction and Stock Prices: High Returns, Low Risk," *Journal of Marketing* 70 (January 2006), pp. 3–14. See also, Thomas S. Gruca and Lopo L. Rego, "Customer Satisfaction, Cash Flow, and Shareholder Value," *Journal of Marketing* 69 (July 2005), pp. 115–30; Eugene W. Anderson, Claes Fornell, and Sanal K. Mazvancheryl, "Customer Satisfaction and Shareholder Value," *Journal of Marketing* 68 (October 2004), pp. 172–85.

13. Thomas O. Jones and W. Earl Sasser Jr., "Why Satisfied Customers Defect," *Harvard Business Review,* November–December 1995, pp. 88–99.

14. Frederick F. Reichheld, "The One Number You Need to Grow," *Harvard Business Review,* December 2003, pp. 46–54.

15. "Genuine Buy-in Is Key to Mystery Shopping," *Marketing,* June 9, 2010, p. 36; James Davey, "JD Sports Eyes World Cup as Profit Tops Hopes," *Reuters,* April 14, 2010, www.reuters.com; Morag Cuddeford-Jones, "Now You're Talking My Language," *Marketing Week,* July 2, 2009, www.marketingweek.co.uk; Jack Hayes, "Industry Execs: Best Customer Feedback Info Is 'Real' Thing," *Nation's Restaurant News,* March 18, 2002, pp. 4; Leslie Wood and Michael Kirsch, "Performing Your Own Satisfaction Survey," *Agency Sales Magazine,* February 2002, p. 26.

16. "Basic Concepts," *ASQ,* www.asq.org/glossary/q.html, December 9, 2010.

17. Robert D. Buzzell and Bradley T. Gale, "Quality Is King," *The PIMS Principles: Linking Strategy to Performance* (New York: Free Press, 1987), pp. 103–34. (PIMS stands for Profit Impact of Market Strategy.)

18. Lerzan Aksoy, Timothy L. Keiningham, and Terry G. Vavra, "Nearly Everything You Know about Loyalty Is Wrong," *Marketing News,* October 1, 2005, pp. 20–21; Timothy L. Keiningham, Terry G. Vavra, Lerzan Aksoy, and Henri Wallard, *Loyalty Myths* (Hoboken, NJ: Wiley, 2005).

19. Werner J. Reinartz and V. Kumar, "The Impact of Customer Relationship Characteristics on Profitable Lifetime Duration," *Journal of Marketing* 67 (January 2003), pp. 77–99; Werner J. Reinartz and V. Kumar, "On the Profitability of Long-Life Customers in a Noncontractual Setting," *Journal of Marketing* 64 (October 2000), pp. 17–35.

20. Rakesh Niraj, Mahendra Gupta, and Chakravarthi Narasimhan, "Customer Profitability in a Supply Chain," *Journal of Marketing* (July 2001), pp. 1–16.

21. Thomas M. Petro, "Profitability: The Fifth 'P' of Marketing," *Bank Marketing,* September 1990, pp. 48–52; "Who Are Your Best Customers?" *Bank Marketing,* October 1990, pp. 48–52.

22. V. Kumar, "Customer Lifetime Value," Rajiv Grover and Marco Vriens, eds., *Handbook of Marketing Research* (Thousand Oaks, CA: Sage Publications, 2006), pp. 602–27; Sunil Gupta, Donald R. Lehmann, and Jennifer Ames Stuart, "Valuing Customers," *Journal of Marketing Research* 61 (February 2004), pp. 7–18; Rajkumar Venkatesan and V. Kumar, "A Customer Lifetime Value Framework for Customer Selection and Resource Allocation Strategy," *Journal of Marketing* 68 (October 2004), pp. 106–25.

23. V. Kumar, "Profitable Relationships," *Marketing Research* 18 (Fall 2006), pp. 41–46.

24. See Michael Haenlein, Andreas M. Kaplan, and Detlef Schoder, "Valuing the Real Option of Abandoning Unprofitable Customers When Calculating Customer Lifetime Value," *Journal of Marketing* 70 (July 2006), pp. 5–20; Teck-Hua Ho, Young-Hoon Park, and Yong-Pin Zhou, "Incorporating Satisfaction into Customer Value Analysis: Optimal Investment in Lifetime Value," *Marketing Science* 25 (May–June 2006), pp. 260–77; Peter S. Fader, Bruce G. S. Hardie, and Ka Lok Lee, "RFM and CLV: Using Iso-Value Curves for Customer Base Analysis," *Journal of Marketing Research* 62 (November 2005), pp. 415–30; V. Kumar, Rajkumar Venkatesan, Tim Bohling, and Denise Beckmann, "The Power of CLV: Managing Customer Lifetime Value at IBM," *Marketing Science* 27, no. 4 (2008), pp. 585–99.

25. For more on CLV, see Sunil Gupta and Donald R. Lehmann, "Models of Customer Value," Berend Wierenga, ed., *Handbook of Marketing Decision Models* (Berlin, Germany: Springer Science and Business Media, 2007); Sunil Gupta and Donald R. Lehmann, "Customers as Assets," *Journal of Interactive Marketing* 17, no. 1 (Winter 2006), pp. 9–24; Sunil Gupta and Donald R. Lehmann, *Managing Customers as Investments* (Upper Saddle River, NJ: Wharton School Publishing, 2005); Sunil Gupta, Donald R. Lehmann, and Jennifer Ames Stuart, "Valuing Customers," *Journal of Marketing Research* 41, no. 1 (February 2004), pp. 7–18.

26. Nicole E. Coviello, Roderick J. Brodie, Peter J. Danaher, and Wesley J. Johnston, "How Firms Relate to Their Markets: An Empirical Examination of Contemporary Marketing Practices," *Journal of Marketing* 66 (July 2002), pp. 33–46. For a comprehensive set of articles from a variety of perspectives on brand relationships, see Deborah J. MacInnis, C. Whan Park, and Joseph R. Preister, eds., *Handbook of Brand Relationships* (Armonk, NY: M.E. Sharpe, 2009).

27. For an academic perspective, see the Special Section on Customer Relationship Management, *Journal of Marketing* 69 (October 2005). For a study of the processes involved, see Werner Reinartz, Manfred Krafft, and Wayne D. Hoyer, "The Customer Relationship Management Process: Its Measurement and Impact on Performance," *Journal of Marketing Research* 61 (August 2004), pp. 293–305.

28. Michael J. Lanning, *Delivering Profitable Value* (New York: Basic Books, 1998).

29. Don Peppers and Martha Rogers, *One-to-One B2B: Customer Development Strategies for the Business-to-Business World* (New York: Doubleday, 2001); Peppers and Rogers, *The One-to-One Future: Building Relationships One Customer at a Time* (London: Piatkus Books, 1996); Don Peppers and Martha Rogers, *The One-to-One Manager: Real-World Lessons in Customer Relationship Management* (New York: Doubleday, 1999); Don Peppers, Martha Rogers, and Bob Dorf, *The One-to-One Fieldbook: The Complete Toolkit for Implementing a One-to-One Marketing Program* (New York: Bantam, 1999); Don Peppers and Martha Rogers, *Enterprise One to One: Tools for Competing in the Interactive Age* (New York: Currency, 1997).

30. Mylene Mangalindan, "New Marketing Style: Clicks and Mortar," *Wall Street Journal*, December 21, 2007, p. B5.

31. Michael Lewis, "Customer Acquisition Promotions and Customer Asset Value," *Journal of Marketing Research* 63 (May 2006), pp. 195–203.

32. Werner Reinartz, Jacquelyn S. Thomas, and V. Kumar, "Balancing Acquisition and Retention Resources to Maximize Customer Profitability," *Journal of Marketing* 69 (January 2005), pp. 63–79.

33. Michael D. Johnson, and Fred Selnes, "Diversifying Your Customer Portfolio," *MIT Sloan Management Review* 46, no. 3 (Spring 2005), pp. 11–14.

34. Sunil Gupta and Carl F. Mela, "What Is a Free Customer Worth," *Harvard Business Review*, November 2008, pp. 102–9.

35. Leonard L. Berry and A. Parasuraman, *Marketing Services: Computing through Quality* (New York: Free Press, 1991), pp. 136–142. For a business-to-business examination, see Robert W. Palmatier, Srinath Gopalakrishna, and Mark B. Houston, "Returns on Business-to-Business Relationship Marketing Investments: Strategies for Leveraging Profits," *Marketing Science* 25 (September–October 2006), pp. 477–93.

36. Frederick F. Reichheld, "Learning from Customer Defections," *Harvard Business Review,* March 3, 2009, pp. 56–69.

37. Utpal M. Dholakia, "How Consumer Self-Determination Influences Relational Marketing Outcomes," *Journal of Marketing Research* 43 (February 2006), pp. 109–20.

38. For a review, see Grahame R. Dowling and Mark Uncles, "Do Customer Loyalty Programs Really Work?" *Sloan Management Review* 38, no. 4 (Summer 1997), pp. 71–82.

39. Joseph C. Nunes and Xavier Drèze, "Feeling Superior: The Impact of Loyalty Program Structure on Consumers' Perception of Status," *Journal of Consumer Research*, 35 (April 2009), pp. 890–905; Joseph C. Nunes and Xavier Drèze, "Your Loyalty Program Is Betraying You," *Harvard Business Review*, April 2006, pp. 124–31.

40. Adam Lashinsky, "The Decade of Steve Jobs," *Fortune*, November 23, 2009, pp. 93–100; Apple, www.apple.com; Peter Burrows, "Apple vs. Google," *BusinessWeek*, January 25, 2010, pp. 28–34.

41. V. Kumar, Rajkumar Venkatesan, and Werner Reinartz, "Knowing What to Sell, When, and to Whom," *Harvard Business Review,* March 2006, pp. 131–37.

chapter 5

Analyzing Consumer Markets

In this chapter, we will address the following questions:

1. How do consumer characteristics influence buying behavior?
2. What major psychological processes influence consumer responses to the marketing program?
3. How do consumers make purchasing decisions?

Marketing Management at LEGO

LEGO of Billund, Denmark, may have been one of the first mass customized brands. Every child who has ever owned a set of LEGO blocks has built his or her own unique and amazing creations, brick by plastic brick. When LEGO decided to become a lifestyle brand and launch theme parks and its own lines of clothes, watches, video games, and other products, however, it neglected its core market of five- to nine-year-old boys. Plunging profits led to layoffs of almost half its employees as the firm streamlined its brand portfolio to emphasize its core businesses.

To better coordinate new product activities, LEGO reorganized into four functional groups managing eight key areas. For example, one group is now responsible for supporting customer communities and tapping into them for product ideas. LEGO also developed Digital Designer software for creating new LEGO sets—software it makes available, as a free download, to customers who want to design, share, and build their own custom LEGO sets. Customers can share their creations online with other enthusiasts or order the sets from LEGO's Connecticut warehouse, including step-by-step building instructions. Appealing to preteens, the new LEGO Universe multiplayer online game also invites customization by allowing players to personalize their avatars and create game characters from virtual LEGO bricks.[1]

Adopting a holistic marketing orientation means understanding customers—gaining a 360-degree view of both their daily lives and the changes that occur during their lifetimes so the right products are marketed to the right customers in the right way and at the right time. This chapter explores individual consumer buying dynamics; the next chapter explores the buying dynamics of business buyers.

What Influences Consumer Behavior?

Consumer behavior is the study of how individuals, groups, and organizations select, buy, use, and dispose of goods, services, ideas, or experiences to satisfy their needs and wants.[2] Marketers must fully understand both the theory and reality of consumer behavior. A consumer's buying behavior is influenced by cultural, social, and personal factors. Of these, cultural factors exert the broadest and deepest influence.

Cultural Factors

Culture, subculture, and social class are particularly important influences on consumer buying behavior. **Culture** is the fundamental determinant of a person's wants and behavior. Through family and other key institutions, a child growing up in the United States is exposed to values such as achievement and success, activity, efficiency and practicality, progress, material comfort, individualism, freedom, external comfort, humanitarianism, and youthfulness.[3]

Each culture consists of smaller *subcultures* that provide more specific identification and socialization for their members. Subcultures include nationalities, religions, racial groups, and geographic regions. When subcultures grow large and affluent enough, companies often design specialized marketing programs to serve them.

Social classes are relatively homogeneous and enduring divisions in a society, hierarchically ordered and with members who share similar values, interests, and behavior. One classic depiction of social classes in the United States defined seven ascending levels: (1) lower lowers, (2) upper lowers, (3) working class, (4) middle class, (5) upper middles, (6) lower uppers, and (7) upper uppers.[4] Social class members show distinct product and brand preferences in many areas, including clothing, home furnishings, leisure activities, and automobiles. There are also language differences—advertising copy and dialogue must ring true to the targeted social class.

Social Factors

In addition to cultural factors, social factors such as reference groups, family, and social roles and statuses affect consumer buying behavior.

Reference Groups   **Reference groups** are all the groups that have a direct (face-to-face) or indirect influence on a customer's attitudes or behavior. Groups having a direct influence are called **membership groups**. Some of these are *primary groups* with whom the person interacts fairly continuously and informally, such as family, friends, neighbors, and coworkers. People also belong to *secondary groups* such as religious, professional, and trade-union groups, which tend to be more formal and require less continuous interaction.

Reference groups expose consumers to new behaviors and lifestyles, influence attitudes and self-concept, and create pressures for conformity that may affect product and brand choices. People are also influenced by groups to which they do *not* belong. **Aspirational groups** are those a person hopes to join; **dissociative groups** are those whose values or behavior an individual rejects.

Where reference group influence is strong, marketers must determine how to reach and influence the group's opinion leaders. An **opinion leader** is the person who offers informal advice or information about a specific product or product category, such as which of several brands is best or how a particular product may be used.[5] Marketers try to reach opinion leaders by identifying their demographic and psychographic characteristics, identifying the media they use, and directing messages to them.

Family   The family is the most important consumer buying organization in society, and family members constitute the most influential primary reference group.[6] The **family of orientation** consists of parents and siblings. From parents a person acquires an orientation toward religion, politics, and economics and a sense of personal ambition, self-worth, and love.[7] A more direct influence on everyday buying behavior is the **family of procreation**—namely, the person's spouse and children. For expensive products and services such as cars, vacations, or housing, the vast majority of husbands and wives engage in joint decision making.[8] Men and women may respond differently to marketing messages, however.[9]

Another shift in buying patterns is an increase in the direct and indirect influence wielded by children and teens. Research has shown that more than two-thirds of 13- to 21-year-olds make or influence family purchase decisions on audio/video equipment, software, and vacation destinations.[10] In total, these teens and young adults spend over $120 billion a year. To make sure they buy the right products, they say they watch what friends say and do as much as what they see or hear in an ad or are told by a salesperson in a store.[11] By the time children are about 2 years old, they can often recognize characters, logos, and brands. They can distinguish between advertising and programming by about ages 6 or 7. A year or so later, they can understand the concept of persuasive intent on the part of advertisers. By 9 or 10, they can perceive discrepancies between message and product.[12]

Roles and Status   We each participate in many groups—family, clubs, organizations. Groups often are an important source of information and help to define norms for behavior. We can define a person's position in each group in terms of role and status. A **role** consists of the activities a person is expected to perform. Each role in turn connotes a **status**. A senior vice president may be seen as having more status than an office clerk, for example. People choose products that reflect and communicate their role and their actual or desired status in society. Marketers must be aware of the status-symbol potential of products and brands.

Personal Factors

Personal characteristics that influence a buyer's decision include age and stage in the life cycle, occupation and economic circumstances, personality and self-concept, and lifestyle and values.

Age and Stage in the Life Cycle   Our taste in food, clothes, furniture, and recreation is often related to our age. Consumption is also shaped by the *family life cycle* and the number, age, and gender of people in the household at any point in time. In addition, *psychological* life-cycle stages may matter. Adults experience certain "passages" or "transformations" as they go through life.[13] Marketers should also consider *critical life events or transitions*—marriage, childbirth, illness, relocation, divorce, first job, career change, retirement, death of a spouse—as giving rise to new needs and buying behaviors.

Occupation and Economic Circumstances   Occupation also influences consumption patterns. Marketers try to identify the occupational groups that have above-average interest in their products and services and even tailor products for certain occupational groups: Software companies, for example, design different products for engineers, lawyers, and physicians. As the recent recession showed, product and brand choice are greatly affected by economic circumstances: spendable income (level, stability, and time pattern), savings and assets, debts, borrowing power, and attitudes toward spending and saving. If economic indicators point to a recession, marketers can take steps to redesign, reposition, and reprice their products or introduce or increase the emphasis on discount brands so they can continue to offer value to target customers.

Personality and Self-Concept   Each person has personality characteristics that influence buying behavior. **Personality** refers to the distinguishing human psychological traits that lead to relatively consistent and enduring responses to environmental stimuli (including buying behavior). We often describe personality in terms of such traits as self-confidence, dominance, autonomy, deference, sociability, defensiveness, and adaptability.[14] Personality can be a useful variable in analyzing consumer brand choices.

Brands also have personalities, and consumers are likely to choose brands whose personalities match their own. We define **brand personality** as the specific mix of human traits that we can attribute to a particular brand. Stanford's Jennifer Aaker has identified five brand personality traits: sincerity, excitement, competence, sophistication, and ruggedness.[15] Cross-cultural studies have found that some but not all of these traits apply outside the United States.[16]

Consumers often choose and use brands with a brand personality consistent with their *actual self-concept* (how we view ourselves), although the match may be based on the consumer's *ideal self-concept* (how we would like to view ourselves) or on *others' self-concept* (how we think others see us).[17] These effects may be more pronounced for publicly consumed products than for privately consumed goods.[18] On the other hand, consumers who are high "self-monitors"—that is, sensitive to how others see them—are more likely to choose brands with personalities that fit the consumption situation.[19] Finally, often consumers have multiple aspects of self (serious professional, caring family member, active fun-lover) that may be evoked differently in different situations or around different types of people.

Lifestyle and Values   People from the same subculture, social class, and occupation may lead quite different lifestyles. A **lifestyle** is a person's pattern of living in the world as expressed in activities, interests, and opinions. It portrays the "whole person" interacting with his or her environment. Marketers search for relationships between their products and lifestyle groups. A computer manufacturer might find that most computer buyers are achievement-oriented and then aim the brand more clearly at the achiever lifestyle. As another example, many marketers are targeting consumers in LOHAS segments—an acronym for *lifestyles of health and sustainability*. These consumers worry about the environment, care about sustainability, and advance their personal health and development through purchases of organic foods, energy-efficient appliances, solar panels, ecotourism, and other LOHAS-related offerings (see Table 5.1).[20]

Lifestyles are shaped partly by whether consumers are *money constrained* or *time constrained*. Companies aiming to serve money-constrained consumers will create lower-cost products and services. In some categories, firms targeting time-constrained consumers need to be aware that these very same people want to believe they're *not* operating within time constraints. Hamburger Helper, for instance, knows that its customers use at least one pot or pan and spend at least 15 minutes cooking, rather than microwaving a meal. The brand constantly introduces new flavors to tap into changing taste trends, and sales rose 9 percent during the recent downturn.[21]

Consumer decisions are also influenced by **core values**, the belief systems that underlie attitudes and behaviors. Core values go much deeper than behavior or attitude and determine, at a basic level, people's choices and desires over the long term. Marketers who target consumers on

TABLE 5.1	LOHAS Market Segments	
Personal Health	**Natural Lifestyles**	
Natural, organic products	Indoor & outdoor furnishings	
Nutritional products	Organic cleaning supplies	
Integrative health care	Compact fluorescent lights	
Dietary supplements	Social change philanthropy	
Mind-body-spirit products	Apparel	
U.S. Market—$118.03 billion	*U.S. Market—$10.6 billion*	
Green Building	**Alternative Transportation**	
Home certification	Hybrid vehicles	
Energy Star appliances	Biodiesel fuel	
Sustainable flooring	Car-sharing programs	
Renewable energy systems	*U.S. Market—$6.12 billion*	
Wood alternatives	**Alternative Energy**	
U.S. Market—$50 billion	Renewable energy credits	
Eco-Tourism	Green pricing	
Eco-tourism travel	*U.S. Market—$380 million*	
Eco-adventure travel		
U.S. Market—$24.17 billion		

Source: Reprinted by permission of LOHAS, www.lohas.com.

the basis of their values believe that with appeals to people's inner selves, it is possible to influence their outer selves—their purchase behavior.

Key Psychological Processes

The starting point for understanding consumer behavior is the stimulus-response model shown in Figure 5.1. Marketing and environmental stimuli enter the consumer's consciousness, and a set of psychological processes combine with certain consumer characteristics to result in decision processes and purchase decisions. The marketer's task is to understand what happens in the consumer's consciousness between the arrival of the outside marketing stimuli and the ultimate purchase decisions. Five key psychological processes—motivation, perception, learning, emotions, and memory—fundamentally influence consumer responses.[22]

Motivation: Freud, Maslow, Herzberg

We all have many needs at any given time. Some needs are *biogenic*; they arise from physiological states of tension such as hunger, thirst, or discomfort. Other needs are *psychogenic*; they arise from psychological states of tension such as the need for recognition, esteem, or belonging.

FIGURE 5.1 Model of Consumer Behavior

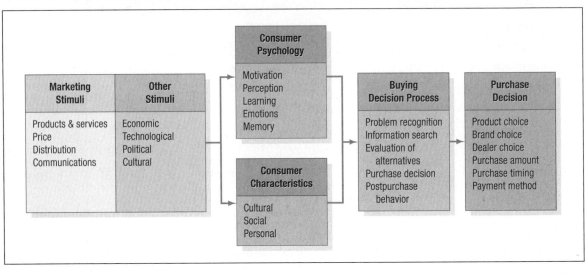

A need becomes a **motive** when it is aroused to a sufficient level of intensity to drive us to act. Motivation has both *direction*—we select one goal over another—and *intensity*—we pursue the goal with more or less vigor. Three of the best-known theories of human motivation—those of Sigmund Freud, Abraham Maslow, and Frederick Herzberg—carry quite different implications for consumer analysis and marketing strategy.

Sigmund Freud assumed the psychological forces shaping people's behavior are largely unconscious, and that a person cannot fully understand his or her own motivations. Someone who examines specific brands will react not only to the stated capabilities, but also to other, less conscious cues such as shape, size, weight, and brand name. A technique called *laddering* lets us trace a person's motivations from the stated instrumental ones to the more terminal ones. Then the marketer can decide at what level to develop the message and appeal.[23]

Abraham Maslow sought to explain why people are driven by particular needs at particular times.[24] His answer is that human needs are arranged in a hierarchy from most to least pressing—physiological needs, safety needs, social needs, esteem needs, and self-actualization needs. People will try to satisfy their most important need first and then try to satisfy the next most important.

Frederick Herzberg developed a two-factor theory that distinguishes *dissatisfiers* (factors that cause dissatisfaction) from *satisfiers* (factors that cause satisfaction).[25] The absence of dissatisfiers is not enough to motivate a purchase; satisfiers must be present. For example, a computer that lacks a warranty would be a dissatisfier. Yet the presence of a product warranty would not act as a satisfier or motivator, because it is not a source of intrinsic satisfaction. Ease of use would be a satisfier. In line with this theory, marketers should avoid dissatisfiers that might unsell a product and identify the major satisfiers of purchase in the market and supply them.

Perception

A motivated person is ready to act—*how* is influenced by his or her perception of the situation. In marketing, perceptions are more important than reality, because perceptions affect consumers' actual behavior. **Perception** is the process by which we select, organize, and interpret information inputs to create a meaningful picture of the world.[26] It depends not only on physical stimuli, but also on the stimuli's relationship to the surrounding environment and on conditions within each of us. People emerge with different perceptions of the same object because of three perceptual processes: selective attention, selective distortion, and selective retention.

Although we're exposed to thousands of ads and other stimuli every day, we screen most stimuli out—a process called **selective attention**. This means marketers must work hard to attract consumers' notice. Research shows that people are more likely to notice stimuli that relate to a current need; this is why car shoppers notice car ads but not DVD ads. Also, people are more likely to notice stimuli they anticipate, such as laptops displayed in a computer store. And people are more likely to notice stimuli whose deviations are large in relationship to the normal size of the stimuli, such as an ad offering a $100 discount, not a $5 discount.

Even noticed stimuli don't always come across in the way senders intend. *Selective distortion* is the tendency to interpret information in a way that fits our preconceptions. Consumers will often distort information to be consistent with prior brand and product beliefs and expectations.[27] Selective distortion can work to the advantage of marketers with strong brands when consumers distort neutral or ambiguous brand information to make it more positive. In other words, coffee may seem to taste better or a car may seem to drive more smoothly, depending on the brand.

Most of us don't remember much of the information to which we're exposed, but we do retain information that supports our attitudes and beliefs. Because of *selective retention*, we're likely to remember good points about a product we like and forget good points about competing products. Selective retention again works to the advantage of strong brands. It also explains why marketers must repeat messages to ensure that information is not overlooked.

Learning

When we act, we learn. **Learning** induces changes in our behavior arising from experience. Most human behavior is learned, although much learning is incidental. Theorists believe learning is produced through the interplay of drives, stimuli, cues, responses, and reinforcement. A **drive** is a strong internal stimulus impelling action. **Cues** are minor stimuli that determine when, where, and how a person responds.

Suppose you buy a Hewlett-Packard computer. If your experience is rewarding, your response to computers and HP will be positively reinforced. When you want to buy a printer, you may assume that because HP makes good computers, it also makes good printers. You have *generalized* your response to similar stimuli. A countertendency to generalization is *discrimination*, in which we learn to recognize differences in sets of similar stimuli and adjust our responses accordingly. Learning theory teaches marketers that they can build demand for a product by associating it with strong drives, using motivating cues, and providing positive reinforcement.

Emotions

Consumer response is not all cognitive and rational; much may be emotional and invoke different kinds of feelings. A brand or product may make a consumer feel proud, excited, or confident. An ad may create feelings of amusement, disgust, or wonder. Ad campaigns from Procter & Gamble, for instance, now link the company's market-leading Tide laundry detergent to positive feelings about using clothing to express personal style and look good.[28]

Memory

Cognitive psychologists distinguish between short-term memory (STM)—a temporary and limited repository of information—and long-term memory (LTM)—a more permanent, essentially unlimited repository. All the information and experiences we encounter as we go through life can end up in our long-term memory.

Most widely accepted views of long-term memory structure assume we form some kind of associative model.[29] For example, the **associative network memory model** views LTM as a set of nodes and links. *Nodes* are stored information connected by *links* that vary in strength. Any type of information can be stored in the memory network, including verbal, visual, abstract, and contextual. A spreading activation process from node to node determines how much we retrieve and what information we can actually recall in any given situation. When a node becomes activated because we're encoding external information (when we read or hear a word or phrase) or retrieving internal information from LTM (when we think about a concept), other nodes are also activated if they're strongly associated with that node.

In this model, we can think of consumer brand knowledge as a node in memory with a variety of linked associations. The strength and organization of these associations will be important determinants of the information we can recall about the brand. **Brand associations** consist of all brand-related thoughts, feelings, perceptions, images, experiences, beliefs, attitudes, and so on that become linked to the brand node.

Some companies create mental maps that depict consumers' knowledge of a particular brand in terms of the key associations likely to be triggered in a marketing setting, and their relative strength, favorability, and uniqueness to consumers. Figure 5.2 displays a simple mental map highlighting brand beliefs for a hypothetical consumer for State Farm insurance.

Memory Processes *Memory encoding* describes how and where information gets into memory. The strength of the resulting association depends on how much we process the information at encoding (how much we think about it, for instance) and in what way.[30] In

FIGURE 5.2 Hypothetical Mental Map

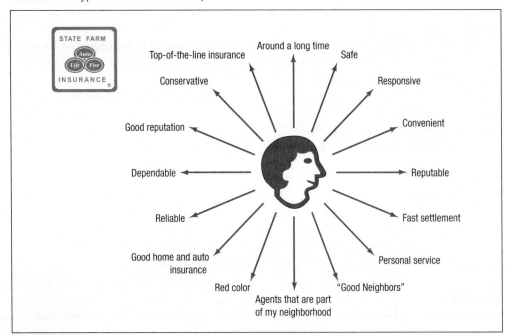

general, the more attention we pay to the meaning of information during encoding, the stronger the resulting associations in memory will be.[31]

Memory Retrieval   *Memory retrieval* is the way information gets out of memory. Marketers should note that the presence of *other* product information in memory can produce interference effects and cause us to overlook or confuse new data. One marketing challenge in a crowded category is that consumers may mix up brands. Also, the time between exposure to information and encoding matters. Once information is stored in memory, its strength of association decays very slowly.

Finally, information may be *available* in memory but not be *accessible* for recall without retrieval cues or reminders. The effectiveness of retrieval cues is one reason marketing *inside* a store is so critical. Product packaging and other in-store cues that remind consumers of advertising and other information conveyed outside the store are prime determinants of consumer decision making.

The Buying Decision Process: The Five-Stage Model

Smart companies try to fully understand customers' buying decision process—all the experiences in learning, choosing, using, and even disposing of a product.[32] Figure 5.3 shows the five stages of the process: problem recognition, information search, evaluation of alternatives, purchase decision, and postpurchase behavior. Clearly, the buying process starts long before the actual purchase and has consequences long afterward.[33] Consumers don't always pass through all five stages—they may skip or reverse some. The model provides a good frame of reference because it captures the full range of considerations that arise when a consumer faces a highly involving new purchase.[34]

Problem Recognition

The buying process starts when the buyer recognizes a problem or need triggered by internal stimuli (such as hunger or thirst) or external stimuli (such as seeing an ad). Marketers need to identify the circumstances that trigger a particular need by gathering information from a number of consumers. They can then develop marketing strategies that spark consumer interest and lead to the second stage in the buying process.

Information Search

Surprisingly, consumers often search for limited amounts of information. Surveys have shown that for durables, half of all consumers look at only one store, and only 30 percent look at more than one brand of appliances. We can distinguish between two levels of engagement in the search. In the milder search state, *heightened attention*, a person simply becomes more receptive

FIGURE 5.3 Five-Stage Model of the Consumer Buying Process

to information about a product. In an *active information search*, a person talks with friends, searches online, and visits stores to learn about the product.

Information sources for consumers fall into four groups: personal (family, friends, neighbors, acquaintances), commercial (advertising, Web sites, salespersons, dealers, packaging, displays), public (mass media, consumer-rating organizations), and experiential (handling, examining, using the product). Although consumers receive the greatest amount of information about a product from commercial (marketer-dominated) sources, the most effective information often comes from personal or experiential sources, or public sources that are independent authorities.

By gathering information, the consumer learns about competing brands and their features. The first box in Figure 5.4 shows the *total set* of brands available. The individual consumer will come to know a subset of these, the *awareness set*. Only some, the *consideration set*, will meet initial buying criteria. As the consumer gathers more information, just a few, the *choice set*, will remain strong contenders. The consumer makes a final choice from these.[35]

Figure 5.4 makes it clear that a company must get its brand into the prospect's awareness, consideration, and choice sets. The company must also identify the other brands in the consumer's choice set so it can plan appropriate competitive appeals. In addition, marketers should identify the consumer's information sources and evaluate their relative importance so it can prepare effective communications.

Evaluation of Alternatives

How does the consumer process competitive brand information and make a final value judgment? There are several processes, and the most current models see the consumer forming judgments largely on a conscious and rational basis.

Some basic concepts will help us understand consumer evaluation processes: First, the consumer is trying to satisfy a need. Second, the consumer is looking for certain benefits from the product solution. Third, the consumer sees each product as a bundle of attributes with varying abilities to deliver the benefits. The attributes of interest to buyers vary by product; the attributes sought in a hotel, for example, might be location, atmosphere, and price. Knowing

FIGURE 5.4 Successive Sets Involved in Consumer Decision Making

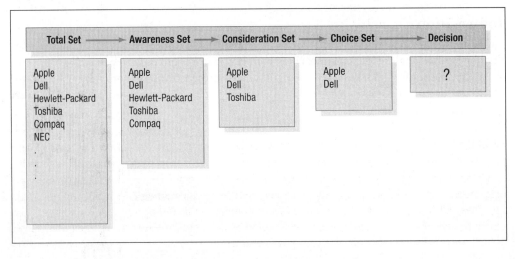

that consumers will pay more attention to attributes that deliver the sought-after benefits, firms can segment their markets according to attributes and benefits important to different consumer groups.

Through experience and learning, people acquire beliefs and attitudes. These in turn influence buying behavior. A **belief** is a descriptive thought that a person holds about something. Just as important are **attitudes**, a person's enduring favorable or unfavorable evaluations, emotional feelings, and action tendencies toward some object or idea.[36] People have attitudes toward almost everything: religion, politics, clothes, music, food. Because attitudes economize on energy and thought, they can be very difficult to change. A company is well advised to fit its product into existing attitudes rather than try to change attitudes.

The consumer arrives at attitudes toward various brands through an attribute evaluation procedure, developing a set of beliefs about where each brand stands on each attribute.[37] The **expectancy-value model** of attitude formation posits that consumers evaluate products and services by combining their brand beliefs—the positives and negatives—according to importance.[38]

Suppose Linda has narrowed her choice set to four laptop computers (A, B, C, and D). Assume she's interested in four attributes: memory capacity, graphics capability, size, and price. If one laptop dominated the others on all the criteria, we could predict that Linda would choose it. But, as is often the case, her choice set consists of brands that vary in their appeal. One brand offers the best memory capacity, another has the best graphics capability, and so on.

If we knew the weights Linda attaches to the four attributes, we could more reliably predict her laptop choice. Suppose she assigned 40 percent of the importance to the laptop's memory capacity, 30 percent to graphics capability, 20 percent to size, and 10 percent to price. To find Linda's perceived value for each laptop, we multiply her weights by her beliefs about each brand's attributes. So for brand A, if she assigns a score of 8 for memory capacity, 9 for graphics capability, 6 for size, and 9 for price, the overall score for A would be:

$$\text{Laptop A} = 0.4(8) + 0.3(9) + 0.2(6) + 0.1(9) = 8.0$$

Calculating the scores for all of the other laptops Linda is considering will show which has the highest perceived value. When a computer marketer knows how buyers form preferences, it can take steps to influence consumer decisions, such as to redesign the laptop (real repositioning), alter beliefs about the brand (psychological repositioning), alter beliefs about competitors (competitive depositioning), alter the importance weights (persuading buyers to attach more importance to attributes in which the brand excels), call attention to neglected attributes (such as styling), or shift the buyer's ideals (persuading buyers to change their ideal levels for one or more attributes).[39]

Purchase Decision

In the evaluation stage, the consumer forms preferences among the brands in the choice set and may also form an intention to buy the most preferred brand. Even if consumers form brand evaluations, two general factors can intervene between the purchase intention and the purchase decision.[40] The first factor is the *attitudes of others*. The influence of another person's attitude depends on two things: (1) the intensity of the other person's negative attitude toward our preferred alternative and (2) our motivation to comply with the other person's wishes.[41] The more intense the other person's negativism and the closer he or she is to us, the more we will adjust our purchase intention. The converse is also true.

The second factor is *unanticipated situational factors* that may erupt to change the purchase intention. Linda might lose her job, some other purchase might become more urgent, or a store salesperson may turn her off. Preferences and even purchase intentions are not completely reliable predictors of purchase behavior.

A consumer's decision to modify, postpone, or avoid a purchase decision is heavily influenced by one or more types of *perceived risk*.[42] The degree of perceived risk varies with the amount of money at stake, the amount of attribute uncertainty, and the level of consumer self-confidence. Consumers develop routines for reducing the uncertainty and negative consequences of risk, such as avoiding decisions, gathering information, and developing preferences for brand names and warranties. Marketers must understand the factors that provoke a feeling of risk in consumers and then provide information and support to reduce perceived risk.

Postpurchase Behavior

After the purchase, the consumer might experience dissonance from noticing certain disquieting features or hearing favorable things about other brands and will be alert to information that supports his or her decision. The marketer's job therefore doesn't end with the purchase. Marketers must monitor postpurchase satisfaction, postpurchase actions, and postpurchase product uses and disposal. "Marketing Skills: Dealing with Customer Defections" discusses how marketers can learn why customers leave and win them back.

A satisfied consumer is more likely to purchase the product again and will tend to say good things about the brand to others. Dissatisfied consumers may abandon or return the product, take public action (complaining to the firm, seeing a lawyer, or complaining to government agencies or other groups), or take private actions (not buying the product or warning friends).[43]

Marketing Skills

DEALING WITH CUSTOMER DEFECTIONS

The road to winning customers back starts with an understanding of when, why, and how they decide to leave. Companies that bill monthly learn quickly when a customer leaves, as do firms that receive complaints or cancellations; those with unscheduled or infrequent customer contact may not notice for some time. Marketers can also use informal contacts (such as phone calls and social media) or formal research (such as an exit interview) to learn why customers defect. The goal is to reveal sources of dissatisfaction that can be addressed to win back and retain customers, demonstrating that the firm listens to, responds to, and values its customers.

EarthLink, a major Internet service provider, uses sophisticated software to segment its customer base, analyze customer behavior, and identify potential defectors. In particular, the company focuses on its most profitable customers, the touch points used to maintain contact, and the warning signs of defection. Its service reps are trained to work with customers to resolve complaints, retain their business, and win back high-profit customers. This has helped EarthLink reduce costly customer churn by 18 percent while reducing marketing expenses.[44]

Postpurchase communications to buyers have been shown to result in fewer product returns and order cancellations. Marketers should also monitor how buyers use and dispose of the product. A key driver of sales frequency is product consumption rate—the more quickly buyers consume a product, the sooner they may be back in the market to repurchase it. One strategy to speed replacement is to tie the act of replacing the product to a certain holiday, event, or time of year. Another strategy is to provide consumers with better information about the time they first used the product and the need to replace it or the product's current level of performance. If consumers throw the product away, the marketer needs to know how they dispose of it, especially if—like a battery—it can damage the environment.

Behavioral Decision Theory and Behavioral Economics

Consumers don't always make buying decisions in a deliberate, rational manner. One of the most active academic research areas in marketing over the past three decades has been *behavioral decision theory* (BDT). Behavioral decision theorists have identified many situations in which consumers make seemingly irrational choices.[45] (For insights from the author of *Predictably Irrational* and *The Upside of Irrationality*, see "Marketing Insight: Predictably Irrational.")

Marketing Insight

PREDICTABLY IRRATIONAL

Behavioral economics expert Dr. Dan Ariely says that seemingly irrational decisions are actually systematic and predictable. Among his thought-provoking insights for marketers are:

- When selling a new product, marketers should compare it with something consumers already know about, even if the new product has few direct comparisons. Consumers find it difficult to judge products in isolation and feel more comfortable if they base a new decision at least in part on a past decision.

- Consumers find the lure of "free" almost irresistible. In one experiment, consumers had to choose between normally high-priced Lindt chocolate truffles for 15 cents and ordinary Hershey kisses for a penny. Seventy-three percent of the customers chose the truffles. When the price of truffles was cut to 14 cents and the kisses were offered for free, however, 69 percent of customers chose the kisses, even though the truffles were a better deal.

- The "optimism bias" or "positivity illusion" is a pervasive effect that transcends gender, age, education, and nationality. People tend to overestimate their chances of experiencing a good outcome (having healthy kids or financial security) but underestimate their chances of experiencing a bad outcome (a heart attack or a parking ticket).

Sources: Dan Ariely, *Predictably Irrational* (New York: HarperCollins, 2008); Dan Ariely, "The Curious Paradox of Optimism Bias," *BusinessWeek*, August 24 and 31, 2009, p. 48; Dan Ariely, "The End of Rational Economics," *Harvard Business Review*, July–August 2009, pp. 78–84; Russ Juskalian, "Not as Rational as We Think We Are," *USA Today*, March 17, 2008; Elizabeth Kolbert, "What Was I Thinking?" *New Yorker*, February 25, 2008.

This academic research reinforces that consumer behavior is very constructive and the context of decisions really matters. The work of researchers has also challenged predictions from economic theory and assumptions about rationality, leading to the emergence of the field of *behavioral economics*.[46] Here, we review some issues in two key areas: decision heuristics and framing.

Decision Heuristics

Consumers often take "mental shortcuts" called **heuristics** or rules of thumb in the decision process. In everyday decision making, when consumers forecast the likelihood of future outcomes or events, they may use one of these heuristics:[47]

1. The *availability heuristic*—Consumers base their predictions on how quickly and easily a particular example of an outcome comes to mind. If an example comes to mind too easily, they might overestimate the likelihood of its happening. For example, a recent product failure may lead a consumer to inflate the likelihood of a future product failure and make him more inclined to purchase a product warranty.

2. The *representativeness heuristic*—Consumers base their predictions on how representative or similar the outcome is to other examples. One reason package appearances may be so similar for different brands in the same product category is that marketers want their products to be seen as representative of the category as a whole.

3. The *anchoring and adjustment heuristic*—Consumers arrive at an initial judgment and then adjust it based on additional information. Marketers therefore strive to make a strong first impression, establishing a favorable anchor so subsequent experiences will be interpreted in a more favorable light.

Framing

Decision framing is the manner in which choices are presented to and seen by a decision maker. A $200 cell phone may not seem that expensive in the context of a set of $400 phones but may seem very expensive if those phones cost $50. Framing effects are pervasive and can be powerful. In fact, research shows that consumers use *mental accounting* when they handle their money, as a way of coding, categorizing, and evaluating the financial outcomes of their choices.[48] The principles of mental accounting are derived in part from *prospect theory*, which holds that consumers frame their decision alternatives in terms of gains and losses according to a value function. In general, consumers are loss-averse. They tend to overweight very low probabilities and underweight very high probabilities.

EXECUTIVE SUMMARY

Consumer behavior is influenced by three factors: cultural (culture, subculture, and social class), social (reference groups, family, and social roles and statuses), and personal (age, stage in the life cycle, occupation, economic circumstances, personality and self-concept, and lifestyle and values). The main psychological processes that affect consumer behavior are motivation, perception, learning, emotions, and memory.

The typical buying process consists of the following sequence of events: problem recognition, information search, evaluation of alternatives, purchase decision, and postpurchase behavior. The marketers' job is to understand the behavior at each stage. The attitudes of others, unanticipated situational factors, and perceived risk may all affect the decision to buy, as will consumers' levels of postpurchase product satisfaction, use, and disposal. Behavioral decision theory helps marketers understand the situations in which consumers make seemingly irrational choices. Two key aspects of behavioral decision theory are decision heuristics and framing.

NOTES

1. Alex Pham, "Lego Universe's Quest: Build on Toy's Offline Success," *Los Angeles Times,* June 29, 2010, http://latimes.com; "Lego's Turnaround: Picking Up the Pieces," *Economist,* October 28, 2006, p. 76; Paul Grimaldi, "Consumers Design Products Their Way," *Knight Ridder Tribune Business News,* November 25, 2006; Michael A. Prospero, "Brick by Brick: Lego's New Building Blocks," *Fast Company,* September 2005, p. 35; David Robertson and Per Hjuler, "Innovating a Turnaround at LEGO," *Harvard Business Review,* September 2009, pp. 20–21; Kim Hjelmgaard, "Lego, Refocusing on Bricks, Builds on Image," *Wall Street Journal,* December 24, 2009.

2. Michael R. Solomon, *Consumer Behavior: Buying, Having, and Being,* 9th ed. (Upper Saddle River, NJ: Prentice Hall, 2011).

3. Leon G. Schiffman and Leslie Lazar Kanuk, *Consumer Behavior,* 10th ed. (Upper Saddle River, NJ: Prentice Hall, 2010).

4. For some classic perspectives, see Richard P. Coleman, "The Continuing Significance of Social Class to Marketing," *Journal of Consumer Research* (December 1983), pp. 265–80; Richard P. Coleman and Lee P. Rainwater, *Social Standing in America: New Dimension of Class* (New York: Basic Books, 1978).

5. Leon G. Schiffman and Leslie Lazar Kanuk, *Consumer Behavior,* 10th ed. (Upper Saddle River, NJ: Prentice Hall, 2010).

6. Elizabeth S. Moore, William L. Wilkie, and Richard J. Lutz, "Passing the Torch: Intergenerational Influences as a Source of Brand Equity," *Journal of Marketing* (April 2002), pp. 17–37; Robert Boutilier, "Pulling the Family's Strings," *American Demographics,* August 1993, pp. 44–48; David J. Burns, "Husband-Wife Innovative Consumer Decision Making: Exploring the Effect of Family Power," *Psychology & Marketing* (May–June 1992), pp. 175–89; Rosann L. Spiro, "Persuasion in Family Decision Making," *Journal of Consumer Research* (March 1983), pp. 393–402. For cross-cultural comparisons of husband–wife buying roles, see John B. Ford, Michael S. LaTour, and Tony L. Henthorne, "Perception of Marital Roles in Purchase-Decision Processes: A Cross-Cultural Study," *Journal of the Academy of Marketing Science* (Spring 1995), pp. 120–31.

7. Kay M. Palan and Robert E. Wilkes, "Adolescent-Parent Interaction in Family Decision Making," *Journal of Consumer Research* 24, no. 2 (March 1997), pp. 159–69; Sharon E. Beatty and Salil Talpade, "Adolescent Influence in Family Decision Making: A Replication with Extension," *Journal of Consumer Research* 21 (September 1994), pp. 332–41.

8. Chenting Su, Edward F. Fern, and Keying Ye, "A Temporal Dynamic Model of Spousal Family Purchase-Decision Behavior," *Journal of Marketing Research* 40 (August 2003), pp. 268–81.

9. Hillary Chura, "Failing to Connect: Marketing Messages for Women Fall Short," *Advertising Age,* September 23, 2002, pp. 13–14.

10. "YouthPulse: The Definitive Study of Today's Youth Generation," *Harris Interactive,* www.harrisinteractive.com, December 9, 2010.

11. Dana Markow, "Today's Youth: Understanding Their Importance and Influence," *Trends & Tudes* 7, no. 1, www.harrisinteractive.com, February 2008.

12. Deborah Roedder John, "Consumer Socialization of Children: A Retrospective Look at Twenty-Five Years of Research," *Journal of Consumer Research* 26 (December 1999), pp. 183–213; Lan Nguyen Chaplin and Deborah Roedder John, "The Development of Self-Brand Connections in Children and Adolescents," *Journal of Consumer Research* 32 (June 2005), pp. 119–29; Lan Nguyen Chaplin and Deborah Roedder John, "Growing Up in a Material World: Age Differences in Materialism in Children and Adolescents," *Journal of Consumer Research* 34 (December 2007), pp. 480–93.

13. Rex Y. Du and Wagner A. Kamakura, "Household Life Cycles and Lifestyles in the United States," *Journal of Marketing Research* 48 (February 2006), pp. 121–32; Lawrence Lepisto, "A Life Span Perspective of Consumer Behavior," Elizabeth Hirshman and Morris Holbrook, eds., *Advances in Consumer Research,* vol. 12 (Provo, UT: Association for Consumer Research, 1985), p. 47; see also, Gail Sheehy, *New*

Passages: Mapping Your Life across Time (New York: Random House, 1995).

14. Harold H. Kassarjian and Mary Jane Sheffet, "Personality and Consumer Behavior: An Update," Harold H. Kassarjian and Thomas S. Robertson, eds., *Perspectives in Consumer Behavior* (Glenview, IL: Scott Foresman, 1981), pp. 160–80.

15. Jennifer Aaker, "Dimensions of Measuring Brand Personality," *Journal of Marketing Research* 34 (August 1997), pp. 347–56.

16. Yongjun Sung and Spencer F. Tinkham, "Brand Personality Structures in the United States and Korea: Common and Culture-Specific Factors," *Journal of Consumer Psychology* 15, no. 4 (December 2005), pp. 334–50; Jennifer L. Aaker, Veronica Benet-Martinez, and Jordi Garolera, "Consumption Symbols as Carriers of Culture: A Study of Japanese and Spanish Brand Personality Constructs," *Journal of Personality and Social Psychology* 81, no. 3 (March 2001), pp. 492–508.

17. M. Joseph Sirgy, "Self Concept in Consumer Behavior: A Critical Review," *Journal of Consumer Research* 9 (December 1982), pp. 287–300.

18. Timothy R. Graeff, "Consumption Situations and the Effects of Brand Image on Consumers' Brand Evaluations," *Psychology & Marketing* 14, no. 1 (January 1997), pp. 49–70; Timothy R. Graeff, "Image Congruence Effects on Product Evaluations: The Role of Self-Monitoring and Public/Private Consumption," *Psychology & Marketing* 13, no. 5 (August 1996), pp. 481–99.

19. Jennifer L. Aaker, "The Malleable Self: The Role of Self-Expression in Persuasion," *Journal of Marketing Research* 36, no. 1 (February 1999), pp. 45–57.

20. "LOHAS Forum Attracts Fortune 500 Companies," *Environmental Leader*, June 22, 2009.

21. Noel C. Paul, "Meal Kits in Home," *Christian Science Monitor,* June 9, 2003, p. 13; Anne D'Innocenzio, "Frugal Times: Hamburger Helper, Kool-Aid in Advertising Limelight," *Associated Press, Seattle Times*, April 29, 2009.

22. For a review of academic research on consumer behavior, see Barbara Loken, "Consumer Psychology: Categorization, Inferences, Affect, and Persuasion," *Annual Review of Psychology* 57 (2006), pp. 453–95. For more about how consumer behavior theory can be applied to policy decisions, see "Special Issue on Helping Consumers Help Themselves: Improving the Quality of Judgments and Choices," *Journal of Public Policy & Marketing* 25, no. 1 (Spring 2006).

23. Thomas J. Reynolds and Jonathan Gutman, "Laddering Theory, Method, Analysis, and Interpretation," *Journal of Advertising Research* (February–March 1988),

pp. 11–34; Thomas J. Reynolds and Jerry C. Olson, *Understanding Consumer Decision-Making: The Means-Ends Approach to Marketing and Advertising* (Mahwah, NJ: Lawrence Erlbaum, 2001); Brian Wansink, "Using Laddering to Understand and Leverage a Brand's Equity," *Qualitative Market Research* 6, no. 2 (2003).

24. Abraham Maslow, *Motivation and Personality* (New York: Harper & Row, 1954), pp. 80–106. For an interesting business application, see Chip Conley, *Peak: How Great Companies Get Their Mojo from Maslow* (San Francisco: Jossey-Bass, 2007).

25. See Frederick Herzberg, *Work and the Nature of Man* (Cleveland: William Collins, 1966); H. Thierry and A. M. Koopman-Iwema "Motivation and Satisfaction," P. J. D. Drenth, H. Thierry, P. J. Willems, and C. J. de Wolff, eds., *A Handbook of Work and Organizational Psychology* (East Sussex, UK: Psychology Press, 1984), pp. 141–42.

26. Bernard Berelson and Gary A. Steiner, *Human Behavior: An Inventory of Scientific Findings* (New York: Harcourt Brace Jovanovich, 1964), p. 88.

27. J. Edward Russo, Margaret G. Meloy, and Victoria Husted Medvec, "The Distortion of Product Information during Brand Choice," *Journal of Marketing Research* 35 (November 1998), pp. 438–52.

28. Stuart Elliott, "A Campaign Linking Clean Clothes with Stylish Living," *New York Times,* January 7, 2010, www.nytimes.com; Ellen Byron, "Tide, Woolite Tout Their Fashion Sense," *Wall Street Journal*, March 11, 2009.

29. Robert S. Wyer Jr. and Thomas K. Srull, "Person Memory and Judgment," *Psychological Review* 96, no. 1 (January 1989), pp. 58–83; John R. Anderson, *The Architecture of Cognition* (Cambridge, MA: Harvard University Press, 1983).

30. For additional discussion, see John G. Lynch Jr. and Thomas K. Srull, "Memory and Attentional Factors in Consumer Choice: Concepts and Research Methods," *Journal of Consumer Research* 9 (June 1982), pp. 18–36; and Joseph W. Alba, J. Wesley Hutchinson, and John G. Lynch Jr., "Memory and Decision Making," Harold H. Kassarjian and Thomas S. Robertson, eds., *Handbook of Consumer Theory and Research* (Englewood Cliffs, NJ: Prentice Hall, 1992), pp. 1–49.

31. Robert S. Lockhart, Fergus I. M. Craik, and Larry Jacoby, "Depth of Processing, Recognition, and Recall," John Brown, ed., *Recall and Recognition* (New York: Wiley, 1976); Fergus I. M. Craik and Endel Tulving, "Depth of Processing and the Retention of Words in Episodic Memory," *Journal of Experimental Psychology* 104, no. 3 (September 1975), pp. 268–94; Fergus I. M. Craik and Robert S. Lockhart, "Levels of Processing:

A Framework for Memory Research," *Journal of Verbal Learning and Verbal Behavior* 11 (1972), pp. 671–84.

32. Benson Shapiro, V. Kasturi Rangan, and John Sviokla, "Staple Yourself to an Order," *Harvard Business Review,* July–August 1992, pp. 113–22. See also, Carrie M. Heilman, Douglas Bowman, and Gordon P. Wright, "The Evolution of Brand Preferences and Choice Behaviors of Consumers New to a Market," *Journal of Marketing Research* (May 2000), pp. 139–55.

33. Marketing scholars have developed several models of the consumer buying process through the years. See Mary Frances Luce, James R. Bettman, and John W. Payne, *Emotional Decisions: Tradeoff Difficulty and Coping in Consumer Choice* (Chicago: University of Chicago Press, 2001); James F. Engel, Roger D. Blackwell, and Paul W. Miniard, *Consumer Behavior,* 8th ed. (Fort Worth, TX: Dryden, 1994); John A. Howard and Jagdish N. Sheth, *The Theory of Buyer Behavior* (New York: Wiley, 1969).

34. William P. Putsis Jr. and Narasimhan Srinivasan, "Buying or Just Browsing? The Duration of Purchase Deliberation," *Journal of Marketing Research* (August 1994), pp. 393–402.

35. Chem L. Narayana and Rom J. Markin, "Consumer Behavior and Product Performance: An Alternative Conceptualization," *Journal of Marketing* (October 1975), pp. 1–6. See also, Lee G. Cooper and Akihiro Inoue, "Building Market Structures from Consumer Preferences," *Journal of Marketing Research* 33, no. 3 (August 1996), pp. 293–306; Wayne S. DeSarbo and Kamel Jedidi, "The Spatial Representation of Heterogeneous Consideration Sets," *Marketing Science* 14, no. 3, pt. 2 (Summer 1995), pp. 326–42.

36. David Krech, Richard S. Crutchfield, and Egerton L. Ballachey, *Individual in Society* (New York: McGraw-Hill, 1962), chapter 2.

37. See Leigh McAlister, "Choosing Multiple Items from a Product Class," *Journal of Consumer Research* (December 1979), pp. 213–24; Paul E. Green and Yoram Wind, *Multiattribute Decisions in Marketing: A Measurement Approach* (Hinsdale, IL: Dryden, 1973), chapter 2; Richard J. Lutz, "The Role of Attitude Theory in Marketing," H. Kassarjian and T. Robertson, eds., *Perspectives in Consumer Behavior* (Lebanon, IN: Scott Foresman, 1981), pp. 317–39.

38. This expectancy-value model was originally developed by Martin Fishbein, "Attitudes and Prediction of Behavior," Martin Fishbein, ed., *Readings in Attitude Theory and Measurement* (New York: Wiley, 1967), pp. 477–92. For a critical review, see Paul W. Miniard and Joel B. Cohen, "An Examination of the Fishbein-Ajzen Behavioral-Intentions Model's Concepts and Measures," *Journal of Experimental Social Psychology* (May 1981), pp. 309–39.

39. Michael R. Solomon, *Consumer Behavior: Buying, Having, and Being,* 9th ed. (Upper Saddle River, NJ: Prentice Hall, 2011).

40. Jagdish N. Sheth, "An Investigation of Relationships among Evaluative Beliefs, Affect, Behavioral Intention, and Behavior," John U. Farley, John A. Howard, and L. Winston Ring, eds., *Consumer Behavior: Theory and Application* (Boston: Allyn & Bacon, 1974), pp. 89–114.

41. Martin Fishbein, "Attitudes and Prediction of Behavior," M. Fishbein, ed., *Readings in Attitude Theory and Measurement* (New York: Wiley, 1967), pp. 477–492.

42. Margaret C. Campbell and Ronald C. Goodstein, "The Moderating Effect of Perceived Risk on Consumers' Evaluations of Product Incongruity: Preference for the Norm," *Journal of Consumer Research* 28 (December 2001), pp. 439–49; Grahame R. Dowling, "Perceived Risk," Peter E. Earl and Simon Kemp, eds., *The Elgar Companion to Consumer Research and Economic Psychology* (Cheltenham, UK: Edward Elgar, 1999), pp. 419–24; Grahame R. Dowling, "Perceived Risk: The Concept and Its Measurement," *Psychology and Marketing* 3 (Fall 1986), pp. 193–210; James R. Bettman, "Perceived Risk and Its Components: A Model and Empirical Test," *Journal of Marketing Research* 10 (May 1973), pp. 184–90; Raymond A. Bauer, "Consumer Behavior as Risk Taking," Donald F. Cox, ed., *Risk Taking and Information Handling in Consumer Behavior* (Boston: Division of Research, Harvard Business School, 1967).

43. Albert O. Hirschman, *Exit, Voice, and Loyalty* (Cambridge, MA: Harvard University Press, 1970).

44. Eric Savitz, "Earthlink Q4 EPS Beats; Churn Down; Stock Gains," *Barron's,* February 4, 2010, www.barrons.com; Lauren McKay, "EarthLink Connects to a World of Loyalty," *CRM Magazine,* December 2009, p. 46; Rhonda Abrams, "Strategies: Make Customer Retention Priority No. 1," *USA Today,* May 29, 2009, www.usatoday.com; Jay Kassing, "Increasing Customer Retention," *Financial Services Marketing* (March–April 2002), pp. 32+.

45. For an overview of some issues involved, see James R. Bettman, Mary Frances Luce, and John W. Payne, "Constructive Consumer Choice Processes," *Journal of Consumer Research* 25 (December 1998), pp. 187–217; and Itamar Simonson, "Getting Closer to Your Customers by Understanding How They Make Choices," *California Management Review* 35 (Summer 1993), pp. 68–84. For classic studies in this area, see Dan Ariely and Ziv Carmon, "Gestalt Characteristics of

Experiences: The Defining Features of Summarized Events," *Journal of Behavioral Decision Making* 13, no. 2 (April 2000), pp. 191–201; Ravi Dhar and Klaus Wertenbroch, "Consumer Choice between Hedonic and Utilitarian Goods," *Journal of Marketing Research* 37 (February 2000), pp. 60–71; Itamar Simonson and Amos Tversky, "Choice in Context: Tradeoff Contrast and Extremeness Aversion," *Journal of Marketing Research* 29 (August 1992), pp. 281–95; Itamar Simonson, "The Effects of Purchase Quantity and Timing on Variety-Seeking Behavior," *Journal of Marketing Research* 27 (May 1990), pp. 150–62.

46. Leon Schiffman and Leslie Kanuk, *Consumer Behavior,* 10th ed. (Upper Saddle River, NJ: Prentice Hall, 2010); Wayne D. Hoyer and Deborah J. MacInnis, *Consumer Behavior,* 5th ed. (Cincinnati, OH: South-Western College Publishing, 2009).

47. For the practical significance of consumer decision making, see Itamar Simonson, "Get Close to Your Customers by Understanding How They Make Their Choices," *California Management Review* 35 (Summer 1993), pp. 78–79.

48. See Richard H. Thaler, "Mental Accounting and Consumer Choice," *Marketing Science* 4, no. 3 (Summer 1985), pp. 199–214; and Richard Thaler, "Mental Accounting Matters," *Journal of Behavioral Decision Making* 12, no. 3 (September 1999), pp. 183–206.

chapter 6

Analyzing Business Markets

In this chapter, we will address the following questions:

1. What is the business market, and how does it differ from the consumer market?
2. What buying situations do organizational buyers face?
3. Who participates in the business-to-business buying process, and how are buying decisions made?
4. How can companies build strong relationships with business customers?

Marketing Management at Oracle

Oracle grew into a high-tech powerhouse by offering a whole range of products and services to satisfy business customers' needs for enterprise software. Known originally for its database management systems, Oracle has spent $30 billion in recent years to buy 56 companies, including $7.4 billion to buy Sun Microsystems, doubling the company's revenue to $24 billion and sending its stock soaring in the process.

To become a one-stop shop for all kinds of business customers, Oracle seeks to provide the widest range of software offerings in the industry. It has also launched "Project Fusion" to unify its different applications, so customers can reap the benefits of consolidating many of their software needs with Oracle. Although the firm's market power has sometimes attracted criticism and raised regulatory concerns, Oracle's many long-time customers appreciate its track record of product innovation and its focus on customer satisfaction.[1]

Organizations such as Oracle do not only sell; they also buy vast quantities of raw materials, manufactured components, equipment, supplies, and business services. To create and capture value, sellers need to understand these organizations' needs, resources, policies, and buying procedures. In this chapter, we will highlight some of the key elements that marketers must analyze in business markets.[2]

What Is Organizational Buying?

Frederick E. Webster Jr. and Yoram Wind define **organizational buying** as the decision-making process by which formal organizations establish the need for purchased products and services and identify, evaluate, and choose among alternative brands and suppliers.[3] Organizational buying occurs within the business market, which differs from the consumer market in a number of ways.

The Business Market versus the Consumer Market

The **business market** consists of all the organizations that acquire goods and services used in the production of other products or services that are sold, rented, or supplied to others. The major industries making up the business market are agriculture, forestry, and fisheries; mining; manufacturing; construction; transportation; communication; public utilities; banking, finance, and insurance; distribution; and services. Table 6.1 shows the unique characteristics of business markets.

TABLE 6.1	Characteristics of Business Markets
Characteristic	**Description**
Fewer, larger buyers	Business marketers normally deal with far fewer, much larger buyers than consumer marketers.
Close supplier–customer relationship	Because of the smaller customer base and the importance and power of the larger customers, suppliers are frequently expected to customize offerings to individual business customer needs.
Professional purchasing	Trained purchasing agents follow formal purchasing policies, constraints, and requirements. Many of the buying instruments—such as proposals and purchase contracts—are not typically found in consumer buying.
Multiple buying influences	More people influence business buying decisions. Business marketers must send well-trained sales representatives and teams to deal with the well-trained buyers and with buying committees.
Multiple sales calls	Because more people are involved, it takes multiple sales calls to win most business orders during a sales cycle often measured in years.
Derived demand	Demand for business goods is ultimately derived from the demand for consumer goods, so business marketers must monitor the buying patterns of ultimate consumers.
Inelastic demand	Total demand for many business offerings is inelastic—that is, not much affected by price changes, especially in the short run, because producers cannot make quick production changes.
Fluctuating demand	Demand for business goods and services tends to be more volatile than demand for consumer goods and services. An increase in consumer demand can lead to a much larger increase in demand for plant and equipment necessary to produce the additional output.
Geographically concentrated buyers	More than half of U.S. business buyers are concentrated in seven states: New York, California, Pennsylvania, Illinois, Ohio, New Jersey, and Michigan.
Direct purchasing	Business buyers often buy directly from manufacturers rather than through intermediaries, especially items that are technically complex or expensive.

As an example of the business market, consider the process of producing and selling a pair of shoes. Hide dealers must sell hides to tanners, who sell leather to shoe manufacturers, who sell shoes to wholesalers, who sell shoes to retailers, who finally sell them to consumers. Each party in the supply chain also buys many other goods and services to support its operations.

Business marketers face many of the same challenges as consumer marketers. In particular, understanding their customers and what they value is of paramount importance to both. A survey of top business-to-business firms also identified other key challenges: identifying new opportunities for organic business growth, improving value management techniques and tools, and developing better metrics for marketing performance and accountability.[4]

Institutional and Government Markets

The overall business market includes institutional and government organizations in addition to profit-seeking companies. The *institutional market* consists of schools, hospitals, nursing homes, and other institutions that provide goods and services to people in their care. Many of these organizations have low budgets and captive clienteles.

For example, hospitals must decide what quality of food to buy for patients. The buying objective here is not profit, because the food is part of the total package; nor is cost minimization the sole objective, because poor food will draw complaints and hurt the hospital's reputation. The hospital must search for vendors whose quality meets or exceeds a certain minimum standard and whose prices are low. Knowing this, many food vendors set up a separate sales division to cater to institutional buyers' special needs. Heinz produces, packages, and prices its ketchup differently to meet the requirements of hospitals, colleges, and prisons. ARAMARK has gained a competitive advantage in this market due to its expert purchasing and supply chain management.[5]

In most countries, government organizations are major buyers of goods and services. The U.S. government is the world's largest customer, buying goods and services valued at more than $220 billion. Although most of the items cost between $2,500 and $25,000, the government also makes purchases in the billions, many in technology. Government organizations typically require suppliers to submit bids and often award the contract to the lowest bidder, sometimes making allowances for superior quality or a reputation for on-time performance. Demonstrating useful experience and successful past performance through case studies, especially with other government organizations, can be influential.[6]

Buying Situations

The business buyer faces many decisions in making a purchase. How many depends on the complexity of the problem being solved, newness of the buying requirement, number of people involved, and time required. Three types of buying situations are the straight rebuy, modified rebuy, and new task.[7]

- Straight rebuy. In a *straight rebuy*, the purchasing department reorders supplies such as bulk chemicals on a routine basis and chooses from suppliers on an approved list. These suppliers make an effort to maintain product and service quality and often propose automatic reordering systems to save time. "Out-suppliers" attempt to offer something new or exploit dissatisfaction with a current supplier. Their goal is to get a small order and then enlarge their purchase share over time.

- Modified rebuy. In a *modified rebuy,* the buyer wants to change product specifications, prices, delivery requirements, or other terms. This usually requires additional participants on both sides. The in-suppliers become nervous and want to protect the account. The out-suppliers see an opportunity to propose a better offer to gain some business.
- New task. A *new-task* purchaser buys a product or service for the first time (an office building, a new security system). The greater the cost or risk, the larger the number of participants, and the greater their information gathering—the longer the time to a decision.[8]

The business buyer makes the fewest decisions in the straight rebuy situation and the most in the new-task situation. Over time, new-buy situations become straight rebuys and routine purchase behavior.

New-task buying passes through several stages: awareness, interest, evaluation, trial, and adoption.[9] Mass media can be most important during the initial awareness stage; salespeople often have their greatest impact at the interest stage; and technical sources can be most important during the evaluation stage. Online selling efforts may be useful at all stages. In the new-task situation, the buyer must determine product specifications, price limits, delivery terms and times, service terms, payment terms, order quantities, acceptable suppliers, and the selected supplier. Different participants influence each decision, and the order in which they make these decisions can vary.

Because of the complicated selling required, many companies use a *missionary sales force* consisting of their most effective salespeople. The brand promise and the manufacturer's brand name recognition will be important in establishing trust and the customer's willingness to consider change.[10] The marketer also tries to reach as many key participants as possible and provide helpful information and assistance.

Systems Buying and Selling

Many business buyers prefer to buy a total problem solution from one seller. Called *systems buying,* this practice originated with government purchases of major weapons and communications systems. The government solicited bids from *prime contractors* that, if awarded the contract, would be responsible for bidding out and assembling the system's subcomponents from *second-tier contractors.* The prime contractor thus provided a turnkey solution, so-called because the buyer simply had to turn one key to get the job done.

Sellers have increasingly recognized that buyers like to purchase in this way, and many have adopted systems selling as a marketing tool. One variant of systems selling is *systems contracting,* in which a single supplier provides the buyer with its entire requirement of MRO (maintenance, repair, and operating) supplies. The customer benefits from reduced procurement and management costs and from price protection during the contract period. The seller benefits from lower operating costs thanks to steady demand and reduced paperwork.

Systems selling is a key marketing strategy in bidding to build large-scale industrial projects such as irrigation systems, sanitation systems, and even new towns. Project engineering firms must compete on price, quality, reliability, and other attributes to win contracts. For example, when the Indonesian government requested bids to build a cement factory near Jakarta, a U.S. firm made a proposal that included choosing the site, designing the factory, hiring the construction crews, assembling the materials and equipment, and turning over the finished factory to the government. The Japanese firm's proposal included all these services, plus hiring and training the workers to run the factory, exporting the cement, and using the cement to build roads and buildings in Jakarta. Although the Japanese proposal was more costly, it won the contract because it took the broadest view of the customer's needs, which is true systems selling.

Participants in the Business Buying Process

Who buys the trillions of dollars' worth of goods and services needed by business organizations? Purchasing agents are influential in straight-rebuy and modified-rebuy situations, whereas other department personnel are more influential in new-buy situations. Engineering personnel usually have a major influence in selecting product components, and purchasing agents dominate in selecting suppliers.[11]

The Buying Center

Frederic Webster and Yoram Wind call the decision-making unit of a buying organization the *buying center.* It consists of "all those individuals and groups who participate in the purchasing decision-making process, who share some common goals and the risks arising from the decisions."[12] The buying center includes all members of the organization who play any of the following seven roles in the purchase decision process.

1. *Initiators*—Users or others in the organization who request that something be purchased.
2. *Users*—Those who will use the product or service. In many cases, the users initiate the buying proposal and help define the product requirements.
3. *Influencers*—People who influence the buying decision (especially technical personnel) by helping define specifications and providing information for evaluating alternatives.
4. *Deciders*—People who decide on product requirements or on suppliers.
5. *Approvers*—People who authorize the proposed actions of deciders or buyers.
6. *Buyers*—People who have formal authority to select the supplier and arrange the purchase terms. Buyers may help shape product specifications, but they play their major role in selecting vendors and negotiating. In more complex purchases, buyers might include high-level managers.
7. *Gatekeepers*—People such as purchasing agents and receptionists who have the power to prevent sellers or information from reaching members of the buying center.

Several people can occupy a given role such as user or influencer, and one person may play multiple roles.[13] A purchasing manager often occupies the roles of buyer, influencer, and gatekeeper simultaneously, determining which sales reps can call on others in the organization; what budget and other constraints to place on the purchase; and which firm will actually get the business, even though others (deciders) might select two or more potential vendors that can meet the firm's requirements. The typical buying center has a minimum of five or six members, including some outside the organization, such as government officials and technical advisors.

Buying Center Influences

Buying centers usually include several participants with differing interests, authority, status, and persuasiveness, and sometimes very different decision criteria. Engineers may want to maximize product performance; production people may want ease of use and reliability of supply; financial

MARKETING ACROSS CULTURES

Marketing Skills

Language differences aside, marketers must assume that business-people from other cultures have different customs, beliefs, preferences, and values, at least until they confirm similarities with their own cultures. Research the other culture to learn how buyers and sellers interact in business and social settings, because in many countries, relationship building is as important as—or more important than—price or other aspects of the offer. Also find out how businesspeople in the other cultures prefer to communicate, how often they want contact, and how they make decisions, and be ready to adapt to these differences throughout the life of the relationship.

When Florida-based Bell Performance wanted to market its fuel additive products in Asia, the president studied local business etiquette before visiting the region. He learned, for example, that in Japan, he should introduce himself to the most senior manager before greeting others in order of their company status. Attention to details such as these—plus the company's product line and customer service—has enabled Bell Performance to expand in more than two dozen nations; today it generates 40 percent of its revenue from international sales.[14]

staff focus on the purchase's economics; purchasing may be concerned with operating and replacement costs; union officials may emphasize safety issues.

Business buyers also have personal motivations, perceptions, and preferences influenced by their age, income, education, job position, personality, attitudes toward risk, and culture (for more about dealing with cultural influences in international business marketing, see "Marketing Skills: Marketing Across Cultures, above"). Buyers definitely exhibit different buying styles. Some conduct rigorous analyses of competitive proposals before choosing a supplier. Others are "toughies" from the old school who pit competing sellers against one another.

Webster cautions that ultimately individuals, not organizations, make purchasing decisions.[15] Individuals are motivated by their own needs and perceptions in attempting to maximize the rewards (pay, advancement, recognition, and feelings of achievement) offered by the organization. Personal needs motivate their behavior, but organizational needs legitimate the buying process and its outcomes.

Thus, businesspeople are actually buying solutions to two problems: the organization's economic and strategic problem and their own personal need for individual achievement and reward. In this sense, industrial buying decisions are both "rational" and "emotional"—they serve both the organization's and the individual's needs.[16] Recognizing these extrinsic, interpersonal influences, more industrial firms have put greater emphasis on strengthening their corporate brand.

Targeting Firms and Buying Centers

Successful business-to-business marketing requires that business marketers know which types of companies to focus on in their selling efforts, as well as who to concentrate on within the buying centers in those organizations. Finding market segments with the greatest growth prospects, most profitable customers, and most promising opportunities is crucial.

Also, marketers should remember that many business-to-business transactions involve products purchased as components or ingredients in products that companies sell to the ultimate end users.

To target their efforts properly, business marketers need to figure out: Who are the major decision participants? What decisions do they influence? What is their level of influence? What evaluation criteria do they use? Small sellers concentrate on reaching the *key buying influencers.* Larger sellers go for *multilevel in-depth selling* to reach as many participants as possible. Their salespeople virtually "live with" high-volume customers. Companies must rely more heavily on their communications programs to reach hidden buying influences and keep current customers informed.[17]

Stages in the Buying Process

The business buying-decision process includes eight stages called *buyphases*, as identified by Patrick J. Robinson and his associates, in the *buygrid* framework (see Table 6.2).[18] In modified-rebuy or straight-rebuy situations, some stages are compressed or bypassed. For example, the buyer normally has a favorite supplier or a ranked list of suppliers and can skip the search and proposal solicitation stages. Here are some important considerations in each of the eight stages.

Problem Recognition

The buying process begins when someone in the company recognizes a problem or need that can be met by acquiring a good or service. The recognition can be triggered by internal or external stimuli. Internal stimuli might include a decision to develop a new product, which requires new equipment and materials; a machine breaking down and requiring new parts; or a decision to search for new vendors, lower prices, or better quality. Externally, the buyer may get new ideas at a trade show, see an ad, visit a Web site, or receive a call from a sales representative who offers a

TABLE 6.2	Buygrid Framework: Major Stages (Buyphases) of the Industrial Buying Process in Relation to Major Buying Situations (Buyclasses)		
		Buyclasses	
		New Task	Modified Rebuy	Straight Rebuy
Buyphases	1. Problem recognition	Yes	Maybe	No
	2. General need description	Yes	Maybe	No
	3. Product specification	Yes	Yes	Yes
	4. Supplier search	Yes	Maybe	No
	5. Proposal solicitation	Yes	Maybe	No
	6. Supplier selection	Yes	Maybe	No
	7. Order-routine specification	Yes	Maybe	No
	8. Performance review	Yes	Yes	Yes

Source: Adapted from Patrick J. Johnson, Charles W. Farris, and Yoram Wind, *Industrial Buying and Creative Marketing* (Boston: Allyn & Bacon, 1967), p. 14.

better product or a lower price. Business marketers can stimulate problem recognition by direct mail, telemarketing, personal selling, and Internet communications.

General Need Description and Product Specification

Next, the buyer determines the needed item's general characteristics and required quantity. For standard items, this is simple. For complex items, the buyer will work with others—engineers, users—to define characteristics such as reliability, durability, or price. Business marketers can help by describing how their products meet or even exceed the buyer's needs.

The buying organization now develops the item's technical specifications. Often, the firm will assign a product-value-analysis engineering team to the project. *Product value analysis (PVA)* is an approach to cost reduction that studies whether components can be redesigned or standardized or made by cheaper methods of production without damaging product performance. The PVA team will identify overdesigned components, for instance, that last longer than the product itself. Tightly written specifications allow the buyer to refuse components that are too expensive or fail to meet specified standards. Suppliers can use PVA as a tool for positioning themselves to win an account.

Supplier Search

The buyer next tries to identify the most appropriate suppliers through trade directories, contacts with other companies, trade advertisements, trade shows, and the Internet.[19] Companies that purchase over the Internet are utilizing electronic marketplaces in several forms (see Table 6.3). Web sites are organized around two types of e-hubs: *vertical hubs* centered on industries (plastics, paper) and *functional hubs* (media buying, energy management).

Moving into e-procurement means more than acquiring software; it requires changing purchasing strategy and structure. However, the benefits are many: Aggregating purchasing across multiple departments yields larger, centrally negotiated volume discounts, a smaller purchasing staff, and less buying of substandard goods from outside the approved list of suppliers.

The supplier's task is to ensure it is considered when customers are—or could be—in the market and searching for a supplier. Identifying good leads and converting them to sales requires

---

TABLE 6.3	Electronic Marketplaces for Business Buying

- *Catalog sites.* Companies can order thousands of items through electronic catalogs distributed by e-procurement software, such as Grainger's.

- *Vertical markets.* Companies buying industrial products (such as plastics) or services (such as media) can go to specialized Web sites such as Plastics.com.

- *"Pure-Play" auction sites.* Online auctions can serve business buyers and sellers worldwide. Ritchie Bros. operates the multilingual rbauction.com auction site, where businesses in many nations can buy or sell.

- *Spot (or exchange) markets.* On spot electronic markets, prices change by the minute. ChemConnect.com is an online exchange for buyers and sellers of bulk chemicals such as benzene.

- *Private exchanges.* Hewlett-Packard, IBM, and Walmart operate private online exchanges to link with specially invited groups of suppliers and partners.

- *Barter markets.* In barter markets, participants offer to trade business goods and services.

- *Buying alliances.* Several companies buying the same goods can join together to form purchasing consortia and gain deeper discounts on volume purchases. TopSource is a buying alliance of grocery-related businesses.

the marketing and sales organizations to take a coordinated, multichannel approach to the role of trusted advisor to prospective customers. Marketing must work together with sales to define what makes a "sales ready" prospect and cooperate to send the right messages via sales calls, trade shows, online activities, PR, events, direct mail, and referrals.[20]

Suppliers that have insufficient production capacity or a poor reputation will be rejected. Those that qualify may be visited by the buyer's agents, who will examine the suppliers' facilities and meet the staff. After evaluating each company, the buyer will end up with a short list of qualified suppliers.

Proposal Solicitation

Next, the buyer invites qualified suppliers to submit proposals. If the item is complex or expensive, the proposal will be written and detailed. After evaluating the proposals, the buyer will invite a few suppliers to make formal presentations. Business marketers must be skilled in researching, writing, and presenting proposals that describe value and benefits in customer terms. Oral presentations must inspire confidence and position the company's capabilities so they stand out from the competition.

Supplier Selection

Before selecting a supplier, the buying center will specify and rank desired supplier attributes. To develop compelling value propositions, business marketers need to better understand how business buyers arrive at their valuations.[21] Researchers studying how business marketers assess customer value found eight different *customer value assessment (CVA)* methods. Companies tended to use the simpler methods, although the more sophisticated ones produce a more accurate picture of customer perceived value.

Despite moves toward strategic sourcing, partnering, and participation in cross-functional teams, buyers still spend a lot of time haggling with suppliers over price. Marketers can counter requests for a lower price in a number of ways. They may be able to show that the life-cycle cost of using their product is lower than for competitors' products. They can cite the value of the services the buyer now receives, especially if these are competitively superior. Service support and personal interactions, as well as a supplier's know-how and ability to improve customers' time to market, can be useful differentiators in achieving key-supplier status.[22] Some firms handle price-oriented buyers by setting a lower price but establishing restrictive conditions: (1) limited quantities, (2) no refunds, (3) no adjustments, and (4) no services.[23]

Companies are increasingly reducing the number of their suppliers. A selected supplier will therefore be responsible for a larger component system, have to deliver continuous quality and performance improvement, and cut prices each year by a given percentage. It will also be expected to work closely with business customers during product development. There is even a trend toward single sourcing.

Order-Routine Specification

After selecting suppliers, the buyer negotiates the final order, listing the technical specifications, the quantity needed, the expected time of delivery, return policies, and so on. In the case of MRO items, buyers are moving toward blanket contracts rather than periodic purchase orders. A blanket contract establishes a long-term relationship in which the supplier promises to resupply the buyer as needed, at set prices, over a set period. Because the seller holds the stock, blanket contracts are sometimes called *stockless purchase plans.* The buyer's computer automatically sends an order to the seller when stock is needed. This makes it difficult for out-suppliers to break in unless the buyer becomes dissatisfied with prices, quality, or service.

Companies that fear a shortage of key materials are willing to buy and hold large inventories. They will sign long-term supply contracts to ensure a steady flow of materials. DuPont, Ford, and several major companies regard long-term supply planning as a major responsibility of their purchasing managers. Business marketers are also setting up extranets with important customers to facilitate and lower the cost of transactions. Customers enter orders that are automatically transmitted to the supplier. Some companies go further and shift the ordering responsibility to their suppliers in systems called *vendor-managed inventory.* These suppliers are privy to the customer's inventory levels and take responsibility for replenishing automatically through *continuous replenishment programs.*

Performance Review

The buyer periodically reviews the performance of the chosen supplier(s) using one of three methods. The buyer may contact end users and ask for their evaluations, rate the supplier on several criteria using a weighted-score method, or aggregate the cost of poor performance to come up with adjusted costs of purchase, including price. The performance review may lead the buyer to continue, modify, or end a supplier relationship.

Managing Business-to-Business Customer Relationships

To improve effectiveness and efficiency, business suppliers and customers are exploring different ways to manage their relationships.[24] Cultivating the right relationships with business is paramount for any holistic marketing program.

The Benefits of Vertical Coordination

Much research has advocated greater vertical coordination between buying partners and sellers, so they can go beyond transactions to engage in activities that create more value for both parties.[25] Building trust is one prerequisite to healthy long-term relationships (see "Marketing Insight: Establishing Corporate Trust, Credibility, and Reputation"). Knowledge that is specific and relevant to a relationship partner is also an important factor in the strength of interfirm ties.[26]

A number of forces influence the development of a relationship between business partners.[27] Four relevant factors are availability of alternatives, importance of supply, complexity of supply, and supply market dynamism. Based on these we can classify buyer–supplier relationships into eight categories:[28]

1. *Basic buying and selling*—These are simple, routine exchanges with moderate levels of cooperation and information exchange.
2. *Bare bones*—These relationships require more adaptation by the seller and less cooperation and information exchange.
3. *Contractual transaction*—These exchanges are defined by formal contract and generally have low levels of trust, cooperation, and interaction.
4. *Customer supply*—In this traditional custom supply situation, competition rather than cooperation is the dominant form of governance.

ESTABLISHING CORPORATE TRUST, CREDIBILITY, AND REPUTATION

Corporate credibility, the extent to which customers believe a firm can design and deliver offerings that satisfy their needs and wants, depends on three factors:

- Corporate expertise—the extent to which a company is seen as able to make, sell, and deliver its offerings.
- Corporate trustworthiness—the extent to which a company is seen as honest, dependable, and sensitive to customer needs.
- Corporate likability—the extent to which a company is seen as likable, attractive, prestigious, and so on.

Trust, the willingness of a firm to rely on a business partner, depends on such factors as the firm's perceived competence, integrity, honesty, and benevolence. Building trust can be tricky in online settings, and firms often impose more stringent requirements on online business partners than on others. Business buyers worry that they won't get products of the right quality delivered to the right place at the right time. Sellers worry about getting paid on time and how much credit they should extend. Over time, as buyers and sellers work with each other, they build trust and strengthen their relationships for mutual benefit.

Sources: Bob Violino, "Building B2B Trust," *Computerworld,* June 17, 2002, p. 32; Richard E. Plank, David A. Reid, and Ellen Bolman Pullins, "Perceived Trust in Business-to-Business Sales: A New Measure," *Journal of Personal Selling and Sales Management* 19, no. 3 (Summer 1999), pp. 61–72; Kevin Lane Keller and David A. Aaker, "Corporate-Level Marketing: The Impact of Credibility on a Company's Brand Extensions," *Corporate Reputation Review* 1 (August 1998), pp. 356–78; Robert M. Morgan and Shelby D. Hunt, "The Commitment–Trust Theory of Relationship Marketing," *Journal of Marketing* 58, no. 3 (July 1994), pp. 20–38; Christine Moorman, Rohit Deshpande, and Gerald Zaltman, "Factors Affecting Trust in Market Research Relationships," *Journal of Marketing* 57 (January 1993), pp. 81–101; Glen Urban, "Where Are You Positioned on the Trust Dimensions?" *Don't Just Relate-Advocate: A Blueprint for Profit in the Era of Customer Power* (Upper Saddle River, NJ: Pearson Education/Wharton School Publishers, 2005).

5. *Cooperative systems*—The partners are united in operational ways, but neither demonstrates structural commitment through legal means or adaptation.
6. *Collaborative*—In collaborative exchanges, much trust and commitment lead to true partnership.
7. *Mutually adaptive*—Buyers and sellers make many relationship-specific adaptations, but without necessarily achieving strong trust or cooperation.
8. *Customer is king*—The seller adapts to meet the customer's needs without expecting much adaptation or change in exchange.

Over time, however, relationship roles may shift or be activated under different circumstances.[29] Some needs can be satisfied with fairly basic supplier performance. Buyers then neither want nor require a close relationship with a supplier. Likewise, some suppliers may not find it worth their while to invest in customers with limited growth potential.

Business Relationships: Risks and Opportunism

Establishing a customer–supplier relationship creates tension between safeguarding (ensuring predictable solutions) and adaptation (allowing for flexibility for unanticipated events). Vertical coordination can facilitate stronger customer–seller ties but at the same time may increase the risk to the customer's and supplier's specific investments. *Specific investments* are those expenditures tailored to a particular company and value chain partner (investments in company-specific training, equipment, and operating procedures or systems).[30] They help firms grow profits and achieve their positioning.[31]

Specific investments, however, entail considerable risk to both customer and supplier. Transaction theory from economics maintains that because these investments are partially sunk, they lock firms into a particular relationship. Sensitive cost and process information may need to be exchanged. A buyer may be vulnerable to holdup because of switching costs; a supplier may be vulnerable because it has dedicated assets and/or technology/knowledge at stake.

When buyers cannot easily monitor supplier performance, the supplier might shirk or cheat and not deliver the expected value. *Opportunism* is "some form of cheating or undersupply relative to an implicit or explicit contract."[32] It may entail blatant self-serving and deliberate misrepresentation that violates contractual agreements. A more passive form of opportunism might be a refusal or unwillingness to adapt to changing circumstances.

Opportunism is a concern because firms must devote resources to control and monitoring that they could otherwise allocate to more productive purposes. Contracts may become inadequate to govern supplier transactions when supplier opportunism becomes difficult to detect, when firms make specific investments in assets they cannot use elsewhere, and when contingencies are harder to anticipate. A supplier with a good reputation will try to avoid opportunism to protect this valuable asset. Finally, to start and strengthen relationships with business-to-business customers, top firms are redesigning Web sites, improving search results, exchanging e-mails, engaging in social media, and launching Webinars and podcasts.

EXECUTIVE SUMMARY

Organizational buying is the decision-making process by which formal organizations establish the need for purchased products and services, then identify, evaluate, and choose among alternative brands and suppliers. The business market consists of all the organizations that acquire goods and services used in the production of other products or services that are sold, rented, or supplied to others. The institutional market consists of schools and other institutions that provide goods and services to people in their care. Government organizations are also major buyers of goods and services. Compared to consumer markets, business markets have fewer and larger buyers, closer customer-supplier relationships, and more geographically concentrated buyers. Demand in the business market is derived from demand in the consumer market and fluctuates with the business cycle.

Three types of buying situations are the straight rebuy, modified rebuy, and new task. The buying center consists of initiators, users, influencers, deciders, approvers, buyers, and gatekeepers. To influence these parties, marketers must be aware of environmental, organizational, interpersonal, and individual factors. The buying process consists of eight buyphases: (1) problem recognition, (2) general need description, (3) product specification, (4) supplier search, (5) proposal solicitation, (6) supplier selection, (7) order-routine specification, and (8) performance review. Business marketers must form strong relationships with their customers and provide added value.

NOTES

1. Chris Kanaracus, "Oracle Gearing Up for More Purchases," *BusinessWeek,* July 13, 2010, www.businessweek.com; Adam Lashinsky, "The Enforcer," *Fortune*, September 28, 2009, pp. 117–24; Steve Hamm, "Oracle Faces Its Toughest Deal Yet," *BusinessWeek*, May 4, 2009, p. 24; Steve Hamm and Aaron Ricadela, "Oracle Has Customers over a Barrel," *BusinessWeek*, September 21, 2009, pp. 52–55.

2. For a comprehensive review, see James C. Anderson and James A. Narus, *Business Market Management: Understanding, Creating, and Delivering Value,* 3rd ed. (Upper Saddle River, NJ: Prentice Hall, 2009).

3. Frederick E. Webster Jr. and Yoram Wind, *Organizational Buying Behavior* (Upper Saddle River, NJ: Prentice Hall, 1972), p. 2. For a review of recent academic literature on the topic, see Håkan Håkansson and Ivan Snehota, "Marketing in Business Markets," Bart Weitz and Robin Wensley, eds., *Handbook of Marketing* (London: Sage Publications, 2002), pp. 513–26; Mark Glynn and Arch Woodside, eds., *Business-to-Business Brand Management: Theory, Research, and Executive Case Study Exercises in Advances in Business Marketing & Purchasing* series, Volume 15 (Bingley, UK: Emerald Group Publishing, 2009).

4. "B-to-B Marketing Trends 2010," *Institute for the Study of Business Markets*, http://isbm.smeal.psu.edu, December 9, 2010.

5. Paul King, "Purchasing: Keener Competition Requires Thinking Outside the Box," *Nation's Restaurant News,* August 18, 2003, p. 87.

6. Bill Gormley, "The U.S. Government Can Be Your Lifelong Customer," *Washington Business Journal,* January 23, 2009; Chris Warren, "How to Sell to Uncle Sam," *BNET Crash Course*, www.bnet.com, December 9, 2010.

7. Patrick J. Robinson, Charles W. Faris, and Yoram Wind, *Industrial Buying and Creative Marketing* (Boston: Allyn & Bacon, 1967).

8. Michele D. Bunn, "Taxonomy of Buying Decision Approaches," *Journal of Marketing* 57 (January 1993), pp. 38–56; Daniel H. McQuiston, "Novelty, Complexity, and Importance as Causal Determinants of Industrial Buyer Behavior," *Journal of Marketing* (April 1989), pp. 66–79; Peter Doyle, Arch G. Woodside, and Paul Mitchell, "Organizational Buying in New Task and Rebuy Situations," *Industrial Marketing Management* (February 1979), pp. 7–11.

9. Urban B. Ozanne and Gilbert A. Churchill Jr., "Five Dimensions of the Industrial Adoption Process," *Journal of Marketing Research* (August 1971), pp. 322–28.

10. For more about business-to-business branding, see Philip Kotler and Waldemar Pfoertsch, *B2B Brand Management* (Berlin, Germany: Springer, 2006).

11. Jeffrey E. Lewin and Naveen Donthu, "The Influence of Purchase Situation on Buying Center Structure and Involvement: A Select Meta-Analysis of Organizational Buying Behavior Research," *Journal of Business Research* 58 (October 2005), pp. 1381–90; R. Venkatesh and Ajay K. Kohli, "Influence Strategies in Buying Centers," *Journal of Marketing* 59 (October 1995), pp. 71–82; Donald W. Jackson Jr., Janet E. Keith, and Richard K. Burdick, "Purchasing Agents' Perceptions of Industrial Buying Center Influence," *Journal of Marketing* (Fall 1984), pp. 75–83.

12. Frederick E. Webster Jr. and Yoram Wind, *Organizational Buying Behavior* (Upper Saddle River, NJ: Prentice Hall, 1972) p. 6.

13. James C. Anderson and James A. Narus, *Business Market Management: Understanding, Creating, and Delivering Value,* 3rd ed. (Upper Saddle River, NJ: Prentice Hall, 2009); Frederick E. Webster Jr. and Yoram Wind, "A General Model for Understanding Organizational Buying Behavior," *Journal of Marketing* 36 (April 1972), pp. 12–19; Frederick E. Webster Jr. and Yoram Wind, *Organizational Buying Behavior* (Upper Saddle River, NJ: Prentice Hall, 1972).

14. Karen J. Bannan, "Going Global with E-mail Marketing," *BtoB*, July 22, 2010, www.btobonline.com; Ian Mount, "Tips for Increasing Sales in International Markets," *New York Times,* April 22, 2010, p. B7; Betsy Cummings, "Selling Around the World," *Sales & Marketing Management,* May 2001, p. 70; Rhonda Coast, "Understanding Cultural Differences Is a Priority," *Pittsburgh Business Times,* February 11, 2000, p. 13.

15. Frederick E. Webster Jr. and Kevin Lane Keller, "A Roadmap for Branding in Industrial Markets," *Journal of Brand Management* 11 (May 2004), pp. 388–402.

16. Scott Ward and Frederick E. Webster Jr., "Organizational Buying Behavior," Tom Robertson and Hal Kassarjian, eds., *Handbook of Consumer Behavior* (Upper Saddle River, NJ: Prentice Hall, 1991), chapter 12, pp. 419–58.

17. Frederick E. Webster Jr. and Yoram Wind, *Organizational Buying Behavior* (Upper Saddle River, NJ: Prentice Hall, 1972), p. 6.

18. Patrick J. Robinson, Charles W. Faris, and Yoram Wind, *Industrial Buying and Creative Marketing* (Boston, MA: Allyn & Bacon, 1967).

19. Rajdeep Grewal, James M. Comer, and Raj Mehta, "An Investigation into the Antecedents of Organizational Participation in Business-to-Business Electronic Markets," *Journal of Marketing* 65 (July 2001), pp. 17–33.

20. Brian J. Carroll, *Lead Generation for the Complex Sale* (New York: McGraw-Hill, 2006).

21. Daniel J. Flint, Robert B. Woodruff, and Sarah Fisher Gardial, "Exploring the Phenomenon of Customers' Desired Value Change in a Business-to-Business Context," *Journal of Marketing* 66 (October 2002), pp. 102–17.

22. Wolfgang Ulaga and Andreas Eggert, "Value-Based Differentiation in Business Relationships: Gaining and Sustaining Key Supplier Status," *Journal of Marketing* 70 (January 2006), pp. 119–36.

23. Nirmalya Kumar, *Marketing as Strategy: Understanding the CEO's Agenda for Driving Growth and Innovation* (Boston: Harvard Business School Press, 2004).

24. For foundational material, see Lloyd M. Rinehart, James A. Eckert, Robert B. Handfield, Thomas J. Page Jr., and Thomas Atkin, "An Assessment of Buyer–Seller Relationships," *Journal of Business Logistics* 25, no. 1 (2004), pp. 25–62; F. Robert Dwyer, Paul Schurr, and Sejo Oh, "Developing Buyer–Supplier Relationships," *Journal of Marketing* 51 (April 1987), pp. 11–28; and Barbara Bund Jackson, *Winning & Keeping Industrial Customers: The Dynamics of Customer Relations* (Lexington, MA: D. C. Heath, 1985).

25. Das Narayandas and V. Kasturi Rangan, "Building and Sustaining Buyer–Seller Relationships in Mature Industrial Markets," *Journal of Marketing* 68 (July 2004), pp. 63–77.

26. Robert W. Palmatier, Rajiv P. Dant, Dhruv Grewal, and Kenneth R. Evans, "Factors Influencing the Effectiveness of Relationship Marketing: A Meta-Analysis," *Journal of Marketing* 70 (October 2006), pp. 136–53; Jean L. Johnson, Ravipreet S. Sohli, and Rajdeep Grewal, "The Role of Relational Knowledge Stores in Interfirm Partnering," *Journal of Marketing* 68 (July 2004), pp. 21–36; Fred Selnes and James Sallis, "Promoting Relationship Learning," *Journal of Marketing* 67 (July 2003), pp. 80–95; Patricia M. Doney and Joseph P. Cannon, "An Examination of the Nature of Trust in Buyer–Seller Relationships," *Journal of Marketing* 61 (April 1997), pp. 35–51; Shankar Ganesan, "Determinants of Long-Term Orientation in Buyer–Seller Relationships," *Journal of Marketing* 58 (April 1994), pp. 1–19.

27. William W. Keep, Stanley C. Hollander, and Roger Dickinson, "Forces Impinging on Long-Term Business-to-Business Relationships in the United States: An Historical Perspective," *Journal of Marketing* 62 (April 1998), pp. 31–45.

28. Joseph P. Cannon and William D. Perreault Jr., "Buyer–Seller Relationships in Business Markets," *Journal of Marketing Research* 36 (November 1999), pp. 439–60.

29. Jan B. Heide and Kenneth H. Wahne, "Friends, Businesspeople, and Relationship Roles: A Conceptual Framework and Research Agenda," *Journal of Marketing* 70 (July 2006), pp. 90–103.

30. Akesel I. Rokkan, Jan B. Heide, and Kenneth H. Wathne, "Specific Investment in Marketing Relationships: Expropriation and Bonding Effects," *Journal of Marketing Research* 40 (May 2003), pp. 210–24.

31. Kenneth H. Wathne and Jan B. Heide, "Relationship Governance in a Supply Chain Network," *Journal of Marketing* 68 (January 2004), pp. 73–89; Douglas Bowman and Das Narayandas, "Linking Customer Management Effort to Customer Profitability in Business Markets," *Journal of Marketing Research* 61 (November 2004), pp. 433–47; Mrinal Ghosh and George John, "Governance Value Analysis and Marketing Strategy," *Journal of Marketing* 63 (Special Issue, 1999), pp. 131–45.

32. Kenneth H. Wathne and Jan B. Heide, "Opportunism in Interfirm Relationships: Forms, Outcomes, and Solutions," *Journal of Marketing* 64 (October 2000), pp. 36–51.

chapter 7

Identifying Market Segments and Targets

In this chapter, we will address the following questions:

1. In what ways can a company divide a consumer or business market into segments?
2. How should a company choose the most attractive target markets?
3. What are the different levels of market segmentation?

Marketing Management at Club Med

One of the most famous leisure travel brands in the world, France's Club Méditerranée, better known as Club Med, has targeted different customer groups through the years. Started in 1950, Club Med was a pioneer of the all-inclusive resort, using exotic locations and bare-bones accommodations to target singles, young couples, and others seeking sea, sand, and a good time. Later, Club Med added family-friendly resort locations and services, with activities ranging from flying-trapeze clinics to body building to snow skiing.

Today Club Med operates in more than 40 countries. Following the recent recession, the firm restructured and invested hundreds of millions of dollars to move upscale and attract wealthier customers by crafting a more sophisticated image. To celebrate its 60th anniversary, the company launched a new advertising campaign, backed by online marketing, proclaiming that Club Med was "Where Happiness Means the World." Soon it will open a series of resorts in China, targeting affluent vacationers in this fast-growing market.[1]

T arget marketing, which Club Med is using, requires that marketers (1) identify and profile distinct groups of buyers who differ in their needs and wants (market segmentation), (2) select one or more market segments to enter (market targeting), and (3) establish and communicate the offering's distinctive benefit(s) to each target segment (market positioning). This chapter focuses on the first two steps; Chapter 9 discusses positioning and competitive dynamics.

Bases for Segmenting Consumer Markets

Market segmentation divides a market into well-defined slices. A *market segment* consists of a group of customers who share a similar set of needs and wants. The marketer's task is to identify the appropriate number and nature of market segments and decide which one(s) to target.

We use two broad groups of variables to segment consumer markets. Some researchers try to define segments by looking at descriptive characteristics: geographic, demographic, and psychographic. Then they examine whether these customer segments exhibit different needs or product responses. Other researchers try to define segments by looking at behavioral considerations, such as consumer responses to benefits, usage occasions, or brands. The researcher then sees whether different characteristics are associated with each consumer-response segment.

Regardless of which type of segmentation scheme we use, the key is adjusting the marketing program to recognize customer differences. The major segmentation variables—geographic, demographic, psychographic, and behavioral segmentation—are summarized in Table 7.1.

Geographic Segmentation

Geographic segmentation divides the market into geographical units such as nations, states, regions, counties, cities, or neighborhoods. The company can operate in one or a few areas, or it can operate in all but pay attention to local variations. In that way it can tailor marketing programs to the needs and wants of local customer groups in trading areas, neighborhoods, even individual stores. In a growing trend called *grassroots marketing,* such activities concentrate on getting as close and personally relevant to individual customers as possible.

More and more, regional marketing means marketing right down to a specific zip code.[2] Some approaches combine geographic data with demographic data to yield richer descriptions of consumers and neighborhoods. Nielsen Claritas has developed a geoclustering approach called PRIZM (Potential Rating Index by Zip Markets) NE that classifies over half a million U.S. residential neighborhoods into 14 distinct groups and 66 distinct lifestyle segments called PRIZM Clusters.[3] The groupings take into consideration 39 factors in five broad categories: (1) education and affluence, (2) family life cycle, (3) urbanization, (4) race and ethnicity, and (5) mobility. The clusters have descriptive titles such as *Blue Blood Estates, Young Digerati, Hometown Retired,* and *Back Country Folks.* The inhabitants in a cluster tend to lead similar lives, drive similar cars, have similar jobs, and read similar magazines.

Demographic Segmentation

In demographic segmentation, we divide the market using variables such as age, family size, family life cycle, gender, income, occupation, education, religion, race, generation, nationality, and social class. Demographic variables are popular with marketers because they're often associated with consumer needs and wants and because they're easy to measure. Even when we describe the target market in nondemographic terms (say, by personality type), we may need the link back to demographic characteristics in order to estimate the size of the market and the media used to reach it.

TABLE 7.1	Major Segmentation Variables for Consumer Markets
Geographic region	Pacific Mountain, West North Central, West South Central, East North Central, East South Central, South Atlantic, Middle Atlantic, New England
City or metro size	Under 5,000; 5,000–20,000; 20,000–50,000; 50,000–100,000; 100,000–250,000; 250,000–500,000; 500,000–1,000,000; 1,000,000–4,000,000; 4,000,000+
Density	Urban, suburban, rural
Climate	Northern, southern
Demographic age	Under 6, 6–11, 12–17, 18–34, 35–49, 50–64, 65+
Family size	1–2, 3–4, 5+
Family life cycle	Young, single; young, married, no children; young, married, youngest child under 6; young, married, youngest child 6 or older; older, married, with children; older, married, no children under 18; older, single; other
Gender	Male, female
Income	Under $10,000; $10,000–$15,000; $15,000–$20,000; $20,000–$30,000; $30,000–$50,000; $50,000–$100,000; $100,000+
Occupation	Professional and technical; managers, officials, and proprietors; clerical sales; craftspeople; forepersons; operatives; farmers; retired; students; homemakers; unemployed
Education	Grade school or less; some high school; high school graduate; some college; college graduate
Religion	Catholic, Protestant, Jewish, Muslim, Hindu, other
Race	White, Black, Asian, Hispanic
Generation	Silent Generation, Baby boomers, Gen X, Gen Y
Nationality	North American, Latin American, British, French, German, Italian, Chinese, Indian, Japanese
Social class	Lower lowers, upper lowers, working class, middle class, upper middles, lower uppers, upper uppers
Psychographic lifestyle	Culture-oriented, sports-oriented, outdoor-oriented
Personality	Compulsive, gregarious, authoritarian, ambitious
Behavioral occasions	Regular occasion, special occasion
Benefits	Quality, service, economy, speed
User status	Nonuser, ex-user, potential user, first-time user, regular user
Usage rate	Light user, medium user, heavy user
Loyalty status	None, medium, strong, absolute
Readiness stage	Unaware, aware, informed, interested, desirous, intending to buy
Attitude toward product	Enthusiastic, positive, indifferent, negative, hostile

Here's how marketers have used certain demographic variables to segment markets.

- Age and life-cycle stage. Consumer wants and abilities change with age. Toothpaste brands such as Crest offer three main lines of products to target kids, adults, and older consumers. Age segmentation can be even more refined. Pampers divides its market into prenatal, new baby (0–5 months), baby (6–12 months), toddler (13–23 months), and preschooler (24 months+). However, age and life cycle can be tricky variables.[4]
- Life stage. People in the same part of the life cycle may still differ in their life stage. **Life stage** defines a person's major concern, such as going through a divorce, going into a

second marriage, taking care of an older parent, deciding to cohabit with another person, deciding to buy a new home, and so on. These life stages present opportunities for marketers who can help people cope with their major concerns.

- Gender. Men and women have different attitudes and behave differently, based partly on genetic makeup and partly on socialization.[5] For example, men often need to be invited to touch a product, whereas women are likely to pick it up without prompting. Many men like to read product information; women may relate to a product on a more personal level.[6] When women shop for cars, they are more interested than men in the environmental impact, interior styling, and features that help drivers survive an accident rather than help avoid one.[7]

- Income. Income segmentation is often used in such categories as automobiles, clothing, cosmetics, financial services, and travel. However, income does not always predict the best customers for a given product. Many marketers are deliberately going after lower-income groups, sometimes finding fewer competitive pressures or greater consumer loyalty.[8] Increasingly, companies are finding their markets are hourglass shaped as middle-market U.S. consumers migrate toward both discount *and* premium products.[9]

- Generation. Each generation or *cohort* is profoundly influenced by the times in which it grows up—the music, movies, politics, and events of that period. Table 7.2 shows the four main U.S. generation cohorts.[10] Marketers often advertise to a cohort by using the icons and images prominent in its shared experiences. Firms also try to develop offerings and marketing approaches suited to a generational target's interests and preferences. Many Gen Y members dislike "hard sell" tactics, for example, so some marketers use online buzz, unconventional sports, and other untraditional means to reach and persuade them.[11]

- Race and culture. *Multicultural marketing* is an approach recognizing that different ethnic and cultural segments have sufficiently different needs and wants to require targeted marketing activities, and that a mass market approach is not refined enough for the diversity of the marketplace. Consider that McDonald's now does 40 percent of its U.S. business with ethnic minorities.[12] The norms, language nuances, buying habits, and business practices of multicultural markets need to be factored into the formulation of a

TABLE 7.2	Profiling U.S. Generation Cohorts		
Generational Cohort	**Birth Range**	**Approximate Size**	**Defining Features**
Millennials (Gen Y)	1979–1994	78 million	Raised with relative affluence, technologically plugged in and concerned with the environment and social issues, they also have a strong sense of independence and a perceived immunity from marketing.
Gen X	1964–1978	50 million	Sometimes seen as falling between the generational cracks, they bridge the technological savvy of Gen Y with the adult realities of the baby boomers.
Baby Boomers	1946–1964	76 million	Still largely in the prime of their consumption cycle, they embrace products and lifestyles that allow them to turn back the hands of time.
Silent Generation	1925–1945	42 million	Defying their advancing age, they maintain active lives, seeking products and marketing that help them to achieve that.

Sources: Kenneth Gronbach, "The 6 Markets You Need to Know Now," *Advertising Age*, June 2, 2008, p. 21; Geoffrey E. Meredith and Charles D. Schewe, *Managing by Defining Moments: America's 7 Generational Cohorts, Their Workplace Values, and Why Managers Should Care* (New York: Hungry Minds, 2002).

marketing strategy, rather than being added as an afterthought.[13] Multicultural marketing can result in different marketing messages, media, channels, and so on.

Psychographic Segmentation

Psychographics is the science of using psychology and demographics to better understand consumers. In *psychographic segmentation*, buyers are divided into different groups on the basis of psychological/personality traits, lifestyle, or values. People within the same demographic group can exhibit very different psychographic profiles.

One of the most popular commercially available classification systems based on psychographic measurements is Strategic Business Insight's VALS™ framework. VALS, signifying values and lifestyles, classifies U.S. adults into eight primary groups based on demographics and attitudes. The VALS system is continually updated with new data from more than 80,000 surveys per year (see Figure 7.1).[14]

The main dimensions of the VALS segmentation framework are consumer motivation and consumer resources. Consumers are inspired by one of three primary motivations: ideals, achievement, and self-expression. Different levels of resources enhance or constrain a person's expression of his or her primary motivation.

FIGURE 7.1 The VALS Segmentation System: An Eight-Part Typology

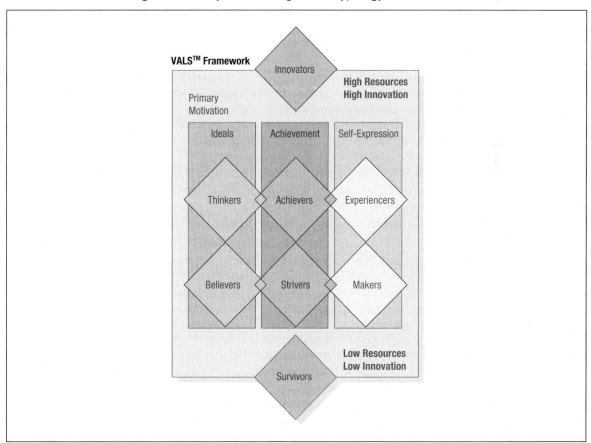

Source: VALS™ © SRI Consulting Business Intelligence. Used with permission.

Behavioral Segmentation

In behavioral segmentation, marketers divide buyers into groups on the basis of their knowledge of, attitude toward, use of, or response to a product. Behavior variables can include needs or benefit, decision roles, or be user and usage-related. Combining different behavioral bases can provide a more comprehensive and cohesive view of a market and its segments.

Needs and Benefits   Not everyone who buys a product has the same needs or wants the same benefits from it. Needs-based or benefit-based segmentation is widely used because it identifies distinct segments with clear marketing implications.

Decision Roles   People can play five roles in a buying decision: *Initiator, Influencer, Decider, Buyer,* and *User.* Assume a wife initiates a purchase by requesting a new treadmill for her birthday. The husband may seek information from many sources, including a friend who has a treadmill and is a key influencer in what models to consider. After presenting the alternative choices to his wife, he buys her preferred model, which ends up being used by the entire family. Different people are playing different decision roles, but all are crucial in the decision process and ultimate consumer satisfaction.

User and Usage   Many marketers believe variables related to various aspects of users or usage—occasions, user status, usage rate, buyer-readiness stage, loyalty status, and attitude—are good starting points for constructing market segments.

- Occasions. Occasions mark a time of day, week, month, year, or other well-defined temporal aspects of a consumer's life. We can distinguish buyers according to the occasions when they develop a need, purchase a product, or use a product. For example, air travel is triggered by occasions related to business, vacation, or family.

- User status. Every product has its nonusers, ex-users, potential users, first-time users, and regular users. Included in the potential-user group are consumers who will become users in connection with some life stage or life event. The key to attracting potential users, or even possibly nonusers, is to understand why they don't use an offering. Do they have deeply held attitudes, beliefs, or behaviors or lack knowledge of the product or benefits? Market leaders tend to focus on attracting potential users because they have the most to gain. Smaller firms focus on trying to attract current users away from the leader.

- Usage rate. We can segment markets into light, medium, and heavy product users. Heavy users are often a small slice but account for a high percentage of total consumption. Marketers would rather attract one heavy user than several light users. A potential problem is that heavy users are often either extremely loyal to one brand or never loyal to any brand and always looking for the lowest price.

- Buyer-readiness stage. Some people are unaware of the product, some are aware, some are informed, some are interested, some desire the product, and some intend to buy. To help characterize how many people are at different stages and how well they have converted people from one stage to another, marketers can employ a *marketing funnel.* Figure 7.2 shows a funnel for two hypothetical brands. Compared to Brand B, Brand A performs poorly at converting one-time users to more recent users (only 46 percent convert for Brand A compared to 61 percent for Brand B). A marketing campaign could make a difference by, for example, highlighting more accessible retail outlets or dispelling incorrect brand beliefs.

- Loyalty status. Marketers usually envision four groups based on brand loyalty status: hard-core loyals (always buy one brand), split loyals (loyal to two or three brands), shifting loyals (shift from one brand to another), and switchers (not loyal to any brand).[15] A firm can study its hard-core loyals to help identify the product's strengths; study split

FIGURE 7.2 Brand Funnel

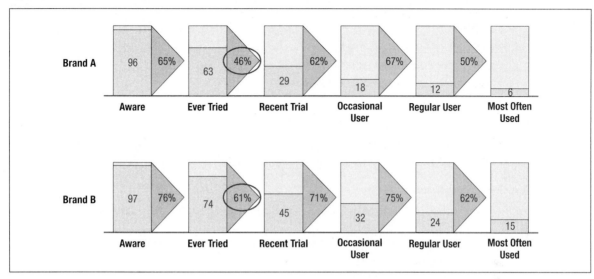

loyals to see which brands are most competitive with its own; and study customers who drop its brand to learn about and correct any marketing weaknesses. One caution: What appear to be brand-loyal buying patterns may reflect habit, indifference, a low price, a high switching cost, or the unavailability of other brands.

- **Attitude.** Five consumer attitudes about products are enthusiastic, positive, indifferent, negative, and hostile. Door-to-door workers in a political campaign use attitude to determine how much time to spend with each voter. They thank enthusiastic voters and remind them to vote, reinforce those who are positively disposed, try to win the votes of indifferent voters, and spend no time trying to change the attitudes of negative and hostile voters.

Bases for Segmenting Business Markets

We can segment business markets with some of the same variables we use in consumer markets, such as geography, benefits sought, and usage rate, but business marketers also use other variables (see Table 7.3). The demographic variables are the most important, followed by the operating variables—down to the personal characteristics of the buyer. Within a chosen target industry, business marketers can further segment by company size and by purchase criteria.

Business marketers generally identify segments through a sequential process. Consider an aluminum company, which first looked at which end-use market to serve: automobile, residential, or beverage containers. It chose the residential market, and it needed to determine the most attractive product application: semifinished material, building components, or aluminum mobile homes. Deciding to focus on building components, it had to consider the best customer size, and it chose large customers. Finally, the firm distinguished among customers buying on price, service, or quality. Because it had a high-service profile, the firm decided to concentrate on the service-motivated segment.

Market Targeting

There are many statistical techniques for developing market segments.[16] Once the firm has identified its market-segment opportunities, it must decide how many and which ones to target. Marketers are increasingly combining several variables in an effort to identify smaller, better-defined target groups.

TABLE 7.3	Major Segmentation Variables for Business Markets

Demographic

1. Industry: Which industries should we serve?
2. Company size: What size companies should we serve?
3. Location: What geographical areas should we serve?

Operating Variables

4. Technology: What customer technologies should we focus on?
5. User or nonuser status: Should we serve heavy users, medium users, light users, or nonusers?
6. Customer capabilities: Should we serve customers needing many or few services?

Purchasing Approaches

7. Purchasing-function organization: Should we serve companies with a highly centralized or decentralized purchasing organization?
8. Power structure: Should we serve companies that are engineering dominated, financially dominated, and so on?
9. Nature of existing relationship: Should we serve companies with which we have strong relationships or simply go after the most desirable companies?
10. General purchasing policies: Should we serve companies that prefer leasing? Service contract? Systems purchases? Sealed bidding?
11. Purchasing criteria: Should we serve companies that are seeking quality? Service? Price?

Situational Factors

12. Urgency: Should we serve companies that need quick and sudden delivery or service?
13. Specific application: Should we focus on a certain application of our product rather than all applications?
14. Size of order: Should we focus on large or small orders?

Personal Characteristics

15. Buyer-seller similarity: Should we serve companies whose people and values are similar to ours?
16. Attitude toward risk: Should we serve risk-taking or risk-avoiding customers?
17. Loyalty: Should we serve companies that show high loyalty to their suppliers?

Source: Adapted from Thomas V. Bonoma and Benson P. Shapiro, *Segmenting the Industrial Market* (Lexington, MA: Lexington Books, 1983).

Thus, a bank may not only identify a group of wealthy retired adults but within that group distinguish several segments depending on current income, assets, and risk preferences. This has led some market researchers to advocate a *needs-based market segmentation approach*. Roger Best proposed the seven-step approach shown in Table 7.4.

Effective Segmentation Criteria

Not all segmentation schemes are useful. Although we could divide buyers of table salt into blond and brunette customers, hair color is irrelevant to the purchase of salt. Furthermore, if all salt buyers buy the same amount of salt each month, believe all salt is the same, and would pay only one price for salt, this market is minimally segmentable from a marketing viewpoint.

TABLE 7.4	Steps in the Segmentation Process
	Description
1. Needs-Based Segmentation	Group customers into segments based on similar needs and benefits sought by customers in solving a particular consumption problem.
2. Segment Identification	For each needs-based segment, determine which demographics, lifestyles, and usage behaviors make the segment distinct and identifiable (actionable).
3. Segment Attractiveness	Using predetermined segment attractiveness criteria (such as market growth, competitive intensity, and market access), determine the overall attractiveness of each segment.
4. Segment Profitability	Determine segment profitability.
5. Segment Positioning	For each segment, create a "value proposition" and product-price positioning strategy based on that segment's unique customer needs and characteristics.
6. Segment "Acid Test"	Create "segment storyboard" to test the attractiveness of each segment's positioning strategy.
7. Marketing-Mix Strategy	Expand segment positioning strategy to include all aspects of the marketing mix: product, price, promotion, and place.

Source: Adapted from Roger J. Best, *Market-Based Management,* 5th ed. (Upper Saddle River, NJ: Prentice Hall, 2009).

Rating Segments   To be useful, market segments must rate favorably on five key criteria:

- Measurable. The size, purchasing power, and characteristics of the segments can be measured.
- Substantial. The segments are large and profitable enough to serve. A segment should be the largest possible homogeneous group worth going after with a tailored marketing program.
- Accessible. The segments can be effectively reached and served.
- Differentiable. The segments are conceptually distinguishable and respond differently to different marketing-mix elements and programs. If two segments respond identically to an offer, they are not separate segments.
- Actionable. Effective programs can be formulated for attracting and serving the segments.

Long-term Segment Attractiveness   Michael Porter has identified five forces that determine the intrinsic long-run attractiveness of a market or market segment. The first is the *threat of intense segment rivalry*. A segment is unattractive if it already contains numerous, strong, or aggressive competitors. It's even more unattractive if it's stable or declining, if plant capacity must be added in large increments, if fixed costs or exit barriers are high, or if competitors have high stakes in staying in the segment.

The second is the *threat of potential entrants*. A segment is most attractive when entry barriers are high and exit barriers are low.[17] Few new firms can enter, and poorly performing firms can easily exit. When both entry and exit barriers are high, profit potential is high, but firms face more risk because poorer-performing firms stay in and fight it out. When entry and exit barriers are low, firms easily enter and leave, and returns are stable but low. The worst case is when entry barriers are low and exit barriers are high, because firms will enter during good times but find it hard to leave during bad times.

The third is the *threat of substitutes*. A segment is unattractive when there are actual or potential substitutes for the product. Substitutes place a limit on prices and on profits. If technology advances or competition increases in these substitute industries, prices and profits are likely to fall.

The fourth is the *threat of buyers' growing bargaining power*. A segment is unattractive if buyers possess strong or growing bargaining power. Buyers' bargaining power grows when they become more concentrated or organized, when the product represents a significant fraction of their costs, when the product is undifferentiated, when buyers' switching costs are low, when buyers are price-sensitive because of low profits, or when they can integrate upstream. To protect themselves, sellers might select buyers who have the least power to negotiate or switch suppliers. A better defense is developing superior offers that strong buyers cannot refuse.

The fifth force is the *threat of suppliers' growing bargaining power*. A segment is unattractive if suppliers can raise prices or reduce quantity supplied. Suppliers tend to be powerful when they are concentrated or organized, when they can integrate downstream, when there are few substitutes, when the supplied product is an important input, and when the costs of switching suppliers are high. The best defenses are to build strong relationships with suppliers or use multiple supply sources.

Evaluating and Selecting Market Segments

In evaluating market segments, the firm must look at the segment's overall attractiveness and its own objectives and capabilities. How well does a potential segment score on the five criteria? Does it have characteristics that make it attractive, such as size, growth, profitability, scale economies, and low risk? Does investing in the segment make sense given the firm's objectives, competencies, and resources? Some attractive segments may not mesh with the company's long-run objectives, or the company may lack the competencies needed to provide superior value (see "Marketing Skills: Evaluating Segments").

Marketing   Skills

EVALUATING SEGMENTS

Because choosing the wrong segment(s) can waste money and divert attention from more profitable segments, marketers must be skilled in evaluating segments. To start, they screen out unsuitable segments by determining which are illegal, too controversial, too risky, or unethical. Next, they evaluate the remaining segments on the basis of the five key criteria and long-term attractiveness, using appropriate market measures such as size, profit, and growth potential; competitive measures such as ease of entry/exit; and accessibility measures such as channel availability. Finally, they rank the segments, using a system such as calculating a total score for each segment, so they can give marketing priority to the highest-scoring segments.

Marketers for Time Warner Cable are experienced in evaluating segments to target consumers and businesses that need specific bundles of cable, Internet, and digital phone services. One segment they've chosen as a marketing priority is affluent households that want to subscribe to a full range of services with top-of-the-line, personalized support. For this segment, Time Warner Cable bundled cable television access with a high-capacity digital video recorder, broadband wireless Internet access, and digital phone. Customers can contact Personal Service Advisors by phone or live chat 24 hours a day, and can have technicians connect as many as 13 wireless-ready devices during the installation process, two benefits they particularly value.[18]

FIGURE 7.3 Possible Levels of Segmentation

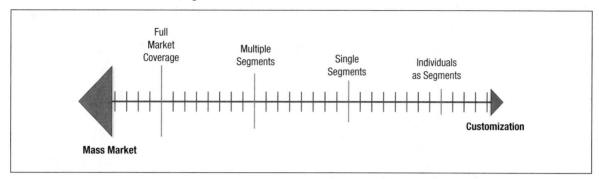

Marketers have a range or continuum of possible levels of segmentation that can guide their target market decisions (see Figure 7.3). At one end is a mass market of essentially one segment; at the other are individuals or segments of one person. Between lie multiple segments and single segments.

Full Market Coverage   The firm attempts to serve all customer groups with all the products they might need. Only very large firms such as Microsoft (software) and Coca-Cola (nonalcoholic beverages) can do this, covering a whole market through undifferentiated or differentiated marketing.

In *undifferentiated* or *mass marketing*, the firm ignores segment differences and goes after the whole market with one offer. It designs a marketing program for a product with a superior image that can be sold to the broadest number of buyers via mass distribution and mass communications. Undifferentiated marketing is appropriate when all consumers have roughly the same preferences and the market shows no natural segments. The narrow product line keeps down the costs of research and development, production, inventory, transportation, advertising, and product management; with lower costs, the firm can lower prices to attract price-sensitive customers. However, many critics point to the increasing splintering of the market, and the proliferation of channels and communication, which make it difficult and expensive to reach a mass audience.

In *differentiated marketing*, the firm sells different products to all the different segments. Differentiated marketing typically creates more total sales than undifferentiated marketing. However, it also increases the costs of doing business. Because differentiated marketing leads to both higher sales and higher costs, no generalizations about its profitability are valid.

Multiple Segment Specialization   With *selective specialization*, a firm selects a subset of all the possible segments, each objectively attractive and appropriate. There may be little or no synergy among the segments, but each promises to be a moneymaker. The multisegment strategy also diversifies the firm's risk. Keeping synergies in mind, companies can try to operate in supersegments rather than in isolated segments. A **supersegment** is a set of segments sharing some exploitable similarity. A firm can also attempt to achieve some synergy with product or market specialization.

- With *product specialization*, the firm sells a certain product to several different market segments. A microscope manufacturer, for instance, sells to university, government, and commercial laboratories, making different instruments for each and building a strong reputation in the specific product area. The risk is that the product may be supplanted by an entirely new technology.
- With *market specialization*, the firm concentrates on serving many needs of a particular customer group, such as by selling an assortment of products only to university laboratories.

The firm gains a strong reputation among this customer group and becomes a channel for additional products its members can use. The risk is that the customer group may suffer budget cuts or shrink in size.

Single-Segment Concentration   With single-segment concentration, the firm markets to only one segment. Through concentrated marketing, it gains deep knowledge of the segment's needs and achieves a strong market presence. It also enjoys operating economies by specializing its production, distribution, and promotion. If it captures segment leadership, the firm can earn a high return on its investment.

A *niche* is a more narrowly defined customer group seeking a distinctive mix of benefits within a segment. Marketers usually identify niches by dividing a segment into subsegments. What does an attractive niche look like? Customers have a distinct set of needs; they will pay a premium to the firm that best satisfies them; the niche has size, profit, and growth potential; it is unlikely to attract many competitors; and the firm can use specialization to gain economies within the niche (see "Marketing Insight: Chasing the Long Tail"). As marketing efficiency increases, niches that were seemingly too small may become more profitable.[19]

Individual Marketing   The ultimate level of segmentation leads to "segments of one," "customized marketing," or "one-to-one marketing."[20] Today, customers are taking more individual initiative in determining what and how to buy, using the Internet to look up product information and evaluations; to contact suppliers, users, and product critics; and in many cases, to design the product they want.

CHASING THE LONG TAIL

The advent of online commerce, made possible by technology and epitomized by Amazon.com, eBay, and Netflix, has led to a shift in consumer buying patterns, according to Chris Anderson, author of *The Long Tail*. In most markets, the distribution of product sales conforms to a curve weighted heavily to one side—the "head"—where the bulk of sales are generated by a few hit products. The curve falls rapidly toward zero and hovers just above it far along the X-axis—the "long tail"—where the vast majority of products generate very little sales. The mass market traditionally focused on generating "hit" products at the head.

Anderson says the Internet is shifting demand "down the tail, from hits to niches" in product categories such as music and books. His theory is based on three premises: (1) Lower distribution costs make it economically easier to sell products without precise demand predictions; (2) The more products available for sale, the greater the likelihood of tapping into demand for niche tastes unreachable through traditional channels; and (3) If enough niche tastes are aggregated, a big new market can result. Although some research supports this theory, other research finds that very low-share products in the tail may be so obscure that they disappear before generating enough purchase volume to justify their existence. Also, the inventory, stocking, and handling costs of physical products may outweigh any financial benefits of chasing the long tail.

Sources: Chris Anderson, *The Long Tail* (New York: Hyperion, 2006); "Reading the Tail," interview with Chris Anderson, *Wired*, July 8, 2006, p. 30; "Wag the Dog: What the Long Tail Will Do," *Economist*, July 8, 2006, p. 77; Erik Brynjolfsson, Yu "Jeffrey" Hu, and Michael D. Smith, "From Niches to Riches: Anatomy of a Long Tail," *MIT Sloan Management Review* (Summer 2006), p. 67; John Cassidy, "Going Long," *New Yorker*, July 10, 2006; www.longtail.com; "Rethinking the Long Tail Theory: How to Define 'Hits' and 'Niches,'" *Knowledge@Wharton*, September 16, 2009.

Jerry Wind and Arvind Rangaswamy see a movement toward "customerizing" the firm.[21] **Customerization** combines operationally driven mass customization with customized marketing in a way that empowers consumers to design the product and service offering of their choice. The firm no longer requires prior information about the customer, nor does it need to own manufacturing. It provides a platform and tools and "rents" to customers the means to design their own products. A company is customerized when it can respond to individual customers by customizing its products, services, and messages on a one-to-one basis.[22]

Customization is certainly not for every company.[23] It may be very difficult to implement for complex products such as automobiles and it can raise the cost of goods by more than customers will pay. Some customers don't know what they want until they see actual products, but they also cannot cancel the order after the company has started to work on it. In spite of this, customization has worked well for some products.

Ethical Choice of Market Targets   Market targeting sometimes generates public controversy when marketers take unfair advantage of vulnerable groups (such as children) or disadvantaged groups (such as poor people) or promote potentially harmful products.[24] Establishing ethical and legal boundaries in marketing to children online and offline continues to be a hot topic as consumer advocates decry the commercialism they believe such marketing engenders. Not all attempts to target children or other special segments draw criticism. For instance, Colgate's SpongeBob toothpaste and toothbrushes are designed to encourage children to brush longer and more often. Thus, the issue is not who is targeted, but how and for what. Socially responsible marketing calls for targeting that serves not only the company's interests, but also the interests of those targeted.

EXECUTIVE SUMMARY

Target marketing includes three activities: market segmentation, market targeting, and market positioning. Market segments are large, identifiable groups of customers who share a similar set of needs and wants. The major segmentation variables for consumer markets are geographic, demographic, psychographic, and behavioral. Marketers use them singly or in combination. Business marketers use all these variables along with operating variables, purchasing approaches, and situational factors. To be useful, market segments must be measurable, substantial, accessible, differentiable, and actionable.

We can target markets at four main levels: mass, multiple segments, single (or niche) segment, and individuals. A mass market approach is adopted only by the biggest companies. Many companies target multiple segments defined in various ways. A niche is a more narrowly defined group within a segment. More companies now practice individual and mass customization. The future is likely to see more individual consumers take the initiative in designing products and brands. Marketers must choose target markets in an ethical and socially responsible manner.

NOTES

1. Wendy Leung, "Club Med Investor Fosun in Talks to Buy Stakes in European Luxury Brands," *Bloomberg News,* July 29, 2010, www.bloomberg.com/news/2010-07-29/club-med-investor-fosun-in-talks-to-buy-stakes-in-european-luxury-brands.html; Jonathan Schneider, "Club Med—Sex, Sand, and Surf," *Brand Channel,* July 21, 2001, www.brandchannel.com; Christina White, "It's Raining Hard on Club Med," *BusinessWeek,* February 4, 2002; *Club Med,* www.clubmed.us; Susan Spano, "Club Med, Swinging into the Future," *Morning Call,* January 15, 2006; Cherisse Beh, "Club Med Unveils Global Branding Push," *Marketing Interactive.com,* March 31, 2008, www.marketing-interactive.com.

2. You can visit the company's sponsored site, MyBestSegments.com, enter zip code, and discover the top five clusters for that area. Note that another leading supplier of geodemographic data is ClusterPlus (Strategic Mapping).

3. Becky Ebenkamp, "Urban America Redefined," *Brandweek,* October 6, 2003, pp. 12–13.

4. Gina Chon, "Car Makers Talk 'Bout G-G-Generations," *Wall Street Journal,* May 9, 2006.

5. For some practical implications, see Marti Barletta, *Marketing to Women: How to Increase Share of the World's Largest Market,* 2nd ed. (New York: Kaplan Business, 2006); Bridget Brennan, *Why She Buys: The New Strategy for Reaching the World's Most Powerful Consumers* (New York: Crown Business, 2009).

6. For more consumer behavior perspectives on gender, see Jane Cunningham and Philippa Roberts, "What Woman Want," *Brand Strategy,* December 2006–January 2007, pp. 40–41; Robert J. Fisher and Laurette Dube, "Gender Differences in Responses to Emotional Advertising," *Journal of Consumer Research* 31 (March 2005), pp. 850–58; Joan Meyers-Levy and Durairaj Maheswaran, "Exploring Males' and Females' Processing Strategies," *Journal of Consumer Research* 18 (June 1991), pp. 63–70; Joan Meyers-Levy and Brian Sternthal, "Gender Differences in the Use of Message Cues and Judgments," *Journal of Marketing Research* 28 (February 1991), pp. 84–96.

7. Aixa Pascual, "Lowe's Is Sprucing Up Its House," *BusinessWeek,* June 3, 2002, pp. 56–57; Pamela Sebastian Ridge, "Tool Sellers Tap Their Feminine Side," *Wall Street Journal,* June 16, 2002.

8. Ian Zack, "Out of the Tube," *Forbes,* November 26, 2001, p. 200.

9. Gregory L. White and Shirley Leung, "Middle Market Shrinks as Americans Migrate toward the Higher End," *Wall Street Journal,* March 29, 2002.

10. Charles D. Schewe and Geoffrey Meredith, "Segmenting Global Markets by Generational Cohort: Determining Motivations by Age," *Journal of Consumer Behavior* 4 (October 2004), pp. 51–63; Geoffrey E. Meredith and Charles D. Schewe, *Managing by Defining Moments: America's 7 Generational Cohorts, Their Workplace Values, and Why Managers Should Care* (New York: Hungry Minds, 2002); Geoffrey E. Meredith, Charles D. Schewe, and Janice Karlovich, *Defining Markets Defining Moments* (New York: Hungry Minds, 2001).

11. Piet Levy, "The Quest for Cool," *Marketing News,* February 28, 2009, p. 6; Michelle Conlin, "Youth Quake," *BusinessWeek,* January 21, 2008, pp. 32–36.

12. Marissa Miley, "Don't Bypass African-Americans," *Advertising Age,* February 2, 2009.

13. Elisabeth Sullivan, "Choose Your Words Wisely," *Marketing News,* February 15, 2008, p. 22; Emily Bryson York, "Brands Prepare for a More Diverse 'General Market,'" *Advertising Age,* November 30, 2009, p. 6.

14. Strategic Business Insights, www.strategicbusinessinsights.com.

15. This classification was adapted from George H. Brown, "Brand Loyalty: Fact or Fiction?" *Advertising Age,* June 1952–January 1953, a series. See also, Peter E. Rossi, Robert E. McCulloch, and Greg M. Allenby, "The Value of Purchase History Data in Target Marketing," *Marketing Science* 15, no. 4 (Fall 1996), pp. 321–40.

16. For a review of methodological issues in developing segmentation schemes, see William R. Dillon and Soumen Mukherjee, "A Guide to the Design and Execution of Segmentation Studies," Rajiv Grover and Marco Vriens, eds., *Handbook of Marketing Research* (Thousand Oaks, CA: Sage, 2006); Michael Wedel and Wagner A. Kamakura, *Market Segmentation: Conceptual and Methodological Foundations* (Boston: Kluwer, 1997).

17. Michael E. Porter, *Competitive Strategy* (New York: Free Press, 1980), pp. 22–23.

18. Mike Robuck, "Time Warner Cable Digs in on Segmentation Strategy," *CED Magazine,* July 21, 2010, www.cedmagazine.com; Marian Burk Wood, *The Marketing Plan Handbook,* 4th ed. (Upper Saddle River, NJ: Prentice Hall, 2011), pp. 73–74; Linda Haugsted, "Segmenting Rings Up Phone Additions," *Multichannel News,* December 18, 2006, p. 18.

19. Robert Blattberg and John Deighton, "Interactive Marketing: Exploiting the Age of Addressability," *Sloan Management Review* 33, no. 1 (Fall 1991), pp. 5–14.

20. Don Peppers and Martha Rogers, *One-to-One B2B: Customer Development Strategies for the Business-To-Business World* (New York: Doubleday, 2001); Jerry Wind and Arvind Rangaswamy, "Customerization: The Next Revolution in Mass Customization," *Journal of Interactive Marketing* 15, no. 1 (Winter 2001), pp. 13–32.

21. James C. Anderson and James A. Narus, "Capturing the Value of Supplementary Services," *Harvard Business Review,* January–February 1995, pp. 75–83.

22. Itamar Simonson, "Determinants of Customers' Responses to Customized Offers: Conceptual Framework and Research Propositions," *Journal of Marketing* 69 (January 2005), pp. 32–45.

23. Joann Muller, "Kmart con Salsa: Will It Be Enough?" *BusinessWeek,* September 9, 2002.

24. Bart Macchiette and Roy Abhijit, "Sensitive Groups and Social Issues," *Journal of Consumer Marketing* 11, no. 4 (Fall 1994), pp. 55–64.

Creating Brand Equity

In this chapter, we will address the following questions:

1. What is a brand, and how does branding work?
2. What is brand equity and how is it built, measured, and managed?
3. What are the important decisions in developing a branding strategy?

Marketing Management at Lululemon

While attending yoga classes, Canadian entrepreneur Chip Wilson decided the cotton-polyester blend clothing most fellow students wore was too uncomfortable. After designing a well-fitting, sweat-resistant black garment to sell, he also decided to open a yoga studio, and lululemon was born. The company has taken a grassroots approach to growth by creating a strong emotional connection with customers.

Before lululemon opens a store in a new city, it identifies influential yoga instructors or other fitness teachers in the area. In exchange for a year's worth of clothing, these teachers serve as "ambassadors," hosting students at lululemon-sponsored classes and sales events. They also give the company product design advice. The cult-like devotion of customers is evident in their willingness to pay a premium for lululemon's clothing, despite competition from Nike and other big brands. With $450 million in North American sales, lululemon is looking to expand by putting its brand on products for other sports, such as running, swimming, and biking.[1]

Strategic brand management combines the design and implementation of marketing activities and programs to build, measure, and manage brands to maximize their value and strengthen customer loyalty. This process involves (1) identifying and establishing brand positioning, (2) planning and implementing brand marketing, (3) measuring and interpreting brand performance, and (4) growing and sustaining brand value.[2] In this chapter we examine brand marketing, brand performance, and brand value; in Chapter 9, we discuss brand positioning and competitive dynamics.

What Is Brand Equity?

The American Marketing Association defines a **brand** as "a name, term, sign, symbol, or design, or a combination of them, intended to identify the goods or services of one seller or group of sellers and to differentiate them from those of competitors." A brand adds dimensions that differentiate the offering in some way from other offerings designed to satisfy the same need. These differences may be functional, rational, or tangible—related to product performance of the brand. They may also be more symbolic, emotional, or intangible—related to what the brand represents.

The Role of Brands

Brands identify the source or maker of a product and allow consumers—either individuals or organizations—to assign responsibility for its performance to a particular manufacturer or distributor. Consumers may evaluate the identical product differently depending on how it is branded. They learn about brands through past experiences with the product and its marketing program, finding out which brands satisfy their needs and which do not. As consumers' lives become more complicated, rushed, and time-starved, a brand's ability to simplify decision making and reduce risk becomes invaluable.[3]

Brands also perform valuable functions for firms.[4] First, they simplify product handling or tracing. Brands help to organize inventory and accounting records. A brand also offers the firm legal protection for unique features or aspects of the product.[5] The brand name can be protected through registered trademarks; manufacturing processes can be protected through patents; and packaging can be protected through copyrights and proprietary designs. These intellectual property rights ensure that the firm can safely invest in the brand and reap the benefits of a valuable asset.

A credible brand signals a certain level of quality so that satisfied buyers can easily choose the product again.[6] Brand loyalty provides predictability and security of demand for the firm, and it creates barriers to entry that make it difficult for other firms to enter the market. Loyalty also can translate into customer willingness to pay a higher price—often 20 percent to 25 percent more than competing brands.[7] Although competitors may duplicate manufacturing processes and product designs, they cannot easily match lasting impressions left in the minds of customers by years of product experience and marketing activity. Thus, branding can be a powerful means to secure a competitive advantage.

The Scope of Branding

Branding is endowing products and services with the power of a brand. It's all about creating differences between products. The firm needs to teach consumers "who" the product is—by giving it a name and other brand elements to identify it—as well as what the product does and why consumers should care. Branding creates mental structures that help consumers organize their knowledge about the offering in a way that clarifies their decision making and provides value to the firm.

For branding strategies to be successful and brand value to be created, consumers must be convinced there are meaningful differences among a category's brands. It's possible to brand a physical good (Ford Flex automobile), a service (Singapore Airlines), a store (Nordstrom), a person (snowboarder Shaun White), a place (the city of Sydney), an organization (American Automobile Association), or an idea (free trade).[8]

Defining Brand Equity

Brand equity is the added value endowed on products and services. It may be reflected in the way consumers think, feel, and act with respect to the brand, as well as in the prices, market share, and profitability the brand commands.[9] Marketers and researchers use various perspectives to study brand equity.[10] *Customer-based brand equity* is the differential effect brand knowledge has on consumer response to that brand's marketing.[11] A brand has positive customer-based brand equity when consumers react more favorably to a product and its marketing when the brand is identified, than when it is not identified. A brand has negative customer-based brand equity if consumers react less favorably to its marketing activity under the same circumstances.

There are three key ingredients of customer-based brand equity. First, brand equity arises from differences in consumer response. If no differences occur, the brand-name product is essentially a commodity, and competition will probably be based on price.[12] Second, differences in response are a result of consumer's **brand knowledge**, all the thoughts, feelings, images, experiences, and beliefs associated with the brand. Brands must create strong, favorable, and unique brand associations with customers. Third, brand equity is reflected in perceptions, preferences, and behavior related to all aspects of the brand's marketing. Stronger brands lead to greater loyalty and revenue, larger profit margins, less vulnerability to competition, and increased marketing communications effectiveness.[13]

Brand knowledge dictates appropriate future directions for the brand. A **brand promise** is the marketer's vision of what the brand must be and do for consumers. Consumers will decide, based on what they think and feel about the brand, where (and how) they believe the brand should go and grant permission (or not) to any marketing action or program. New products such as Cracker Jack cereal failed because consumers found them inappropriate extensions for the brand.

Brand Equity Models

Brand equity models offer differing perspectives on branding.

- BrandAsset Valuator. Advertising agency Young and Rubicam's model of brand equity, the BrandAsset Valuator, measures four pillars of brand equity (see Figure 8.1) Strong new brands show higher levels of differentiation and energy than relevance, whereas both esteem and knowledge are lower still. Leadership brands show high levels on all pillars; declining brands show high knowledge, a lower level of esteem, and even lower relevance, energy, and differentiation.
- BrandZ. Marketing research consultants Millward Brown and WPP have developed the BrandZ model of brand strength. According to this model, brand building follows a series of steps leading from a weak to a strong brand relationship (see Figure 8.2). "Bonded" consumers at the top of the pyramid build stronger relationships with and spend more on the brand than those at lower levels.

FIGURE 8.1 BrandAsset® Valuator Model

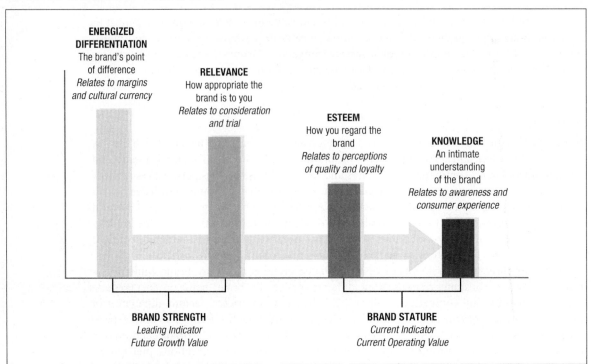

Source: Courtesy of BrandAsset® Consulting, a division of Young & Rubicam.

- Brand Resonance Model. The brand resonance model also views brand building as an ascending series of steps. Enacting these four steps means establishing a pyramid of six "brand building blocks" (see Figure 8.3). The model emphasizes the duality of brands: the rational route to brand building is on the left side and the emotional route is on the right side.[14]

FIGURE 8.2 BrandDynamics™ Pyramid

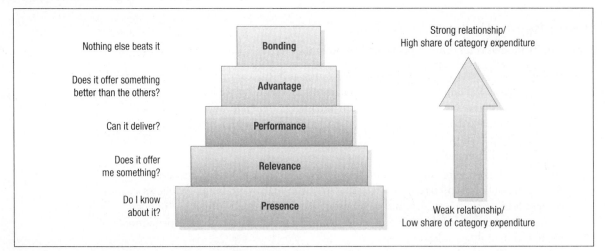

Source: BrandDynamics™ Pyramid. Reprinted by permission of Millward Brown.

FIGURE 8.3 Brand Resonance Pyramid

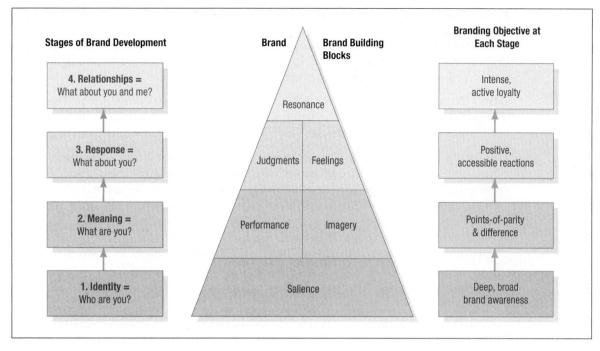

Building Brand Equity

Marketers build brand equity by creating the right brand knowledge structures with the right consumers. This process depends on *all* brand-related contacts—whether marketer-initiated or not.[15] From a marketing management perspective, however, there are three main sets of *brand equity drivers:*

1. *The initial choices for the brand elements or identities making up the brand (brand names, URLs, logos, symbols, characters, spokespeople, slogans, jingles, packages, and signage)*— Microsoft chose the name Bing for its search engine because the name conveys search and the "aha" moment of finding what a person is looking for. It is also short, appealing, memorable, active, and effective multiculturally.[16]

2. *The product and service and all accompanying marketing activities and supporting marketing programs*—Liz Claiborne's fastest-growing clothing brand is Juicy Couture, marketed as affordable luxury with an edgy lifestyle appeal and limited distribution.[17]

3. *Other associations indirectly transferred to the brand by linking it to some other entity (a person, place, or thing)*—The brand name of New Zealand vodka 42BELOW refers to both a latitude that runs through New Zealand and the percentage of its alcohol content. The packaging leverages the country's perceived purity while communicating the brand's positioning.[18]

The following sections will look at each of these three brand-equity drivers.

Choosing Brand Elements

Brand elements are trademarkable devices that identify and differentiate the brand. For example, Nike has the distinctive "swoosh" logo and the "Nike" name from the winged goddess of victory. The test of brand building is what consumers would think or feel about the product *if* the brand element were all they knew. Based on its name alone, for instance, a consumer might expect Panasonic Toughbook laptops to be durable and reliable.

Brand Element Choice Criteria   Table 8.1 shows the six criteria for choosing brand elements. The first three—memorable, meaningful, and likable—build the brand. The latter three—transferable, adaptable, and protectable—help leverage and preserve brand equity.

Developing Brand Elements   Brand elements can play a number of brand-building roles.[19] If consumers don't examine much information in making decisions, brand elements should be easy to recall and inherently descriptive and persuasive. The likability of brand elements may also increase awareness and associations.[20] The less concrete brand benefits are, the more important that brand elements capture intangible characteristics. This is why many insurance firms use symbols of strength for their brands (such as Prudential's Rock of Gibraltar). However, choosing a name with inherent meaning may make it harder to add a different meaning or update the positioning.[21]

Designing Holistic Marketing Activities

Customers come to know a brand through a range of contacts and touch points: advertising, personal observation and use, word of mouth, interactions with employees, online or telephone experiences, and payment transactions. A **brand contact** is any information-bearing experience, whether positive or negative, a customer or prospect has with the brand, its product category, or its market.[22] The company must put as much effort into managing these experiences as into producing its ads.[23]

Integrated marketing is about mixing and matching marketing activities to maximize their individual and collective effects.[24] To achieve it, marketers need a variety of different marketing activities that consistently reinforce the brand promise. Successful cult brands are built on creative and consistent integrated marketing (see "Marketing Skills: Building a Cult Brand").

Leveraging Secondary Associations

The third and final way to build brand equity is to "borrow" it by linking the brand to other information in memory that conveys meaning to consumers. As Figure 8.4 shows, these "secondary" brand associations can link to sources such as the company itself; employees and spokespersons

TABLE 8.1 Criteria for Choosing Brand Elements	
For Building the Brand	**For Defending the Brand**
Memorable: Is the element easily recalled and recognized at purchase and consumption? Example: Tide	*Transferable:* Can the element introduce new products in the same category or other categories? Does it add brand equity across geographic boundaries and segments? Example: Amazon.com
Meaningful: Is the element credible and suggestive of the category? Does it suggest something about an ingredient or a brand user? Example: DieHard	*Adaptable:* Can the element be adapted and updated? Example: Betty Crocker image
Likable: Is the element appealing and inherently likable visually, verbally, and in other ways? Example: Flickr	*Protectable:* Is the element legally and competitively protectable? Can the firm retain trademark rights? Example: Yahoo!

BUILDING A CULT BRAND

Building a cult brand can significantly increase sales and profits without expensive promotions and without appealing to a mass market, making this skill important for marketers launching unconventional or niche goods or services. To build or sustain a cult brand, marketers need the ability to create a "buzz" among opinion leaders. They should also know how to enhance the brand's appeal through supply and distribution. A product that is available everywhere will seem less special. In addition, marketers can establish a framework for brand-based communities, bringing enthusiasts together for special events that make the brand experience more relevant and encourage long-term loyalty.

Harley-Davidson knows how to nurture the cult status of its motorcycle brand to attract new customers and strengthen ties with current customers. When entering India, it planned exclusive activities for Harley owners, opened only a few dealerships, and introduced a limited number of models. In the U.S. market, Harley has enlisted the help of opinion leaders such as the rock group Korn to design trendy bikes that appeal to younger buyers. Few brands have as loyal a following as Harley-Davidson—and the company is skilled at making the most of their brand enthusiasm.[25]

FIGURE 8.4 Secondary Sources of Brand Knowledge

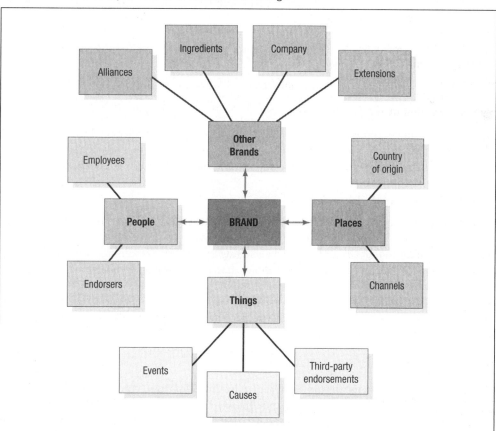

who endorse the brand; geographical regions and channels; plus sporting or cultural events, causes, and other third-party sources.

Internal Branding

Marketers must "walk the walk" to deliver the brand promise. They must adopt an *internal* perspective to be sure employees and marketing partners appreciate and understand basic branding notions and how they can help—or hurt—brand equity.[26] *Internal branding* consists of activities and processes that help inform and inspire employees.[27] Holistic marketers go even further, training and encouraging distributors to serve their customers well.

Brand Communities

Thanks in part to the Internet, companies are collaborating with consumers to create value through communities built around brands. A **brand community** is a specialized community of consumers and employees whose identification and activities focus around the brand.[28] Three characteristics identify brand communities: (1) a sense of connection to the brand, firm, product, or other community members; (2) shared rituals, stories, and traditions that help convey meaning; and (3) shared responsibility or duty to the community and individual members.[29] The Harley Owners Group is a brand community, for example.

A strong brand community results in a more loyal, committed customer base. Its advocacy can substitute to some degree for activities the firm would otherwise engage in, increasing marketing effectiveness and efficiency.[30] A brand community can also be a source of ideas for product improvements or innovations.

Measuring and Managing Brand Equity

How do we measure brand equity? An *indirect* approach assesses potential sources of brand equity by identifying and tracking consumer brand knowledge structures.[31] A *direct* approach assesses the actual impact of brand knowledge on consumer response to different marketing aspects. For brand equity to guide strategy and decisions, marketers need to fully understand (1) the sources of brand equity and how they affect outcomes of interest, and (2) how these sources and outcomes change, if at all, over time. Brand audits are important for the former; brand tracking for the latter.

Brand Audits and Brand Tracking

A **brand audit** is a consumer-focused series of procedures to assess the health of the brand, uncover its sources of brand equity, and suggest ways to improve and leverage its equity. Marketers should conduct a brand audit when setting up marketing plans and when considering strategic shifts. Conducting regular audits allows marketers to manage their brands proactively and responsively. *Brand-tracking studies* collect quantitative data from consumers over time to provide baseline information about how brands and marketing programs are performing. Tracking studies show where, how much, and in what ways brand value is being created, to facilitate marketing decision making.

Brand Valuation

Marketers should distinguish brand equity from **brand valuation**, which is the job of estimating the total financial value of the brand. In some well-known companies, brand value accounts for over half the total market capitalization. Top brand-management firm Interbrand

WHAT IS A BRAND WORTH?

Interbrand uses brand value assessments as a strategic tool to identify and maximize return on brand investment across numerous areas. Its process for valuing a brand follows five steps:

1. *Market Segmentation*—Divide the market(s) in which the brand is sold into mutually exclusive segments that help determine variances in the brand's economic value.

2. *Financial Analysis*—Assess purchase price, volume, and frequency to forecast future brand revenues. Deduct all associated operating costs to derive earnings before interest and tax (EBIT). Also deduct taxes and a charge for the capital employed to operate the underlying business, which leaves Intangible Earnings, those attributed to the firm's intangible assets.

3. *Role of Branding*—The Role of Branding assessment, based on market research, represents the percentage of Intangible Earnings the brand generates. Multiplying the Role of Branding by Intangible Earnings yields Brand Earnings.

4. *Brand Strength*—Interbrand assesses the brand's strength profile to determine the likelihood that the brand will realize forecasted Brand Earnings. For each segment, Interbrand determines a brand-risk premium and adds this premium to the risk-free rate, represented by government-bond yield. Applying the Brand Discount Rate to the Brand Earnings forecast yields the net present value of Brand Earnings.

5. *Brand Value Calculation*—Brand Value is the net present value (NPV) of the forecasted Brand Earnings, discounted by the Brand Discount Rate. This NPV calculation reflects the ability of brands to continue generating future earnings.

Source: Interbrand, the Interbrand Brand Glossary, and Interbrand's Nik Stucky and Rita Clifton.

has developed a model to estimate the dollar value of a brand (see "Marketing Insight: What Is a Brand Worth?").

Managing Brand Equity

Because responses to marketing activity depend on what consumers know and remember about a brand, a firm's short-term marketing actions, by changing brand knowledge, necessarily increase or decrease the long-term success of future marketing actions.

Brand Reinforcement   Marketers can reinforce brand equity by consistently conveying the brand's meaning in terms of (1) what products it represents, what core benefits it supplies, and what needs it satisfies, and (2) how the brand makes products superior, and which strong, favorable, and unique brand associations should exist in consumers' minds.[32] The brand must always be moving forward in the right direction, with new and compelling offerings and marketing. While there is little need to deviate from a successful position, many tactical changes may be necessary to maintain the strategic thrust and direction of the brand over time. When change *is* necessary, marketers should vigorously preserve and defend sources of brand equity.

Brand Revitalization   Any new development in the marketing environment can affect a brand's fortunes. Nevertheless, a number of brands have managed to make impressive comebacks in recent years.[33] After some hard times, Burberry, Fiat, and Volkswagen have all turned their brand fortunes around to varying degrees.

Often, the first thing to do in revitalizing a brand is to understand the original sources of brand equity. Are positive associations losing their strength or uniqueness? Have negative associations become linked to the brand? Then decide whether to retain the same positioning or create a new one. Sometimes the marketing program is a problem, because it fails to deliver on the brand promise; here, a "back to basics" strategy may make sense. In other cases, the old positioning may no longer be viable and a reinvention strategy will be needed. In the continuum of revitalization strategies, pure "back to basics" is at one end and pure "reinvention" is at the other. The challenge is to change enough to attract new customers but not enough to alienate old customers. Brand revitalization of almost any kind starts with the product.[34]

Devising a Branding Strategy

A firm's **branding strategy** reflects the number and nature of both common and distinctive brand elements. Deciding how to brand new products is especially critical. A firm has three main choices: (1) develop new brand elements for the new product, (2) apply some of its existing brand elements, or (3) use a combination of new and existing brand elements (see definitions in Table 8.2).

Branding Decisions

Today, hardly anything goes unbranded. Assuming a firm decides to brand its offerings, it must choose which brand names to use. Three general strategies are:

- Individual or separate family brand names. If a product fails or seems to be low quality, the company's reputation is not hurt because the brands are separate. Firms often use different brand names for different quality lines within the same product class. General Mills largely uses individual brand names, such as Nature Valley granola bars and Wheaties cereal.

TABLE 8.2	Branding New Products
Concept	**Definition**
Brand extension	Using an established brand to launch a new product
Sub-brand	Combining a new brand with an existing brand
Parent brand	An existing brand that gives birth to a brand extension or sub-brand
Master or family brand	A parent brand that is associated with multiple brand extensions
Line extension	Using a parent brand on a new product within a category it currently serves (such as new flavors or colors)
Category extension	Using a parent brand to enter a different category from the one it currently serves
Brand line	All products (including line and category extensions) sold under a particular brand
Brand mix	The set of all brand lines that a particular seller offers
Branded variants	Specific brand lines supplied to specific retailers or distribution channels
Licensed product	Using the brand name licensed from one firm on a product made by another firm

- Corporate umbrella or company brand name. Many firms, such as Heinz and GE, use their corporate brand as an umbrella brand across their entire range of products.[35] Development costs are lower, and sales are likely to be strong if the manufacturer's name is good. Corporate-image associations of innovativeness, expertise, and trustworthiness have been shown to directly influence consumer evaluations.[36]
- Sub-brand name. Sub-brands combine two or more of the corporate brand, family brand, or individual product brand names. Kellogg does this by combining the corporate brand with individual product brands, as with Kellogg's Rice Krispies. The company name legitimizes, and the individual name individualizes, the new product.

The use of individual or separate family brand names has been referred to as a "house of brands" strategy, whereas the use of an umbrella corporate or company brand name has been referred to as a "branded house" strategy. These two strategies represent two ends of a brand relationship continuum. A sub-brand strategy falls somewhere between, depending on which component of the sub-brand receives more emphasis.

Brand Portfolios

The **brand portfolio** is the set of all brands and brand lines a particular firm offers for sale in a particular category or market segment. The basic principle is to maximize market coverage so no potential customers are being ignored, but minimize brand overlap so brands are not competing for customer approval. Each brand should be clearly differentiated and appealing to a sizable enough segment to justify its marketing and production costs.[37] Marketers must carefully monitor brand portfolios over time to identify weak brands and kill unprofitable ones.[38]

Brands can also play a number of specific roles as part of a portfolio.

- Flankers—Flanker or "fighter" brands are positioned with respect to competitors' brands so that more important (and more profitable) *flagship brands* can retain their desired positioning. Fighter brands must be neither so attractive that they take sales away from their higher-priced comparison brands nor designed so cheaply that they reflect poorly on them.
- Cash cows—Some brands may be retained despite dwindling sales because they remain profitable with virtually no marketing support. Companies can "milk" these "cash cow" brands by capitalizing on their reservoir of brand equity.
- Low-end entry level—The role of a relatively low-priced brand in the portfolio may be to attract customers to the brand franchise. Retailers feature these "traffic builders" because they are able to "trade up" customers to a higher-priced brand.
- High-end prestige—A relatively high-priced brand can add prestige and credibility to the entire portfolio.

Brand Extensions

Many firms leverage their most valuable asset by introducing new products under their strongest brand names. In fact, most new products are line extensions—typically 80 percent to 90 percent in any one year. Moreover, many of the most successful new products are extensions, although numerous new products are introduced as new brands.

Advantages of Brand Extensions   Brand extensions can improve the odds of new-product success, because consumers form expectations about a new product based on what they know about the parent brand and the extent to which they feel this information is relevant.[39] By setting up positive expectations, extensions reduce risk.[40] It also may be easier to convince retailers to stock and promote a brand extension. An introductory campaign for an extension need not create awareness of both the brand *and* the new product; it can concentrate on the new product itself.[41]

Extensions can thus reduce launch costs, important given that establishing a new brand name for a U.S. consumer packaged good can cost over $100 million! Extensions also avoid the difficulty—and expense—of coming up with a new name. Extensions allow for packaging and labeling efficiencies and provide the brand with more prominence in the store.[42] With a portfolio of brand variants within a category, consumers who want a change can switch to a different product type without leaving the brand family.

A second advantage is that brand extensions can provide feedback benefits.[43] They can help to clarify the meaning of a brand and its core values or improve loyalty to the company behind the extension.[44] Line extensions can renew interest in and liking for the brand and benefit the parent brand by expanding market coverage. A successful extension may also generate subsequent extensions.[45]

Disadvantages of Brand Extensions   Line extensions may cause the brand name to be less strongly identified with any one product.[46] **Brand dilution** occurs when consumers no longer associate a brand with a specific product or highly similar set of products and start thinking less of the brand. If consumers think an extension is inappropriate, they may question the brand's integrity, become confused, or become frustrated: Which version is the "right one" for them? Retailers reject many new products and brands because they lack shelf or display space. Also, the firm itself may become overwhelmed. One more disadvantage of brand extensions is that the firm forgoes the chance to create a new brand with a unique image and equity.

The worst possible scenario is for an extension to fail and harm the parent brand in the process. Fortunately, such events are rare. "Marketing failures," in which too few consumers were attracted to a brand, are typically much less damaging than "product failures," in which the brand fundamentally fails to live up to its promise. Product failures dilute brand equity only when the extension is seen as very similar to the parent brand.

Even if a brand extension's sales meet targets, the revenue may be coming from consumers switching to the extension from existing parent-brand offerings, cannibalizing the parent brand. Intrabrand shifts in sales may not be undesirable if they're a form of preemptive cannibalization. In other words, consumers might have switched to a competing brand if the line extension hadn't been introduced. Tide laundry detergent maintains the same market share it had 50 years ago because of the sales contributions of its many line extensions.

Success Characteristics   Marketers must judge each potential brand extension by how effectively it fits with and leverages existing brand equity from the parent brand, as well as how it contributes to the parent brand's equity and to profitability.[47] One major mistake in evaluating extension opportunities is failing to take *all* consumers' brand knowledge structures into account and focusing instead on one or a few brand associations as a potential basis of fit.[48]

Customer Equity

Finally, we can relate brand equity to one other important marketing concept, *customer equity*. The aim of customer relationship management (CRM) is to produce high customer equity.[49] Although we can calculate it in different ways, one definition is "the sum of lifetime values of all customers."[50]

The brand equity and customer equity perspectives share many common themes.[51] Both emphasize the importance of customer loyalty and the notion that we create value by having as many customers as possible pay as high a price as possible. However, customer equity focuses on bottom-line financial value and offers limited guidance for go-to-market strategies and brand-building, not fully accounting for competitive actions, social network effects, word of mouth, and customer-to-customer recommendations.

Brand equity, on the other hand, emphasizes strategic issues in managing brands and creating and leveraging brand awareness and image, providing guidance for marketing activities. Still, with a focus on brands, managers don't always develop detailed customer analyses in terms of the brand equity they achieve or the long-term profitability they create.[52] Brand equity approaches could benefit from the sharper segmentation afforded by customer-level analyses and more considera-tion of how to develop personalized, customized marketing programs for individual customers.

Nevertheless, both brand equity and customer equity matter. Brands serve as the "bait" that retailers and other channel intermediaries use to attract customers from whom they extract value. Customers are the tangible profit engine for brands to monetize their brand value.

EXECUTIVE SUMMARY

A brand is a name, term, sign, symbol, design, or some combination of these elements, intended to identify the offerings of one seller or seller group and to differentiate these offerings from competitive offerings. Brands offer a number of benefits to customers and firms and need to be managed carefully. Brand equity should be defined in terms of marketing effects uniquely attrib-utable to a brand. Three drivers of brand equity are: (1) The initial choices for the brand elements or identities making up the brand; (2) the way the brand is integrated into the supporting marketing program; and (3) the associations indirectly transferred to the brand by links to some other entity.

A branding strategy identifies which brand elements a firm chooses to apply across its various products. In a brand extension, a firm puts an established brand name on a new product. Potential extensions must be judged by how well they leverage existing brand equity as well as how they contribute to the equity of the parent brand. Customer equity is a complementary concept to brand equity that reflects the sum of lifetime values of all customers for a brand.

NOTES

1. Suzy Evans, "Om: National Yoga Month," *Fast Company,* September 1, 2010, www.fastcompany. com/magazine/148/om.html; Jen Aronoff, "Health and Happiness: Lululemon's Yoga-inspired Athletic Apparel Brands Its Way into Charlotte's Heart," *Charlotte Observer,* July 1, 2010, www.charlotteobserver.com; Alli McConnon, "Lululemon's Next Workout," *BusinessWeek,* June 9, 2008, pp. 43–44; Danielle Sacks, "Lululemon's Cult of Selling," *Fast Company,* March 2009; Bryant Urstadt, "Lust for Lulu," *New York Magazine,* July 26, 2009.

2. For foundational work on branding, see Jean-Noel Kapferer, *The New Strategic Brand Management,* 4th ed. (New York: Kogan Page, 2008); David A. Aaker and Erich Joachimsthaler, *Brand Leadership* (New York: Free Press, 2000); David A. Aaker, *Building Strong Brands*

(New York: Free Press, 1996); David A. Aaker, *Managing Brand Equity* (New York: Free Press, 1991).

3. Rajneesh Suri and Kent B. Monroe, "The Effects of Time Pressure on Consumers' Judgments of Prices and Products," *Journal of Consumer Research* 30 (June 2003), pp. 92–104.

4. Rita Clifton and John Simmons, eds., *The Economist on Branding* (New York: Bloomberg Press, 2004); Rik Riezebos, *Brand Management: A Theoretical and Practical Approach* (Essex, England: Pearson Education, 2003); and Paul Temporal, *Advanced Brand Management: From Vision to Valuation* (Singapore: Wiley, 2002).

5. Constance E. Bagley, *Managers and the Legal Environment: Strategies for the 21st Century,* 3rd ed. (Cincinnati, OH: South-Western College/West

Publishing, 2005). For a marketing academic point of view of some important legal issues, see Judith Zaichkowsky, *The Psychology behind Trademark Infringement and Counterfeiting* (Mahwah, NJ: LEA Publishing, 2006) and Maureen Morrin and Jacob Jacoby, "Trademark Dilution: Empirical Measures for an Elusive Concept," *Journal of Public Policy & Marketing* 19, no. 2 (May 2000), pp. 265–76; Maureen Morrin, Jonathan Lee, and Greg M. Allenby, "Determinants of Trademark Dilution," *Journal of Consumer Research* 33 (September 2006), pp. 248–57.

6. Tulin Erdem, "Brand Equity as a Signaling Phenomenon," *Journal of Consumer Psychology* 7, no. 2 (1998), pp. 131–57; Joffre Swait and Tulin Erdem, "Brand Effects on Choice and Choice Set Formation under Uncertainty," *Marketing Science* 26, no. 5 (September–October 2007), pp. 679–97; Tulin Erdem, Joffre Swait, and Ana Valenzuela, "Brands as Signals: A Cross-Country Validation Study," *Journal of Marketing* 70 (January 2006), pp. 34–49.

7. Scott Davis, *Brand Asset Management: Driving Profitable Growth through Your Brands* (San Francisco: Jossey-Bass, 2000); Mary W. Sullivan, "How Brand Names Affect the Demand for Twin Automobiles," *Journal of Marketing Research* 35 (May 1998), pp. 154–65; D. C. Bello and M. B. Holbrook, "Does an Absence of Brand Equity Generalize across Product Classes?" *Journal of Business Research* 34 (October 1996), pp. 125–31.

8. For a discussion of how consumers become strongly attached to people as brands, see Matthew Thomson, "Human Brands: Investigating Antecedents to Consumers' Stronger Attachments to Celebrities," *Journal of Marketing* 70 (July 2006), pp. 104–19. For branding tips from the world of sports, see Irving Rein, Philip Kotler, and Ben Shields, *The Elusive Fan: Reinventing Sports in a Crowded Marketplace* (New York: McGraw-Hill, 2006).

9. Kevin Lane Keller, *Strategic Brand Management*, 3rd ed. (Upper Saddle River, NJ: Prentice Hall, 2008); David A. Aaker and Erich Joachimsthaler, *Brand Leadership* (New York: Free Press 2000); David A. Aaker, *Building Strong Brands* (New York: Free Press, 1996); David A. Aaker, *Managing Brand Equity* (New York: Free Press, 1991).

10. Other approaches are based on economic principles of signaling, for example, Tulin Erdem, "Brand Equity as a Signaling Phenomenon," *Journal of Consumer Psychology* 7, no. 2 (1998), pp. 131–57; or a sociological, anthropological, or biological perspective (e.g., Grant McCracken, *Culture and Consumption II: Markets, Meaning, and Brand Management* (Bloomington: Indiana University Press, 2005); Susan Fournier,

"Consumers and Their Brands: Developing Relationship Theory in Consumer Research," *Journal of Consumer Research* 24 (September 1998), pp. 343–73; Craig J. Thompson, Aric Rindfleisch, and Zeynep Arsel, "Emotional Branding and the Strategic Value of the Doppelganger Brand Image," *Journal of Marketing* 70 (January 2006), pp. 50–64.

11. Kevin Lane Keller, *Strategic Brand Management*, 3rd ed. (Upper Saddle River, NJ: Prentice Hall, 2008).

12. Theodore Levitt, "Marketing Success through Differentiation—of Anything," *Harvard Business Review*, January–February 1980, pp. 83–91.

13. Kusum Ailawadi, Donald R. Lehmann, and Scott Neslin, "Revenue Premium as an Outcome Measure of Brand Equity," *Journal of Marketing* 67 (October 2003), pp. 1–17.

14. Kevin Lane Keller, "Building Customer-Based Brand Equity: A Blueprint for Creating Strong Brands," *Marketing Management* 10 (July–August 2001), pp. 15–19.

15. M. Berk Ataman, Carl F. Mela, and Harald J. van Heerde, "Building Brands," *Marketing Science* 27, no. 6 (November–December 2008), pp. 1036–54.

16. Walter Mossberg, "Is Bing the Thing?" *Wall Street Journal*, June 2, 2009, p. R4; Burt Heim, "The Dubbing of 'Bing,'" *BusinessWeek*, June 15, 2009, p. 23; Todd Wasserman, "Why Microsoft Chose the Name 'Bing,'" *Brandweek*, June 1, 2009, p. 33.

17. Rachel Dodes, "From Tracksuits to Fast Track," *Wall Street Journal*, September 13, 2006.

18. "42 Below," www.betterbydesign.org.nz, September 14, 2007.

19. Alina Wheeler, *Designing Brand Identity* (Hoboken, NJ: Wiley, 2003).

20. Pat Fallon and Fred Senn, *Juicing the Orange: How to Turn Creativity into a Powerful Business Advantage* (Cambridge, MA: Harvard Business School Press, 2006); Eric A. Yorkston and Geeta Menon, "A Sound Idea: Phonetic Effects of Brand Names on Consumer Judgments," *Journal of Consumer Research* 31 (June), pp. 43–51; Tina M. Lowery and L. J. Shrum, "Phonetic Symbolism and Brand Name Preference," *Journal of Consumer Research* 34 (October 2007), pp. 406–14.

21. John R. Doyle and Paul A. Bottomly, "Dressed for the Occasion: Font-Product Congruity in the Perception of Logotype," *Journal of Consumer Psychology* 16, no. 2 (2006), pp. 112–23; Kevin Lane Keller, Susan Heckler, and Michael J. Houston, "The Effects of Brand Name Suggestiveness on Advertising Recall," *Journal of Marketing* 62 (January 1998), pp. 48–57. For more on how brand names get developed, see Alex Frankel,

Wordcraft: The Art of Turning Little Words into Big Business (New York: Crown Publishers, 2004).

22. Don Schultz and Heidi Schultz, *IMC: The Next Generation* (New York: McGraw-Hill, 2003); Don E. Schultz, Stanley I. Tannenbaum, and Robert F. Lauterborn, *Integrated Marketing Communications* (Lincolnwood, IL: NTC Business Books, 1993).

23. Mohanbir Sawhney, "Don't Harmonize, Synchronize," *Harvard Business Review,* July–August 2001, pp. 101–8.

24. Dawn Iacobucci and Bobby Calder, eds., *Kellogg on Integrated Marketing* (New York: Wiley, 2003).

25. Jonathan Welsh, "Harley-Davidson Seeks Young Buyers at Concerts," *Wall Street Journal,* July 13, 2010, www.wsj.com; "Harley Davidson to Bring HOG to India for Cruise Biking," *Times of India,* July 14, 2010, http://timesofindia.indiatimes.com; "Can India Have Cult Brands?" *Business Standard (India),* May 29, 2007, www.business-standard.com/india.

26. Michael Dunn and Scott Davis, "Building Brands from the Inside," *Marketing Management* (May–June 2003), pp. 32–37; Scott Davis and Michael Dunn, *Building the Brand-Driven Business* (New York: Wiley, 2002).

27. Stan Maklan and Simon Knox, *Competing on Value* (Upper Saddle River, NJ: Financial Times, Prentice Hall, 2000).

28. James H. McAlexander, John W. Schouten and Harold F. Koenig, "Building Brand Community," *Journal of Marketing* 66 (January 2002), pp. 38–54. For examinations of brand communities, see René Algesheimer, Utpal M. Dholakia, and Andreas Herrmann, "The Social Influence of Brand Community: Evidence from European Car Clubs," *Journal of Marketing* 69 (July 2005), pp. 19–34; Albert M. Muniz Jr. and Hope Jensen Schau, "Religiosity in the Abandoned Apple Newton Brand Community," *Journal of Consumer Research* 31, no. 4 (2005), pp. 412–32; Robert Kozinets, "Utopian Enterprise: Articulating the Meanings of *Star Trek*'s Culture of Consumption," *Journal of Consumer Research* 28 (June 2001), pp. 67–87; John W. Schouten and James H. McAlexander, "Subcultures of Consumption: An Ethnography of New Bikers," *Journal of Consumer Research* 22 (June 1995), pp. 43–61.

29. Albert M. Muniz Jr. and Thomas C. O'Guinn, "Brand Community," *Journal of Consumer Research* 27 (March 2001), pp. 412–32.

30. Scott A. Thompson and Rajiv K. Sinha, "Brand Communities and New Product Adoption: The Influence and Limits of Oppositional Loyalty," *Journal of Marketing* 72 (November 2008), pp. 65–80.

31. Deborah Roeddder John, Barbara Loken, Kyeong-Heui Kim, and Alokparna Basu Monga, "Brand Concept Maps: A Methodology for Identifying Brand Association Networks," *Journal of Marketing Research* 43 (November 2006), pp. 549–63.

32. For a discussion of factors determining long-term branding success, see Allen P. Adamson, *Brand Simple* (New York: Palgrave Macmillan, 2006).

33. Larry Light and Joan Kiddon, *Six Rules for Brand Revitalization* (Upper Saddle River, NJ: Wharton School Publishing, 2009).

34. Rebecca J. Slotegraaf and Koen Pauwels, "The Impact of Brand Equity and Innovation on the Long-term Effectiveness of Promotions," *Journal of Marketing Research* 45 (June 2008), pp. 293–306.

35. For corporate branding guidelines, see James R. Gregory, *The Best of Branding: Best Practices in Corporate Branding* (New York: McGraw-Hill, 2004). For international perspectives, see Majken Schultz, Mary Jo Hatch, and Mogens Holten Larsen, eds., *The Expressive Organization: Linking Identity, Reputation, and Corporate Brand* (Oxford, UK: Oxford University Press, 2000); and Majken Schultz, Yun Mi Antorini, and Fabian F. Csaba, eds., *Corporate Branding: Purpose, People, and Process* (Denmark: Copenhagen Business School Press, 2005).

36. Guido Berens, Cees B. M. van Riel, and Gerrit H. van Bruggen, "Corporate Associations and Consumer Product Responses: The Moderating Role of Corporate Brand Dominance," *Journal of Marketing* 69 (July 2005), pp. 35–48; Zeynep Gürhan-Canli and Rajeev Batra, "When Corporate Image Affects Product Evaluations: The Moderating Role of Perceived Risk," *Journal of Marketing Research* 41 (May 2004), pp. 197–205; Kevin Lane Keller and David A. Aaker, "Corporate-Level Marketing: The Impact of Credibility on a Company's Brand Extensions," *Corporate Reputation Review* 1 (August 1998), pp. 356–78; Thomas J. Brown and Peter Dacin, "The Company and the Product: Corporate Associations and Consumer Product Responses," *Journal of Marketing* 61 (January 1997), pp. 68–84; Gabriel J. Biehal and Daniel A. Sheinin, "The Influence of Corporate Messages on the Product Portfolio," *Journal of Marketing* 71 (April 2007), pp. 12–25.

37. Jack Trout, *Differentiate or Die: Survival in Our Era of Killer Competition* (New York: Wiley, 2000); Kamalini Ramdas and Mohanbir Sawhney, "A Cross-Functional Approach to Evaluating Multiple Line Extensions for Assembled Products," *Management Science* 47, no. 1 (January 2001), pp. 22–36.

38. Nirmalya Kumar, "Kill a Brand, Keep a Customer," *Harvard Business Review,* December 2003, pp. 87–95.

39. Byung-Do Kim and Mary W. Sullivan, "The Effect of Parent Brand Experience on Line Extension Trial and Repeat Purchase," *Marketing Letters* 9 (April 1998), pp. 181–93.

40. John Milewicz and Paul Herbig, "Evaluating the Brand Extension Decision Using a Model of Reputation Building," *Journal of Product & Brand Management* 3, no. 1 (January 1994), pp. 39–47; Kevin Lane Keller and David A. Aaker, "The Effects of Sequential Introduction of Brand Extensions," *Journal of Marketing Research* 29 (February 1992), pp. 35–50.

41. Valarie A. Taylor and William O. Bearden, "Ad Spending on Brand Extensions: Does Similarity Matter?" *Journal of Brand Management* 11 (September 2003), pp. 63–74; Sheri Bridges, Kevin Lane Keller, and Sanjay Sood, "Communication Strategies for Brand Extensions: Enhancing Perceived Fit by Establishing Explanatory Links," *Journal of Advertising* 29 (Winter 2000), pp. 1–11; Daniel C. Smith, "Brand Extension and Advertising Efficiency: What Can and Cannot Be Expected," *Journal of Advertising Research* (November–December 1992), pp. 11–20; Daniel C. Smith and C. Whan Park, "The Effects of Brand Extensions on Market Share and Advertising Efficiency," *Journal of Marketing Research* 29 (August 1992), pp. 296–313.

42. Ralf van der Lans, Rik Pieters, and Michel Wedel, "Competitive Brand Salience," *Marketing Science* 27, no. 5 (September–October 2008), pp. 922–31.

43. Subramanian Balachander and Sanjoy Ghose, "Reciprocal Spillover Effects: A Strategic Benefit of Brand Extensions," *Journal of Marketing* 67, no. 1 (January 2003), pp. 4–13.

44. Bharat N. Anand and Ron Shachar, "Brands as Beacons: A New Source of Loyalty to Multiproduct Firms," *Journal of Marketing Research* 41 (May 2004), pp. 135–50.

45. Kevin Lane Keller and David A. Aaker, "The Effects of Sequential Introduction of Brand Extensions," *Journal of Marketing Research* 29 (February 1992), pp. 35–50. For consumer processing implications, see Huifung Mao and H. Shanker Krishnan, "Effects of Prototype and Exemplar Fit on Brand Extension Evaluations: A Two-Process Contingency Model," *Journal of Consumer Research* 33 (June 2006), pp. 41–49; Byung Chul Shine, Jongwon Park, and Robert S. Wyer Jr., "Brand Synergy Effects in Multiple Brand Extensions," *Journal of Marketing Research* 44 (November 2007), pp. 663–70.

46. Maureen Morrin, "The Impact of Brand Extensions on Parent Brand Memory Structures and Retrieval Processes," *Journal of Marketing Research* 36, no. 4 (November 1999), pp. 517–25; John A. Quelch and David Kenny, "Extend Profits, Not Product Lines," *Harvard Business Review*, September–October 1994, pp. 153–60; Perspectives from the Editors, "The Logic of Product-Line Extensions," *Harvard Business Review*, November–December 1994, pp. 53–62.

47. Deborah Roedder John, Barbara Loken, and Christopher Joiner, "The Negative Impact of Extensions: Can Flagship Products Be Diluted," *Journal of Marketing*, January 1998, pp. 19–32; Susan M. Broniarcyzk and Joseph W. Alba, "The Importance of the Brand in Brand Extension," *Journal of Marketing Research* (May 1994), pp. 214–28; Barbara Loken and Deborah Roedder John, "Diluting Brand Beliefs: When Do Brand Extensions Have a Negative Impact?" *Journal of Marketing* (July 1993), pp. 71–84. See also, Chris Pullig, Carolyn Simmons, and Richard G. Netemeyer, "Brand Dilution: When Do New Brands Hurt Existing Brands?" *Journal of Marketing* 70 (April 2006), pp. 52–66; R. Ahluwalia and Z. Gürhan-Canli, "The Effects of Extensions on the Family Brand Name: An Accessibility-Diagnosticity Perspective," *Journal of Consumer Research* 27 (December 2000), pp. 371–81; Z. Gürhan-Canli and M. Durairaj, "The Effects of Extensions on Brand Name Dilution and Enhancement," *Journal of Marketing Research* 35 (November 1998), pp. 464–73; S. J. Milberg, C. W. Park, and M. S. McCarthy, "Managing Negative Feedback Effects Associated with Brand Extensions: The Impact of Alternative Branding Strategies," *Journal of Consumer Psychology* 6 (1997), pp. 119–40; Franziska Völckner and Henrik Sattler, "Drivers of Brand Extension Success," *Journal of Marketing* 70 (April 2006), pp. 1–17.

48. Pierre Berthon, Morris B. Holbrook, James M. Hulbert, and Leyland F. Pitt, "Viewing Brands in Multiple Dimensions," *MIT Sloan Management Review* (Winter 2007), pp. 37–43.

49. Roland T. Rust, Valerie A. Zeithaml, and Katherine A. Lemon, "Measuring Customer Equity and Calculating Marketing ROI," Rajiv Grover and Marco Vriens, eds., *Handbook of Marketing Research* (Thousand Oaks, CA: Sage Publications, 2006), pp. 588–601; Roland T. Rust, Valerie A. Zeithaml, and Katherine A. Lemon, *Driving Customer Equity* (New York: Free Press, 2000).

50. Robert C. Blattberg and John Deighton, "Manage Marketing by the Customer Equity Test," *Harvard Business Review*, July–August 1996, pp. 136–44.

51. Much of this section is based on Robert Leone, Vithala Rao, Kevin Lane Keller, Man Luo, Leigh McAlister, and Rajendra Srivatstava, "Linking Brand Equity to Customer Equity," *Journal of Service Research* 9 (November 2006), pp. 125–38.

52. Niraj Dawar, "What Are Brands Good For?" *MIT Sloan Management Review* (Fall 2004), pp. 31–37.

chapter 9

Crafting the Brand Positioning and Competing Effectively

1. How can a firm develop and establish an effective positioning?
2. How are brands successfully differentiated?
3. How can marketers identify and analyze competition?
4. How can market leaders, challengers, followers, and nichers compete effectively?

Marketing Management at Method

Method Products is the brainchild of former high school buddies Eric Ryan and Adam Lowry. They realized that although the category of cleaning and household products was huge, it was incredibly boring. So Ryan and Lowry designed a sleek, uncluttered soap container that also had a functional advantage—the bottle was built to let soap flow out the bottom, so users never have to turn it upside down.

By creating a unique line of nontoxic, biodegradable household cleaning products with bright colors and sleek designs, Method has grown beyond $100 million in revenues. Its big break came when it placed its products in Target, which partners with well-known designers to offer stand-out products at affordable prices. Now Method's challenge is to differentiate beyond design to compete effectively and avoid copycats eroding the brand's cachet. The company, on a limited marketing budget, is capitalizing on interest in green products by emphasizing its earth-friendly ingredients.[1]

Creating a compelling, well-differentiated brand position, as Method has done, requires a keen understanding of consumer needs and wants, customer capabilities, and competitive actions. In this chapter, we outline a process by which marketers can uncover the most powerful brand positioning. We also examine the role of competition and how to manage brands based on their market position.

Developing and Establishing a Brand Positioning

All marketing strategy is built on segmentation, targeting, and positioning. A company discovers different needs and groups in the marketplace, targets those it can satisfy in a superior way, and then positions its offerings so the target market recognizes the company's distinctive offerings and images.

Positioning is the act of designing a company's offering and image to occupy a distinctive place in the minds of the target market.[2] The goal is to locate the brand in the minds of consumers to maximize the potential benefit to the firm. A good brand positioning helps guide marketing strategy by clarifying the brand's essence, identifying the goals it helps the consumer achieve, and showing how it does so in a unique way. The real trick is striking the right balance between what the brand is and what it could be.

The result of positioning is the successful creation of a *customer-focused value proposition*, a cogent reason why the target market should buy the product. Table 9.1 shows how three firms have defined their value proposition, given their target customers, benefits, and prices.[3]

Deciding on a positioning requires (1) determining a frame of reference, (2) identifying the optimal points-of-parity and points-of-difference brand associations, and (3) creating a brand mantra to summarize the positioning.

Competitive Frame of Reference

The **competitive frame of reference** defines which other brands a brand competes with and therefore which brands should be the focus of competitive analysis. A good starting point is to determine **category membership**—the products or sets of products with which a brand competes and which function as close substitutes. The range of a company's actual and potential competitors can be much broader than the obvious. For a brand to grow by entering new markets, a broader or maybe more aspirational competitive frame may be necessary to reflect possible future competitors. In fact, a firm is more likely to be hurt by emerging competitors or new technologies than by current competitors.

TABLE 9.1	Examples of Value Propositions			
Company and Product	**Target Customers**	**Key Benefits**	**Price**	**Value Proposition**
Perdue (chicken)	Quality-conscious consumers of chicken	Tenderness	10% premium	More tender golden chicken at a moderate premium price
Volvo (station wagon)	Safety-conscious upscale families	Durability and safety	20% premium	The safest, most durable wagon in which your family can ride
Domino's (pizza)	Convenience-minded pizza lovers	Delivery speed and good quality	15% premium	A good hot pizza, delivered promptly to your door, at a moderate price

We can examine competition from both an industry and a market point of view.[4] An **industry** is a group of firms offering a product or class of products that are close substitutes for one another. Using the market approach, we define *competitors* as companies that satisfy the same customer need. Jeffrey F. Rayport and Bernard J. Jaworski suggest profiling direct and indirect competitors by mapping the buyer's steps in obtaining and using the product, to highlight the firm's opportunities and challenges.[5] See "Marketing Insight: High Growth Through Value Innovation" for a discussion of competing through value innovation.

Once a firm has identified its main competitors, it must ask: What is each competitor seeking in the marketplace? What drives each competitor's behavior? Many factors shape a competitor's objectives, including size, history, current management, and financial situation. If the competitor is a part of a larger firm, is the parent running it for growth or for profits, or milking it?[6] Based on all this analysis, marketers must formally define the competitive frame of reference to guide positioning. In stable markets with little short-term change likely, it may be easy to define one, two, or three key competitors. In dynamic categories where competition may exist or arise in a variety of forms, multiple frames of reference may arise.

Points-of-Difference and Points-of-Parity

Once marketers have fixed the competitive frame of reference, they can define the appropriate points-of-difference and points-of-parity associations.[7] **Points-of-difference (PODs)** are attributes or benefits that consumers strongly associate with a brand, positively evaluate, and believe they could not find to the same extent with a competitive brand. Strong brands may have multiple points-of-difference. Two examples are Apple (*design, ease-of-use,* and *irreverent attitude*) and Southwest Airlines (*value, reliability,* and *fun personality*). Creating

Marketing Insight

HIGH GROWTH THROUGH VALUE INNOVATION

INSEAD professors W. Chan Kim and Renée Mauborgne advocate "blue-ocean thinking," creating offerings for which there are no direct competitors. Instead of searching within the conventional boundaries of industry competition, managers should look for unoccupied market positions that represent real value innovation. Classic blue-ocean thinking involves designing creative business ventures to positively affect both a company's cost structure and its value proposition to consumers.

Kim and Mauborgne propose that marketers ask four questions to guide blue-ocean thinking: (1) Which of the factors that our industry takes for granted should we eliminate? (2) Which factors should we reduce well *below* the industry's standard? (3) Which factors should we raise well *above* the industry's standard? (4) Which factors should we create that the industry has never offered?

Sources: W. Chan Kim and Renée Mauborgne, *Blue-Ocean Strategy* (Cambridge, MA: Harvard Business School Press, 2005); W. Chan Kim and Renée Mauborgne, "Creating New Market Space," *Harvard Business Review,* January–February 1999; W. Chan Kim and Renée Mauborgne, "Value Innovation: The Strategic Logic of High Growth," *Harvard Business Review,* January–February 1997.

strong, favorable, and unique associations is a real challenge, but an essential one for competitive brand positioning.

Three criteria determine whether a brand association can function as a point-of-difference:

1. *Desirable to consumer*—Consumers must see the brand association as personally relevant to them.

2. *Deliverable by the company*—The company must have the resources an[...] ment to feasibly and profitably create and maintain the brand associat[...] minds of consumers. The ideal brand association is preemptive, defensible[...] cult to attack.

3. *Differentiating from competitors*—Consumers must see the brand association as distinctive and superior to competitors.[8]

Points-of-parity (**POPs**) are attributes or benefit associations that are not necessarily unique to the brand but may be shared with other brands.[9] These types of associations come in two forms: category and competitive. *Category points-of-parity* are associations that consumers view as essential to a credible offering within a certain category, although not necessarily sufficient conditions for brand choice. Category points-of-parity may change over time due to technological advances, legal developments, or consumer trends.

Competitive points-of-parity are associations designed to overcome perceived weaknesses of the brand. A competitive point-of-parity may be required to negate *competitors'* perceived points-of-difference or negate a perceived vulnerability of the brand. If, in the eyes of consumers, a brand can "break even" in those areas where it appears to be at a disadvantage *and* achieve advantages in other areas, the brand should be in a strong—and perhaps unbeatable— competitive position. For an offering to achieve a point-of-parity on a particular attribute or benefit, a sufficient number of consumers must believe the brand is "good enough" on that dimension.

It is not uncommon for a brand to identify more than one frame of reference, if competition widens or the firm expands into new categories. A company may straddle two frames of reference with one set of points-of-difference and points-of-parity. In these cases, the points-of-difference for one category become points-of-parity for the other and vice versa. Subway restaurants are positioned as offering healthy, good-tasting sandwiches. This allows the brand to create a POP on taste and a POD on health with respect to quick-serve restaurants such as McDonald's and, at the same time, a POP on health and a POD on taste with respect to health food restaurants. Straddle positions allow brands to expand their market coverage and potential customer base. However, if the POP and POD are not credible, the brand may not be viewed as a legitimate player in either category.

Choosing POPs and PODs

Marketers typically focus on brand benefits in choosing the POPs and PODs that make up their brand positioning. Brand attributes generally play more of a supporting role by providing "reasons to believe" or "proof points" as to why a brand can credibly claim it offers certain benefits. Multiple attributes may support a certain benefit, and they may change over time. For choosing specific benefits as POPs and PODs to position a brand, marketers may use *perceptual maps,* visual representations of consumer perceptions and preferences. These provide quantitative portrayals of market situations and consumer perceptions along various dimensions, revealing "openings" that suggest unmet consumer needs and marketing opportunities.

FIGURE 9.1 Hypothetical Beverage Perceptual Map

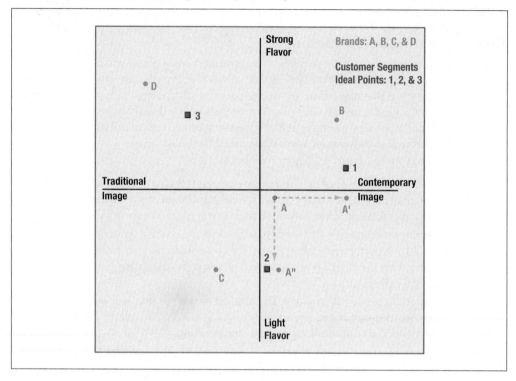

For example, Figure 9.1 shows a hypothetical perceptual map for a beverage category. The four brands—A, B, C, and D—vary in terms of how consumers view their flavor (light versus strong) and image (contemporary versus modern). Also displayed on the map are ideal point "configurations" for three market segments (1, 2, and 3). The ideal points represent each segment's most preferred ("ideal") combination of taste and imagery. Brand A is seen as more balanced in terms of both taste and imagery, although no market segment seems to desire this balance.

On Figure 9.1 are two possible repositioning strategies for Brand A. By making its image more contemporary, Brand A could move to A' to target consumers in Segment 1 and achieve a point-of-parity on image and maintain point-of-difference on taste with respect to Brand B. By offering a lighter flavor, Brand A could move to A" to target consumers in Segment 2 and achieve a point-of-parity on flavor and maintain point-of-difference on image with respect to Brand C. Deciding which repositioning is most promising and profitable would require detailed consumer and competitive analysis.

Brand Mantras

A *brand mantra* is an articulation of the brand essence and promise, economically communicating what the brand is and what it is *not* in short, three- to five-word phrases. For brands seeking growth, it is helpful to define the product or benefit space in which the brand would like to compete, as Nike did with "athletic performance." This helps employees and marketing partners understand the brand so they can act accordingly. A good brand mantra should communicate the category and clarify the brand's uniqueness; be vivid and memorable; and stake out ground that is meaningful and relevant.

Establishing Brand Positioning

Establishing the brand positioning requires that consumers understand what the brand offers and what makes it a superior competitive choice. The typical approach is to inform consumers of a brand's category membership before stating its point-of-difference. Presumably, consumers need to know what a product is and what function it serves before deciding whether it is superior to competing brands. For new products, initial advertising often concentrates on creating brand awareness, and subsequent advertising attempts to create the brand image.

Three ways to convey a brand's category membership are:

1. *Announcing category benefits*—To reassure consumers that a brand will deliver on the fundamental reason for using a category, marketers frequently use benefits to announce category membership. Thus, industrial tools might claim to have durability.
2. *Comparing to exemplars*—Well-known, noteworthy brands in a category can help a brand specify its category membership. When Tommy Hilfiger was an unknown, advertising announced his membership as a great U.S. designer by associating him with recognized category members such as Calvin Klein.
3. *Relying on the product descriptor*—The product descriptor that follows the brand name is a concise means of conveying category origin. Amazon.com calls its Kindle a "wireless reading device" to communicate category membership.

One common difficulty in creating a strong, competitive brand positioning is that many of the attributes or benefits that make up the points-of-parity and points-of-difference are negatively correlated. For example, it might be difficult to position a brand as both "inexpensive" and "top quality." Moreover, individual attributes and benefits often have positive *and* negative aspects. Unfortunately, consumers typically want to maximize *both* of the negatively correlated attributes or benefits. The best approach clearly is to develop a product or service that performs well on both dimensions.

Some marketers have adopted other approaches to address attribute or benefit trade-offs: launching two different marketing campaigns, each one devoted to a different brand attribute or benefit; linking themselves to any kind of person, place, or thing that possesses the right kind of equity as a means to establish an attribute or benefit as a POP or POD; and even attempting to convince consumers that the negative relationship between attributes and benefits, if they consider it differently, is in fact positive.

Differentiation Strategies

To avoid the commodity trap, marketers must start with the belief that anything can be differentiated. **Competitive advantage** is a company's ability to perform in one or more ways that competitors cannot or will not match. Although few competitive advantages are sustainable, a *leverageable advantage* can be used as a springboard to new advantages, much as Microsoft leveraged its operating system to Microsoft Office and then to networking applications.

For a brand to be effectively positioned, customers must see any competitive advantage as a *customer advantage*. For example, if a company claims its product works faster than its competitors, it will be a customer advantage only if customers value speed. Companies must focus on customer advantages to deliver high customer value and satisfaction, which leads to repeat purchasing and ultimately to high profitability.[10]

Dimensions of Differentiation

The obvious means of differentiation, and often the most compelling to consumers, relate to aspects of the product and service. In competitive markets, firms may need to consider other dimensions:

- Employee differentiation—Companies can have better-trained employees who provide superior customer service. Singapore Airlines is well regarded in large part because of its flight attendants.
- Channel differentiation—Companies can design their channels' coverage, expertise, and performance to make buying easier, more enjoyable, and more rewarding for customers.
- Image differentiation—Companies can craft powerful, compelling images that appeal to consumers' social and psychological needs.
- Services differentiation—A service firm can differentiate itself by delivering more effective and efficient solutions to consumers.

Rational and Emotional Components of Differentiation

Many marketing experts believe a brand positioning should have both rational and emotional components, with points-of-difference and points-of-parity that appeal to the head and the heart. Saatchi & Saatchi CEO Kevin Roberts advocates that brands strive to become lovemarks, commanding consumer respect and love through a combination of mystery, sensuality, and intimacy.[11] A person's emotional response to a brand and its marketing will depend on many factors, including authenticity.[12] Brands such as Hershey's, Crayola, and Johnson & Johnson that are seen as authentic and genuine can evoke trust, affection, and strong loyalty.[13]

Therefore, the firm should analyze potential competitive threats by monitoring:

- Share of market—The competitor's share of the target market.
- Share of mind—The percentage of customers who named the competitor in responding to the statement, "Name the first company that comes to mind in this industry."
- Share of heart—The percentage of customers who named the competitor in responding to the statement, "Name the company from which you would prefer to buy the product."

Companies that make steady gains in mind share and heart share will inevitably make gains in market share and profitability. Firms such as Timberland and Wegmans are reaping the benefits of providing emotional, experiential, social, and financial value to satisfy customers and all their constituents.[14]

Competitive Strategies for Market Leaders

Suppose a market is occupied by the firms shown in Figure 9.2. The *market leader* holds 40 percent; another 30 percent belongs to a *market challenger*; and 20 percent is claimed by a *market follower* willing to maintain its share and not rock the boat. *Market nichers,* serving small segments larger firms don't reach, hold the remaining 10 percent.

A market leader such as McDonald's has the largest market share in its industry and usually leads in price changes, new-product introductions, distribution coverage, and promotional intensity. Although marketers assume well-known brands are distinctive in consumers'

FIGURE 9.2 Hypothetical Market Structure

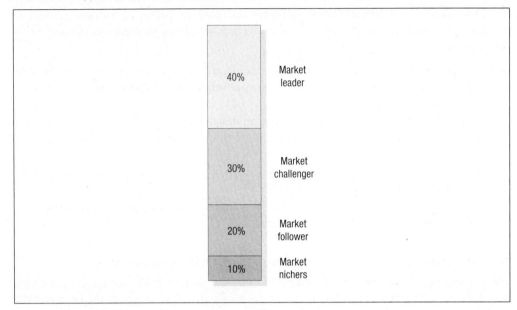

minds, unless a dominant firm enjoys a legal monopoly, it must maintain constant vigilance. A powerful product innovation may come along; a competitor might find a fresh marketing angle or launch a major marketing investment; or the leader's cost structure might spiral upward.

Companies offering both low prices and high quality are capturing customers all over the world. More than half the U.S. population now shops weekly at mass merchants such as Target, for instance. Such value-oriented firms often focus on one or a few consumer segments; provide better delivery or just one additional benefit; and match low prices with highly efficient operations to keep costs down, changing consumer expectations about the trade-off between quality and price.

To compete, mainstream firms need greater intensity of focus on cost control and product differentiation, plus flawless execution. Differentiation becomes less about the abstract goal of rising above competitive clutter and more about identifying openings left by the value players' business models. Effective pricing means waging a transaction-by-transaction perception battle for consumers predisposed to believe value-oriented competitors are always cheaper.[15]

To stay number one, the market leader must find ways to expand total market demand, protect its current share through good defensive and offensive actions, and increase market share, even if market size remains constant.

Expanding the Total Market

When the total market expands, the dominant firm usually gains the most. If Heinz can convince more people to use ketchup, or to use ketchup with more meals, or to use more ketchup on each occasion, the firm will benefit because it already sells almost two-thirds of the country's ketchup. In general, the market leader should look for new customers or more usage from existing customers. A company can search for new users among three groups: those who might use it but do not *(market-penetration strategy)*, those who have never used it *(new-market segment strategy)*, or those who live elsewhere *(geographical-expansion strategy)*.

Marketers can also try to increase the amount, level, or frequency of product consumption. They can sometimes boost the *amount* of consumption through packaging or product redesign; larger packages increase the amount that consumers use at one time, for example.[16] Consumers use more of impulse products such as soft drinks when the product is made more available. Increasing *frequency* of consumption, on the other hand, requires either (1) identifying additional opportunities to use the brand in the same way or (2) identifying completely new and different ways to use the brand.

Protecting Market Share

While trying to expand total market size, the dominant firm must actively defend its current business: Boeing against Airbus, and Google against Microsoft.[17] The most constructive response to protecting market share is *continuous innovation*. The firm should lead the industry in developing new products and customer services, distribution effectiveness, and cost cutting. Comprehensive solutions increase its competitive strength and value to customers. Even when it does not launch offensives, the market leader must leave no major flanks exposed. Defensive strategy reduces the probability of attack, diverts attacks to less-threatened areas, and lessens their intensity. A leading firm can use six defense strategies.[18]

- Position Defense—This means occupying the most desirable market space in consumers' minds, making the brand almost impregnable, as Procter & Gamble has done with Tide detergent.
- Flank Defense—The market leader should erect outposts to protect a weak front or support a possible counterattack, the way Procter & Gamble's Luvs diapers have played strategic offensive and defensive roles.
- Preemptive Defense—A more aggressive maneuver is to attack first, perhaps with guerrilla action—hitting one competitor here, another there—and keeping everyone off balance. Another is to achieve broad market envelopment that signals competitors not to attack.[19] Yet another preemptive defense is to introduce a stream of new products and announce them in advance.[20]
- Counteroffensive Defense—The market leader can meet an attacker frontally so the rival will have to defend itself or exercise economic or political clout. The leader may try to crush a competitor by subsidizing lower prices for the vulnerable product with revenue from more profitable products, preannouncing a product upgrade to prevent customers from buying a competing product, or lobbying for political action to inhibit the competition.
- Mobile Defense—Here, the leader stretches into new territories through market broadening and market diversification. *Market broadening* shifts focus from the current product to the underlying generic need, the way "petroleum" companies recast themselves as "energy" companies. *Market diversification* means shifting into unrelated industries, the way Altria, which owns the tobacco company Philip Morris, has moved into wine.
- Contraction Defense—Sometimes large companies can no longer defend all their territory. In *planned contraction* (also called *strategic withdrawal*), they give up weaker markets and reassign resources to stronger ones. Motorola sold its network equipment business to Nokia Siemens Networks so it could concentrate on other communications equipment.[21]

Increasing Market Share

In many markets, one share point can be worth tens of millions of dollars, which means that much depends on the company's strategy for expanding share.[22] Because the cost of buying higher market share may far exceed its revenue value, firms should consider four factors first:

1. *The possibility of provoking antitrust action*—Frustrated competitors are likely to cry "monopoly" and seek legal action if a dominant firm makes further inroads. Microsoft and Intel have had to fend off legal challenges as a result of what some feel are inappropriate or illegal practices and abuse of market power.

2. *Economic cost*—After a certain point, profitability might fall, not rise, with market share gains. The cost of gaining further share might exceed the value if holdout customers dislike the firm, are loyal to competitors, have unique needs, or prefer dealing with smaller firms. Pushing for higher share is less justifiable when there are unattractive segments, buyers who want multiple sources of supply, high exit barriers, and few economies of scale. Some market leaders have even increased profitability by selectively *decreasing* market share in weaker areas.[23]

3. *Pursuing the wrong marketing activities*—Firms that gain share typically outperform competitors in three areas: new-product activity, relative product quality, and marketing expenditures.[24] Those that cut prices more deeply than competitors typically don't achieve significant gains, because rivals meet the price cuts or offer other values to keep customers.

4. *The effect of increased market share on actual and perceived quality*[25]—Too many customers can strain the firm's resources, hurting product value and service delivery.

Other Competitive Strategies

Firms that are not industry leaders are often called runner-up or trailing firms. Some, such as Ford, are quite large in their own right. These firms can either attack the leader and other competitors in an aggressive bid for further market share as *market challengers*, or they can not "rock the boat" as *market followers*.

Market-Challenger Strategies

Many market challengers have gained ground or even overtaken the leader. A market challenger must first define its strategic objective, usually to increase market share. The challenger must decide whom to attack. Attacking the leader is a high-risk but potentially high-payoff strategy if the leader is not serving the market well. The challenger can attack firms of its own size that are underperforming and underfinanced, have aging products or high prices, or aren't satisfying customers in other ways. Or it can attack small local and regional firms.

Given clear opponents and objectives, five attack strategies for challengers are:

1. *Frontal attack*—The attacker matches its opponent's product, advertising, price, and distribution. A modified frontal attack, such as cutting price, can work if the market leader doesn't retaliate, and if the competitor convinces the market its product is equal to the leader's.

2. *Flank attack*—A *flanking* strategy is another name for identifying shifts that are causing gaps to develop, then filling the gaps. Flanking is particularly attractive to a challenger

with fewer resources and more likely to succeed than frontal attacks. In a geographic attack, the challenger spots areas where the opponent is underperforming. Another flanking strategy is to serve uncovered market needs.

3. *Encirclement Attack—Encirclement* attempts to capture a wide slice of territory by launching a grand offensive on several fronts; this makes sense when the challenger has superior resources.

4. *Bypass Attack—Bypassing* the enemy to attack easier markets offers three lines of approach: diversifying into unrelated products; diversifying into new geographical markets; and leapfrogging into new technologies, shifting the battleground to an advance where the challenger has an advantage.

5. *Guerrilla Attacks—Guerrilla* attacks are small, intermittent attacks, both conventional and unconventional, including selective price cuts, intense promotional blitzes, and occasional legal action, to harass the opponent and secure footholds (see "Marketing Skills: Guerilla Marketing"). A guerrilla campaign must be backed by a stronger attack to beat the opponent.

Any aspect of marketing can serve as the basis for attack, such as lower-priced or discounted products, new or improved offerings, a wider variety of offerings, and innovative distribution. A challenger's success depends on combining several, more specific, strategies to improve its position over time.

Market-Follower Strategies

Theodore Levitt has argued that a strategy of *product imitation* might be as profitable as a strategy of *product innovation*.[26] The innovator bears the expense of developing the new product, getting it

Marketing Skills

GUERRILLA MARKETING

Who needs guerrilla marketing skills? Any marketer who wants to grab share from the leader without risking the higher cost and provocation of a frontal attack. Guerrilla marketers must think creatively about how to attract maximum customer attention and achieve marketing objectives with limited resources. They should test the idea internally and/or locally to spot potential problems before implementation, and be prepared to change or drop a nonperforming guerrilla campaign. Finally, guerrilla marketers should anticipate stakeholders' reactions to controversial techniques or messages and be sensitive to legal and ethical concerns.

For example, Cluck-U, a family-friendly fried-chicken chain with 25 units, doesn't attack market-leader KFC or other major competitors head on. Instead, it uses guerrilla marketing to reach its target audience. Cluck-U employees, dressed in chicken costumes, march in local parades and roam nearby streets giving away discount coupons. The mascots attract attention, bring smiles to people's faces, and draw crowds to the restaurants. "Twenty-five percent of what we bring in is because of those chickens," says Cluck-U's CEO.[27]

into distribution, and informing the market. The reward for all this work and risk is normally market leadership. However, another firm can then copy or improve on the new product. Although it probably will not overtake the leader, the follower can achieve high profits because it did not bear any of the innovation expense.

Many companies prefer to follow rather than challenge the market leader, especially in industries such as steel and chemicals, where few opportunities for product differentiation and image differentiation exist, service quality is comparable, and price sensitivity runs high. Short-run grabs for market share provoke retaliation, so most firms present similar offers to buyers, usually by copying the leader, which keeps market shares stable.

Some followers use a counterfeiter strategy, duplicating the leader's product and packages and selling on the black market or through disreputable dealers. Some are cloners, emulating the leader's products, name, and packaging, with slight variations. Some are imitators, copying a few things from the leader but maintaining differentiation of packaging, advertising, pricing, or location. The leader doesn't mind as long as the imitator doesn't attack aggressively. Finally, some followers become adapters, taking the leader's products and adapting or improving them, perhaps for different markets.

Normally, a follower earns less than the leader. Therefore, followership is often not a rewarding path.

Market-Nicher Strategies

An alternative to being a follower in a large market is to be a leader in a small market or niche. Smaller firms normally avoid competing with larger firms by targeting small markets of little or no interest to larger rivals. But large, profitable firms also use niching strategies for some of their business units or companies. A niche might dry up or be attacked, however, so nichers must seek to create new niches, expand existing niches, and protect their niches. Table 9.2 shows the specialist roles open to nichers.

TABLE 9.2	Niche Specialist Roles
Niche Specialty	**Description**
End-user specialist	The firm specializes in serving one type of end-use customer.
Vertical-level specialist	The firm specializes at some vertical level of the production-distribution value chain.
Customer-size specialist	The firm concentrates on either small, medium, or large customers.
Specific-customer specialist	The firm limits its selling to one or a few customers.
Geographic specialist	The firm sells only in a certain locality, region, or area of the world.
Product or product-line specialist	The firm carries or produces only one product line or product.
Product-feature specialist	The firm specializes in a certain type of product or product feature.
Job-shop specialist	The firm customizes its products for individual customers.
Quality-price specialist	The firm operates at the low- or high-quality ends of the market.
Service specialist	The firm offers one or more services not available from other firms.
Channel specialist	The firm specializes in serving only one channel of distribution.

EXECUTIVE SUMMARY

To develop an effective positioning, a company must study competitors as well as actual and potential customers. A company should identify competitors by using both industry- and market-based analyses. Developing a positioning requires the determination of a frame of reference—by identifying the target market and the resulting nature of the competition—and the optimal points-of-parity and points-of-difference brand associations. The key to competitive advantage is relevant brand differentiation based on the product or service itself or on considerations such as employees, channels, image, or services. Emotional branding is becoming an important way to connect with customers and create differentiation.

Market leaders stay number one by expanding total market demand, protecting current share through good defensive and offensive actions, and increasing market share, even if market size remains constant. Firms that are not market leaders can bid aggressively for more share as market challengers by attacking the leader and other competitors, or they can be market followers rather than challenging the leader. An alternative to being a follower in a large market is to be a leader in a small market or niche.

NOTES

1. Elaine Wong, "With Leering Bubbles and Sexy Detergent, Method Embraces Madness," *Adweek*, June 7, 2010, p. 22; Ilana DeBare, "Cleaning Up without Dot-coms," *San Francisco Chronicle*, October 8, 2006; "Marketers of the Next Generation," *Brandweek*, April 17, 2006, p. 30.
2. Al Ries and Jack Trout, *Positioning: The Battle for Your Mind, 20th Anniversary Edition* (New York: McGraw-Hill, 2000).
3. Michael J. Lanning and Lynn W. Phillips, "Building Market-Focused Organizations," Gemini Consulting White Paper, 1991.
4. Allan D. Shocker, "Determining the Structure of Product-Markets: Practices, Issues, and Suggestions," Barton A. Weitz and Robin Wensley, eds., *Handbook of Marketing* (London: Sage, 2002), pp. 106–25. See also, Bruce H. Clark and David B. Montgomery, "Managerial Identification of Competitors," *Journal of Marketing* 63 (July 1999), pp. 67–83.
5. Jeffrey F. Rayport and Bernard J. Jaworski, *e-Commerce* (New York: McGraw-Hill, 2001), p. 53.
6. For discussion of some long-term implications of marketing, see Koen Pauwels, "How Dynamic Consumer Response, Competitor Response, Company Support, and Company Inertia Shape Long-Term Marketing Effectiveness," *Marketing Science* 23 (Fall 2004), pp. 596–610; Koen Pauwels, Dominique M. Hanssens, and S. Siddarth, "The Long-term Effects of Price Promotions on Category Incidence, Brand Choice, and Purchase Quantity,"

Journal of Marketing Research 34 (November 2002), pp. 421–39; and Marnik Dekimpe and Dominique Hanssens, "Sustained Spending and Persistent Response: A New Look at Long-term Marketing Profitability," *Journal of Marketing Research* 36 (November 1999), pp. 397–412.
7. Kevin Lane Keller, Brian Sternthal, and Alice Tybout, "Three Questions You Need to Ask about Your Brand," *Harvard Business Review*, September 2002, pp. 80–89.
8. Michael Applebaum, "Comfy to Cool: A Brand Swivel," *Brandweek*, May 2, 2005, pp. 18–19.
9. Thomas A. Brunner and Michaela Wänke, "The Reduced and Enhanced Impact of Shared Features on Individual Brand Evaluations," *Journal of Consumer Psychology* 16 (April 2006), pp. 101–11.
10. Patrick Barwise, *Simply Better: Winning and Keeping Customers by Delivering What Matters Most* (Cambridge, MA: Harvard Business School Press, 2004).
11. Kevin Roberts, *Lovemarks: The Future Beyond Brands*, expanded edition (New York: Powerhouse Books, 2005); Kevin Roberts, *The Lovemarks Effect: Winning in the Consumer Revolution* (New York: Powerhouse Books, 2005); "The Lovemarks Heart Beat: January 2010," *Lovemarks*, www.lovemarks.com.
12. James H. Gilmore and B. Joseph Pine II, *Authenticity: What Consumers Really Want* (Cambridge, MA: Harvard Business School Press, 2007); Lynn B. Upshaw, *Truth: The New Rules for Marketing in a Skeptical World* (New York: AMACOM, 2007).

13. Owen Jenkins, "Gimme Some Lovin'," *Marketing News*, May 15, 2009, p. 19.

14. Rajendra S. Sisodia, David B. Wolfe, and Jagdish N. Sheth, *Firms of Endearment: How World-Class Companies Profit from Passion & Purpose* (Upper Saddle River, NJ: Wharton School Publishing, 2007).

15. Nirmalya Kumar, "Strategies to Fight Low-Cost Rivals," *Harvard Business Review,* December 2006, pp. 104–12; Robert J. Frank, Jeffrey P. George, and Laxman Narasimhan, "When Your Competitor Delivers More for Less," *McKinsey Quarterly* (Winter 2004), pp. 48–59. See also, Jan-Benedict E.M. Steenkamp and Nirmalya Kumar, "Don't Be Undersold," *Harvard Business Review,* December 2009, pp. 90–95.

16. Brian Wansink, "Can Package Size Accelerate Usage Volume?" *Journal of Marketing* 60 (July 1996), pp. 1–14; See also, Priya Raghubir and Eric A. Greenleaf, "Ratios in Proportion: What Should the Shape of the Package Be?" *Journal of Marketing* 70 (April 2006), pp. 95–107; and Valerie Folkes and Shashi Matta, "The Effect of Package Shape on Consumers' Judgments of Product Volume: Attention as a Mental Contaminant," *Journal of Consumer Research* 31 (September 2004), pp. 390–401.

17. George Stalk Jr. and Rob Lachanauer, "Hardball: Five Killer Strategies for Trouncing the Competition," *Harvard Business Review* 82 (April 2004), pp. 62–71; Richard D'Aveni, "The Empire Strikes Back: Counterrevolutionary Strategies for Industry Leaders," *Harvard Business Review,* November 2002, pp. 66–74.

18. These six defense strategies and the five attack strategies are from Philip Kotler and Ravi Singh, "Marketing Warfare in the 1980s," *Journal of Business Strategy* (Winter 1981), pp. 30–41.

19. Michael E. Porter, *Market Signals, Competitive Strategy: Techniques for Analyzing Industries and Competitors* (New York: Free Press, 1998), pp. 75–87; Jaideep Prabhu and David W. Stewart, "Signaling Strategies in Competitive Interaction: Building Reputations and Hiding the Truth," *Journal of Marketing Research* 38 (February 2001), pp. 62–72.

20. Roger J. Calantone and Kim E. Schatzel, "Strategic Foretelling: Communication-Based Antecedents of a Firm's Propensity to Preannounce," *Journal of Marketing* 64 (January 2000), pp. 17–30; Jehoshua Eliashberg and Thomas S. Robertson, "New Product Preannouncing Behavior: A Market Signaling Study," *Journal of Marketing Research* 25 (August 1988), pp. 282–92.

21. Wailin Wong, "Motorola Is Selling Wireless Networks Unit to Nokia Siemens," *Los Angeles Times,* July 19, 2010, www.latimes.com.

22. J. Scott Armstrong and Kesten C. Green, "Competitor-Oriented Objectives: The Myth of Market Share," *International Journal of Business* 12, no. 1 (Winter 2007), pp. 115–34; Stuart E. Jackson, *Where Value Hides: A New Way to Uncover Profitable Growth for Your Business* (New York: Wiley, 2006).

23. Nirmalya Kumar, *Marketing as Strategy* (Cambridge, MA: Harvard Business School Press, 2004); Philip Kotler and Paul N. Bloom, "Strategies for High-Market-Share Companies," *Harvard Business Review,* November–December 1975, pp. 63–72.

24. Robert D. Buzzell and Frederick D. Wiersema, "Successful Share-Building Strategies," *Harvard Business Review,* January–February 1981, pp. 135–44.

25. Linda Hellofs and Robert Jacobson, "Market Share and Customer's Perceptions of Quality: When Can Firms Grow Their Way to Higher versus Lower Quality?" *Journal of Marketing* 63 (January 1999), pp. 16–25.

26. Theodore Levitt, "Innovative Imitation," *Harvard Business Review,* September–October 1966, pp. 63. See also, Steven P. Schnaars, *Managing Imitation Strategies: How Later Entrants Seize Markets from Pioneers* (New York: Free Press, 1994).

27. Steve Randazzo, "To Guerilla or Not Guerilla," *Promo,* July 8, 2010, http://promomagazine.com; Lauren Comiteau, "Marketing 0.0: Forget Social Media," *Adweek,* March 22, 2010, p. 10; Cary Hatch, "When Should You Try Guerilla Marketing?" *ABA Bank Marketing,* March 2005, p. 53; Shari Caudron, "Guerrilla Tactics," *IndustryWeek,* July 16, 2001, pp. 53ff.

Setting Product Strategy and Marketing Through the Life Cycle

In this chapter, we will address the following questions:

1. What are the characteristics of products, and how do marketers classify products?
2. How can companies differentiate products?
3. How can a company build and manage its product mix and product lines?
4. How can companies use packaging, labeling, warranties, and guarantees as marketing tools?
5. What strategies are appropriate for new product development and through the product life cycle?

Marketing Management at Ford

Ford Motor Company endured tough times during the years when gas prices were going up and vehicle sales were going down. Perhaps the biggest concern was public perception that Ford products were not high quality. Rejecting government bailouts during the recent recession created some goodwill, but the CEO knew reliable, stylish, and affordable vehicles that performed well would make or break the company's fortunes. A redesigned high-mileage Ford Fusion with innovative electronics and an environmentally friendly hybrid option caught customers' attention, as did the hip, urban-looking seven-seat Ford Flex SUV.

The CEO planned to use Ford's vast infrastructure and scale to create vehicles that, with small adjustments, could easily be sold all over the world. The result of extensive global research, the Ford Fiesta hatchback was a striking example of this world-car concept. The company knew it had a winner when the Fiesta was well received in China, Europe, and the United States. Ford also relied on experiential and social media marketing. Before the U.S. launch, Ford sent 150 Fiestas on tour for test drives and gave 100 to bloggers who shared their experiences online. At a time when the rest of the U.S. auto industry was struggling, the Fiesta garnered thousands of preorders and helped Ford return to profitability.[1]

The customer will judge the offering by three basic elements: product features and quality, services mix and quality, and price, which must be meshed into a competitively attractive offering. To achieve market leadership, firms must offer products and services of superior quality that provide unsurpassed customer value. This chapter discusses product concepts and decisions, new product development, and the product life cycle. Chapter 11 examines services and Chapter 12 explores price.

Product Characteristics and Classifications

A **product** is anything that can be offered to a market to satisfy a want or need, including physical goods, services, experiences, events, persons, places, properties, organizations, information, and ideas.

Product Levels

In planning its market offering, the marketer needs to address five product levels (see Figure 10.1).[2] Each level adds more customer value, and the five constitute a **customer-value hierarchy**. The fundamental level is the *core benefit*: the service or benefit the customer is really buying. A hotel guest is buying rest and sleep. The purchaser of a drill is buying holes. Marketers must see themselves as benefit providers.

At the second level, the marketer must turn the core benefit into a *basic product*. Thus a hotel room includes a bed, bathroom, and towels. At the third level, the marketer prepares an *expected product*, a set of attributes and conditions buyers normally expect when they purchase this product. Hotel guests expect a clean bed, fresh towels, and so on. At the fourth level, the marketer prepares an *augmented product* that exceeds customer expectations. In developed countries, brand positioning and competition take place at this level. In developing and emerging markets, competition takes place mostly at the expected product level. At the fifth level is the *potential product*, all the possible augmentations and transformations the offering might

FIGURE 10.1 Five Product Levels

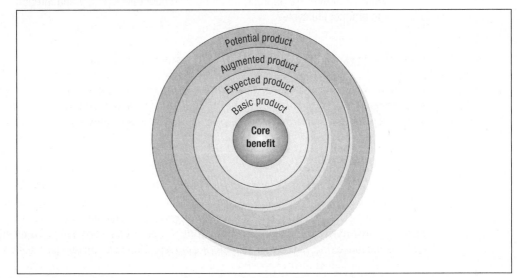

undergo in the future. Here is where companies search for new ways to satisfy customers and distinguish their offering.

Differentiation arises and competition increasingly occurs on the basis of product augmentation, which also leads the marketer to look at the user's total *consumption system*: the way the user gets and uses products and related services.[3] Each augmentation adds cost, however, and augmented benefits soon become expected benefits, forcing competitors to search for still other features and benefits to differentiate themselves. As some companies raise the price of their augmented product, others offer a stripped-down version for less.

Product Classifications

Marketers classify products on the basis of durability, tangibility, and use (consumer or industrial). Each type has an appropriate marketing-mix strategy.[4]

- Durability and tangibility. *Nondurable goods* are tangible goods normally consumed in one or a few uses, such as beer and shampoo. Because these are purchased frequently, the appropriate strategy is to make them available in many locations, charge a small markup, and advertise to induce trial and build preference. *Durable goods* are tangible goods (such as appliances) that survive many uses, require personal selling and service, command a higher margin, and require more seller guarantees. *Services* are intangible, inseparable, variable, and perishable products (such as legal advice) that normally require more quality control, supplier credibility, and adaptability.

- Consumer-goods classification. Classified according to shopping habits, these products include **convenience goods** (such as soft drinks), which are purchased frequently, immediately, and with minimal effort; **shopping goods** (such as major appliances) that consumers compare on the basis of suitability, quality, price, and style; **specialty goods** (such as cars) with unique characteristics or brand identification for which enough buyers are willing to make a special purchasing effort; and **unsought goods** (such as smoke detectors), which the consumer does not know about or normally think of buying.

- Industrial-goods classification. *Materials and parts* are goods that enter the manufacturer's product completely. *Raw materials* can be *farm products* (wheat) or *natural products* (iron ore). *Manufactured materials and parts* can be either component materials (cement) or component parts (small motors). **Capital items** are long-lasting goods that facilitate developing or managing the finished product, including *installations* (factories) and *equipment* (trucks). *Supplies and business services* are short-term goods and services that facilitate developing or managing the finished product.

Product and Services Differentiation

To be branded, products must be differentiated. At one extreme are products that allow little variation, such as chicken, aspirin, and steel. Yet even here, some differentiation is possible: Perdue chickens, Bayer aspirin, and India's Tata Steel have carved out distinct identities. At the other extreme are products capable of high differentiation, such as automobiles and furniture.

Product Differentiation

Marketers face an abundance of differentiation possibilities, including form, features, customization, performance quality, conformance quality, durability, reliability, repairability, and style.[5]

- Form. **Form** refers to the product's size, shape, or physical structure. For example, aspirin can be differentiated by dosage size, shape, color, coating, or action time.
- Features. Most products can be offered with varying **features** that supplement their basic function. A company can identify and select new features by surveying buyers and calculating *customer value* versus *company cost* for each potential feature. It should consider how many people want each feature, the time needed to introduce it, and whether competitors could easily copy it.[6] To avoid "feature fatigue," the company must prioritize features and tell consumers how to use and benefit from them.[7]
- Customization. With **mass customization** a company meets each customer's requirements, on a mass basis, by individually designing products, services, programs, and communications.[8] Customers must know how to express their personal product preferences, however, or be given assistance to best customize a product.[9]
- Performance quality. **Performance quality** is the level at which the product's primary characteristics operate. Firms should design a performance level appropriate to the target market and competition (which is not necessarily the highest level possible) and manage performance quality over time.
- Conformance quality. Buyers expect a high **conformance quality**, the degree to which all produced units are identical and meet promised specifications. A product with low conformance quality will disappoint some buyers.
- Durability. *Durability*, a measure of the product's expected operating life under natural or stressful conditions, is a valued attribute for vehicles and other durable goods. The extra price for durability must not be excessive, however, and the product must not be subject to rapid technological obsolescence.
- Reliability. Buyers normally will pay a premium for *reliability*, a measure of the probability that a product will not malfunction or fail within a specified period.
- Repairability. *Repairability* measures the ease of fixing a product when it malfunctions or fails. Ideal repairability would exist if users could fix the product themselves with little cost in money or time.
- Style. *Style* describes the product's look and feel to the buyer. It creates distinctiveness that is hard to copy, although strong style doesn't always mean high performance. Style plays a key role in the marketing of many brands, including Apple.

Services Differentiation

When the physical product cannot easily be differentiated, the key to competitive success may lie in adding valued services and improving their quality. The main service differentiators are ordering ease, delivery, installation, customer training, customer consulting, and maintenance and repair.

- Ordering ease. How easy is it for the customer to place an order with the company?
- Delivery. How well is the offering delivered to the customer? Today's customers have grown to expect speed: eyeglasses made in one hour. Accuracy and care are important, as well.

- Installation. How is the product made operational in its planned location? Ease of installation is a true selling point for buyers of complex products like heavy equipment.
- Customer training. Training helps the customer's employees use the vendor's equipment properly and efficiently.
- Customer consulting. Sellers can offer data, information systems, and advice services to buyers. Tech firms such as IBM and Oracle have found consulting to be an increasingly essential—and profitable—part of their business.
- Maintenance and repair. Maintenance and repair programs help customers keep purchased products in good working order. Hewlett-Packard and other firms now offer online technical support for customers.

Product returns are an unavoidable reality of doing business, especially with online purchases. One basic service strategy is to eliminate the root causes of controllable returns while developing processes for handling uncontrollable returns.

Design Differentiation

As competition intensifies, design offers a potent way to differentiate and position a company's products and services.[10] **Design** is the totality of features that affect how a product looks, feels, and functions to a consumer. Design offers functional and aesthetic benefits and appeals to both our rational and emotional sides.[11] To the company, a well-designed product is easy to manufacture and distribute. To the customer, a well-designed product is pleasant to look at and easy to open, install, use, repair, and dispose of. The designer must take all these factors into account.[12] Design should penetrate all aspects of the marketing program. In search of a universal identity scheme, Coca-Cola's vice president of global design established four core principles. Each design should reflect bold simplicity, real authenticity, the power of red, and a "familiar yet surprising" nature.[13]

Product and Brand Relationships

Each product can be related to other products to ensure that a firm is offering and marketing the optimal set of products. A **product system** is a group of diverse but related items that function in a compatible manner. For example, the extensive iPod product system includes headphones and headsets, cables and docks, armbands, cases, power and car accessories, and speakers. A **product mix** (also called a **product assortment**) is the set of all products and items a particular seller offers for sale.

A product mix consists of various **product lines**, each a group of products within a product class that is closely related because they perform similar functions, are sold to the same customer groups, are marketed through the same channels, or fall within given price ranges. Michelin has three main product lines: tires, maps, and restaurant-rating services. A *product type* is a group of items within a line that share one of several possible product forms, while an *item* is a distinct unit within a line distinguishable by size, appearance, or another attribute.

The *width* of a product mix refers to how many different product lines the company carries. The *length* of a product mix refers to the total number of items in the mix. The *depth* of a product mix refers to how many variants are offered of each product in the line. The *consistency* of the product mix describes how closely related the various product lines are in end use, production requirements, distribution, or some other way. These four product-mix dimensions permit the company to expand by adding new product lines (widening its product mix), lengthening each product line, adding product variants (deepening its product mix), and pursuing more product-line consistency. Marketers need to conduct product-line analysis to support these decisions.

Product-Line Analysis

In offering a product line, companies normally develop a basic platform and modules that can be added to meet different customer requirements, the way car manufacturers build cars around a basic platform. Product-line managers need to know the sales and profits of each item in their line to determine which items to build, maintain, harvest, or divest.[14] To understand each product line's market profile, marketers use a *product map* to see which competitors' items are competing against their own items. Product mapping also identifies market segments and shows how well the company is positioned to serve the needs of each. Product-line analysis provides information for decisions about length and modernization.

Product-Line Length

Companies seeking high market share and market growth will generally carry longer product lines. Companies that emphasize high profitability will carry shorter lines consisting of carefully chosen items. Increasingly, consumers are growing weary of dense product lines, overextended brands, and feature-laden products (see "Marketing Insight: When Less Is More").

A company lengthens its product line in two ways: line stretching and line filling. **Line stretching** occurs when a company lengthens its product line beyond its current range, whether down-market, up-market, or both ways. A firm may choose a down-market stretch—introducing a lower-priced line—to attract value-priced buyers, battle low-end competitors, or avoid a stagnating middle market. With an up-market stretch, companies seek to achieve more growth, realize higher margins, or position themselves as full-line manufacturers. Firms serving the middle market might stretch their line in both directions.

With *line filling*, a firm adds more items within the product line's present range. Motives for line filling include reaching for incremental profits, satisfying dealers who complain about lost sales because of items missing from the line, utilizing excess capacity, trying to become the leading full-line company, and plugging holes to keep out competitors.

Line Modernization, Featuring, and Pruning

Product lines need to be modernized. Companies plan improvements to encourage customer migration to higher-valued, higher-priced items. They time improvements so they do not appear too early (damaging sales of the current line) or too late (giving competitors time to establish a strong reputation).[15] The firm typically features one item or a few select items in the line or features a high-end item to lend prestige to the line. In addition, marketers must periodically review the entire line for pruning, identifying weak items through sales and cost analysis. One study found that for a big Dutch retailer, a major assortment reduction led to a short-term drop in category sales—yet it attracted new category buyers at the same time, partially offsetting the sales losses among former buyers of the delisted items.[16] Many multibrand companies concentrate resources on their biggest and most established brands.

Product-Mix Pricing

Marketers must modify their price-setting logic when the product is part of a product mix. In **product-mix pricing**, the firm searches for a set of prices that maximizes profits on the total mix. Pricing is difficult because the various products have demand and cost interrelationships and are subject to different degrees of competition. Six product-mix pricing situations are shown in Table 10.1 (on page 176).

WHEN LESS IS MORE

With thousands of new products introduced each year, consumers find it ever harder to navigate store aisles. Recent research indicates that the average shopper spends 40 seconds or more in the supermarket soda aisle, compared to 25 seconds six or seven years ago. Although consumers may think greater product variety increases their likelihood of finding the right product for them, the reality is often different. In one study, although consumers expressed greater interest in shopping with a larger assortment of 24 flavored jams than a smaller assortment of 6, they were 10 times more likely to actually make a selection with the smaller assortment.

Similarly, if the product quality in an assortment is high, consumers would actually prefer a smaller than a larger set of choices. Although consumers with well-defined preferences may benefit from more differentiated products that offer specific benefits to better suit their needs, too much product choice may cause other consumers frustration, confusion, and regret. Also, exposing customers to constant product changes and introductions may nudge them into reconsidering and perhaps switching to a competitor's product. Finally, some products are too complicated for the average consumer. Royal Philips Electronics asked managers to take Philips products home one weekend and see whether they could make them work. The number of executives who returned frustrated and angry spoke volumes about the challenges the ordinary consumer faced.

Sources: Dimitri Kuksov and J. Miguel Villas-Boas, "When More Alternatives Lead to Less Choice," *Marketing Science*, 2010, in press; Kristin Diehl and Cait Poynor, "Great Expectations?! Assortment Size, Expectations, and Satisfaction," *Journal of Marketing Research* 46 (April 2009), pp. 312–22; Joseph P. Redden and Stephen J. Hoch, "The Presence of Variety Reduces Perceived Quantity," *Journal of Consumer Research* 36 (October 2009), pp. 406–17; Alexander Chernev and Ryan Hamilton, "Assortment Size and Option Attractiveness in Consumer Choice Among Retailers," *Journal of Marketing Research* 46 (June 2009), pp. 410–20; Richard A. Briesch, Pradeep K. Chintagunta, and Edward J. Fox, "How Does Assortment Affect Grocery Store Choice," *Journal of Marketing Research* 46 (April 2009), pp. 176–89; Aner Sela, Jonah Berger, and Wendy Liu, "Variety, Vice and Virtue: How Assortment Size Influences Option Choice," *Journal of Consumer Research* 35 (April 2009), pp. 941–51; Susan M. Broniarczyk, "Product Assortment," Curt P. Haugtvedt, Paul M. Herr, and Frank R. Kardes, eds., *Handbook of Consumer Psychology* (New York: Taylor & Francis, 2008), pp. 755–79; Cassie Mogilner, Tamar Rudnick, and Sheena S. Iyengar, "The Mere Categorization Effect," *Journal of Consumer Research* 35 (August 2008), pp. 202–15; Alexander Chernev, "The Role of Purchase Quantity in Assortment Choice," *Journal of Marketing Research* 45 (April 2008), pp. 171–81; John Gourville and Dilip Soman, "Overchoice and Assortment Type: When and Why Variety Backfires," *Marketing Science* 24 (Summer 2005), pp. 382–95; Barry Schwartz, *The Paradox of Choice: Why More Is Less* (New York: HarperCollins Ecco, 2004); Alexander Chernev, "When More Is Less and Less Is More," *Journal of Consumer Research* 30 (September 2003), pp. 170–83; Sheena S. Iyengar and Mark R. Lepper, "When Choice Is Demotivating: Can One Desire Too Much of a Good Thing?" *Journal of Personality and Social Psychology* 79, no. 6 (December 2000), pp. 995–1006.

Co-Branding and Ingredient Branding

Marketers often combine their products with products from other companies in various ways. In **co-branding**—also called dual branding or brand bundling—two or more well-known brands are combined into a joint product or marketed together in some fashion.[17] One form of co-branding is *same-company co-branding*, as when General Mills advertises Trix cereal and Yoplait yogurt. Other forms include *joint-venture co-branding*, *multiple-sponsor co-branding*, and *retail co-branding*.

TABLE 10.1   Product-Mix Pricing Situations

1. *Product-line pricing.* Many sellers introduce price steps within a product line. The seller's task is to establish perceived quality differences that justify the price differences.

2. *Optional-feature pricing.* Automakers and other firms offer optional products, features, and services with their main product. Firms must decide which options to include in the standard price and which to offer separately.

3. *Captive-product pricing.* Some products require the use of ancillary or *captive products*. Manufacturers of razors often price them low and set high markups on blades. If the captive product is priced too high, however, counterfeiting and substitutions can erode sales.

4. *Two-part pricing.* Many service firms charge a fixed fee plus a variable usage fee. For instance, cell phone users pay a monthly fee plus charges for calls that exceed their allotted minutes. The seller must decide how much to charge for basic service and variable usage.

5. *By-product pricing.* The production of certain goods (such as meats) often results in by-products that should be priced on their value. Income from the by-products will make it easier for the firm to charge less for its main product if competition forces it to do so.

6. *Product-bundling pricing. Pure bundling* occurs when a firm offers its products only as a bundle. In *mixed bundling*, the seller offers goods both individually and in bundles, normally charging less for the bundle than for the items purchased separately. Savings on the price bundle must be enough to induce customers to buy it.

Co-branding's main advantage is that a product can be convincingly positioned by virtue of the multiple brands, generating greater sales from the existing market and opening opportunities for new consumers and channels. It can also reduce the cost of product introduction, because it combines two well-known images and speeds adoption. And co-branding may be a valuable means to learn about consumers and how other companies approach them. The potential disadvantages are the risks and lack of control in becoming aligned with another brand. Consumer expectations of co-brands are likely to be high, so unsatisfactory performance could have negative repercussions for both brands. With a high number of co-branding arrangements, overexposure may dilute the transfer of any association and result in a lack of focus on existing brands. Consumers may feel less sure of what they know about the brand.[18]

Ingredient branding is a special case of co-branding.[19] It creates brand equity for materials, components, or parts that are necessarily contained within other branded products. Intel microprocessors and GORE-TEX water-resistant fibers are two successful examples. An interesting take on ingredient branding is "self-branded ingredients" that companies advertise and even trademark. Westin Hotels advertises its own "Heavenly Bed" and "Heavenly Shower." An ingredient brand must create awareness and preference for its product so consumers will not buy a "host" product that doesn't contain it.[20]

Packaging, Labeling, Warranties, and Guarantees

Many marketers have called packaging a fifth P, along with price, product, place, and promotion. Most, however, treat packaging and labeling as an element of product strategy. Warranties and guarantees can also be an important part of the product strategy.

Packaging

Packaging includes all the activities of designing and producing the container for a product. Packages might have up to three layers, a primary package inside a box (secondary package) and then a shipping package for one or more packaged units. The package is the buyer's first encounter with the product, so it must draw the consumer in and encourage product choice. Packaging also affects consumers' experiences when they open the package and use the product at home. Distinctive packaging like that for Altoids mints is an important part of a brand's equity.[21] Of course, marketers have to take into account environmental and safety concerns when planning packaging.

Packaging must achieve a number of objectives.[22] It must identify the brand, convey descriptive and persuasive information, facilitate product transportation and protection, assist at-home storage, and aid product consumption. Aesthetic considerations relate to a package's size and shape, material, color, text, and graphics. The packaging elements must harmonize with each other and with all other parts of the marketing program. Redesigning or updating packaging can be risky: If consumers don't like the new package or confuse it with other brands, they won't buy. After PepsiCo introduced new packaging for its Tropicana juice, sales dropped so much that the firm quickly reverted to the old packaging.[23]

Labeling

The label can be a simple attached tag or an elaborately designed graphic that is part of the package. It might carry a great deal of information, or only the brand name. A label performs several functions. First, it *identifies* the product or brand—for instance, the name Sunkist stamped on oranges. It might also *grade* the product; canned peaches are grade-labeled A, B, and C. The label might *describe* the product: who made it, where and when, what it contains, how it is to be used, and how to use it safely. Finally, the label might *promote* the product through attractive graphics.

Labels eventually need freshening up. The label on Ivory soap has been redone at least 18 times in 120 years, with gradual changes in the lettering. Legal and regulatory requirements must also be considered. For example, processed foods must carry nutritional labeling stating the amounts of protein, fat, carbohydrates, and calories, as well as vitamin and mineral content as a percentage of the recommended daily allowance.[24]

Warranties and Guarantees

All sellers are legally responsible for fulfilling a buyer's normal or reasonable expectations. **Warranties** are formal statements of expected product performance by the manufacturer, and legally enforceable. Products under warranty can be returned to the manufacturer or a repair center for repair, replacement, or refund. Guarantees reduce the buyer's perceived risk and suggest that the product is of high quality and the company and its service performance are dependable. This is especially helpful when the firm or product is not well known or when the product's quality is superior to that of competitors.

Managing New Products

A company can add new products through acquisition (buying another firm, patents from other firms, or a license or franchise) or organically through development from within (using its own laboratories, contracting with independent researchers, or hiring a new-product development firm).[25] New products range from new-to-the-world products that create an entirely new market to minor improvements or revisions of existing products. Most new-product activity is devoted to improving existing products. In contrast, new-to-the-world products incur the greatest cost and risk. Although radical innovations can hurt the company's bottom line in the short run, if they succeed they can create a greater sustainable competitive advantage than ordinary products and produce significant financial rewards as a result.[26]

The Innovation Imperative and New Product Success

New products fail for many reasons: ignored or misinterpreted market research; overestimates of market size; high development costs; poor design or ineffectual performance; incorrect positioning, advertising, or price; insufficient distribution support; competitors who fight back hard; and inadequate ROI or payback. In an economy of rapid change, continuous innovation is a necessity. Highly innovative firms are able to identify and quickly seize new market opportunities. Innovative firms create a positive attitude toward innovation and risk taking, routinize the innovation process, practice teamwork, and allow their people to experiment and even fail. Companies that fail to develop new products leave their existing offerings vulnerable to changing customer needs and tastes, new technologies, shortened product life cycles, and increased competition.

New product specialists Robert Cooper and Elko Kleinschmidt found that unique, superior products succeed 98 percent of the time, compared to products with a moderate advantage (58 percent success) and those with a minimal advantage (18 percent success). Other factors include a well-defined product concept, well-defined target market and benefits, technological and marketing synergy, quality execution, and market attractiveness.[27]

Most established companies focus on *incremental innovation*, entering new markets by tweaking products for new customers, introducing variations on a core product, and creating interim solutions for industry-wide problems. Newer companies create *disruptive technologies* that are cheaper and more likely to alter the competitive space. Established companies can be slow to react or invest in these disruptive technologies because they threaten their investment. Then they suddenly find themselves facing formidable new competitors, and many fail.[28] To avoid this trap, incumbent firms must carefully monitor customer preferences and uncover evolving, difficult-to-articulate needs.[29]

New Product Development

The stages in new product development are shown in Figure 10.2 and discussed next.

Idea Generation   The process starts with the search for ideas (see "Marketing Skills: Finding New Product Ideas"). Some experts believe the greatest opportunities and highest leverage with new products are found by uncovering the best possible set of unmet customer needs or technological innovation.[30] Ideas can come from interacting with customers, scientists, employees, and other groups; from using creativity techniques; and from studying competitors. Companies are increasingly turning to "crowdsourcing" to generate new ideas by inviting the Internet community to help create content or software, often with prize money or a moment of glory as an incentive.[31] Getting the right customers engaged in the right way is critical.[32]

Idea Screening   The next step is to screen out poor ideas early, because product-development costs rise substantially with each successive development stage. Most companies require new-product ideas to be described on a standard form for a new-product committee's review. The description states the product idea, the target market, and the competition, and roughly estimates market size, product price, development time and costs, manufacturing costs, and rate of return. The executive committee then reviews each idea against criteria such as: Does the product meet a need and offer superior value? Can it be distinctively advertised? Does the company have the necessary know-how and capital? Will the new product deliver the expected sales volume, sales growth, and profit? The company also estimates each idea's overall probability of success and determines which warrant continued development.

FIGURE 10.2 The New-Product Development Decision Process

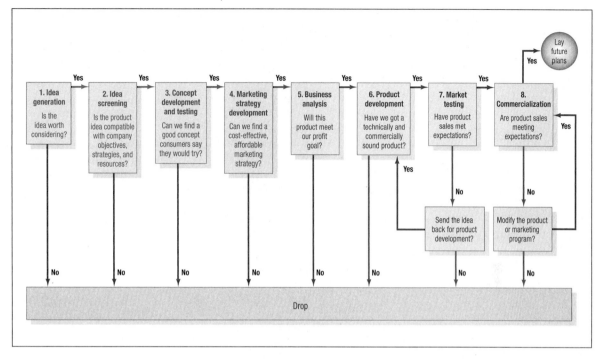

FINDING NEW PRODUCT IDEAS

How do marketers find promising new product ideas? First, view every customer contact as an opportunity to identify unmet or emerging needs, find new ways to solve old problems, or innovatively apply existing technology and techniques to new problems. Observe how customers use the firm's product (and competing products); ask customers to speak up about their likes and dislikes; and tap into feedback gathered by salespeople, service reps, and other employees. Finally, maintain a new-idea database so marketers can review and reassess ideas at any time.

A growing number of marketers are obtaining product ideas through customer interaction on Web sites and in social media. Dell, for example, set up IdeaStorm (www.ideastorm.com) as a central site where customers can post their tech product ideas. Inspired by Dell, Starbucks created a Web site and a Twitter account where customers can share their product ideas (http://mystarbucksidea.force.com, http://twitter.com/mystarbucksidea). Coca-Cola's marketers get product ideas from comments on the brand's Facebook page (www.facebook.com/cocacola). And Philips, the electrical goods manufacturer, collects product ideas through multiple connections on LinkedIn (www.linkedin.com/companies/philips).[33]

FIGURE 10.3 Product and Brand Positioning

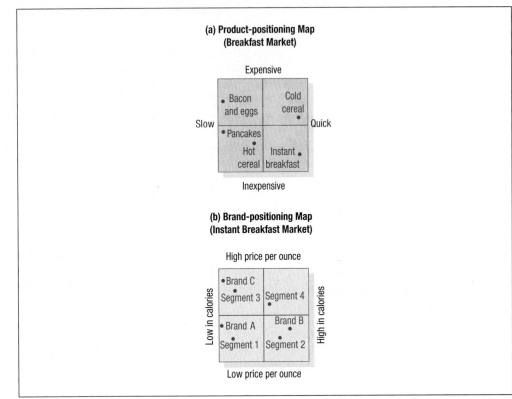

Concept Development   A *product idea* is a possible product the company might offer to the market. A *product concept* is an elaborated version of the idea expressed in consumer terms. A product idea can be turned into several concepts by asking: Who will use this product? What primary benefit should it provide? When will people consume or use it? By answering these questions, a company can form several concepts, select the most promising concept, and create a *product-positioning map* for it. Figure 10.3(a) shows the positioning of a product concept, a low-cost instant breakfast drink, compared to other available breakfast foods. These contrasts can be useful in communicating and promoting a concept to the market.

Next, the product concept is turned into a *brand concept.* To transform the low-cost instant breakfast drink concept into a brand concept, the firm must decide how much to charge and how calorific to make the drink. Figure 10.3(b) shows the positions of three instant breakfast drink brands. The new concept would have to be distinctive in the medium-price, medium-calorie market or the high-price, high-calorie market.

Concept Testing   Concept testing means presenting the product concept to target consumers, physically or symbolically, and getting their reactions. The more the tested concepts resemble the final product or experience, the more dependable concept testing is. In the past, creating physical prototypes was costly and time consuming, but today firms can use *rapid prototyping* to design products on a computer and then produce rough models to show potential consumers for their reactions.

Companies are also using *virtual reality* to test product concepts. Respondents are shown different hypothetical offers formed by combining varying levels of the attributes, then asked to rank the various offers. Management can identify the most appealing offer and its estimated market share and profit. Note that the most customer-appealing offer is not always the most profitable offer for the firm.

Marketing Strategy Development   After a successful concept test, the firm drafts a preliminary three-part strategy for introducing the new product. The first part describes the target market's size, structure, and behavior; the planned product positioning; and the sales, market share, and profit goals sought in the first few years. The second part outlines the planned price, distribution strategy, and marketing budget for the first year. The third part describes the long-run sales and profit goals and marketing-mix strategy over time. This plan forms the basis for the next step, the business analysis.

Business Analysis   The firm evaluates the proposed product's business attractiveness by preparing sales, cost, and profit projections to determine whether they satisfy company objectives. If they do, the concept can move to the development stage. As new information comes in, the business analysis will undergo revision and expansion.

Total estimated sales are the sum of estimated first-time sales, replacement sales, and repeat sales. Sales-estimation methods depend on whether the product is purchased once (such as an engagement ring), infrequently, or often. For one-time products, sales rise at the beginning, peak, and approach zero as the number of potential buyers is exhausted; if new buyers keep entering the market, the curve will not drop to zero. Infrequently purchased products such as automobiles exhibit replacement cycles dictated by physical wear or obsolescence associated with changing styles, features, and performance; therefore, sales forecasting calls for estimating first-time sales and replacement sales separately. For frequently purchased products, the number of first-time buyers initially increases and then decreases as fewer buyers are left (assuming a fixed population). Repeat purchases occur soon, providing the product satisfies some buyers. The sales curve eventually plateaus, representing a level of steady repeat-purchase volume; by this time, the product is no longer a new product. As part of their financial analysis, firms may conduct a breakeven or risk analysis.

Product Development   Up to now, the product has existed only as a word description, a drawing, or a prototype. The next step represents a jump in investment that dwarfs the costs incurred so far. The company will determine whether the product idea can translate into a technically and commercially feasible product.

The job of translating target customer requirements into a working prototype is helped by a set of methods known as *quality function deployment* (QFD). The methodology takes the list of desired *customer attributes* (CAs) generated by market research and turns them into a list of *engineering attributes* (EAs) that engineers can use. For example, customers of a proposed truck may want a certain acceleration rate (CA). Engineers can turn this into the required horsepower and other engineering equivalents (EAs). QFD improves communication between marketers, engineers, and manufacturing people.[34]

The R&D department will develop a prototype that embodies the key attributes in the product-concept statement, performs safely under normal use and conditions, and can be produced within budgeted manufacturing costs; this process is being speeded by virtual reality technology and the Web. When the prototypes are ready, they undergo rigorous functional and customer tests before they enter the marketplace. *Alpha testing* tests the product within the firm to see how it performs in different applications. After refining the prototype further, the company moves to *beta testing* with customers. Consumer testing can take many forms, from bringing consumers into a laboratory to giving them samples to use at home.

Market Testing   After management is satisfied with functional and psychological performance, the product is ready to be branded with a name, logo, and packaging and go into a market test.

TABLE 10.2	Four Methods of Market Testing Consumer Goods
Method	**Description**
Sales-wave research	Consumers who initially try the product at no cost are reoffered it, or a competitor's product, at slightly reduced prices. The offer may be made as many as five times (sales waves), while the company notes how many customers select it again and their reported level of satisfaction.
Simulated test marketing	Thirty to 40 qualified shoppers are asked about brand familiarity and preferences in a specific product category and attend a brief screening of ads. The consumers receive a small amount of money and are invited into a store to shop. The firm notes how many buy the new brand and competing brands and asks consumers why they bought or did not buy. Those who did not buy the new item are given a free sample and are reinterviewed later to determine attitudes, usage, satisfaction, and repurchase intention.
Controlled test marketing	A research firm delivers the product to a panel of participating stores and controls shelf position, pricing, and number of facings, displays, and point-of-purchase promotions to test sales, the impact of local advertising, and determine customers' impressions of the product.
Test markets	The company chooses a few representative cities, sells the trade on carrying the product, and puts on a full marketing communications campaign in those markets. Marketers must decide on the number of test cities, the test duration, and the data to be collected. At the conclusion, they must decide what action to take.

Not all firms undertake market testing. The amount is influenced by the investment cost and risk on the one hand, and the time pressure and research cost on the other. Consumer-products tests seek to estimate four variables: *trial, first repeat, adoption,* and *purchase frequency.* Table 10.2 shows four methods of consumer-goods testing, starting with the least costly and progressing to the most costly.

Business goods also benefit from market testing. Expensive industrial goods and new technologies will normally undergo alpha and beta testing. During beta testing, the company's technical people observe how customers use the product, a practice that often exposes unanticipated problems and alerts the company to customer training and servicing requirements. At trade shows the company can observe how much interest buyers show in the new product, how they react to various features, and how many express purchase intentions or place orders. In distributor and dealer display rooms, products may stand next to the manufacturer's other products and possibly competitors' products, yielding preference and pricing information in the product's normal selling atmosphere. However, customers who come in might not represent the target market, or they might want to place early orders that cannot be filled.

Commercialization   At commercialization, which is the costliest stage in the process, the firm contracts for manufacture or builds or rents a manufacturing facility. It also prepares its communications campaign, which can cost $25 million to $100 million for the first year of a new consumer packaged good introduced nationally.

Market timing is critical. If a firm learns that a competitor is readying a new product, it can choose *first entry* (being first to market, locking up key distributors and customers, and gaining a leadership advantage, although this can backfire if the product hasn't been thoroughly debugged), *parallel entry* (launching at the same time as the competitor may gain both products more attention[35]), or *late entry* (delaying until after the competitor has borne the cost of educating the market and revealed problems to avoid).

Most companies will develop a planned market rollout over time, choosing markets based on potential, the company's local reputation, the cost of filling the pipeline, the cost of communication media, the influence of the area on other areas, and competitive penetration. Small firms select an attractive city and put on a blitz campaign, entering other cities one at a time. Large firms usually launch into a whole region and then move to the next. Companies with national distribution networks, such as auto companies, launch new models nationally. Increasingly, firms are rolling out new products simultaneously across the globe; masterminding a global launch poses challenges, however, and a sequential rollout may still be the best option.[36] Within the rollout markets, the company must target initial distribution and promotion to the best prospect groups.

Because new-product launches often take longer and cost more than expected, it's important to allocate sufficient time and resources—yet not overspend—as the new product gains traction in the marketplace.[37] To coordinate the many tasks in launching a new product, management can use network-planning techniques such as *critical path scheduling (CPS),* which uses a master chart showing the simultaneous and sequential activities that must take place. By estimating how much time each activity takes, planners can estimate project completion time. Any delay in an activity on the critical path will delay the project.[38]

The Consumer-Adoption Process

Adoption is an individual's decision to become a regular user of a product and is followed by the *consumer-loyalty process*. New-product marketers typically aim at early adopters and use the theory of innovation diffusion and consumer adoption to identify them.

Stages in the Adoption Process

An **innovation** is any good, service, or idea that someone *perceives* as new, no matter how long its history. Everett Rogers defines the **innovation diffusion process** as "the spread of a new idea from its source of invention or creation to its ultimate users or adopters."[39] The *consumer-adoption process* covers the mental steps through which an individual passes from first hearing about an innovation to final adoption.[40] These five stages are (1) *awareness* (consumer becomes aware of the innovation but lacks information about it), (2) *interest* (consumer is stimulated to seek information), (3) *evaluation* (consumer considers whether to try the innovation), (4) *trial* (the consumer tries the innovation to estimate its value), and (5) *adoption* (the consumer decides to make full and regular use of the innovation).

Factors Influencing Adoption

Everett Rogers defines a person's level of innovativeness as "the degree to which an individual is relatively earlier in adopting new ideas than the other members of his social system." As Figure 10.4 shows, innovators are the first to adopt something new, while laggards are the last. After a slow start, an increasing number of people adopt the innovation, the number reaches a peak, and then it diminishes as fewer nonadopters remain. The five adopter groups differ in their value orientations and their motives for adopting or resisting the new product.[41]

Personal influence, the effect one person has on another's attitude or purchase probability, has greater significance in some situations and for some individuals than others, and it is more important in evaluation than the other adoption stages. It has more power over late than early adopters and in risky situations.

FIGURE 10.4 Adopter Categorization on the Basis of Relative Time of Adoption of Innovations

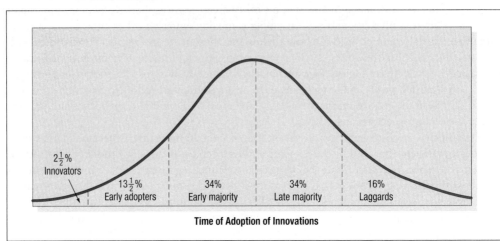

Source: Tungsten, http://en.wikipedia.org/wiki/Everett_Rogers. Based on Everett M. Rogers, *Diffusion of Innovations* (New York: Free Press, 1962).

Five characteristics influence an innovation's rate of adoption. The first is *relative advantage*—the degree to which the innovation appears superior to existing products. The second is *compatibility*—the degree to which the innovation matches the values and experiences of the individuals. Third is *complexity*—the degree to which the innovation is difficult to understand or use. Fourth is *divisibility*—the degree to which the innovation can be tried on a limited basis. Fifth is *communicability*—the degree to which the benefits of use are observable or describable to others. Other characteristics that influence the rate of adoption are cost, risk and uncertainty, scientific credibility, and social approval.

Finally, adoption is associated with variables in the organization's environment (community progressiveness, community income), the organization itself (size, profits, pressure to change), and the administrators (education level, age, sophistication). Other forces come into play in trying to get a product adopted into organizations that receive the bulk of their funding from the government, such as public schools. A controversial or innovative product can be squelched by negative public opinion.

Marketing through the Product Life Cycle

A company's positioning and differentiation strategy must change as the product, market, and competitors change over the *product life cycle (PLC)*. To say a product has a life cycle is to assert that (1) products have a limited life; (2) product sales pass through distinct stages, each posing different challenges and opportunities to the seller; (3) profits rise and fall at different stages; and (4) products require different marketing, financial, manufacturing, purchasing, and human resource strategies in each stage.

Product Life Cycles

Most product life-cycle curves are portrayed as bell-shaped (see Figure 10.5). This curve is typically divided into four stages: introduction, growth, maturity, and decline. In *introduction*, sales grow

FIGURE 10.5 Sales and Profit Life Cycles

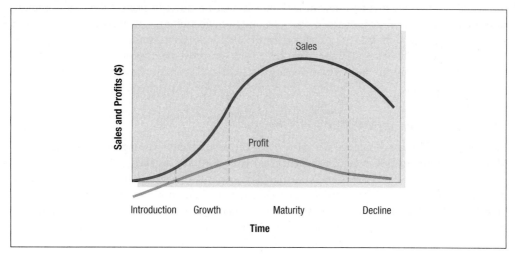

slowly as the product is introduced; profits are nonexistent because of heavy introduction expenses. *Growth* is a period of rapid market acceptance and substantial profit improvement. In *maturity,* sales growth slows because the product has achieved acceptance by most potential buyers, and profits stabilize or decline because of higher competition. In *decline,* sales drift downward and profits erode.

Marketing Strategies: Introduction Stage and the Pioneer Advantage

Because it takes time to roll out a new product, work out the technical problems, fill dealer pipelines, and gain consumer acceptance, sales growth tends to be slow during the introduction.[42] Profits are negative or low, and promotional expenditures are at their highest ratio to sales because of the need to (1) inform potential consumers, (2) induce product trial, and (3) secure distribution.[43]

Being the first to enter the market with a new product can be rewarding, but risky and expensive.[44] When Steven Schnaars studied industries where imitators surpassed innovators, he found several weaknesses among the failing pioneers.[45] These included new products that were too crude, were improperly positioned, or appeared before there was strong demand; development costs that exhausted the innovator's resources; insufficient resources to compete against larger rivals; and managerial incompetence or complacency. Successful imitators offered lower prices, improved the product continuously, or used brute market power to overtake the pioneer.

Gerald Tellis and Peter Golder have identified five factors underpinning long-term market leadership: vision of a mass market, persistence, relentless innovation, financial commitment, and asset leverage.[46] Other research has highlighted the importance of the novelty of the product innovation.[47]

Marketing Strategies: Growth Stage

The growth stage is marked by a rapid climb in sales; early adopters like the product and additional consumers start buying it. As new competitors enter, they introduce new features and expand distribution, and prices stabilize or fall slightly, depending on how fast demand increases. Companies maintain or increase promotional expenditures to meet competition, but sales rise faster than costs. Profits increase as promotion costs are spread over a larger volume, and unit manufacturing costs fall faster than price declines.

To sustain rapid market share growth, the firm must improve product quality, add new features, and improve styling; add new models and flanker products to protect the main product; enter new market segments; increase distribution coverage and enter new channels; shift from awareness and trial communications to preference and loyalty communications; and cut price to attract price-sensitive buyers. By spending on product improvement, promotion, and distribution, the firm can capture a dominant position, trading off maximum current profit for high market share and the hope of greater profits in the next stage.

Marketing Strategies: Maturity Stage

At some point, the rate of sales growth slows, and the product enters a stage of relative maturity. Most products are in this stage of the life cycle, which normally lasts longer than the preceding ones. Three ways to change a brand's course in maturity are market, product, and marketing program modifications. A firm might try to expand the market by increasing the number of brand users (converting nonusers, entering new segments, or attracting competitors' customers) and increasing usage rates among users (getting current customers to use the product on more occasions, use more on each occasion, or use the product in new ways). Managers can also try to stimulate sales by improving the quality, features, or style. Finally, brand managers might try to stimulate sales by modifying nonproduct marketing elements—price, distribution, and communications in particular.

Marketing Strategies: Decline Stage

Sales decline for a number of reasons, including technological advances, shifts in consumer tastes, and increased competition. All can lead to overcapacity, increased price cutting, and profit erosion. As sales and profits decline over a long period of time, some firms withdraw. Those remaining may reduce the number of products they offer, withdraw from smaller segments and weaker channels, cut marketing budgets, and reduce prices further. Unless strong reasons for retention exist, carrying a weak product is often very costly.

A strong competitor in an unattractive industry should consider shrinking selectively; a strong competitor in an attractive industry should consider strengthening its investment. Companies that successfully restage or rejuvenate a mature product often do so by adding value to it. Two other options are harvesting and divesting. *Harvesting* calls for gradually reducing a product or business's costs while trying to maintain sales. When a firm wants to *divest* a product with strong distribution and residual goodwill, it can probably sell the item to another firm. If the company can't find any buyers, it must decide whether to liquidate the brand quickly or slowly.

Critique of the Product Life-Cycle Concept

Table 10.3 summarizes the characteristics, objectives, and strategies in the four product life-cycle stages. In general, the PLC concept helps marketers interpret product and market dynamics, conduct planning and control, and do forecasting. However, critics say that life-cycle patterns are too variable in shape and duration to be generalized, and that marketers can seldom tell what stage their product is in. A product may appear mature when it has actually reached a plateau prior to another upsurge. Critics also say that the PLC pattern is the result of marketing, and that skillful marketing can lead to continued growth.[48] Firms need to visualize a *market's* evolutionary path as it is affected by new needs, competitors, technology, channels, and other developments, then change product and brand positioning to keep pace.[49]

TABLE 10.3	Summary of Product Life-Cycle Characteristics, Objectives, and Strategies			
	Introduction	Growth	Maturity	Decline
Characteristics				
Sales	Low sales	Rapidly rising sales	Peak sales	Declining sales
Costs	High cost per customer	Average cost per customer	Low cost per customer	Low cost per customer
Profits	Negative	Rising profits	High profits	Declining profits
Customers	Innovators	Early adopters	Middle majority	Laggards
Competitors	Few	Growing number	Stable number beginning to decline	Declining number
Marketing Objectives				
	Create product awareness and trial	Maximize market share	Maximize profit while defending market share	Reduce expenditure and milk the brand
Strategies				
Product	Offer a basic product	Offer product extensions, service, warranty	Diversify brands and items	Phase out weak products
Price	Charge cost-plus	Price to penetrate market	Price to match or best competitors'	Cut price
Distribution	Build selective distribution	Build intensive distribution	Build more intensive distribution	Go selective: phase out unprofitable outlets
Communications	Build product awareness and trial among early adopters and dealers	Build awareness and interest in the mass market	Stress brand differences and benefits and encourage brand switching	Reduce to minimal level needed to retain hard-core loyals

Sources: Chester R. Wasson, *Dynamic Competitive Strategy and Product Life Cycles* (Austin, TX: Austin Press, 1978); John A. Weber, "Planning Corporate Growth with Inverted Product Life Cycles," *Long Range Planning* (October 1976), pp. 12–29; Peter Doyle, "The Realities of the Product Life Cycle," *Quarterly Review of Marketing* (Summer 1976).

EXECUTIVE SUMMARY

A product is anything that can be offered to a market to satisfy a want or need. In planning the market offering, the marketer needs to think through the five levels of the product: the core benefit, the basic product, the expected product, the augmented product, and the potential product. Marketers classify products on the basis of durability, tangibility, and use (consumer or industrial). To be branded, products and services must be differentiated. A product mix can be classified according to width, length, depth, and consistency. Physical products must be packaged and labeled, have well-designed packages, and may come with warranties and guarantees.

The new product development process consists of idea generation, idea screening, concept development and testing, marketing strategy development, business analysis, product development, market testing, and commercialization. The adoption process—by which customers learn about, evaluate, and try new products, then adopt or reject them—is influenced by many factors. Each product life-cycle stage (introduction, growth, maturity, and decline) calls for different marketing strategies.

NOTES

1. Guy Bird, "Creating a New Roadmap for One Ford's Marketing," *Marketing Week,* October 28, 2010, www.marketingweek.co.uk/in-depth-analysis/features/creating-a-new-roadmap-for-one-ford%E2%80%99s-marketing/3019775.article; John Frank, "Beep! Beep! Coming Through," *Marketing News,* September 30, 2009, pp. 12–14; David Kiley, "Ford's Savior?" *BusinessWeek*, March 16, 2009, pp. 31–34; Alex Taylor III, "Fixing Up Ford," *Fortune*, May 25, 2009, pp. 45–50; David Kiley, "One Ford for the Whole Wide World," *BusinessWeek*, June 15, 2009, pp. 58–59; "Ford's European Arm Lends a Hand," *Economist*, March 8, 2008, pp. 72–73.

2. This discussion is adapted from a classic article: Theodore Levitt, "Marketing Success through Differentiation: Of Anything," *Harvard Business Review,* January–February 1980, pp. 83–91. The first level, core benefit, has been added to Levitt's discussion.

3. Harper W. Boyd Jr. and Sidney Levy, "New Dimensions in Consumer Analysis," *Harvard Business Review,* November–December 1963, pp. 129–40.

4. For some definitions, see Peter D. Bennett, ed., *Dictionary of Marketing Terms* (Chicago: American Marketing Association, 1995). See also, Patrick E. Murphy and Ben M. Enis, "Classifying Products Strategically," *Journal of Marketing* (July 1986), pp. 24–42.

5. Some of these bases are discussed in David A. Garvin, "Competing on the Eight Dimensions of Quality," *Harvard Business Review,* November–December 1987, pp. 101–9.

6. Marco Bertini, Elie Ofek, and Dan Ariely, "The Impact of Add-on Features on Product Evaluations," *Journal of Consumer Research* 36 (June 2009), pp. 17–28; Tripat Gill, "Convergent Products: What Functionalities Add More Value to the Base," *Journal of Marketing* 72 (March 2008), pp. 46–62; Robert J. Meyer, Sheghui Zhao, and Jin K. Han, "Biases in Valuation vs. Usage of Innovative Product Features," *Marketing Science* 27 (November–December 2008), pp. 1083–96.

7. Paul Kedrosky, "Simple Minds," *Business 2.0,* April 2006, p. 38; Debora Viana Thompson, Rebecca W. Hamilton, and Roland Rust, "Feature Fatigue," *Journal of Marketing Research* 42 (November 2005), pp. 431–42.

8. James H. Gilmore and B. Joseph Pine, *Markets of One* (Boston: Harvard Business School Press, 2000).

9. Nikolaus Franke, Peter Keinz, and Christoph J. Steger, "Testing the Value of Customization," *Journal of Marketing* 73 (September 2009), pp. 103–21.

10. Bruce Nussbaum, "The Power of Design," *BusinessWeek,* May 17, 2004, pp. 88–94; "Masters of Design," *Fast Company*, June 2004, pp. 61–75. See also, Philip Kotler, "Design: A Powerful but Neglected Strategic Tool," *Journal of Business Strategy* (Fall 1984), pp. 16–21.

11. Ravindra Chitturi, Rajagopal Raghunathan, and Vijay Mahajan, "Delight by Design: The Role of Hedonic Versus Utilitarian Benefits," *Journal of Marketing* 72 (May 2008), pp. 48–63.

12. Ulrich R. Orth and Keven Malkewitz, "Holistic Package Design and Consumer Brand Impressions," *Journal of Marketing* 72 (May 2008), pp. 64–81; Mark Borden, "Less Hulk, More Bruce Lee," *Fast Company*, April 2007, pp. 86–91.

13. Linda Tischler, "Pop Artist David Butler," *Fast Company*, October 2009, pp. 91–97; Jessie Scanlon, "Coca-Cola's New Design Direction," *BusinessWeek*, August 25, 2008.

14. A Yesim Orhun, "Optimal Product Line Design When Consumers Exhibit Choice Set-Dependent Preferences," *Marketing Science* 28 (September–October 2009), pp. 868–86; Robert Bordley, "Determining the Appropriate Depth and Breadth of a Firm's Product Portfolio," *Journal of Marketing Research* 40 (February 2003), pp. 39–53; Peter Boatwright and Joseph C. Nunes, "Reducing Assortment: An Attribute-Based Approach," *Journal of Marketing* 65 (July 2001), pp. 50–63.

15. Brett R. Gordon, "A Dynamic Model of Consumer Replacement Cycles in the PC Processor Industry," *Marketing Science* 28 (September–October 2009), pp. 846–67; Raghunath Singh Rao, Om Narasimhan, and George John, "Understanding the Role of Trade-Ins in Durable Goods Markets," *Marketing Science* 28 (September–October 2009), pp. 950–67.

16. Laurens M. Sloot, Dennis Fok, and Peter Verhoef, "The Short- and Long-Term Impact of an Assortment Reduction on Category Sales," *Journal of Marketing Research* 43 (November 2006), pp. 536–48.

17. Akshay R. Rao, Lu Qu, and Robert W. Ruekert, "Signaling Unobservable Quality through a Brand Ally," *Journal of Marketing Research* 36 (May 1999), pp. 258–68; Akshay R. Rao and Robert W. Ruekert, "Brand Alliances as Signals of Product Quality," *Sloan Management Review* (Fall 1994), pp. 87–97.

18. Tansev Geylani, J. Jeffrey Inman, and Frenkel Ter Hofstede, "Image Reinforcement or Impairment: The Effects of Co-Branding on Attribute Uncertainty,"

Marketing Science 27 (July–August 2008), pp. 730–44; Ed Lebar, Phil Buehler, Kevin Lane Keller, Monika Sawicka, Zeynep Aksehirli, and Keith Richey, "Brand Equity Implications of Joint Branding Programs," *Journal of Advertising Research* 45 (December 2005).

19. Philip Kotler and Waldermar Pfoertsch, *Ingredient Branding: Making the Invisible Visible* (Heidelberg, Germany: Springer-Verlag, 2011).

20. Joe Tradii, "Ingredient Branding: Time to Check That Recipe Again," *Brandweek*, March 29, 2010, p. 44; Piet Levy, "B-to-B-to-C," *Marketing News*, September 30, 2009, pp. 15–20.

21. Fred Richards, "Memo to CMOs: It's The Packaging, Stupid," *Brandweek*, August 17, 2009, p. 22.

22. Susan B. Bassin, "Value-Added Packaging Cuts through Store Clutter," *Marketing News,* September 26, 1988, p. 21.

23. Stuart Elliott, "Tropicana Discovers Some Buyers Are Passionate About Packaging," *New York Times*, February 23, 2009; Natalie Zmuda, "Tropicana Line's Sales Plunge 20% Post-Rebranding," *Advertising Age*, April 2, 2009.

24. John C. Kozup, Elizabeth H. Creyer, and Scot Burton, "Making Healthful Food Choices: The Influence of Health Claims and Nutrition Information on Consumers' Evaluations of Packaged Food Products and Restaurant Menu Items," *Journal of Marketing* 67 (April 2003), pp. 19–34; Siva K. Balasubramanian and Catherine Cole, "Consumers' Search and Use of Nutrition Information," *Journal of Marketing* 66 (July 2002), pp. 112–27.

25. For an overview of different industry approaches, see Frank T. Rothaermel and Andrew M. Hess, "Innovation Strategies Combined," *MIT Sloan Management Review* (Spring 2010), pp. 13–15. See also, Stephen J. Carson, "When to Give Up Control of Outsourced New-Product Development," *Journal of Marketing* 71 (January 2007), pp. 49–66.

26. Shuba Srinivasan, Koen Pauwels, Jorge Silva-Risso, and Dominique M. Hanssens, "Product Innovations, Advertising and Stock Returns," *Journal of Marketing* 73 (January 2009), pp. 24–43; Alina B. Sorescu and Jelena Spanjol, "Innovation's Effect on Firm Value and Risk: Insights from Consumer Packaged Goods," *Journal of Marketing* 72 (March 2008), pp. 114–32; Sungwook Min, Manohar U. Kalwani, and William T. Robinson, "Market Pioneer and Early Follower Survival Risks," *Journal of Marketing* 70 (January 2006), pp. 15–33; C. Page Moreau, Arthur B. Markman, and Donald R. Lehmann, "'What Is It?' Category Flexibility and Consumers' Response to Really New Products," *Journal of Consumer Research* 27 (March 2001), pp. 489–98.

27. Robert G. Cooper and Elko J. Kleinschmidt, *New Products: The Key Factors in Success* (Chicago: American Marketing Association, 1990).

28. Clayton M. Christensen, *Disrupting Class: How Disruptive Innovation Will Change the Way the World Learns* (New York: McGraw-Hill, 2008); Clayton M. Christensen, *The Innovator's Solution: Creating and Sustaining Successful Growth* (Boston: Harvard University Press, 2003); Clayton M. Christensen, *The Innovator's Dilemma* (Boston: Harvard University Press, 1997).

29. Ely Dahan and John R. Hauser, "Product Development: Managing a Dispersed Process," Bart Weitz and Robin Wensley, eds., *Handbook of Marketing* (London: Sage, 2002), pp. 179–222.

30. John Hauser, Gerard J. Tellis, and Abbie Griffin, "Research on Innovation: A Review and Agenda for Marketing Science," *Marketing Science* 25 (November–December 2006), pp. 687–717.

31. Jeff Howe, *Crowdsourcing: Why the Power of the Crowd Is Driving the Future of Business* (New York: Crown Business, 2008).

32. Helena Yli-Renko and Ramkumar Janakiraman, "How Customer Portfolio Affects New Product Development in Technology-Based Firms," *Journal of Marketing* 72 (September 2008), pp. 131–48; Donna L. Hoffman, Praveen K. Kopalle, and Thomas P. Novak, "The 'Right' Consumers for Better Concepts," *Journal of Marketing Research,* 47 (October 2010), in press.

33. Mark Choueke, "Q&A with Alexandra Wheeler of Starbucks," *Marketing Week*, August 12, 2010, www.marketingweek.co.uk; Sean Hargrave, "Social Media Research," *New Media Age,* August 5, 2010, www.nma.co.uk; Steve Hamm, "Speed Demons," *BusinessWeek,* March 27, 2006, pp. 69–76.

34. John Hauser, "House of Quality," *Harvard Business Review,* May–June 1988, pp. 63–73. Customer-driven engineering is also called "quality function deployment." See, Lawrence R. Guinta and Nancy C. Praizler, *The QFD Book: The Team Approach to Solving Problems and Satisfying Customers through Quality Function Deployment* (New York: AMACOM, 1993); and V. Srinivasan, William S. Lovejoy, and David Beach, "Integrated Product Design for Marketability and Manufacturing," *Journal of Marketing Research* 34, no. 1 (February 1997), pp. 154–63.

35. Remco Prins and Peter C. Verhoef, "Marketing Communication Drivers of Adoption Timing of a New E-Service among Existing Customers," *Journal of Marketing* 71 (April 2007), pp. 169–83.

36. Yvonne van Everdingen, Dennis Folk, and Stefan Stremersch, "Modeling Global Spillover in New

Product Takeoff," *Journal of Marketing Research*, 46 (October 2009), pp. 637–52; Katrijn Gielens and Jan-Benedict E. M. Steenkamp, "Drivers of Consumer Acceptance of New Packaged Goods," *International Journal of Research in Marketing* 24 (June 2007), pp. 97–111; Marc Fischer, Venkatesh Shankar, and Michael Clement, "Can a Late Mover Use International Market Entry Strategy to Challenge the Pioneer?" Marketing Science Institute Working Paper 05-118, Cambridge, MA; Venkatesh Shankar, Gregory S. Carpenter, and Lakshman Krishnamukthi, "Late Mover Advantages," *Journal of Marketing Research* 35 (February 1998), pp. 54–70.

37. Mark Leslie and Charles A. Holloway, "The Sales Learning Curve," *Harvard Business Review*, July–August 2006, pp. 114–23.

38. For details, see Keith G. Lockyer, *Critical Path Analysis and Other Project Network Techniques* (London: Pitman, 1984); see also, Arvind Rangaswamy and Gary L. Lilien, "Software Tools for New-Product Development," *Journal of Marketing Research* 34, no. 1 (February 1997), pp. 177–84.

39. The following discussion leans heavily on Everett M. Rogers, *Diffusion of Innovations* (New York: Free Press, 1962). Also see his third edition, published in 1983.

40. C. Page Moreau, Donald R. Lehmann, and Arthur B. Markman, "Entrenched Knowledge Structures and Consumer Response to New Products," *Journal of Marketing Research* 38 (February 2001), pp. 14–29.

41. Everett M. Rogers, *Diffusion of Innovations* (New York: Free Press, 1962), p. 192; Geoffrey A. Moore, *Crossing the Chasm: Marketing and Selling High-Tech Products to Mainstream Customers* (New York: HarperBusiness, 1999); for an interesting application with services, see Barak Libai, Eitan Muller, and Renana Peres, "The Diffusion of Services," *Journal of Marketing Research* 46 (April 2009), pp. 163–75.

42. Robert D. Buzzell, "Competitive Behavior and Product Life Cycles," John S. Wright and Jack Goldstucker, eds., *New Ideas for Successful Marketing* (Chicago: American Marketing Association, 1956), p. 51.

43. Rajesh J. Chandy, Gerard J. Tellis, Deborah J. MacInnis, and Pattana Thaivanich, "What to Say When: Advertising Appeals in Evolving Markets," *Journal of Marketing Research* 38 (November 2001), pp. 399–414.

44. Glen L. Urban et al., "Market Share Rewards to Pioneering Brands," *Management Science* (June 1986), pp. 645–59; William T. Robinson and Claes Fornell, "Sources of Market Pioneer Advantages in Consumer Goods Industries," *Journal of Marketing Research* (August 1985), pp. 305–17.

45. Steven P. Schnaars, *Managing Imitation Strategies* (New York: Free Press, 1994). See also, Jin K. Han, Namwoon Kim, and Hony-Bom Kin, "Entry Barriers: A Dull-, One-, or Two-Edged Sword for Incumbents?" *Journal of Marketing* (January 2001), pp. 1–14.

46. Gerald Tellis and Peter Golder, *Will and Vision: How Latecomers Can Grow to Dominate Markets* (New York: McGraw-Hill, 2001); Rajesh K. Chandy and Gerald J. Tellis, "The Incumbent's Curse? Incumbency, Size, and Radical Product Innovation," *Journal of Marketing Research* (July 2000), pp. 1–17.

47. Sungwook Min, Manohar U. Kalwani, and William T. Robinson, "Market Pioneer and Early Follower Survival Risks," *Journal of Marketing* 70 (January 2006), pp. 15–35. See also, Raji Srinivasan, Gary L. Lilien, and Arvind Rangaswamy, "First In, First Out? The Effects of Network Externalities on Pioneer Survival," *Journal of Marketing* 68 (January 2004), pp. 41–58.

48. Youngme Moon, "Break Free from the Product Life Cycle," *Harvard Business Review,* May 2005, pp. 87–94.

49. Hubert Gatignon and David Soberman, "Competitive Response and Market Evolution," Barton A. Weitz and Robin Wensley, eds., *Handbook of Marketing* (London, UK: Sage Publications, 2002), pp. 126–47; Robert D. Buzzell, "Market Functions and Market Evolution," *Journal of Marketing* 63 (Special Issue 1999), pp. 61–63.

chapter 11

Designing and Managing Services

In this chapter, we will address the following questions:

1. How are services defined and classified?
2. What are the new services realities?
3. How can firms improve service quality?
4. How can goods marketers improve customer-support services?

Marketing Management at Cirque du Soleil

Cirque du Soleil (French for "circus of the sun") puts traditional circus elements such as trapeze artists, clowns, and contortionists into a nontraditional setting with lavish costumes, new age music, and spectacular stage designs. Each production is loosely tied together with a theme such as "a tribute to the nomadic soul" (Varekai). The group has grown from its Quebec street-performance roots to become a global service enterprise with 5,000 employees on four continents entertaining millions of people annually.

The company creates one new production each year. In addition to Cirque's mix of media and local promotion, an extensive interactive e-mail program to its million-plus-member Cirque Club creates an online community of fans—and 20 percent to 30 percent of all ticket sales come from club members. Generating $800 million in revenue annually, the Cirque du Soleil brand has expanded to encompass a record label, a retail operation, and resident productions in Las Vegas, Orlando, Tokyo, and other cities.[1]

Many product marketers find significant profitability in delivering superior service, whether that means on-time delivery, better and faster answering of inquiries, or quicker complaint resolution. Top service providers such as Cirque du Soleil know these advantages well and also how to create memorable customer experiences.[2] In this chapter, we systematically analyze services and how to market them most effectively.

The Nature of Services

Service industries are everywhere. The *government sector* has courts, employment services, military services, police and fire departments, postal service, regulatory agencies, and schools. Services in the *private nonprofit sector* include museums, charities, churches, colleges, and hospitals. A good part of the *business sector,* with its airlines, banks, hotels, law firms, consulting firms, plumbing repair companies, and real estate firms, is in the service business. Many workers in the *manufacturing sector,* such as accountants and legal staff, are service providers, making up a "service factory" providing services to the "goods factory." And those in the *retail sector,* such as cashiers and salespeople, are also providing a service.

A **service** is any act or performance one party can offer to another that is essentially intangible and does not result in the ownership of anything. Its production may or may not be tied to a physical product. Increasingly, manufacturers, distributors, and retailers are providing value-added services or excellent customer service, to differentiate themselves. Many pure service firms are now using the Internet to reach customers; some are only online.

Categories of Service Mix

The service component can be a major or minor part of the total offering. Five categories of offerings are:

1. *Pure tangible good*—a tangible good such as toothpaste, with no accompanying services.
2. *Tangible good with accompanying services*—a tangible good, like a cell phone, accompanied by one or more services. Typically, the more technologically advanced the product, the greater the need for high-quality supporting services.
3. *Hybrid*—an offering, like a restaurant meal, of equal parts goods and services.
4. *Major service with accompanying minor goods and services*—a major service, like air travel, with additional services or supporting goods such as drinks.
5. *Pure service*—primarily an intangible service, such as babysitting or psychotherapy.

Customers cannot judge the technical quality of some services even after they have received them, as shown in Figure 11.1.[3] At the left are goods high in *search qualities*—that is, characteristics the buyer can evaluate before purchase. In the middle are goods and services high in *experience qualities*—characteristics the buyer can evaluate after purchase. At the right are goods and services high in *credence qualities*—characteristics the buyer normally finds hard to evaluate even after consumption.[4]

Because services are generally high in experience and credence qualities, there is more risk in their purchase. As a result, service consumers generally rely on word of mouth rather than advertising. They also rely heavily on price, provider, and physical cues to judge quality, and are highly loyal to service providers who satisfy them. Finally, because switching costs are high, consumer inertia can make it challenging to entice business away from a competitor.

FIGURE 11.1 Continuum of Evaluation for Different Types of Products

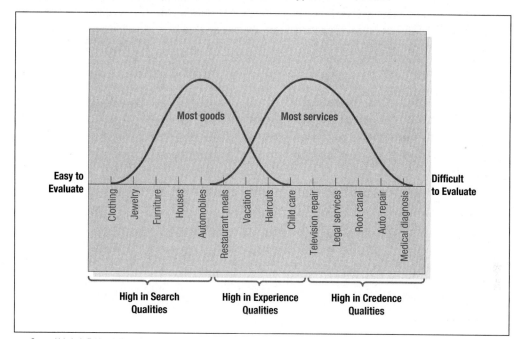

Source: Valarie A. Zeithaml, "How Consumer Evaluation Processes Differ Between Goods and Services," in *Marketing of Services,* ed. James H. Donnelly and William R. George, (Chicago: American Marketing Association, 1981). Reprinted with permission of the American Marketing Association.

Distinctive Characteristics of Services

Four distinctive service characteristics greatly affect the design of marketing programs: *intangibility, inseparability, variability,* and *perishability.*

Intangibility   Unlike physical products, services cannot be seen, tasted, felt, heard, or smelled before they are bought. A person getting cosmetic surgery cannot see the results before the purchase, for instance. To reduce uncertainty, buyers will look for evidence of quality by drawing inferences from the place, people, equipment, facilities, communications, symbols, and price. Therefore, the service provider's task is to "manage the evidence," to "tangibilize the intangible."[5] Service firms can try to demonstrate their service quality through *physical evidence* and *presentation.*[6]

Inseparability   Whereas physical goods are manufactured, then inventoried, then distributed, and later consumed, services are typically produced and consumed simultaneously.[7] Because the client is often present, provider–client interaction is a special feature of services marketing. Several strategies exist for getting around the limitations of inseparability. When clients have strong provider preferences, the service provider can raise its price to ration its limited time. The provider can also work with larger groups, work faster, or train more providers and build up client confidence.

Variability   Services are highly variable because the quality depends on who provides them, when and where, and to whom. To reassure customers, some firms offer *service guarantees* that may reduce perceptions of risk.[8] Three steps to increase the quality control of services are to (1) invest in good hiring and training procedures, (2) standardize the service-performance process, and (3) monitor customer satisfaction. Firms can also develop customer information databases and systems for more personalized service, especially online.[9] Knowing that services are a subjective experience, service firms can design communications so consumers learn more about the brand beyond what they get from service encounters alone.

Perishability   Services cannot be stored, so their perishability can be a problem when demand fluctuates. Public transportation companies must own much more equipment because of rush-hour demand than if demand were even throughout the day. Demand or yield management is critical—the right services must be available to the right customers at the right places at the right times and right prices to maximize profitability.

Several strategies can produce a better match between service demand and supply.[10] On the demand side, these include shifting some demand from peak to off-peak periods (such as pricing morning movies lower), cultivating nonpeak demand (the way McDonald's promotes breakfast service), offering complementary services as alternatives (the way banks offer ATMs), and using reservation systems to manage demand (airlines do this). On the supply side, strategies include adding part-time employees to handle peak demand, having employees perform only essential tasks during peak periods, increasing consumer participation (having shoppers bag their own groceries), sharing services (hospitals sharing medical-equipment purchases), and having facilities for future expansion.

The New Services Realities

Although service firms once lagged behind manufacturers in their use of marketing, now service firms are among the most skilled marketers. Yet in many service industries, such as airlines, banks, stores, and hotels, customer satisfaction in the United States has not significantly improved—or in some cases actually dropped—in recent years.[11] This is just one indicator of the shifting relationship between service providers and their customers.

A Shifting Customer Relationship

Savvy services marketers must recognize three new services realities: the newly empowered customer, customer coproduction, and the need to engage employees as well as customers.

Customer Empowerment   Customers are more sophisticated about buying support services and are pressing for "unbundled services" so they can select the elements they want. Customers also dislike having to deal with a multitude of service providers handling different types of equipment. The Internet has empowered customers by letting them vent their rage about bad service—or reward good service—with a mouse click. Although a person who has a good service experience is more likely to talk about it, someone who has a bad experience will talk to more people.[12] No wonder most companies respond quickly and work hard to prevent and correct dissatisfaction (see "Marketing Skills: Service Recovery").

Customer Coproduction   The reality is that customers do not merely purchase and use a service; they play an active role in its delivery.[13] Their words and actions affect the quality of their service experiences and those of others, and the productivity of frontline employees. This coproduction can put stress on employees, however, and reduce their satisfaction, especially if they differ culturally or in other ways from customers.[14] One study estimated that one-third of all service problems are caused by the customer.[15]

Marketing Skills

SERVICE RECOVERY

With good service recovery skills, marketers can turn a bad service experience into an opportunity for strengthening bonds with customers. Service recovery starts with an intense focus on understanding and meeting customers' needs so marketers can anticipate potential problems and plan appropriate solutions. Many firms use cross-training and empower frontline employees to solve problems on the spot. Service employees must listen carefully, ask tactful questions to clarify the situation, apologize when appropriate, and promptly offer a solution acceptable both to the customer and the company. Finally, the firm should inform customers of what will happen and when—and follow up to ensure satisfaction.

A growing number of companies have customer-service specialists monitoring dedicated social media accounts to quickly respond to complaints and problems. Delta Air Lines, for example, has a Twitter account devoted to service issues (http://twitter.com/DeltaAssist). Customers who post messages about lost luggage, missed connections, and other concerns get a speedy, friendly response from Delta's customer-service reps, with details exchanged via direct message to protect customer privacy. "The whole idea is to work to address issues so they don't escalate," says a Delta spokesperson.[16]

Preventing service failures is crucial, since recovery is always challenging. Although many firms have well-designed and executed procedures to deal with their own failures, they find managing customer failures much more difficult. Figure 11.2 (on page 196) displays the four broad causes of customer failures. Solutions include redesigning processes and customer roles to simplify service encounters; using technology to aid customers and employees; enhancing customer role clarity, motivation, and ability; and encouraging customers to help each other.[17]

Satisfying Employees as Well as Customers Excellent service companies know that positive employee attitudes will promote stronger customer loyalty.[18] Instilling a strong customer orientation in employees can also increase their job satisfaction and commitment. Employees thrive in customer-contact positions when they have an internal drive to (1) pamper customers, (2) accurately read customer needs, (3) develop a personal relationship with customers, and (4) deliver quality service to solve customers' problems.[19] Given the importance of positive employee attitudes to customer satisfaction, service companies must attract the best employees they can find. They need to market a career, design a sound training program, audit job satisfaction, and support and reward good performance.

Marketing Excellence

The increased importance of the service industry has sharpened the focus on what it takes to excel in the marketing of services.[20] In this sector, marketing requires excellence in three broad areas: external, internal, and interactive marketing.[21] *External marketing* describes the normal work of preparing, pricing, distributing, and promoting the service to customers. *Internal marketing* describes training and motivating employees to serve customers well. The marketing department must be "exceptionally clever in getting everyone else in the organization to practice marketing."[22]

FIGURE 11.2 Root Causes of Customer Failure

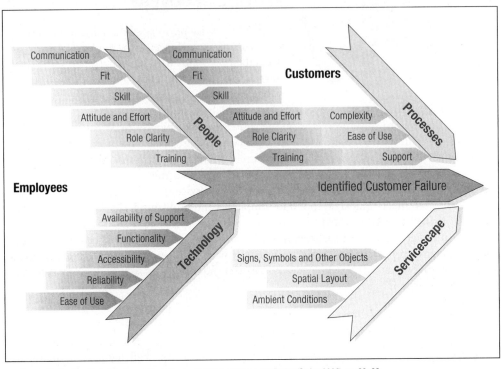

Source: Stephen Tax, Mark Colgate, and David Bowen, *MIT Sloan Management Review* (Spring 2006), pp. 30–38.

Interactive marketing describes the employees' skill in serving the client. Clients judge service not only by its *technical quality* (Was the surgery successful?), but also by its *functional quality* (Did the surgeon show concern and inspire confidence?).[23] In interactive marketing, teamwork is often key, and delegating authority to frontline employees can allow for greater service flexibility and adaptability.[24] Technology also has great power to make service workers more productive.

Companies must avoid pushing productivity so hard that they reduce perceived quality. Some methods lead to too much standardization. Service providers must deliver "high touch" as well as "high tech." Amazon.com has some of the most amazing technological innovations in online retailing, but it also keeps customers extremely satisfied when a problem arises even if they don't actually talk to an Amazon.com employee.[25]

In achieving marketing excellence, well-managed service companies share a strategic concept, a history of top-management commitment to quality, high standards, profit tiers, and systems for monitoring service performance and customer complaints.

Strategic Concept   Top service companies are "customer obsessed." They have a clear sense of their target customers and their needs and have developed a distinctive strategy for satisfying these needs.

Top-Management Commitment   Companies such as Marriott and USAA have a thorough commitment to service quality. Their managements look monthly not only at financial performance, but also at service performance. Sam Walton of Walmart required the following employee pledge: "I solemnly swear and declare that every customer that comes within 10 feet of me, I will smile, look them in the eye, and greet them, so help me Sam."

High Standards   The best service providers set high quality standards. The standards must be set *appropriately* high. A 98 percent accuracy standard may sound good, but it would result in 3 million lost USPS mail pieces each day and no electricity 8 days per year.

Profit Tiers   Firms have decided to raise fees and lower services to those customers who barely pay their way, and to coddle big spenders to retain their patronage as long as possible. Customers in high-profit tiers get special discounts, promotional offers, and lots of service; customers in lower-profit tiers may get more fees, stripped-down service, and voice messages to process their inquiries. Companies that provide differentiated levels of service must be careful about claiming superior service, however—customers who receive lesser treatment will bad-mouth the company and injure its reputation.

Monitoring Systems   Top firms audit service performance, both their own and competitors', on a regular basis. They collect *voice of the customer (VOC) measurements* to probe customer satisfiers and dissatisfiers. They use comparison shopping, mystery or ghost shopping, customer surveys, suggestion and complaint forms, service-audit teams, and customers' letters to the president.

Satisfying Customer Complaints   On average, 40 percent of customers who suffer through a bad service experience stop doing business with the company.[26] Companies that encourage disappointed customers to complain—and also empower employees to remedy the situation on the spot—have been shown to achieve higher revenues and greater profits than companies without a systematic approach for addressing service failures.[27] Customers evaluate complaint incidents in terms of the outcomes they receive, the procedures used to arrive at those outcomes, and the nature of interpersonal treatment during the process.[28] Companies also are increasing the quality of their call centers and their customer service representatives (see "Marketing Insight: Improving Company Call Centers," page 198).

Differentiating Services

Marketers can differentiate their service offerings in many ways. What the customer expects is called the *primary service package*. The provider can then add *secondary service features* to the package. In the hotel industry, various chains have introduced such secondary service features as free breakfast buffets and loyalty programs. The major challenge is that most service offerings and innovations are easily copied. Still, the company that regularly introduces innovations will gain a succession of temporary advantages over competitors. Moreover, many companies are using the Web to offer primary or secondary service features that were never possible before.

Managing Service Quality

Service quality is tested at each service encounter. According to one study, the factors that cause customers to switch services fall into eight categories: pricing, inconvenience, core service failure, service encounter failures, response to service failure, competition, ethical problems, and involuntary switching.[29] Two important considerations in delivering service quality are managing customer expectations and incorporating self-service technologies.

Marketing   Insight

IMPROVING COMPANY CALL CENTERS

Many firms have learned the hard way that empowered customers will no longer put up with poor service when contacting companies. After Sprint and Nextel merged, they ran their call centers as cost centers, rather than a means to enhance customer loyalty. Employees were rewarded for keeping calls short, and when management started to monitor even bathroom trips, morale sank. With customer churn spinning out of control, Sprint Nextel began emphasizing good service over efficiency and rewarding call center employees for solving problems on a customer's first call, rather than for keeping calls short.

Some firms are getting smarter about the type of calls they send to overseas call centers. They are investing more in training as well as sending more complex calls to highly experienced domestic customer service reps. Managing the number of customer service reps is also important. One study found that if just four reps are cut from a call center of three dozen, the number of customers put on hold for four minutes or more will soar from zero to eighty. Finally, cross-training is boosting productivity. USAA, for example, cross-trains call center reps so that agents who answer customers' investment queries can also respond to insurance-related calls.

Sources: Penny Crosman, "Citi, USAA Execs Share Social Media Best Practices," *Bank Systems & Technology,* May 14, 2010, www.banktech.com; Michael Sanserino and Cari Tuna, "Companies Strive Harder to Please Customers," *Wall Street Journal,* July 27, 2009, p. B4; Spencer E. Ante, "Sprint's Wake-Up Call," *BusinessWeek,* March 3, 2008, pp. 54–57; Jena McGregor, "Customer Service Champs," *BusinessWeek,* March 5, 2007; Jena McGregor, "When Service Means Survival," *BusinessWeek,* March 2, 2009, pp. 26–30.

Managing Customer Expectations

Customers form service expectations from many sources, such as past experiences, word of mouth, and advertising. In general, customers compare the *perceived service* with the *expected service.*[30] If the perceived service falls below the expected service, customers are disappointed. Successful companies add benefits to their offering that not only *satisfy* customers but surprise and *delight* them.[31] The service-quality model in Figure 11.3 highlights five gaps that can cause unsuccessful service delivery:[32]

1. *Gap between consumer expectation and management perception*—Management does not always correctly perceive what customers want. Hospital administrators may think patients want better food, but patients may be more concerned with nurse responsiveness.

2. *Gap between management perception and service-quality specification*—Management might correctly perceive customers' wants but not set a performance standard. Hospital administrators may tell the nurses to give "fast" service without specifying it in minutes.

3. *Gap between service-quality specifications and service delivery*—Employees might be poorly trained, or unable or unwilling to meet the standard; they may be held to conflicting standards, such as taking time to listen to customers and serving them fast.

FIGURE 11.3 Service-Quality Model

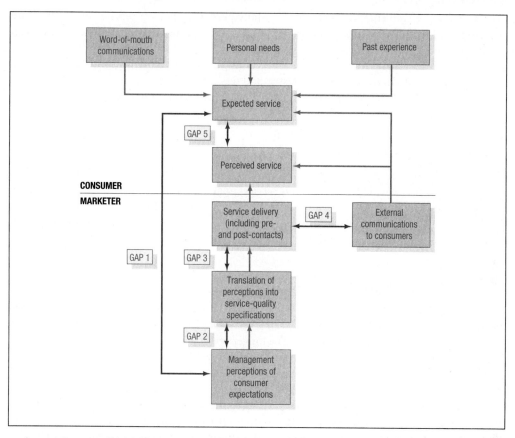

Sources: A. Parasuraman, Valarie A. Zeithaml, and Leonard L. Berry, "A Conceptual Model of Service Quality and Its Implications for Future Research," *Journal of Marketing* (Fall 1985), pp. 41–50. Reprinted with permission of the American Marketing Association. The model is more fully discussed or elaborated in Valarie Zeithaml, Mary Jo Bitner, and Dwayne D. Gremler, *Services Marketing: Integrating Customer Focus across the Firm*, 4th ed. (New York: McGraw-Hill, 2006).

4. *Gap between service delivery and external communications*—Consumer expectations are affected by statements made by company representatives and ads. If a hospital brochure shows a beautiful room but the patient finds it unappealing, communications have distorted the customer's expectations.

5. *Gap between perceived service and expected service*—This gap occurs when the consumer misperceives the service quality. The physician may keep visiting the patient to show care, but the patient may interpret this as an indication that something really is wrong.

Based on this model, researchers identified five determinants of service quality. In order of importance, they are reliability, responsiveness, assurance, empathy, and tangibles.[33] They also note there is a *zone of tolerance,* or a range where a service dimension would be deemed satisfactory, anchored by the minimum level consumers are willing to accept and the level they believe can and should be delivered.

Incorporating Self-Service Technologies

Consumers value convenience in services.[34] Many person-to-person service interactions are being replaced by self-service technologies (SSTs). To the traditional vending machines we can add automated teller machines (ATMs), self-pumping at gas stations, and a variety of online activities, such as ticket purchasing. Not all SSTs improve service quality, but they can make transactions more accurate, convenient, faster, and less costly. One technology firm, Comverse, estimates the cost to answer a query through a call center at $7, but only 10 cents online, which is why so many firms are adding Web-based SSTs.[35]

Managing Product-Support Services

Manufacturers of equipment—small appliances, office machines, tractors, mainframes, airplanes—all must provide *product-support services,* making this a battleground for competitive advantage. Some equipment companies, such as Caterpillar and John Deere, make a significant percentage of their profits from product-support services.[36] In the global marketplace, companies that make a good product but provide poor local service support are seriously disadvantaged.

Identifying and Satisfying Customer Needs

In general, customers have three worries about product service.[37] First, they worry about reliability and *failure frequency.* A farmer may tolerate a combine that breaks down once a year, but not more often. The second issue is *downtime.* The longer the downtime, the higher the cost, which is why buyers count on a seller's *service dependability*—the seller's ability to fix the product quickly or at least provide a loaner. The third issue is *out-of-pocket costs.* How much will maintenance and repairs cost?

A buyer considers all these factors and tries to estimate the **life-cycle cost**, which is the product's purchase cost plus the discounted cost of maintenance and repair less the discounted salvage value. To provide the best support, a manufacturer must identify the services customers value most and their relative importance. Manufacturers of expensive equipment may offer *facilitating services* such as installation, staff training, and financing. They may also add *value-augmenting services* that extend beyond the product's functioning and performance.

A manufacturer can offer, and charge for, product-support services in different ways. One chemical company provides a standard offering plus a basic level of services. If the business customer wants additional services, it can pay extra or increase its annual purchases to a higher level, in which case additional services are included. Many companies offer *service contracts* (also called *extended warranties*), agreeing to provide free maintenance and repair services for a specified period at a specified contract price.

Product companies must understand their strategic intent and competitive advantage in developing services. Are service units supposed to support or protect existing product businesses or to grow as an independent platform? Are the sources of competitive advantage based on economies of scale or economies of skill?[38]

Postsale Service Strategy

Although customers generally take the initiative in requesting service after a purchase, some firms proactively contact customers to provide postsale service.[39] In devising a postsale service strategy, manufacturers usually start by running their own parts-and-service departments so they can stay close to the equipment and know its problems. They also find it expensive and time consuming to train others and find they can profit from parts and service if they are the only supplier and can charge a premium price. In fact, many equipment manufacturers price their equipment low and charge high prices for parts and service.

Over time, manufacturers switch more maintenance and repair service to authorized distributors and dealers. These intermediaries are closer to customers, operate in more locations, and can offer quicker service. Still later, independent service firms emerge and offer a lower price or faster service. Independent service organizations handle computers, telecommunications equipment, and a variety of other equipment lines.

Customer-service choices are increasing rapidly and manufacturers must determine how to make money on their equipment, independent of service contracts. Some new-car warranties now cover 100,000 miles before servicing. The increase in disposable or never-fail equipment makes customers less inclined to pay 2 percent to 10 percent of the purchase price every year for a service. Some business customers might find it cheaper to have their own service people on-site.

EXECUTIVE SUMMARY

A service is any act or performance that one party can offer to another that is essentially intangible and does not result in the ownership of anything. It may or may not be tied to a physical product. The service component can be a major or minor part of the total offering. Services are intangible, inseparable, variable, and perishable, and each characteristic poses marketing challenges. Marketers must find ways to give tangibility to intangibles, to increase the productivity of service providers, to increase and standardize the quality of the service provided, and to match the supply of services with demand.

Marketers of services face new realities in the 21st century due to customer empowerment, customer coproduction, and the need to satisfy employees as well as customers. Marketers can differentiate their service offerings through primary and secondary service features as well as continual innovation. Superior service delivery requires managing customer expectations and incorporating self-service technologies. To offer the best support, a manufacturer must identify the services customers value most and their relative importance. It should also plan for delivering service after the purchase.

NOTES

1. "Call of the Circus: Daniel Lamarre, President and Chief Executive, Cirque du Soleil," *New York Times,* June 20, 2010, p. 8; Matt Krantz, "Tinseltown Gets Glitzy New Star," *USA Today,* August 24, 2009; Linda Tischler, "Join the Circus," *Fast Company,* July 2005, pp. 53–58; "Cirque du Soleil," *America's Greatest Brands* 3 (2004); Geoff Keighley, "The Factory," *Business 2.0,* February 2004, p. 102.

2. Leonard L. Berry, *On Great Service: A Framework for Action* (New York: Free Press, 2006); Leonard L. Berry, *Discovering the Soul of Service Success* (New York: Free Press, 1999); Fred Wiersema, ed., *Customer Service: Extraordinary Results at Southwest Airlines, Charles Schwab, Lands' End, American Express, Staples, and USAA* (New York: HarperBusiness, 1998).

3. Valarie A. Zeithaml, "How Consumer Evaluation Processes Differ between Goods and Services," J. Donnelly and W. R. George, eds., *Marketing of Services* (Chicago: American Marketing Association, 1981), pp. 186–90.

4. Amy Ostrom and Dawn Iacobucci, "Consumer Trade-Offs and the Evaluation of Services," *Journal of Marketing* (January 1995), pp. 17–28.

5. Theodore Levitt, "Marketing Intangible Products and Product Intangibles," *Harvard Business Review,* May–June 1981, pp. 94–102; Leonard L. Berry, "Services Marketing Is Different," *Business,* May–June 1980, pp. 24–29.

6. B. H. Booms and M. J. Bitner, "Marketing Strategies and Organizational Structures for Service Firms," J. Donnelly and W. R. George, eds., *Marketing of Services* (Chicago: American Marketing Association, 1981), pp. 47–51.

7. For some emerging research results on the effects of creating time and place service separation, see Hean Tat Keh and Jun Pang, "Customer Reaction to Service Separation," *Journal of Marketing* 74 (March 2010), pp. 55–70.

8. Gila E. Fruchter and Eitan Gerstner, "Selling with 'Satisfaction Guaranteed,'" *Journal of Service Research* 1, no. 4 (May 1999), pp. 313–23. See also, Rebecca J. Slotegraaf and J. Jeffrey Inman, "Longitudinal Shifts in the Drivers of Satisfaction with Product Quality: The Role of Attribute Resolvability," *Journal of Marketing Research* 41 (August 2004), pp. 269–80.

9. Jeffrey F. Rayport, Bernard J. Jaworski, and Ellie J. Kyung, "Best Face Forward: Improving Companies' Service Interface with Customers," *Journal of Interactive Marketing* 19 (Autumn 2005), pp. 67–80; Asim Ansari and Carl F. Mela, "E-Customization," *Journal of Marketing Research* 40 (May 2003), pp. 131–45.

10. W. Earl Sasser, "Match Supply and Demand in Service Industries," *Harvard Business Review,* November–December 1976, pp. 133–40.

11. Diane Brady, "Why Service Stinks," *BusinessWeek,* October 23, 2000, pp. 119–28.

12. Elisabeth Sullivan, "Happy Endings Lead to Happy Returns," *Marketing News,* October 30, 2009, p. 20.

13. Stephen S. Tax, Mark Colgate, and David Bowen, "How to Prevent Your Customers from Failing," *MIT Sloan Management Review* (Spring 2006), pp. 30–38; Mei Xue and Patrick T. Harker, "Customer Efficiency: Concept and Its Impact on E-Business Management," *Journal of Service Research* 4, no. 4 (May 2002), pp. 253–67; Matthew L. Meuter, Amy L. Ostrom, Robert I. Roundtree, and Mary Jo Bitner, "Self-Service Technologies: Understanding Customer Satisfaction with Technology-Based Service Encounters," *Journal of Marketing* 64, no. 3 (July 2000), pp. 50–64.

14. Kimmy Wa Chan, Chi Kin (Bennett) Yim, and Simon S. K. Lam, "Is Customer Participation in Value Creation a Double-Edged Sword?" *Journal of Marketing* 74 (May 2010), pp. 48–64.

15. Valarie Zeithaml, Mary Jo Bitner, and Dwayne D. Gremler, *Services Marketing: Integrating Customer Focus across the Firm,* 4th ed. (New York: McGraw-Hill, 2006).

16. Mary Jane Credeur, "Delta Monitors Twitter to Remedy Customer Complaints," *BusinessWeek,* August 16, 2010, www.businessweek.com; "Customer Service: Disaffected Nation," *Marketing,* June 8, 2005, p. 32; Robert Geier, "How to Create Disaster Recovery Plans for Customer Contact Operations," *Customer Contact Management Report,* May 2002, pp. 36+.

17. Stephen S. Tax, Mark Colgate, and David Bowen, "How to Prevent Your Customers from Failing," *MIT Sloan Management Review* (Spring 2006), pp. 30–38; Michael Sanserino and Cari Tuna, "Companies Strive Harder to Please Customers," *Wall Street Journal,* July 27, 2009, p. B4.

18. James L. Heskett, W, Earl Sasser Jr., and Joe Wheeler, *Ownership Quotient: Putting the Service Profit Chain to Work for Unbeatable Competitive Advantage* (Boston, MA: Harvard Business School Press, 2008).

19. D. Todd Donovan, Tom J. Brown, and John C. Mowen, "Internal Benefits of Service Worker Customer Orientation: Job Satisfaction, Commitment, and Organizational Citizenship Behaviors," *Journal of Marketing* 68 (January 2004), pp. 128–46.

20. Frances X. Frei, "The Four Things a Service Business Must Get Right," *Harvard Business Review*, April 2008, pp. 70–80.

21. Christian Gronroos, "A Service-Quality Model and Its Marketing Implications," *European Journal of Marketing* 18, no. 4 (1984), pp. 36–44.

22. Leonard Berry, "Big Ideas in Services Marketing," *Journal of Consumer Marketing* (Spring 1986), pp. 47–51. See also, Jagdip Singh, "Performance Productivity and Quality of Frontline Employees in Service Organizations," *Journal of Marketing* 64 (April 2000), pp. 15–34; Detelina Marinova, Jun Ye, and Jagdip Singh, "Do Frontline Mechanisms Matter? Impact of Quality and Productivity Orientations on Unit Revenue, Efficiency, and Customer Satisfaction," *Journal of Marketing* 72 (March 2008), pp. 28–45; John R. Hauser, Duncan I. Simester, and Birger Wernerfelt, "Internal Customers and Internal Suppliers," *Journal of Marketing Research* (August 1996), pp. 268–80; Walter E. Greene, Gary D. Walls, and Larry J. Schrest, "Internal Marketing: The Key to External Marketing Success," *Journal of Services Marketing* 8, no. 4 (1994), pp. 5–13.

23. Christian Gronroos, "A Service-Quality Model and Its Marketing Implications," *European Journal of Marketing* 18, no. 4 (1984), pp. 36–44; Michael D. Hartline, James G. Maxham III, and Daryl O. McKee, "Corridors of Influence in the Dissemination of Customer-Oriented Strategy to Customer-Contact Service Employees," *Journal of Marketing*, April 2000, pp. 35–50.

24. Ad de Jong, Ko de Ruyter, and Jos Lemmink, "Antecedents and Consequences of the Service Climate in Boundary-Spanning Self-Managing Service Teams," *Journal of Marketing* 68 (April 2004), pp. 18–35; Michael D. Hartline and O. C. Ferrell, "The Management of Customer-Contact Service Employees," *Journal of Marketing* 60 (October 1996), pp. 52–70; Christian Homburg, Jan Wieseke, and Torsten Bornemann, "Implementing the Marketing Concept at the Employee-Customer Interface: The Role of Customer Need Knowledge," *Journal of Marketing* 73 (July 2009), pp. 64–81; Chi Kin (Bennett) Yim, David K. Tse, and Kimmy Wa Chan, "Strengthening Customer Loyalty through Intimacy and Passion," *Journal of Marketing Research* 45 (December 2008), pp. 741–56.

25. Heather Green, "How Amazon Aims to Keep You Clicking," *BusinessWeek*, March 2, 2009, pp. 34–40.

26. Dave Dougherty and Ajay Murthy, "What Service Customers Really Want," *Harvard Business Review*, September 2009, p. 22; for a contrarian point of view, see Edward Kasabov, "The Compliant Customer," *MIT Sloan Management Review* (Spring 2010), pp. 18–19.

27. Jeffrey G. Blodgett and Ronald D. Anderson, "A Bayesian Network Model of the Customer Complaint Process," *Journal of Service Research* 2, no. 4 (May 2000), pp. 321–38; Stephen S. Tax and Stephen W. Brown, "Recovering and Learning from Service Failures," *Sloan Management Review* (Fall 1998), pp. 75–88; Claes Fornell and Birger Wernerfelt, "A Model for Customer Complaint Management," *Marketing Science* 7 (Summer 1988), pp. 271–86.

28. Stephen S. Tax, Stephen W. Brown, and Murali Chandrashekaran, "Customer Evaluations of Service Complaint Experiences: Implications for Relationship Marketing," *Journal of Marketing* 62 (April 1998), pp. 60–76; Stephen S. Tax and Stephen W. Brown, "Recovering and Learning from Service Failures," *Sloan Management Review* (Fall 1998), pp. 75–88.

29. Susan M. Keaveney, "Customer Switching Behavior in Service Industries: An Exploratory Study," *Journal of Marketing* (April 1995), pp. 71–82. See also, Jaishankar Ganesh, Mark J. Arnold, and Kristy E. Reynolds, "Understanding the Customer Base of Service Providers," *Journal of Marketing* 64 (July 2000), pp. 65–87; Michael D. Hartline and O. C. Ferrell, "The Management of Customer-Contact Service Employees," *Journal of Marketing* (October 1996), pp. 52–70; Linda L. Price, Eric J. Arnould, and Patrick Tierney, "Going to Extremes: Managing Service Encounters and Assessing Provider Performance," *Journal of Marketing* (April 1995), pp. 83–97; Lois A. Mohr, Mary Jo Bitner, and Bernard H. Booms, "Critical Service Encounters: The Employee's Viewpoint," *Journal of Marketing* (October 1994), pp. 95–106.

30. Glenn B. Voss, A. Parasuraman, and Dhruv Grewal, "The Role of Price, Performance, and Expectations in Determining Satisfaction in Service Exchanges," *Journal of Marketing* 62 (October 1998), pp. 46–61.

31. Roland T. Rust and Richard L. Oliver, "Should We Delight the Customer?" *Journal of the Academy of Marketing Science* 28, no. 1 (Fall 2002), pp. 86–94.

32. A. Parasuraman, Valarie A. Zeithaml, and Leonard L. Berry, "A Conceptual Model of Service Quality and Its Implications for Future Research," *Journal of Marketing* (Fall 1985), pp. 41–50. See also, Michael K. Brady and J. Joseph Cronin Jr., "Some New Thoughts on Conceptualizing Perceived Service Quality," *Journal of Marketing* 65 (July 2001), pp. 34–49; Susan J. Devlin and H. K. Dong, "Service Quality from the Customers' Perspective," *Marketing Research* (Winter 1994), pp. 4–13.

33. Leonard L. Berry and A. Parasuraman, *Marketing Services: Competing through Quality* (New York: Free Press, 1991), p. 16.

34. Leonard L. Berry, Kathleen Seiders, and Dhruv Grewal, "Understanding Service Convenience," *Journal of Marketing* 66 (July 2002), pp. 1–17.

35. "Help Yourself," *Economist*, July 2, 2009, pp. 62–63.

36. Eric Fang, Robert W. Palmatier, and Jan-Benedict E. M. Steenkamp, "Effect of Service Transition Strategies on Firm Value," *Journal of Marketing* 72 (September 2008), pp. 1–14.

37. Mark Vandenbosch and Niraj Dawar, "Beyond Better Products: Capturing Value in Customer Interactions," *MIT Sloan Management Review* 43 (Summer 2002),

pp. 35–42; Milind M. Lele and Uday S. Karmarkar, "Good Product Support Is Smart Marketing," *Harvard Business Review*, November–December 1983, pp. 124–32.

38. Byron G. Auguste, Eric P. Harmon, and Vivek Pandit, "The Right Service Strategies for Product Companies," *McKinsey Quarterly* 1 (2006), pp. 41–51.

39. Goutam Challagalla, R. Venkatesh, and Ajay K. Kohli, "Proactive Postsales Service: When and Why Does It Pay Off?" *Journal of Marketing* 73 (March 2009), pp. 70–87.

chapter 12

Developing Pricing Strategies and Programs

In this chapter, we will address the following questions:

1. How do consumers process and evaluate prices?
2. How should a company set prices initially for products or services?
3. How should a company adapt prices to meet varying circumstances and opportunities?
4. How should a company initiate a price change and respond to a competitor's price change?

Marketing Management at Tiffany & Co.

For more than 170 years, the Tiffany name has connoted diamonds and luxury. A cultural icon— its Tiffany Blue color is even trademarked—Tiffany has survived the economy's numerous ups and downs through the years. With the emergence in the late 1990s of the notion of "affordable luxuries," Tiffany seized the moment by creating a line of cheaper silver jewelry. Earnings skyrocketed for the next five years, but the affordable jewelry brought both an image and a pricing crisis for the company.

Starting in 2002, the company hiked prices, launched higher-end collections, renovated stores to feature expensive items, and expanded aggressively into new cities and shopping malls. When the recession began in 2008, the firm knew it had to be careful not to dilute its high-end appeal. Tiffany offset softer sales largely with cost-cutting and inventory management, and quietly lowered prices on best-selling engagement rings by roughly 10 percent. By 2010, Tiffany was planning new stores in China, where status brands are highly coveted, and in Europe, where it earns better profit margins than it does in the Americas.[1]

Price is the one element of the marketing mix that produces revenue; the other elements produce costs. Price is perhaps the easiest element of the marketing program to adjust; product features, channels, and even communications take more time. Holistic marketers take many factors into account when making pricing decisions—the company, the customers, the competition, the marketing environment, the firm's marketing strategy, and its target markets. This chapter discusses how marketers set and adjust prices.

Understanding Pricing

Price is not just a number on a tag. It comes in many forms and performs many functions, whether it's called rent, tuition, fares, fees, or tolls. Throughout most of history, prices were set by negotiation between buyers and sellers. Setting one price for all buyers is a relatively modern idea that arose with the development of large-scale retailing at the end of the nineteenth century. Tiffany & Co. and other stores advertised a "strictly one-price policy," because they carried so many items and had so many employees.

A Changing Pricing Environment

Pricing practices have changed significantly. During the recent recession, a combination of environmentalism, renewed frugality, and concern about jobs and home values forced many U.S. consumers to replace luxury purchases with basics; eat at home more often; favor small, fuel-efficient vehicles; and cut back spending on hobbies and sports.[2]

Downward price pressure from a changing economic environment coincided with some longer-term trends in the technological environment. For some years now, the Internet has allowed sellers to discriminate between buyers, and buyers to discriminate between sellers.[3] Sellers can monitor buyer behavior and tailor offers to individuals as well as giving special prices to certain customers. Both buyers and sellers can negotiate prices in online auctions, exchanges, or in person. Buyers can compare prices from thousands of vendors, name their price and have it met, and get products free. Another challenge is how to compete with free products. "Marketing Skills: Giving It Away" describes how marketers can profit in such situations.

How Companies Price

In small companies, the boss often sets prices. In large companies, division and product-line managers do it. Even here, top management sets general pricing objectives and policies and often approves lower management's proposals. In industries where pricing is a key factor (aerospace, railroads), companies often establish a pricing department to set or assist others in setting appropriate prices. This department reports to the marketing department, finance department, or top management. Others who influence pricing include sales managers, production managers, finance managers, and accountants.

Pricing can be a big headache for executives. Some firms focus on costs and strive for the industry's traditional margins. Other common mistakes are not revising price often enough to capitalize on market changes; setting price independently of the rest of the marketing program rather than as an intrinsic element of market-positioning strategy; and not varying price enough for different product items, market segments, distribution channels, and purchase occasions.

Effective pricing requires a thorough understanding of consumer pricing psychology and a systematic approach to setting, adapting, and changing prices.

GIVING IT AWAY

Giving away products has long been an effective marketing tactic, and technology has only increased the possibilities. In a digital marketplace, companies can actually make money with a "freemium" strategy. For instance, Flickr offers free basic online photo management while selling the FlickrPro version to highly involved users. This strategy can be tricky, however: "Only one in ten companies will succeed at pulling this off," says Howard Anderson of the MIT Entrepreneurship Center. How can marketers profit from giving things away? First, the offering must be superior and the fee-based extras should be part of the plan from the beginning. Second, never change a free offering to a fee offering, because that will alienate loyal customers. Finally, have a number of revenue sources to cover the cost of the free offering.

The European discount airline Ryanair has profited by virtually giving away seats on its flights and charging for almost everything else; if regulators would permit it, passengers would get a spot to stand on (free or cheap) instead of a seat. About 25 percent of Ryanair's seats are free, except for fees and taxes, yet Ryanair's net margin is better than that of Southwest Airlines, because extras generate so much revenue at such a low cost. Ryanair even sells other companies advertising space on its boarding passes and Web site.[4]

Consumer Psychology and Pricing

Many economists assume that consumers accept prices as given. Marketers recognize that consumers often actively process price information, interpreting it from the context of prior purchasing experience, formal communications (advertising, sales calls, and brochures), informal communications (friends, colleagues, or family members), point-of-purchase or online resources, and other factors.[5] Purchase decisions are based on how consumers perceive prices and what they consider the current actual price to be—*not* on the marketer's stated price. Customers may have a lower price threshold below which prices signal inferior or unacceptable quality and an upper price threshold above which a product appears not worth the money. Consumer attitudes about pricing took a dramatic shift in the recent economic downturn as many found themselves unable to sustain their lifestyles.[6] Yet some firms can still command a price premium if their offerings are unique and relevant to a large segment.

Three key topics for understanding how consumers arrive at their perceptions of prices are:

- Reference prices. Although consumers may have fairly good knowledge of price ranges, surprisingly few can accurately recall specific prices.[7] When examining products, however, they often employ a **reference price**, comparing an observed price to an internal reference price they remember or an external frame of reference such as a posted "regular retail price."[8] Sellers may manipulate reference prices by situating a product among expensive competitors to imply that it belongs in the same class, stating a high manufacturer's suggested price, or pointing to a rival's high price.[9]

- Price-quality inferences. Many consumers use price as an indicator of quality. Image pricing is especially effective with ego-sensitive products such as perfumes and expensive cars. A $100 bottle of perfume might contain $10 worth of scent, but gift givers pay $100 to communicate their high regard for the receiver. When information about true quality is available, price is a less significant indicator of quality. For luxury-goods customers who desire uniqueness, demand may actually increase with high price, because they believe fewer others can afford the product.[10]

- **Price endings.** Consumers see an item priced at $299 as being in the $200 rather than the $300 range; they tend to process prices "left-to-right" rather than by rounding.[11] Price encoding in this fashion is important if there is a mental price break at the higher, rounded price. Prices ending in odd numbers suggest a discount or bargain, so if a company wants a high-price image, it should probably avoid the odd-ending tactic.[12]

Setting the Price

A firm must set a price for the first time when it develops a new product, when it introduces its regular product into a new distribution channel or geographical area, and when it enters bids on new contract work. The firm must consider many factors in setting its pricing policy.[13] The six-step procedure for pricing is: (1) select the pricing objective; (2) determine demand; (3) estimate costs; (4) analyze competitors' costs, prices, and offers; (5) select a pricing method; and (6) select the final price.

Step 1: Selecting the Pricing Objective

Five major pricing objectives are survival, maximum current profit, maximum market share, maximum market skimming, and product-quality leadership. Companies pursue *survival* as their major short-term objective if they are plagued with overcapacity, intense competition, or changing consumer wants. As long as prices cover variable costs and some fixed costs, the company stays in business. To *maximize current profit,* firms estimate the demand and costs associated with alternative prices and choose the price that produces maximum current profit, cash flow, or return on investment. However, the firm may sacrifice long-run performance by ignoring the effects of other marketing variables, competitors' reactions, and legal restraints on price.

Some companies want to *maximize their market share,* believing that a higher sales volume will lead to lower unit costs and higher long-run profit. With **market-penetration pricing**, firms set the lowest price, assuming the market is price sensitive. This is appropriate when (1) the market is highly price sensitive and a low price stimulates market growth, (2) production and distribution costs fall with accumulated production experience, and (3) a low price discourages competition.

Companies unveiling a new technology favor setting high prices to *maximize market skimming.* **Market-skimming pricing**, in which prices start high and slowly drop over time, makes sense when (1) a sufficient number of buyers have a high current demand, (2) the unit costs of producing a small volume are not so high that they cancel the advantage of charging what the traffic will bear, (3) the high initial price does not attract more competitors, and (4) the high price communicates the image of a superior product. A company might aim to be the *product-quality leader* in the market, offering affordable luxuries or superpremium products combining quality, taste, and status with appropriately high prices.

Nonprofit and public organizations may have other pricing objectives. A university aims for *partial cost recovery,* knowing that it must rely on private gifts and public grants to cover its remaining costs.

Step 2: Determining Demand

Each price will lead to a different level of demand and have a different impact on a company's marketing objectives. The normally inverse relationship between price and demand is captured in a demand curve. The higher the price, the lower the demand. For prestige goods, the demand curve sometimes slopes upward, because some consumers take the higher price to signify a better product. However, if the price is too high, demand may fall.

Price Sensitivity   The demand curve shows the market's probable purchase quantity at alternative prices, summing the reactions of many individuals with different price sensitivities. The first step in estimating demand is to understand what affects price sensitivity. In general, customers are less price-sensitive to low-cost items or items they buy infrequently. Yet a seller can successfully charge a higher price than competitors if customers are convinced it offers the lowest *total cost of ownership* (TCO).

Of course, companies prefer customers who are less price-sensitive. Table 12.1 lists some characteristics associated with decreased price sensitivity. Although the Internet has the potential to *increase* price sensitivity, targeting only price-sensitive consumers may mean "leaving money on the table."

Estimating Demand Curves   Companies can measure their demand curves using several different methods. First, they can use surveys to explore how many units consumers would buy at different proposed prices. Consumers might understate their purchase intentions at higher prices to discourage the company from pricing high, but they also tend to actually exaggerate their willingness to pay for new products or services.[14] Second, the firm can experiment by charging different prices for the same product in similar territories or on different Web sites to see how the change affects sales, doing so carefully to avoid alienating customers or violating regulatory requirements. A third method is to statistically analyze past prices, quantities sold, and other factors to reveal their relationships; this approach requires considerable skill.

In measuring the price-demand relationship, the marketer must control for various factors that will influence demand.[15] The competitor's response will make a difference. Also, if the company changes other aspects of the marketing program besides price, the effect of the price change itself will be hard to isolate.

Price Elasticity of Demand   Marketers need to know how responsive, or elastic, demand is to a change in price. If demand hardly changes with a small change in price, we say the demand is

---

TABLE 12.1	Factors Leading to Less Price Sensitivity

- The product is more distinctive.
- Buyers are less aware of substitutes.
- Buyers cannot easily compare the quality of substitutes.
- The expenditure is a smaller part of the buyer's total income.
- The expenditure is small compared to the total cost of the end product.
- Part of the cost is borne by another party.
- The product is used in conjunction with assets previously bought.
- The product is assumed to have more quality, prestige, or exclusiveness.
- Buyers cannot store the product.

Source: Based on information from Thomas T. Nagle, John E. Hogan, and Joseph Zale, *The Strategy and Tactics of Pricing,* 5th ed. (Upper Saddle River, NJ: Prentice Hall, 2011).

inelastic. If demand changes considerably, it is *elastic.* The higher the elasticity, the greater the volume growth resulting from a 1 percent price reduction. If demand is elastic, sellers will consider lowering the price to produce more total revenue, especially when their costs for selling more units do not increase disproportionately.[16]

Price elasticity depends on the magnitude and direction of the contemplated price change. It may be negligible with a small price change and substantial with a large price change. It may differ for a price cut versus a price increase, and there may be a range within which price changes have little or no effect. Long-run price elasticity may differ from short-run elasticity. Buyers may continue to buy from a current supplier after a price increase but eventually switch suppliers. The distinction between short-run and long-run elasticity means that sellers will not know the total effect of a price change until time passes.

One study reviewing a 40-year period of academic research that investigated price elasticity yielded interesting findings.[17] Price elasticity magnitudes were higher for durable goods than for other goods, and higher for products in the introduction/growth stages of the product life cycle than in the mature/decline stages. In addition, promotional price elasticities were higher than actual price elasticities in the short run (although the reverse was true in the long run).

Step 3: Estimating Costs

Whereas demand sets a ceiling on the price of a company's product, costs set the floor. The company wants to charge a price that covers its cost of producing, distributing, and selling the product, including a fair return for its effort and risk.

Types of Costs and Levels of Production   A company's costs take two forms. **Fixed costs**, also known as *overhead,* do not vary with production level or sales revenue. A company must pay bills each month for rent, salaries, and so on, regardless of output. **Variable costs** vary directly with the level of production. For example, each calculator produced by Texas Instruments (TI) incurs the cost of plastic, microprocessor chips, and packaging. These costs tend to be constant per unit produced, but they're called variable because their total varies with the number of units produced. **Total costs** are the sum of the fixed and variable costs for a given level of production. **Average cost** is the cost per unit at that level of production; it equals total costs divided by production. Management wants to charge a price that will at least cover the total production costs at a given level of production.

To price intelligently, management needs to know how its costs vary with different levels of production. The cost per unit is high if few units are produced per day, but as production increases, the average cost falls because the fixed costs are spread over more units. Short-run average cost increases at some point because the plant becomes inefficient (due to problems such as machines breaking down more often). By calculating costs for plants of different sizes, a firm can identify the optimal size and production level to achieve economies of scale and lower average cost. To estimate the real profitability of selling to different types of retailers or customers, firms should use *activity-based cost (ABC) accounting* instead of standard cost accounting.

Accumulated Production   Suppose a TI plant produces 3,000 calculators per day. As TI gains experience producing calculators, its methods improve. Workers learn shortcuts, materials flow more smoothly, and procurement costs fall. The result is that average cost falls with accumulated production experience. Assume the average cost of producing the first 100,000 hand calculators is $10 per calculator. When TI has produced the first 200,000 calculators, the average cost falls to $9. After its accumulated production experience doubles again to 400,000, the average cost is $8.

FIGURE 12.1 Cost per Unit as a Function of Accumulated Production: The Experience Curve

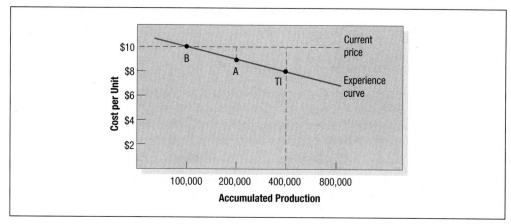

This decline in the average cost with accumulated production experience is called the **experience curve** or *learning curve.*

Now suppose TI competes with firms A and B in this industry, as shown in Figure 12.1. TI is the lowest-cost producer at $8, having produced 400,000 units in the past. If all three firms sell the calculator for $10, TI makes $2 profit per unit, A makes $1 per unit, and B breaks even. The smart move for TI would be to lower its price to $9 to drive B out of the market; even A may consider leaving. TI will pick up the business that would have gone to B (and possibly A). Also, price-sensitive customers will enter the market at the lower price. As production increases beyond 400,000 units, TI's costs will drop further, restoring profits even at a price of $9. TI has used this pricing strategy repeatedly to gain share and drive out rivals.

Experience-curve pricing nevertheless is risky because aggressive pricing might give the product a cheap image. It also assumes competitors are weak followers, and it leads the company to build more plants to meet demand. If a competitor innovates with a lower-cost technology, the market leader is now stuck with the old technology.

Target Costing   Costs change with production scale and experience. They can also change as a result of a concentrated effort by designers, engineers, and purchasing agents to reduce them through **target costing.**[18] Market research establishes a new product's desired functions and the price at which it will sell, given its appeal and competitors' prices. This price less desired profit margin leaves the target cost the marketer must achieve. The firm must examine each cost element—design, engineering, manufacturing, sales—and bring down costs so the final cost projections are in the target range. Companies can cut costs in many ways, including applying what they learn from making affordable products with scarce resources in developing countries.[19]

Step 4: Analyzing Competitors' Costs, Prices, and Offers

Within the range of possible prices determined by market demand and company costs, the firm must take competitors' costs, prices, and possible price reactions into account. If the firm's offer contains features not offered by the nearest competitor, it should evaluate their worth to the customer and add that value to the competitor's price. If the competitor's offer contains some features not offered by the firm, the firm should subtract their value from its own price. Now the firm can decide whether it can charge more than, the same as, or less than the competitor, remembering that pricing can provoke responses from customers, competitors, distributors, suppliers, and even the government.

Step 5: Selecting a Pricing Method

Figure 12.2 summarizes the three major considerations in price setting: Costs set a floor to the price. Competitors' prices and the price of substitutes provide an orienting point. Customers' assessment of unique features establishes the price ceiling. We will examine six price-setting methods: markup pricing, target-return pricing, perceived-value pricing, value pricing, going-rate pricing, and auction-type pricing.

Markup Pricing   The most elementary pricing method is to add a standard **markup** to the product's cost. Construction companies submit job bids by estimating the total project cost and adding a standard markup for profit.

FIGURE 12.2 The Three Cs Model for Price Setting

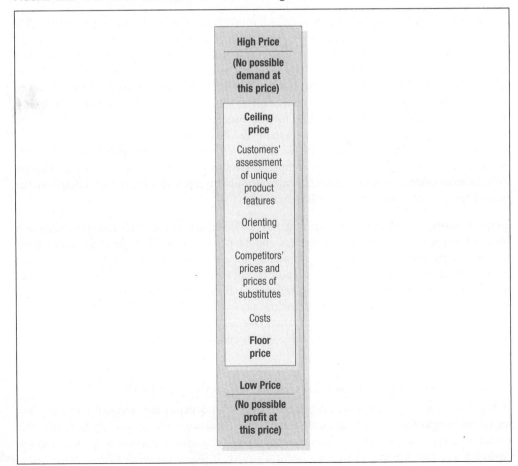

Suppose a toaster manufacturer has the following costs and sales expectations:

Variable cost per unit	$10
Fixed costs	$300,000
Expected unit sales	50,000

The manufacturer's unit cost is given by:

$$\text{Unit cost} = \text{variable cost} + \frac{\text{fixed costs}}{\text{unit sales}} = \$10 + \frac{\$300,000}{50,000} = \$16$$

If the manufacturer wants to earn a 20 percent markup on sales, its markup price is given by:

$$\text{Markup price} = \frac{\text{unit cost}}{(1 - \text{desired return on sales})} = \frac{\$16}{1 - 0.2} = \$20$$

The manufacturer will charge dealers $20 per toaster and make a profit of $4 per unit. If dealers want to earn 50 percent on their selling price, they will mark up the toaster 100 percent to $40.

Does the use of standard markups make logical sense? Generally, no. Any pricing method that ignores current demand, perceived value, and competition is not likely to lead to the optimal price. Markup pricing works only if the marked-up price actually brings in the expected level of sales. Still, markup pricing remains popular. First, sellers can determine costs much more easily than they can estimate demand. By tying the price to cost, sellers simplify the pricing task. Second, where all firms in the industry use this pricing method, prices tend to be similar and price competition is minimized. Third, many people feel that cost-plus pricing is fairer to both buyers and sellers. Sellers do not take advantage of buyers when demand becomes acute, and sellers earn a fair return on investment.

Target-Return Pricing   In **target-return pricing**, the firm determines the price that yields its target rate of return on investment. Suppose the toaster manufacturer has invested $1 million in the business and wants to set a price to earn a 20 percent ROI, specifically $200,000. The target-return price is given by the following formula:

$$\text{Target-return price} = \text{unit cost} + \frac{\text{desired return} \times \text{invested capital}}{\text{unit sales}}$$

$$= \$16 + \frac{.20 \times \$1,000,000}{50,000} = \$20$$

The manufacturer will realize this 20 percent ROI provided its costs and estimated sales are accurate. But what if sales don't reach 50,000 units? The manufacturer can prepare a break-even chart to learn what would happen at other sales levels (see Figure 12.3). Fixed costs are stable, regardless of sales volume, and variable costs (not shown in the figure) rise with volume. Total costs equal the sum of fixed and variable costs; the total revenue curve starts at zero and rises with each unit sold.

FIGURE 12.3 Break-Even Chart for Determining Target-Return Price
and Break-Even Volume

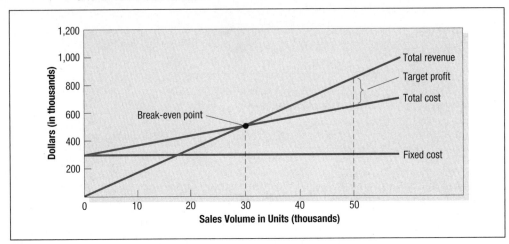

The total revenue and total cost curves cross at 30,000 units. This is the break-even volume, which can be verified by the following formula:

$$\text{Break-even volume} = \frac{\text{fixed cost}}{(\text{price} - \text{variable cost})} = \frac{\$300,000}{\$20 - \$10} = 30,000$$

If the manufacturer sells 50,000 units at $20, it earns $200,000 on its $1 million investment, but much depends on price elasticity and competitors' prices. Unfortunately, target-return pricing tends to ignore these considerations. The manufacturer needs to consider different prices and estimate their probable impacts on sales volume and profits. It should also find ways to lower its fixed or variable costs, because lower costs will decrease its required break-even volume.

Perceived-Value Pricing   Many firms now base their price on the customer's *perceived value*. Perceived value is made up of several inputs, such as the buyer's image of the product performance, the channel deliverables, the warranty quality, customer support, and softer attributes such as the supplier's reputation and trustworthiness. Companies must deliver the value promised by their value proposition, and the customer must perceive this value. Firms use the other marketing program elements, such as advertising and the Internet, to communicate and enhance perceived value in buyers' minds.[20]

Even when a company claims its offering delivers more total value, not all customers will respond positively. A segment of buyers will always care only about price, although another segment typically cares about quality. The key to perceived-value pricing is to deliver more unique value than the competitor and to demonstrate this to prospective buyers. Table 12.2 shows key considerations in developing value-based pricing.

Value Pricing   **Value pricing** is a method in which the firm wins loyal customers by charging a fairly low price for a high-quality offering. Value pricing is not a matter of simply setting lower prices; it means reengineering the company's operations to become a low-cost producer without sacrificing quality, to attract a large number of value-conscious customers.

An important type of value pricing is **everyday low pricing** (**EDLP**). Under EDLP pricing, a retailer charges a constant low price with little or no price promotions and special sales. Constant

TABLE 12.2	A Framework of Questions for Practicing Value-Based Pricing

1. What is the market strategy for the segment? (What does the supplier want to accomplish? What would the supplier like to have happen?)

2. What is the differential value that is *transparent* to target customers? (*Transparent* means that target customers easily understand how the supplier calculates the differential value between its offering and the next best alternative, and that the differential value can be verified with the customer's own data.)

3. What is the price of the next best alternative offering?

4. What is the cost of the supplier's market offering?

5. What pricing tactics will be used initially or eventually? ("Pricing tactics" are changes from a price that a supplier has set for its marketing offering—such as discounts—that motivate customers to take actions that benefit the supplier.)

6. What is the customer's expectation of a "fair" price?

Source: James C. Anderson, Marc Wouters, and Wouter Van Rossum, "Why the Highest Price Isn't the Best Price," *MIT Sloan Management Review* (Winter 2010), pp. 69–76.

prices eliminate week-to-week price uncertainty and the "high-low" pricing of promotion-oriented competitors. In **high-low pricing**, the retailer charges higher prices on an everyday basis but runs frequent promotions with prices temporarily lower than the EDLP level.[21]

The most important reason retailers adopt EDLP is that constant sales and promotions are costly and have eroded consumer confidence in everyday shelf prices. Consumers also have less time and patience for past traditions like watching for supermarket specials and clipping coupons. Yet, promotions do create excitement and draw shoppers, so EDLP does not guarantee success. Some supermarkets use a combination of high-low and everyday low pricing strategies, with increased advertising and promotions, to combat competition from store rivals and alternative channels.

Going-Rate Pricing   In **going-rate pricing**, the firm bases its price largely on competitors' prices. The firm might charge the same, more, or less than major competitors. Going-rate pricing is quite popular. Where costs are difficult to measure or competitive response is uncertain, firms adopt the going price solution because it is thought to reflect the industry's collective wisdom.

Auction-Type Pricing   Auction-type pricing is growing more popular, especially online. *English auctions*, with ascending bids, have one seller and many buyers; bidders raise the offer price until the highest bidder gets the item. There are two types of *Dutch auctions,* which feature descending bids. In the first, the auctioneer announces a high price for a product and then lowers the price until a bidder accepts; in the second, buyers announce something they want to buy, and potential sellers compete to offer the lowest price. In *sealed-bid auctions,* would-be suppliers submit only one bid and do not know the other bids. The U.S. government often uses this method to procure supplies. A supplier will not bid below its cost but cannot bid too high for fear of losing the job. The net effect of these two pulls is the bid's *expected profit.*[22]

Step 6: Selecting the Final Price

Pricing methods narrow the range from which the company selects its final price. In selecting that price, the company must consider factors such as the impact of other marketing activities, company pricing policies, gain-and-risk-sharing pricing, and the impact of price on other parties.

Impact of Other Marketing Activities   The final price must take into account the brand's quality and advertising relative to the competition. When Paul Farris and David Reibstein examined the relationships among relative price, relative quality, and relative advertising for 227 consumer businesses, they found that brands with average relative quality but high relative advertising budgets could charge premium prices, because consumers would pay more for known products.[23] In fact, brands with high relative quality and high relative advertising obtained the highest prices, while brands with low quality and low advertising charged the lowest prices. For market leaders, the positive relationship between high prices and high advertising held most strongly in the later stages of the product life cycle.

Company Pricing Policies   The price must be consistent with company pricing policies. Marketers must apply policies judiciously and try not to alienate customers (see "Marketing Insight: Stealth Price Increases"). Many companies set up a pricing department to develop policies and establish or approve decisions. The aim is to ensure that salespeople quote prices that are reasonable to customers and profitable to the company.

Gain-and-Risk-Sharing Pricing   Buyers may resist accepting a seller's proposal because of a high perceived level of risk. The seller has the option of offering to absorb part or all the risk if it does not deliver the full promised value. Baxter Healthcare, a medical products firm, secured a contract for an information management system from a health care provider by guaranteeing several million dollars in savings over an eight-year period. An increasing number of firms, especially business marketers who promise great savings with their equipment, may have to stand ready to guarantee the promised savings but also participate in the upside if the gains are greater than expected.

Impact of Price on Other Parties   How will distributors and dealers feel about the contemplated price?[24] If they don't make enough profit, they may choose not to bring the product

Marketing Insight

STEALTH PRICE INCREASES

As companies try to increase revenue without really raising prices, they often resort to adding fees for once-free features. Although some consumers abhor "nickel-and-dime" pricing strategies, small additional charges can mean big money. The telecommunications industry has been adding fees for setup, service termination, directory assistance, and other services, costing consumers billions of dollars. Fees for consumers who pay bills online, bounce checks, or use credit cards overseas bring banks billions of dollars annually. State and local governments have also been using an array of fees, fines, and penalties to raise revenue.

This explosion of fees has a number of implications. Given that list prices stay fixed, they may understate inflation. They also make it harder for consumers to compare competitive offerings. Companies justify the fees as the only fair and viable way to cover expenses without losing customers. Many argue that it makes sense to charge a premium for added services that cost more to provide. Companies also use fees to weed out unprofitable customers or get them to change their behavior. Ultimately, the viability of extra fees will be decided in the marketplace, where consumers vote with their wallets.

Sources: Sandra Guy, "Watch Out for New Credit Card Fees," *Chicago Sun-Times,* August 5, 2010, www.suntimes.com; Brian Burnsed, "A New Front in the Credit Card Wars," *BusinessWeek,* November 9, 2009, p. 60; Kathy Chu, "Credit Card Fees Can Suck You In," *USA Today,* December 15, 2006; Michael Arndt, "Fees! Fees! Fees!" *BusinessWeek,* September 29, 2003, pp. 99–104; "The Price Is Wrong," *Economist,* May 25, 2002, pp. 59–60.

to market. Will the sales force be willing to sell at that price? How will competitors react? Will suppliers raise their prices when they see the company's price? Will the government intervene and prevent this price from being charged? Many federal and state statutes protect consumers against deceptive pricing practices. For example, it is illegal for a company to set artificially high "regular" prices, then announce a "sale" at prices close to previous everyday prices.

Adapting the Price

Companies usually do not set a single price but rather develop a pricing structure that reflects variations in geographical demand and costs, market-segment requirements, purchase timing, order levels, delivery frequency, guarantees, service contracts, and other factors. As a result of discounts, allowances, and promotional support, a company rarely realizes the same profit from each unit of a product that it sells. Here we will examine several price-adaptation strategies: geographical pricing, price discounts and allowances, promotional pricing, and differentiated pricing.

Geographical Pricing (Cash, Countertrade, Barter)

In geographical pricing, the company decides how to price its products to different customers in different locations and countries. Should the company charge higher prices to distant customers to cover the higher shipping costs or set a lower price to win additional business? How should it account for exchange rates and the strength of different currencies?

Another question is how to get paid. This issue is critical when buyers lack sufficient hard currency to pay for their purchases. Many buyers want to offer other items in payment, a practice known as **countertrade**. U.S. companies are often forced to engage in countertrade if they want the business. One form of countertrade is *barter,* in which the buyer and seller directly exchange goods, with no money or third party involved. A second form is a *compensation deal,* in which the seller receives some percentage of the payment in cash and the rest in products. A third form is a *buyback agreement,* such as when a firm sells a plant, equipment, or technology to another country and accepts as partial payment products manufactured with the supplied equipment. A fourth form of countertrade is *offset,* where the seller receives full cash payment but agrees to spend much of the money in that country within a stated period.

Price Discounts and Allowances

Most firms will adjust their list price and give discounts and allowances for early payment, volume purchases, and off-season buying (see Table 12.3). Companies must do this carefully or find that their profits are much lower than planned.[25] Some product categories self-destruct by always being on sale. Manufacturers should consider the implications of supplying retailers at a discount, because they may end up losing long-run profits in an effort to meet short-run volume goals. Higher levels of management should conduct a *net price analysis* to arrive at the offering's "real price," which is affected by discounts and other expenses that reduce the realized price.

Promotional Pricing

Companies can use several pricing techniques to stimulate early purchase:

- *Loss-leader pricing.* Stores often drop the price on well-known brands to stimulate store traffic, which pays off if the revenue on the additional sales compensates for the lower margins on the loss-leader items. However, manufacturers of loss-leader brands typically object because this can dilute the brand image and bring complaints from retailers who charge the list price.

TABLE 12.3	Price Discounts and Allowances
Discount	A price reduction to buyers who pay bills promptly. A typical example is "2/10, net 30," which means that payment is due within 30 days and that the buyer can deduct 2 percent by paying the bill within 10 days.
Quantity Discount	A price reduction to those who buy large volumes. A typical example is "$10 per unit for fewer than 100 units; $9 per unit for 100 or more units." Quantity discounts must be offered equally to all customers and must not exceed the cost savings to the seller. They can be offered on each order placed or on the number of units ordered over a given period.
Functional Discount	Discount (also called *trade discount*) offered by a manufacturer to trade-channel members if they will perform certain functions, such as selling and storing. Manufacturers must offer the same functional discounts within each channel.
Seasonal Discount	A price reduction to those who buy merchandise or services out of season. Hotels and airlines offer seasonal discounts in slow selling periods.
Allowance	An extra payment designed to gain reseller participation in special programs. *Trade-in allowances* are granted for turning in an old item when buying a new one. *Promotional allowances* reward dealers for participating in advertising and sales support programs.

- Special event pricing. Sellers establish special prices in certain seasons to draw in more customers, such as back-to-school sales.
- Special customer pricing. Sellers offer special prices exclusively to certain customers, such as members of a brand community.
- Cash rebates. Auto companies and others offer cash rebates to encourage purchase of the manufacturers' products within a specified period, clearing inventories without cutting the stated list price.
- Low-interest financing. Instead of cutting its price, the company can offer customers low-interest financing.
- Longer payment terms. Sellers such as auto companies can stretch loans over longer periods, lowering the buyer's monthly payments. Consumers often worry less about the cost (the interest rate) of a loan, and more about whether they can afford the monthly payment.
- Warranties and service contracts. Companies can promote sales by adding a free or low-cost warranty or service contract.
- Psychological discounting. The firm sets an artificially high price and then offers the product at substantial savings; for example, "Was $359, now $299." The Federal Trade Commission and Better Business Bureaus fight illegal discount tactics.

Promotional-pricing strategies are often a zero-sum game. If they work, competitors copy them and they lose their effectiveness. If they don't work, they waste money that could have been put into other marketing tools, such as building up product quality and service or strengthening product image through advertising.

Differentiated Pricing

Companies often adjust their basic price to accommodate differences in customers, products, locations, and so on. **Price discrimination** occurs when a company sells a product or service at two or more prices that do not reflect a proportional difference in costs. In first-degree price discrimination, the seller charges a separate price to each customer depending on the intensity of his or her demand. In second-degree price discrimination, the seller charges less to buyers of larger volumes. In third-degree price discrimination, the seller charges different amounts to different classes of buyers:

- Customer-segment pricing. Different customer groups pay different prices for the same product or service. For example, museums often charge a lower admission fee to students.
- Product-form pricing. Different versions of the product are priced differently, but not proportionately to their costs. Evian may price a 48-ounce bottle of mineral water at $2 and 1.7 ounces of water as a moisturizer spray at $6.
- Image pricing. Some companies price the same product at two different levels based on image differences. A perfume manufacturer can put the perfume in one bottle, give it a name and image, and price it at $10 an ounce; the price for the same perfume in a different bottle with a different name and image might be $30 an ounce.
- Channel pricing. Coca-Cola carries a different price depending on whether the consumer purchases it in a fine restaurant, a fast-food restaurant, or a vending machine.
- Location pricing. The same product is priced differently at different locations even though the cost of offering it at each location is the same. A theater varies its seat prices according to audience preferences for different locations.
- Time pricing. Prices are varied by season, day, or hour. Utilities vary energy rates to commercial users by time of day and weekend versus weekday.

The airline and hospitality industries use yield management systems and *yield pricing,* offering discounted but limited early purchases, higher-priced late purchases, and the lowest rates on unsold inventory just before it expires.[26] Airlines charge different fares to passengers on the same flight, depending on the seating class, time of day, day of the week, and so on.

The phenomenon of offering different pricing schedules to different consumers and dynamically adjusting prices is exploding.[27] Price discrimination works when (1) the market is segmentable and the segments show different intensities of demand; (2) members in the lower-price segment cannot resell the product to the higher-price segment; (3) rivals cannot undersell the firm in the higher-price segment; (4) the cost of segmenting and policing the market does not exceed the extra revenue derived from price discrimination; (5) the practice does not breed customer resentment and ill will; and (6) the particular form of price discrimination is not illegal.[28]

Initiating and Responding to Price Changes

Companies often need to cut or raise prices in certain situations.

Initiating Price Cuts

Several circumstances might lead a firm to cut prices. One is *excess plant capacity*: The firm needs additional business and cannot generate it through increased sales effort or other measures. Firms sometimes initiate price cuts *to dominate the market through lower costs.* Either the company starts with lower costs than its competitors, or it initiates price cuts in the hope of gaining market share and lower costs. Price-cutting can lead to other possible traps: (1) customers assume quality is low; (2) a low price buys market share but not market loyalty because customers will shift to lower-priced firms; (3) higher-priced competitors match the lower prices but have longer staying power because of deeper cash reserves; and (4) a price war may be triggered.[29]

Initiating Price Increases

A successful price increase can raise profits considerably. If the company's profit margin is 3 percent of sales, a 1 percent price increase will increase profits by 33 percent if sales volume is unaffected. Sometimes firms increase prices due to *cost inflation,* when profit margins are squeezed by rising costs unmatched by productivity gains. Companies often raise their prices by more than the cost increase, in anticipation of further inflation, in a practice called *anticipatory pricing.*

Another factor leading to price increases is *overdemand.* When a company cannot supply all its customers, it can use one of these pricing techniques:

- Delayed quotation pricing. The company does not set a final price until the product is finished or delivered. This pricing is prevalent in industries with long production lead times.
- Escalator clauses. The company requires the customer to pay today's price and all or part of any inflation increase that takes place before delivery.
- Unbundling. The company maintains its price but removes or prices separately one or more elements that were part of the former offer, such as free delivery or installation.
- Reduction of discounts. The company no longer offers its usual cash and quantity discounts.

Generally, consumers prefer small, regular price increases to sudden, sharp increases, and they can turn against firms they perceive as price gougers. Price hikes without corresponding investments in the brand's value will increase vulnerability to lower-priced competition. To avoid a hostile reaction to a price increase, marketers should maintain a sense of fairness, such as by giving advance notice so customers can do forward buying or shop around. And sharp price increases need to be explained to customers in understandable terms.

Responding to Competitors' Price Changes

In deciding how to respond to a competitor's price cut, the firm must consider the product's life-cycle stage, its position in the product portfolio, the competitor's intentions and resources, the market's price and quality sensitivity, the behavior of costs with volume, and the firm's alternative opportunities. In markets characterized by high product homogeneity, the firm can search for ways to enhance its augmented product; otherwise, it may need to meet the price reduction. If the competitor raises its price in a homogeneous product market, other firms might not match it unless the increase will benefit the industry as a whole. Then the leader will need to roll back the increase.

In nonhomogeneous product markets, a firm should consider why the competitor changed the price. Was it to steal the market, utilize excess capacity, meet changing cost conditions, or lead an industry-wide price change? Is the competitor's price change temporary or permanent? What will happen to the company's market share and profits if it does not respond? Are other companies likely to respond? What are the competitors' and other firms' responses likely to be to each possible reaction? To be prepared, marketers should anticipate possible competitors' price changes and plan contingent responses.

EXECUTIVE SUMMARY

Price is the only element that produces revenue; the others produce costs. In setting pricing policy, a company follows six steps: (1) select the pricing objective; (2) determine demand; (3) estimate costs; (4) analyze competitors' costs, prices, and offers; (5) select a pricing method; and (6) select the final price. To adapt prices, firms can use geographical pricing, price discounts and allowances, promotional pricing, and differentiated pricing.

Firms often need to change their prices. A price decrease might be brought about by situations such as excess plant capacity or a desire to dominate the market through lower costs. A price increase might be brought about by cost inflation or overdemand. Companies must carefully manage customer perceptions when raising prices. They should also anticipate competitors' price changes and prepare contingent responses, which may depend on whether the products are homogeneous or nonhomogeneous.

NOTES

1. Andria Cheng, "Tiffany Hints at Cautious Consumers as 2Q Net Rises," *Wall Street Journal,* August 27, 2010, www.wsj.com; Miriam Gottfried, "Tiffany Is Diamond in Stock-Market Rough," *Barron's,* July 22, 2010, http://online.barrons.com; Brian Burnsed, "Where Discounting Can Be Dangerous," *BusinessWeek,* August 3, 2009, p. 49; "Tiffany's Profit Tops Expectations," *Associated Press,* November 26, 2009; Cintra Wilson, "If Bling Had a Hall of Fame," *New York Times,* July 30, 2009; Ellen Byron, "Fashion Victim: To Refurbish Its Image, Tiffany Risks Profits," *Wall Street Journal,* January 10, 2007, p. A1.

2. Rick Newman, "The Great Retail Revolution," *U.S. News & World Report,* March 2010, pp. 19–20; Philip Moeller, "Tough Times Are Molding Tough Consumers," *U.S. News & World Report,* March 2010, pp. 22–25; Steve Hamm, "The New Age of Frugality," *BusinessWeek,* October 20, 2008, pp. 55–60; Timothy W. Martin, "Frugal Shoppers Drive Grocers Back to Basics," *Wall Street Journal,* June 24, 2009, p. B1.

3. For a discussion of some of the academic issues involved, see Florian Zettelmeyer, "Expanding to the Internet: Pricing and Communication Strategies when Firms Compete on Multiple Channels," *Journal of Marketing Research* 37 (August 2000), pp. 292–308; John G. Lynch Jr. and Dan Ariely, "Wine Online: Search Costs Affect Competition on Price, Quality, and Distribution," *Marketing Science* 19, no. 1 (Winter 2000), pp. 83–103; Rajiv Lal and Miklos Sarvary, "When and How Is the Internet Likely to Decrease Price Competition?" *Marketing Science* 18, no. 4 (Fall 1999), pp. 485–503.

4. Andrew Davidson, "We Don't Mind If You Hate Us, Just Keep Flying," *Sunday Times (London),* July 25, 2010, p. 6; Chris Anderson, *Free: The Future of a Radical Price* (New York: Hyperion, 2009); Katherine Heires, "Why It Pays to Give Away the Store," *Business 2.0,* October 2006, pp. 36–37; Ju-Young Kim, Martin Natter, and Martin Spann, "Pay What You Want: A New Participative Pricing Mechanism," *Journal of Marketing* 73 (January 2009), pp. 44–58; Koen Pauwels and Allen Weiss, "Moving from Free to Fee: How Online Firms Market to Change Their Business Model Successfully," *Journal of Marketing* 72 (May 2008), pp. 14–31;

Matthew Maier, "A Radical Fix for Airlines: Make Flying Free," *Business 2.0,* April 2006, pp. 32–34.

5. For a thorough, up-to-date review of pricing research, see Chezy Ofir and Russell S. Winer, "Pricing: Economic and Behavioral Models," Bart Weitz and Robin Wensley, eds., *Handbook of Marketing* (London: Sage Publications, 2002).

6. Bruce Horovitz, "Sale, Sale, Sale: Today Everyone Wants a Deal," *USA Today,* April 21, 2010, pp. 1A, 2A.

7. Peter R. Dickson and Alan G. Sawyer, "The Price Knowledge and Search of Supermarket Shoppers," *Journal of Marketing* 54, no. 3 (July 1990), pp. 42–53. For a methodological qualification, however, see Hooman Estalami, Alfred Holden, and Donald R. Lehmann, "Macro-Economic Determinants of Consumer Price Knowledge: A Meta-Analysis of Four Decades of Research," *International Journal of Research in Marketing* 18 (December 2001), pp. 341–55.

8. For a comprehensive review, see Tridib Mazumdar, S. P. Raj, and Indrajit Sinha, "Reference Price Research: Review and Propositions," *Journal of Marketing* 69 (October 2005), pp. 84–102. For a different point of view, see Chris Janiszewski and Donald R. Lichtenstein, "A Range Theory Account of Price Perception," *Journal of Consumer Research* 25, no. 4 (March 1999), pp. 353–68.

9. K. N. Rajendran and Gerard J. Tellis, "Contextual and Temporal Components of Reference Price," *Journal of Marketing* 58, no. 1 (January 1994), pp. 22–34; Gurumurthy Kalyanaram and Russell S. Winer, "Empirical Generalizations from Reference-Price Research," *Marketing Science* 14, no. 3 (Summer 1995), pp. G161–69. See also, Ritesh Saini, Raghunath Singh Rao, and Ashwani Monga, "Is the Deal Worth My Time? The Interactive Effect of Relative and Referent Thinking on Willingness to Seek a Bargain," *Journal of Marketing* 74 (January 2010), pp. 34–48.

10. Wilfred Amaldoss and Sanjay Jain, "Pricing of Conspicuous Goods: A Competitive Analysis of Social Effects," *Journal of Marketing Research* 42, no. 1 (February 2005); Angela Chao and Juliet B. Schor, "Empirical Tests of Status Consumption," *Journal of Economic Psychology* 19, no. 1 (January 1998), pp. 107–31.

11. Mark Stiving and Russell S. Winer, "An Empirical Analysis of Price Endings with Scanner Data," *Journal of Consumer Research* 24 (June 1997), pp. 57–68.

12. Eric T. Anderson and Duncan Simester, "Effects of $9 Price Endings on Retail Sales: Evidence from Field Experiments," *Quantitative Marketing and Economics* 1, no. 1 (March 2003), pp. 93–110.

13. Shantanu Dutta, Mark J. Zbaracki, and Mark Bergen, "Pricing Process as a Capability: A Resource-Based Perspective," *Strategic Management Journal* 24, no. 7 (July 2003), pp. 615–30.

14. Joo Heon Park and Douglas L. MacLachlan, "Estimating Willingness to Pay with Exaggeration Bias-Corrected Contingent Valuation Method," *Marketing Science* 27 (July–August 2008), pp. 691–98.

15. Thomas T. Nagle and Reed K. Holden, *The Strategy and Tactics of Pricing,* 3rd ed. (Upper Saddle River, NJ: Prentice Hall, 2002).

16. For a summary of elasticity studies, see Dominique M. Hanssens, Leonard J. Parsons, and Randall L. Schultz, *Market Response Models: Econometric and Time Series Analysis* (Boston: Kluwer, 1990), pp. 187–91.

17. Tammo H. A. Bijmolt, Harald J. Van Heerde, and Rik G. M. Pieters, "New Empirical Generalizations on the Determinants of Price Elasticity," *Journal of Marketing Research* 42 (May 2005), pp. 141–56.

18. Michael Sivy, "Japan's Smart Secret Weapon," *Fortune,* August 12, 1991, p. 75.

19. Reena Jane, "From India, the Latest Management Fad," *Bloomberg BusinessWeek,* December 14, 2009, p. 57; Julie Jargon, "General Mills Takes Several Steps to Combat High Commodity Costs," *Wall Street Journal,* September 20, 2007; Mina Kimes, "Cereal Cost Cutters," *Fortune,* November 10, 2008, p. 24.

20. Tung-Zong Chang and Albert R. Wildt, "Price, Product Information, and Purchase Intention," *Journal of the Academy of Marketing Science* 22, no. 1 (Winter 1994), pp. 16–27. See also, G. Dean Kortge and Patrick A. Okonkwo, "Perceived Value Approach to Pricing," *Industrial Marketing Management* 22, no. 2 (May 1993), pp. 133–40.

21. Stephen J. Hoch, Xavier Dreze, and Mary J. Purk, "EDLP, Hi-Lo, and Margin Arithmetic," *Journal of Marketing* 58, no. 4 (October 1994), pp. 16–27; Rajiv Lal and R. Rao, "Supermarket Competition: The Case of Everyday Low Pricing," *Marketing Science* 16, no. 1 (Winter 1997), pp. 60–80; Michael Tsiros and David M. Hardesty, "Ending a Price Promotion: Retracting It in One Step or Phasing It Out Gradually," *Journal of Marketing* 74, 1 (January 2010), pp. 49–64.

22. Using expected profit for setting price makes sense for the seller that makes many bids. The seller who bids only occasionally or who needs a particular contract badly will not find it advantageous to use expected profit. This criterion does not distinguish between a $1,000 profit with a 0.10 probability and a $125 profit with a 0.80 probability. Yet the firm that wants to keep production going would prefer the second contract to the first.

23. Paul W. Farris and David J. Reibstein, "How Prices, Expenditures, and Profits Are Linked," *Harvard Business Review,* November–December 1979, pp. 173–84. See also, Makoto Abe, "Price and Advertising Strategy of a National Brand against Its Private-Label Clone," *Journal of Business Research* 33, no. 3 (July 1995), pp. 241–50.

24. Joel E. Urbany, "Justifying Profitable Pricing," *Journal of Product and Brand Management* 10, no. 3 (2001), pp. 141–57; Charles Fishman, "The Wal-Mart You Don't Know," *Fast Company,* December 2003, pp. 68–80.

25. Michael V. Marn and Robert L. Rosiello, "Managing Price, Gaining Profit," *Harvard Business Review,* September–October 1992, pp. 84–94. See also, Kusum L. Ailawadi, Scott A. Neslin, and Karen Gedenk, "Pursuing the Value-Conscious Consumer: Store Brands versus National-Brand Promotions," *Journal of Marketing* 65 (January 2001), pp. 71–89; Gerard J. Tellis, "Tackling the Retailer Decision Maze: Which Brands to Discount, How Much, When, and Why?" *Marketing Science* 14, no. 3, pt. 2 (Summer 1995), pp. 271–99.

26. Ramarao Deesiraju and Steven M. Shugan, "Strategic Service Pricing and Yield Management," *Journal of Marketing* 63 (January 1999), pp. 44–56; Robert E. Weigand, "Yield Management: Filling Buckets, Papering the House," *Business Horizons* 42, no. 5 (September–October 1999), pp. 55–64.

27. Charles Fishman, "Which Price Is Right?" *Fast Company,* March 2003, pp. 92–102; Bob Tedeschi, "E-Commerce Report," *New York Times,* September 2, 2002; Faith Keenan, "The Price Is Really Right," *BusinessWeek,* March 31, 2003, pp. 62–67; Peter Coy, "The Power of Smart Pricing," *BusinessWeek,* April 10, 2000, pp. 160–64. For a review of recent and seminal work linking pricing decisions with operational insights, see Moritz Fleischmann, Joseph M. Hall, and David F. Pyke, "Research Brief: Smart Pricing," *MIT Sloan Management Review* (Winter 2004), pp. 9–13.

28. For more information on specific types of price discrimination that are illegal, see Henry Cheeseman, *Business Law,* 6th ed. (Upper Saddle River, NJ: Prentice Hall, 2007).

29. Harald J. Van Heerde, Els Gijsbrechts, and Koen Pauwels, "Winners and Losers in a Major Price War," *Journal of Marketing Research* 45 (October 2008), pp. 499–518.

Designing and Managing Integrated Marketing Channels

In this chapter, we will address the following questions:

1. What is a marketing channel system and value network?
2. What work do marketing channels perform?
3. What decisions do companies face in designing, managing, and integrating their channels?
4. What key issues do marketers face with e-commerce and m-commerce?

Marketing Management at Netflix

Convinced that DVDs were the home video medium of the future, Netflix founder Reed Hastings came up with a form of DVD rental distribution in 1997 different from the brick-and-mortar stores used by Blockbuster, then the market leader. Netflix's strong customer loyalty and positive word of mouth is a result of the service's distinctive capabilities: affordable subscription fees, no late fees, (mostly) overnight mail delivery, and a catalog of over 100,000 movie and television titles. The service also has proprietary software that allows customers to easily search for obscure films and discover new ones.

With increased competition from Redbox's 22,000 DVD-rental kiosks in supermarkets and other locations—and higher postage costs—Netflix is putting more emphasis on streaming videos and instantaneous delivery mechanisms. But it still sees growth in DVD rentals from its over 15 million subscribers. Netflix's success has also captured Hollywood's attention. Its online communities of customers who provide and read reviews and feedback can be an important source of fans for films.[1]

Successful value creation depends on successful value delivery. Holistic marketers are increasingly taking a value network view of their businesses, examining the entire supply chain that links raw materials, components, and manufactured goods and shows how they move toward the final consumers. This chapter examines the strategic and tactical issues of marketing channels and value networks; Chapter 14 explores marketing channels from the perspective of retailers, wholesalers, and physical distribution agencies.

Marketing Channels and Value Networks

Most producers do not sell their goods directly to the final users; between them stands a set of intermediaries performing a variety of functions. These are **marketing channels** (also called trade channels or distribution channels), sets of interdependent organizations participating in the process of making a product or service available for use or consumption. They are the set of pathways a product or service follows after production, culminating in purchase and consumption by the final end user.[2]

The Importance of Channels

A **marketing channel system** is the particular set of marketing channels a firm employs, and decisions about it are among the most critical ones management faces. In the United States, channel members collectively earn margins that account for 30 percent to 50 percent of the ultimate selling price, whereas advertising typically accounts for less than 7 percent of the final price.[3] Marketing channels also represent a substantial opportunity cost because they do not just *serve* markets, they must also *make* markets.[4]

The channels chosen affect all other marketing decisions. The company's pricing depends on whether it uses online discounters or high-quality boutiques. Its sales force and advertising decisions depend on how much training and motivation dealers need. In addition, channel decisions include relatively long-term commitments with other firms as well as a set of policies and procedures. When an automaker signs up independent dealers to sell its automobiles, it cannot buy them out the next day and replace them with company-owned outlets. Holistic marketers ensure that marketing decisions in all these areas are made to collectively maximize value.

In managing its intermediaries, the firm must decide how much effort to devote to push versus pull marketing. A **push strategy** uses the manufacturer's sales force, trade promotion money, or other means to induce intermediaries to carry, promote, and sell the product to end users. This is appropriate when there is low brand loyalty in a category, brand choice is made in the store, the product is an impulse item, and product benefits are well understood. In a **pull strategy** the manufacturer uses advertising and other communications to persuade consumers to demand the product from intermediaries, thus inducing the intermediaries to order it. This strategy is appropriate when there is high brand loyalty and high involvement in the category, consumers perceive differences between brands, and brand choices are made before a trip to the store. Top marketing companies such as Coca-Cola and Nike skillfully employ both push and pull strategies.

Hybrid Channels and Multichannel Marketing

Today's successful companies typically employ hybrid channels and multichannel marketing, multiplying the number of "go-to-market" channels in any one market area. **Hybrid channels or multichannel marketing** occurs when a single firm uses two or more marketing channels to reach customer segments. Hewlett-Packard uses its sales force for large accounts, outbound telemarketing for medium-sized accounts, direct mail with an inbound number for small accounts, retailers for still smaller accounts, and the Internet for specialty items.

In multichannel marketing, each channel targets a different segment of buyers, or different need states for one buyer, and delivers the right products in the right places in the right way at the least cost. Companies must make sure their multiple channels work well together and match each target segment's preferred ways of doing business. Customers expect *channel integration* so they can (1) order online and pick up at a convenient retail location; (2) return an online-ordered product to a nearby store; (3) receive discounts and promotional offers based on all channel purchases.

Value Networks

The company should first think of the target market, however, and then design the supply chain backward from that point, a strategy called **demand chain planning**.[5] A broader view sees a company at the center of a **value network**—a system of partnerships and alliances that a firm creates to source, augment, and deliver its offerings. A value network includes a firm's suppliers and its suppliers' suppliers, its immediate customers, and their end customers. The value network includes valued relationships with others such as university researchers and government approval agencies.

Demand chain planning yields several insights.[6] First, the company can estimate whether more money is made upstream or downstream so it can integrate backward or forward. Second, the company can detect supply-chain disturbances that might change costs, prices, or supplies. Third, companies can go online with business partners to speed communications, transactions, and payments; reduce costs; and increase accuracy.

The Role of Marketing Channels

Why would a producer delegate some of the selling job to intermediaries, relinquishing control over how and to whom products are sold? Through their contacts, experience, specialization, and scale of operation, intermediaries make goods available and accessible to target markets, usually more effectively and efficiently than the producer can achieve on its own.[7] Many producers lack the financial resources and expertise to sell directly. The William Wrigley Jr. Company would not find it practical to establish retail gum shops or sell gum by mail order. It is easier to work through the extensive network of privately owned distribution organizations. Even Ford would be hard-pressed to replace all the tasks done by its almost 12,000 dealer outlets worldwide.

Channel Functions and Flows

A marketing channel performs the work of moving goods from producers to consumers. It overcomes the time, place, and possession gaps that separate goods and services from those who need or want them. Members of the marketing channel perform a number of key functions (see Table 13.1).

Some functions (storage and movement, title, and communications) constitute a *forward flow* of activity from the company to the customer; other functions (ordering and payment) constitute a *backward flow* from customers to the company. Still others (information, negotiation, finance, and risk taking) occur in both directions. Five flows for the marketing of forklift trucks

TABLE 13.1	Channel Member Functions

- Gather information about potential and current customers, competitors, and other actors and forces in the marketing environment.
- Develop and disseminate persuasive communications to stimulate purchasing.
- Reach agreements on price and other terms so that transfer of ownership or possession can be made.
- Place orders with manufacturers.
- Acquire the funds to finance inventories at different levels in the marketing channel.
- Assume risks connected with carrying out channel work.
- Provide for the successive storage and movement of physical products.
- Provide for buyers' payment of their bills through banks and other financial institutions.
- Oversee actual transfer of ownership from one organization or person to another.

are illustrated in Figure 13.1. If these flows were superimposed in one diagram, we would see the tremendous complexity of even simple marketing channels.

A manufacturer selling a physical product and services might require three channels: a *sales channel,* a *delivery channel,* and a *service channel.* The question is not *whether* various channel functions need to be performed—they must be—but rather, *who* is to perform them. All channel functions use up scarce resources, can often be performed better through specialization, and can be shifted among channel members. Shifting some functions to intermediaries lowers the producer's costs and prices, but the intermediary must add a charge to cover its work. If the intermediaries are more efficient than the manufacturer, prices to consumers should be lower. If consumers perform some functions themselves, they should enjoy even lower prices.

Channel Levels

The producer and the final customer are part of every channel. We will use the number of intermediary levels to designate the length of a channel. Figure 13.2(a) illustrates several consumer-goods marketing channels of different lengths, while Figure 13.2(b) illustrates industrial marketing channels.

A **zero-level channel**, also called a **direct marketing channel**, consists of a manufacturer selling directly to final customers through door-to-door sales, home parties, mail order, telemarketing, TV selling, Internet selling, manufacturer-owned stores, and other methods. A *one-level channel* contains one selling intermediary. A *two-level channel* contains two intermediaries; in consumer markets, these are typically a wholesaler and a retailer. A *three-level channel* contains three intermediaries. Obtaining information about end users and exercising control becomes more difficult for the producer as the number of channel levels increases.

Channels normally describe a forward movement of products from source to user, but *reverse-flow channels* are also important (1) to reuse products or containers (such as reusable bottles), (2) to refurbish products for resale (such as computers), (3) to recycle products (such as paper), and (4) to dispose of products and packaging. Reverse-flow intermediaries include manufacturers' redemption centers, community groups, trash-collection specialists, and recycling centers.

Service Sector Channels

As Internet and other technologies advance, service industries such as banking and travel are operating through new channels. Kodak offers its customers four ways to print their digital photos— mini-labs in retail outlets, home printers, online services at its Web site, and self-service kiosks.

FIGURE 13.1 Five Marketing Flows in the Marketing Channel for Forklift Trucks

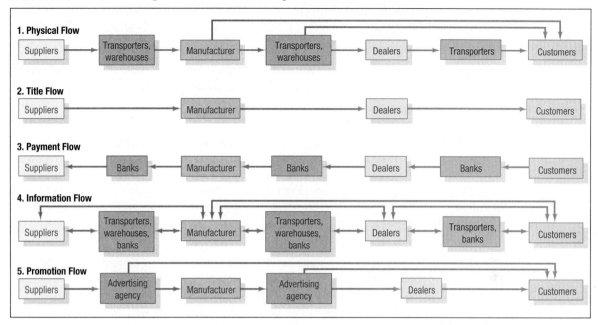

With 80,000 kiosks, Kodak makes money by selling the units and supplying the chemicals and paper used to print photos.[8]

Marketing channels also keep changing in "person marketing." Besides live and programmed entertainment, musicians and other artists can reach fans online in many ways—their own Web sites, social media such as Facebook and Twitter, and third-party Web sites. In addition, nonprofit

FIGURE 13.2 Consumer and Industrial Marketing Channels

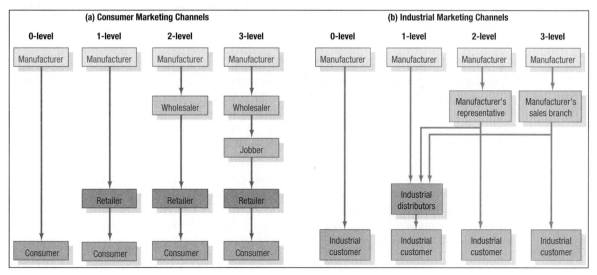

service organizations such as schools are developing "educational-dissemination systems" and hospitals are developing "health-delivery systems" to reach their target markets.

Channel-Design Decisions

To design a marketing channel system, marketers must analyze customer needs and wants, establish objectives and constraints, and identify and evaluate major channel alternatives.

Analyzing Customer Needs and Wants

Consumers may choose the channels they prefer based on price, product assortment, and convenience, as well as their own shopping goals (economic, social, or experiential).[9] As with products, segmentation exists, and marketers must be aware that different consumers have different needs during the purchase process. Even the same consumer may choose different channels for different functions in a purchase, browsing a catalog before visiting a store or test driving a car at a dealer before ordering online.

Channels produce five service outputs:

1. *Lot size*—The number of units the channel permits a typical customer to purchase on one occasion. In buying cars for its fleet, Hertz prefers a channel from which it can buy a large lot size; a household wants a channel that permits a lot size of one.

2. *Waiting and delivery time*—The average time customers wait for receipt of goods. Customers increasingly prefer faster delivery channels.

3. *Spatial convenience*—The degree to which the marketing channel makes it easy for customers to purchase the product.

4. *Product variety*—The assortment provided by the marketing channel. Normally, customers prefer a greater assortment, although too many choices can sometimes create a negative effect.[10]

5. *Service backup*—Add-on services (credit, delivery, installation, repairs) provided by the channel.

Providing greater service outputs also means increasing channel costs and raising prices. The success of discounters (offline and online) indicates that many consumers will accept smaller service outputs if they can save money.

Establishing Objectives and Constraints

Marketers should state their channel objectives in terms of service output levels and associated cost and support levels, adapting objectives to the larger environment. Under competitive conditions, channel members will arrange their functional tasks to minimize costs and still provide desired levels of service.[11] Usually, planners can identify several market segments based on desired service and choose the best channels for each.

Channel objectives vary with product characteristics. Bulky products, such as building materials, require channels that minimize shipping distance and handling. Products requiring installation or maintenance services, such as heating and cooling systems, are usually sold and maintained by the company or franchised dealers. High-unit-value products such as turbines are often sold through a company sales force rather than through intermediaries. Legal regulations and restrictions also affect channel design.

Identifying Major Channel Alternatives

Each channel—from sales forces to agents, distributors, dealers, direct mail, telemarketing, and the Internet—has unique strengths and weaknesses. Channel alternatives differ in three ways: the types of intermediaries, the number needed, and the terms and responsibilities of each.

Types of Intermediaries   Some intermediaries—*merchants* such as wholesalers and retailers—buy, take title to, and resell the merchandise. *Agents* such as brokers, manufacturers' representatives, and sales agents search for customers and may negotiate on the producer's behalf but do not take title to the goods. *Facilitators*—transportation companies, independent warehouses, banks, advertising agencies—assist in distribution but neither take title to goods nor negotiate purchases or sales. Sometimes a firm chooses a new or unconventional channel because of the difficulty, cost, or ineffectiveness of working with the dominant channel.

Number of Intermediaries   The number of intermediaries depends on whether a firm uses exclusive distribution, selective distribution, or intensive distribution. **Exclusive distribution** means severely limiting the number of intermediaries, appropriate when the producer wants to control resellers' service level and outputs. In many cases, this includes *exclusive dealing* arrangements, by which the producer hopes to obtain more dedicated, knowledgeable selling.

Selective distribution relies on only some of the intermediaries willing to carry a particular product. Here, the company need not worry about having too many outlets; it can gain adequate market coverage with more control and less cost than intensive distribution. **Intensive distribution** places offerings in as many outlets as possible, a good strategy for snack foods, soft drinks, newspapers, candies, and gum—products consumers buy frequently or in a variety of locations.

Terms and Responsibilities of Channel Members   The main elements in the "trade-relations mix" are price policies, conditions of sale, territorial rights, and specific services to be performed by each party. *Price policy* calls for the producer to establish a price list and schedule of discounts and allowances that intermediaries see as equitable and sufficient. *Conditions of sale* are payment terms and producer guarantees. Most producers give distributors cash discounts for early payment; they might also offer a guarantee against defective goods or price declines. *Distributors' territorial rights* define the distributors' territories and the terms under which the producer will add other distributors. Distributors normally expect to receive full credit for all sales in their territory, whether or not they did the selling. *Mutual services and responsibilities* must be carefully spelled out, especially in franchised and exclusive-agency channels.

Evaluating Major Channel Alternatives

Each channel alternative needs to be evaluated against economic, control, and adaptive criteria. Figure 13.3 shows how six different sales channels stack up in terms of the value added per sale and the cost per transaction. Marketers should estimate how many sales each alternative will likely generate and the costs of selling different volumes through each channel, then compare sales and costs. Firms will try to align customers and channels to maximize demand at the lowest overall cost, replacing high-cost channels with low-cost channels as long as the value added per sale is sufficient.

Control can be an important factor, especially for channels that are not direct. For example, sales agents may concentrate on the customers who buy the most, not necessarily those who buy

FIGURE 13.3 The Value-Adds versus Costs of Different Channels

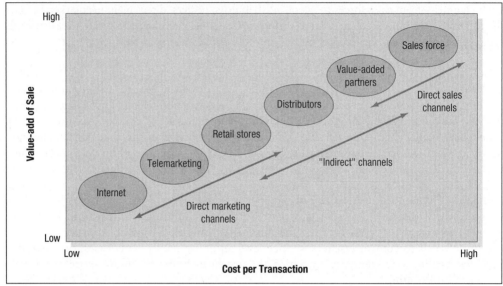

Source: Oxford Associates, adapted from Dr. Rowland T. Moriarty, Cubex Corp.

the manufacturer's goods. They might not master the technical details of the company's product or handle its promotion materials effectively. Finally, to develop a channel, members must commit to each other for a specified period. This reduces the producer's ability to respond to change and uncertainty, even though it needs channel structures and policies that are adaptable.

Channel-Management Decisions

After a firm has chosen a channel system, it must select, train, motivate, and evaluate individual intermediaries for each channel. It may also modify channel design and arrangements over time.

Selecting Channel Members

To customers, the channels are the company. Consider the negative impression customers would get of Mercedes-Benz if its dealerships appeared dirty or inefficient. Producers should determine what characteristics distinguish the better intermediaries—number of years in business, other lines carried, growth and profit record, financial strength, cooperativeness, and reputation. If the intermediaries are sales agents, producers should evaluate the number and character of other lines carried and the size and quality of the sales force. If the intermediaries want exclusive distribution, their locations, future growth potential, and type of clientele will matter.

Training and Motivating Channel Members

A company should view its intermediaries the same way it views its end users—determining their needs and wants and tailoring its channel offering to give them superior value. Carefully implemented training, market research, and other capability-building programs can motivate and improve intermediaries' performance. The company must constantly communicate that intermediaries are crucial partners in a joint effort to satisfy the product's end users.

Producers vary greatly in **channel power**, the ability to alter channel members' behavior so they take actions they would not have taken otherwise.[12] Most producers see gaining intermediaries' cooperation as a huge challenge. In many cases, retailers hold the power, so manufacturers must know the acceptance criteria used by retail buyers and store managers. More sophisticated companies try to forge a long-term partnership with distributors.[13] The manufacturer clearly communicates what it wants from its distributors in the way of market coverage and other channel issues and may introduce a compensation plan for adhering to these policies.

Evaluating Channel Members

Producers must periodically evaluate intermediaries' performance against such standards as sales-quota attainment, average inventory levels, customer delivery time, treatment of damaged and lost goods, and cooperation in promotional and training programs (see "Marketing Skills: Evaluating Channel Members"). Underperformers need to be counseled, retrained, motivated, or terminated.

Modifying Channel Design and Arrangements

A producer must periodically review and modify its channel design and arrangements.[14] A new firm typically starts as a local operation selling in a fairly circumscribed market, using a few existing intermediaries. Here, the problem is to convince the available intermediaries to handle the firm's line. If the firm is successful, it might branch into new markets with different channels. Over time, the channel may need modification as buying patterns change, the market expands, new competition arises, innovative channels emerge, and the product moves into later life-cycle stages.[15] Adding or dropping channel members requires an incremental analysis, which may be performed using sophisticated tools.[16] A basic question is: What would the firm's sales and profits look like with and without this intermediary?

EVALUATING CHANNEL MEMBERS

How important is it for marketers to evaluate and manage suppliers, retailers, and other channel members? One firm found that unpredictable supplier deliveries were causing it to hold $200 million in excess inventory. By evaluating suppliers on standards such as on-time delivery, this firm slashed its costs. To start, determine how suppliers (and their suppliers) as well as distributors can influence the company's performance. Also, translate companywide strategic goals and measurements into specific targets and measures for channel partners throughout the supply chain. Finally, continually measure and reward performance to keep channels efficient, responsive, and reliable.

A growing number of manufacturers and retailers are including environmental sustainability measures in their channel evaluations. Walmart, for example, reviews its suppliers' performance on specific environmental goals and standards such as reducing harmful emissions and eliminating excess packaging. Similarly, Procter & Gamble has introduced a sustainability scorecard to evaluate the environmental performance of the 75,000 firms that make up its global supply chain, encouraging progressively more eco-friendly practices from year to year.[17]

Global Channel Considerations

International markets pose distinct challenges, including variations in customers' shopping habits, but also open opportunities.[18] Many top global retailers such as the United Kingdom's Tesco and Spain's Zara have tailored their image to local needs and wants when entering a new market. Getting close to customers is essential to effective global channel planning. For example, to adapt its clothing for European tastes, Philadelphia-based Urban Outfitters set up a separate design and merchandising unit in London before opening any European stores. Despite higher costs, the blended American and European looks helped the retailer stand out.[19]

Channel Integration and Systems

Distribution channels don't stand still. We'll look at the recent growth of vertical, horizontal, and multichannel marketing systems; the next section examines how these systems cooperate, conflict, and compete.

Vertical Marketing Systems

A *conventional marketing channel* consists of an independent producer, wholesaler(s), and retailer(s). Each is a separate business seeking to maximize its own profits, even if this goal reduces profit for the system as a whole. No channel member has complete or substantial control over other members.

A **vertical marketing system (VMS)**, by contrast, includes the producer, wholesaler(s), and retailer(s) acting as a unified system. One channel member, the *channel captain*, owns or franchises

Marketing Insight

THE IMPORTANCE OF CHANNEL STEWARDS

Harvard's V. Kasturi Rangan believes firms should adopt a new approach to going to market: channel stewardship. Rangan defines *channel stewardship* as the ability of a given participant in a distribution channel—a steward—to create a go-to-market strategy that simultaneously addresses customers' best interests and drives profits for all channel partners. The channel steward accomplishes coordination by persuading channel partners to act in the best interest of all. A channel steward might be the maker of the good or service (Procter & Gamble), the maker of a key component (Intel), the supplier or assembler (Dell), the distributor (W. W. Grainger), or the retailer (Walmart).

Channel stewardship (1) expands value for the steward's customers, enlarging the market or existing customers' purchases through the channel, and (2) creates a tightly woven and yet adaptable channel, rewarding valuable members and weeding out less-valuable members. An evolutionary approach to channel change, stewardship requires constant monitoring, learning, and adaptation, all in the best interests of customers, channel partners, and channel steward.

Sources: V. Kasturi Rangan, *Transforming Your Go-to-Market Strategy: The Three Disciplines of Channel Management* (Boston: Harvard Business School Press, 2006); Kash Rangan, "Channel Stewardship: An Introductory Guide," www.channelstewardship.com; Partha Rose and Romit Dey, "Channel Stewardship: Driving Profitable Revenue Growth in High-Tech with Multi-Channel Management," *Infosys ViewPoint,* August 2007.

the others or has so much power that they all cooperate. "Marketing Insight: The Importance of Channel Stewards" shows how *channel stewards*, a closely related concept, can work.

Vertical marketing systems (VMSs) arose from strong channel members' attempts to control channel behavior and eliminate conflict over independent members pursuing their own objectives. VMSs achieve economies through size, bargaining power, and elimination of duplicated services. In fact, VMSs have become the dominant mode of distribution in the U.S. consumer marketplace.

There are three types of VMS: corporate, administered, and contractual. A *corporate VMS* combines successive stages of production and distribution under one owner. An *administered VMS* coordinates successive stages of production and distribution through one member's size and power, the way Gillette and other big brands secure strong reseller cooperation and support. A *contractual VMS* consists of independent firms at different levels of production and distribution, integrating their programs on a contractual basis to obtain more economies or sales impact than they could achieve alone.[20] These include:

1. *Wholesaler-sponsored voluntary chains* that organize groups of independent retailers to better compete with large chains through standardized selling practices and buying economies.

2. *Retailer cooperatives* in which retailers take the initiative and organize a business entity to carry on wholesaling and possibly some production. Members concentrate their purchases through the co-op and jointly plan advertising, with profits passing back to members in proportion to purchases.

3. *Franchise organizations* in which a *franchisor* links several successive stages in the production-distribution process: the manufacturer-sponsored retailer franchise (Ford and its dealers), the manufacturer-sponsored wholesaler franchise (Coca-Cola and its bottlers), and the service-firm-sponsored retailer franchise (McDonald's and its franchises).

Horizontal Marketing Systems

Another channel development is the **horizontal marketing system**, in which two or more unrelated companies put together resources or programs to exploit an emerging marketing opportunity. Each company lacks the capital, know-how, production, or marketing resources to venture alone, or it is afraid of the risk. The companies might work together on a temporary or permanent basis or create a joint venture company. For example, many supermarket chains have arrangements with local banks to offer in-store banking.

Integrating Multichannel Marketing Systems

An **integrated marketing channel system** is one in which the strategies and tactics of selling through one channel reflect the strategies and tactics of selling through one or more other channels. One benefit of adding more channels is increased market coverage. Not only are more customers able to shop for the company's products in more places, but those who buy in more than one channel are often more profitable than single-channel customers.[21] A second benefit is lower channel cost—selling by phone is cheaper than personal selling to small customers. A third benefit is more customized selling, such as by adding a technical sales force to sell complex equipment. However, new channels typically introduce conflict and problems with control and cooperation.

Multichannel marketers also need to decide how much of their product to offer in each channel. Patagonia views the Web as the ideal channel for showing off its entire line, given that its stores have space to offer only a selection, and even its catalog promotes less than 70 percent of its total merchandise.[22] Other marketers limit their online offerings, theorizing that customers look to Web sites and catalogs for a "best of" array of merchandise and don't want to have to click through dozens of pages.

Conflict, Cooperation, and Competition

No matter how well channels are designed and managed, there will be some conflict, if only because the interests of independent business entities do not always coincide. **Channel conflict** is generated when one channel member's actions prevent another channel member from achieving its goal. **Channel coordination** occurs when channel members are brought together to advance the channel's goals, as opposed to their own potentially incompatible goals.[23] Here we examine three questions: What types of conflict arise in channels? What causes conflict? How can it be managed?

Types of Conflict and Competition

Horizontal channel conflict occurs between channel members at the same level. *Vertical channel conflict* occurs between different levels of the channel. Greater retailer consolidation has led to increased price pressure and influence from retailers.[24] Walmart, for example, is the principal buyer for many manufacturers, including Disney, and can command reduced prices or quantity discounts from suppliers.[25] *Multichannel conflict* exists when the manufacturer has two or more channels that sell to the same market.[26] It's likely to be especially intense when the members of one channel get a lower price (based on larger-volume purchases) or work with a lower margin.

Causes of Channel Conflict

One major cause of channel conflict is *goal incompatibility.* The manufacturer may want to achieve rapid market penetration through a low-price policy, but dealers may want high margins for short-run profitability. Another cause is *unclear roles and rights.* HP may sell computers to large accounts through its own sales force, but its licensed dealers may also be trying to sell to large accounts. Territory boundaries and credit for sales often produce conflict.

Conflict can also stem from *differences in perception,* as when a producer is optimistic about the economy and wants dealers to carry higher inventory, but its dealers are pessimistic. At times, conflict can occur because of intermediaries' *dependence* on the manufacturer. For example, the fortunes of exclusive dealers, such as auto dealers, are profoundly affected by the manufacturer's product and pricing decisions.

Managing Channel Conflict

Some channel conflict can be constructive and lead to better adaptation to a changing environment, but too much is dysfunctional.[27] The challenge is to manage conflict well, through mechanisms such as strategic justification (showing channels or members how each serves distinctive segments); dual compensation (paying existing channels for sales made through new channels); superordinate goals (for mutual benefit); employee exchange (between channel levels); joint memberships (in trade groups); co-optation (including leaders in advisory councils and other groups); diplomacy, mediation, or arbitration (when conflict is chronic or acute); and legal recourse (if nothing else proves effective).[28]

Dilution and Cannibalization

Marketers must be careful not to dilute their brands through inappropriate channels. This is particularly important for luxury brands whose images often rest on exclusivity and personalized service. High-end fashion brands such as Oscar de la Renta have been creating and upgrading e-commerce sites as a way for time-pressured affluent shoppers to research and buy items, as well as to help combat fakes sold online. Given the way these brands pamper in-store customers, they have had to work hard to provide a high-quality experience online.[29]

Legal and Ethical Issues in Channel Relations

Companies are generally free to develop whatever channel arrangements suit them. In fact, the law seeks to prevent them from using exclusionary tactics that might keep competitors from using a channel. Here we briefly consider the legality of certain practices, including exclusive dealing, exclusive territories, tying agreements, and dealers' rights.

With *exclusive distribution*, only certain outlets are allowed to carry a seller's products. Requiring that these dealers not handle competitors' products is called *exclusive dealing*. The seller obtains more loyal and dependable outlets, and the dealers obtain a steady supply of special products and stronger support. Exclusive arrangements are legal as long as they are voluntary and do not substantially lessen competition or tend to create a monopoly.

Exclusive dealing often includes exclusive territorial agreements. The producer may agree not to sell to other dealers in a given area, or the buyer may agree to sell only in its own territory. The first practice increases dealer enthusiasm and is perfectly legal. However, whether a producer can keep a dealer from selling outside its territory has become a major legal issue. Producers of a strong brand sometimes sell to dealers only if they will take some or all of the rest of the line (*full-line forcing*). Such *tying agreements* are not necessarily illegal, but they do violate U.S. law if they tend to lessen competition substantially. In general, sellers cannot drop dealers if, for example, they refuse to cooperate in a doubtful legal arrangement, such as tying agreements.

E-Commerce and M-Commerce Marketing Practices

E-commerce uses a Web site to transact or facilitate the sale of goods and services online. Online retailers provide convenient, informative, and personalized experiences for vastly different types of consumers and businesses. By saving the cost of retail floor space, staff, and inventory, online retailers can profitably sell low-volume products to niche markets. Online retailers compete in three key aspects of a transaction: (1) customer interaction with the Web site, (2) delivery, and (3) ability to address problems when they occur.[30]

Pure-click companies are those that have launched a Web site without any previous existence as a firm; **brick-and-click** companies are existing companies that have added an online site for information or e-commerce.

E-Commerce and Pure-Click Companies

There are several kinds of pure-click companies: search engines, Internet service providers (ISPs), commerce sites, transaction sites, content sites, and enabler sites. Customer service is critical for pure-click companies, and their Web sites should be fast, simple, and easy to use. Something as simple as enlarging on-screen product images can increase perusal time and the amount customers buy.[31] Research suggests that the most significant inhibitors of online shopping are the absence of pleasurable experiences, social interaction, and personal consultation with a company representative.[32] Thus, online retailers are trying blogs, social networks, and mobile marketing to attract shoppers. Online security and privacy are also important; investments in Web site design and processes can help reassure customers sensitive to online risk.[33]

B2B sites make markets more efficient, giving buyers easy access to a great deal of information from (1) supplier Web sites; (2) *infomediaries,* third parties that add value by aggregating information about alternatives; (3) *market makers,* third parties that link buyers and sellers; and (4) *customer communities*, where buyers can swap stories about suppliers' products and services.[34] Firms are using B2B auction sites, spot exchanges, online catalogs, barter sites, and other online resources to obtain better prices, with the result that prices are now more transparent.[35]

E-Commerce and Brick-and-Click Companies

Although many brick-and-mortar companies initially debated whether to add an e-commerce channel for fear of channel conflict, most eventually added the Internet after seeing how much business was generated online.[36] Even Procter & Gamble, which used traditional physical channels of distribution exclusively for years, now sells some big brands online, in part to observe consumer shopping habits more closely.[37] Managing online and offline channels has thus become a priority for many firms.[38]

Adding an e-commerce channel creates the possibility of a backlash from retailers, brokers, and other intermediaries. In selling through intermediaries and online, marketers may decide to (1) offer different brands or products on the Internet, (2) offer offline partners higher commissions to cushion the negative impact on sales, or (3) take orders online but have retailers deliver and collect payment.

M-Commerce Marketing

Because of the widespread penetration of cell phones and smart phones, many see a big future in *m-commerce* (*m* for *mobile*).[39] Mobile channels and media can keep consumers connected and interacting with a brand throughout their day-to-day lives. GPS-type features can help consumers identify shopping or purchase opportunities for their favorite brands. By 2015, more people will be accessing the Internet with mobile phones than with PCs.[40]

In the United States, mobile marketing is becoming more prevalent and taking all forms.[41] Retailers such as CVS have launched m-commerce sites that allow consumers to buy medicine and other items from their smart phones. The travel industry has used m-commerce to target businesspeople who need to book air or hotel reservations while on the move.[42] One Nordstrom salesperson increased the amount of merchandise he sold by 37 percent by sending text messages and e-mails of promotions to his customers' cell phones.[43] However, mobile marketing and the fact that a company can potentially pinpoint a customer or employee's location with GPS technology also raises privacy issues.

EXECUTIVE SUMMARY

Most producers do not sell their goods directly to final users. Between producers and final users stand one or more marketing channels, a host of marketing intermediaries performing a variety of functions. Producers use intermediaries when they lack the financial resources to carry out direct marketing, when direct marketing is not feasible, and when they can earn more by doing so. The most important functions performed by intermediaries are information, promotion, negotiation, ordering, financing, risk taking, physical possession, payment, and title.

Manufacturers can sell direct or use one-, two-, or three-level channels, depending on customer needs, channel objectives, and the types and number of intermediaries involved. Effective channel management calls for selecting intermediaries, training them, and motivating them to build a profitable partnership. Three key trends are the growth of vertical marketing systems, horizontal marketing systems, and multichannel marketing systems. All channels have the potential for conflict and competition. In channel design, marketers must consider legal and ethical issues such as exclusive dealing or territories, tying agreements, and dealers' rights. As e-commerce and m-commerce grow in importance, companies are managing their online and offline selling through channel integration.

NOTES

1. Farhad Manjoo, "Netflix. Meet Hulu. Now, How About Merging Together?" *Fast Company,* October 1, 2010, www.fastcompany.com; Andrew Bary, "An Overnight Hollywood Success," *Barron's,* August 18, 2010, http://online.barrons.com; Brad Tuttle, "Movies for Cheap," *Time,* March 8, 2010, p. 50; Jefferson Graham, "Netflix Is Still Renting Strong," *USA Today*, July 1, 2009, p. 2B; Ronald Grover, Adam Satariano, and Ari Levy, "Honest, Hollywood, Netflix Is Your Friend," *Bloomberg BusinessWeek*, January 11, 2010, pp. 54–55; Michael V. Copeland, "Tapping Tech's Beautiful Minds," *Fortune*, October 12, 2009, pp. 35–36; Jessica Mintz, "Redbox Machines Take on Netflix's Red Envelope," *USA Today*, June 22, 2009; Michael Kraus, "How Redbox Is Changing Retail," *Marketing News*, November 15, 2009, p. 23.

2. Anne T. Coughlan, Erin Anderson, Louis W. Stern, and Adel I. El-Ansary, *Marketing Channels,* 7th ed. (Upper Saddle River, NJ: Prentice Hall, 2007).

3. Louis W. Stern and Barton A. Weitz, "The Revolution in Distribution," *Long Range Planning* 30, no. 6 (December 1997), pp. 823–29.

4. See Erin Anderson and Anne T. Coughlan, "Channel Management: Structure, Governance, and Relationship Management," Bart Weitz and Robin Wensley, eds., *Handbook of Marketing* (London: Sage, 2001), pp. 223–47; and Gary L. Frazier, "Organizing and Managing Channels of Distribution," *Journal of the Academy of Marketing Sciences* 27, no. 2 (Spring 1999), pp. 226–40.

5. Chekitan S. Dev and Don E. Schultz, "In the Mix: A Customer-Focused Approach Can Bring the Current Marketing Mix into the 21st Century," *Marketing Management* 14 (January–February 2005).

6. Robert Shaw and Philip Kotler, "Rethinking the Chain," *Marketing Management* (July/August 2009), pp. 18–23.

7. Anne T. Coughlan, "Channel Management," Bart Weitz and Robin Wensley, eds., *Handbook of Marketing* (London: Sage, 2001), pp. 223–47.

8. William M. Bulkeley, "Kodak Revamps Wal-Mart Kiosks," *Wall Street Journal*, September 6, 2006, p. B2; Faith Keenan, "Big Yellow's Digital Dilemma," *BusinessWeek,* March 24, 2003, pp. 80–81.

9. Asim Ansari, Carl F. Mela, and Scott A. Neslin, "Customer Channel Migration," *Journal of Marketing Research* 45 (February 2008), pp. 60–76; Jacquelyn S. Thomas and Ursula Y. Sullivan, "Managing Marketing Communications," *Journal of Marketing* 69 (October 2005), pp. 239–51; Sridhar Balasubramanian, Rajagopal Raghunathan, and Vijay Mahajan, "Consumers in a Multichannel Environment," *Journal of Interactive Marketing* 19, no. 2 (Spring 2005), pp. 12–30; Edward J. Fox, Alan L. Montgomery, and Leonard M. Lodish, "Consumer Shopping and Spending across Retail Formats," *Journal of Business* 77, no. 2 (April 2004), pp. S25–S60.

10. Susan Broniarczyk, "Product Assortment," Curtis Haugtvedt, Paul Herr, and Frank Kardes, eds., *Handbook of Consumer Psychology* (New York: Lawrence Erlbaum Associates, 2008), pp. 755–79; Alexander Chernev and Ryan Hamilton, "Assortment Size and Option Attractiveness in Consumer Choice among Retailers," *Journal of Marketing Research* 46 (June 2009), pp. 410–20; Richard A. Briesch, Pradeep K. Chintagunta, and Edward J. Fox, "How Does Assortment Affect Grocery Store Choice," *Journal of Marketing Research* 46 (April 2009), pp. 176–89.

11. Louis P. Bucklin, *A Theory of Distribution Channel Structure* (Berkeley: Institute of Business and Economic Research, University of California, 1966).

12. Anderson and Coughlan, "Channel Management," *Handbook of Marketing* (London: Sage Publications, 2002), pp. 223–47; Michaela Draganska, Daniel Klapper, and Sofia B. Villa-Boas, "A Larger Slice or a Larger Pie? An Empirical Investigation of Bargaining Power in the Distribution Channel," *Marketing Science* 29 (January–February 2010), pp. 57–74.

13. Joydeep Srivastava and Dipankar Chakravarti, "Channel Negotiations with Information Asymmetries," *Journal of Marketing Research* 46 (August 2009), pp. 557–72.

14. See Jennifer Shang, Tuba Pinar Yildirim, Pandu Tadikamalla, Vikas Mittal, and Lawrence Brown, "Distribution Network Redesign for Marketing Competitiveness," *Journal of Marketing* 73 (March 2009), pp. 146–63.

15. Xinlei Chen, George John, and Om Narasimhan, "Assessing the Consequences of a Channel Switch," *Marketing Science* 27 (May–June 2008), pp. 398–416.

16. Thomas H. Davenport and Jeanne G. Harris, *Competing on Analytics: The New Science of Winning* (Boston: Harvard Business School Press, 2007).

17. "P&G Launches Supplier Sustainability Scorecard," *Environmental Leader,* May 12, 2010, www.environmentalleader.com; "Wal-Mart Taps CDP for Emissions Reporting in Sustainability Index," *Environmental Leader,* July 16, 2009, www.environmentalleader.com; "Wal-Mart Rolls Out Packaging Scorecard," *Environmental Leader*, February 1, 2008, www.environmentalleader.com; Miles Cook and Rob Tyndall, "Lessons from the Leaders," *Supply Chain Management Review* (November–December 2001), pp. 22+.

18. Bruce Einhorn, "China: Where Retail Dinosaurs Are Thriving," *Bloomberg BusinessWeek*, February 1 and 8, 2010, p. 64.

19. Michael Arndt, "Urban Outfitters Grow-Slow Strategy," *Bloomberg BusinessWeek*, March 1, 2010, p. 56; Michael Arndt, "How to Play It: Apparel Makers," *Bloomberg BusinessWeek*, March 1, 2010, p. 61.

20. Russell Johnston and Paul R. Lawrence, "Beyond Vertical Integration: The Rise of the Value-Adding Partnership," *Harvard Business Review,* July–August 1988, pp. 94–101. See also, Arnt Bovik and George John, "When Does Vertical Coordination Improve Industrial Purchasing Relationships," *Journal of Marketing* 64 (October 2000), pp. 52–64; Judy A. Siguaw, Penny M. Simpson, and Thomas L. Baker, "Effects of Supplier Market Orientation on Distributor Market Orientation and the Channel Relationship," *Journal of Marketing* (July 1998), pp. 99–111.

21. Rajkumar Venkatesan, V. Kumar, and Nalini Ravishanker, "Multichannel Shopping: Causes and Consequences," *Journal of Marketing* 71 (April 2007), pp. 114–32.

22. Susan Casey, "Eminence Green," *Fortune,* April 2, 2007, pp. 64–70.

23. Anne Coughlan and Louis Stern, "Marketing Channel Design and Management," Dawn Iacobucci, ed., *Kellogg on Marketing* (New York: Wiley, 2001), pp. 247–69.

24. Matthew Boyle, "Brand Killers," *Fortune,* August 11, 2003, pp. 51–56; for an opposing view, see Anthony J. Dukes, Esther Gal-Or, and Kannan Srinivasan, "Channel Bargaining with Retailer Asymmetry," *Journal of Marketing Research* 43 (February 2006), pp. 84–97.

25. Jerry Useem, Julie Schlosser, and Helen Kim, "One Nation under Wal-Mart," *Fortune* (Europe), March 3, 2003.

26. Sreekumar R. Bhaskaran and Stephen M. Gilbert, "Implications of Channel Structure for Leasing or Selling Durable Goods," *Marketing Science* 28 (September–October 2009), pp. 918–34.

27. Some conflict can be helpful; see Anil Arya and Brian Mittendorf, "Benefits of Channel Discord in the Sale of Durable Goods," *Marketing Science* 25 (January–February 2006), pp. 91–96; and Nirmalya Kumar, "Living with Channel Conflict," *CMO Magazine,* October 2004.

28. This section draws on Coughlan, Anderson, Stern, and El-Ansary, *Marketing Channels,* Chapter 9. See also, Jonathan D. Hibbard, Nirmalya Kumar, and Louis W. Stern, "Examining the Impact of Destructive Acts in Marketing Channel Relationships," *Journal of Marketing Research* 38 (February 2001), pp. 45–61; Kersi D. Antia and Gary L. Frazier, "The Severity of Contract Enforcement in Interfirm Channel Relationships," *Journal of Marketing* 65 (October 2001), pp. 67–81; James R. Brown, Chekitan S. Dev, and Dong-Jin Lee, "Managing Marketing Channel Opportunism," *Journal of Marketing* 64 (April 2001), pp. 51–65; Alberto Sa Vinhas and Erin Anderson, "How Potential Conflict Drives Channel Structure," *Journal of Marketing Research* 42 (November 2005), pp. 507–15.

29. "Selling Luxury Goods Online: The Chic Learn to Click," *Economist,* July 24, 2010, p. 61; Christina Passriello, "Fashionably Late?" *Wall Street Journal,* May 19, 2006.

30. Joel C. Collier and Carol C. Bienstock, "How Do Customers Judge Quality in an E-tailer," *MIT Sloan Management Review* (Fall 2006), pp. 35–40.

31. Jeff Borden, "The Right Tools," *Marketing News,* April 15, 2008, pp. 19–21.

32. Alexis K. J. Barlow, Noreen Q. Siddiqui, and Mike Mannion, "Development in Information and Communication Technologies for Retail Marketing Channels," *International Journal of Retail and Distribution Management* 32 (March 2004), pp. 157–63; G&J Electronic Media Services, *7th Wave of the GfK-Online-Monitor* (Hamburg: GfK Press, 2001).

33. Ann E. Schlosser, Tiffany Barnett White, and Susan M. Lloyd, "Converting Web Site Visitors into Buyers." *Journal of Marketing* 70 (April 2006), pp. 133–48.

34. Ronald Abler, John S. Adams, and Peter Gould, *Spatial Organizations: The Geographer's View of the World* (Upper Saddle River, NJ: Prentice Hall, 1971), pp. 531–32.

35. See John G. Lynch Jr. and Dan Ariely, "Wine Online: Search Costs and Competition on Price, Quality, and Distribution," *Marketing Science* 19 (Winter 2000), pp. 83–103.

36. Andrea Chang, "Retailers Fuse Stores with E-Commerce," *Los Angeles Times*, June 27, 2010.

37. Anjali Cordeiro, "Procter & Gamble Sees Aisle Expansion on the Web," *Wall Street Journal*, September 2, 2009, p. B6A; Anjali Cordeiro and Ellen Byron, "Procter & Gamble to Test Online Store to Study Buying Habits," *Wall Street Journal*, January 15, 2010.

38. Xubing Zhang, "Retailer's Multichannel and Price Advertising Strategies," *Marketing Science* 28 (November–December 2009), pp. 1080–94.

39. Venkatesh Shankar and Sridhar Balasubramanian, "Mobile Marketing: A Synthesis and Prognosis," *Journal of Interactive Marketing* 23, no. 2 (2009), pp. 118–29; Douglas Lamont, *Conquering the Wireless World: The Age of M-Commerce* (New York: Wiley, 2001); Herbjørn Nysveen, Per E. Pedersen, Helge Thorbjørnsen, and Pierre Berthon, "Mobilizing the Brand: The Effects of Mobile Services on Brand Relationships and Main Channel Use," *Journal of Service Research* 7, no. 3 (2005), pp. 257–76; Venkatesh Shankar, Alladi Venkatesh, Charles Hofacker, and Prasad Naik, "Mobile Marketing in the Retailing Environment," special issue, *Journal of Interactive Marketing*, co-editors Venkatesh Shankar and Manjit Yadav, forthcoming.

40. "The Mobile Internet Report," *Morgan Stanley*, www.morganstanley.com, May 7, 2010.

41. Adam Cahill, Lars Albright, and Carl Howe, "Mobile Advertising and Branding," session as part of the Britt Technology Impact Series, Tuck School of Business, Dartmouth College, March 31, 2010; Alexandre Mars, "Importing Mobile Marketing Tools," *Brandweek*, February 15, 2010, p. 17.

42. Reena Jana, "Retailers Are Learning to Love Smartphones," *BusinessWeek*, October 26, 2009, www.businessweek.com.

43. Nanette Byrnes, "More Clicks at the Bricks," *BusinessWeek*, December 17, 2007, pp. 50–51.

chapter 14

Managing Retailing, Wholesaling, and Logistics

In this chapter, we will address the following questions:

1. What major types of marketing intermediaries occupy this sector and what marketing decisions do they face?
2. What are the major trends with marketing intermediaries?
3. What does the future hold for private label brands?

Marketing Management at Zappos

Superior customer service is a hallmark of Zappos, the online retailer founded in 1999 to sell footwear. With free shipping and returns, 24/7 customer service, and fast turnaround on a wide selection of products and styles, Zappos finds that three-fourths of its purchases are by repeat customers. Unlike many other firms, Zappos has not outsourced its call centers; in fact, its customer service reps are encouraged to take their time and are empowered to solve problems. When a customer called to complain that a pair of boots was leaking after a year of use, the rep sent out a new pair even though the company's policy is that only unworn shoes are returnable.

Half the interview process for potential new hires is devoted to finding out whether they are sufficiently outgoing, open-minded, and creative to be a good cultural fit for the company. Bought by Amazon.com in 2009 but still run separately, Zappos now also sells clothing, handbags, and other accessories. Thanks to its success, it even offers two-day, $4,000 seminars to business executives eager to learn the secrets behind the retailer's unique corporate culture and approach to customer service.[1]

While innovative retailers such as Zappos have thrived in recent years, others such as Gap and Kmart have struggled. Successful intermediaries know how to use strategic planning, advanced information systems, and sophisticated marketing tools. They segment their markets, improve their market targeting and positioning, and pursue expansion and diversification strategies. In this chapter, we consider marketing excellence in retailing, wholesaling, and logistics.

Retailing

Retailing includes all the activities in selling goods or services directly to final consumers for personal, nonbusiness use. A **retailer** or *retail store* is any business enterprise whose sales volume comes primarily from retailing. Any organization selling to final consumers—whether it is a manufacturer, wholesaler, or retailer—is in retailing. It doesn't matter *how* the goods or services are sold (in person, by mail, telephone, vending machine, or online) or *where* (in a store, on the street, or in the consumer's home).

Types of Retailers

Consumers today can shop at store retailers, nonstore retailers, and retail organizations. Table 14.1 shows the major types of store retailers. Different formats of store retailers will have different competitive and price dynamics. Discount stores, for example, compete much more intensely with each other than other formats.[2]

Retailers can position themselves as offering one of four levels of service:

1. *Self-service*—Self-service is the cornerstone of all discount operations. Many customers carry out their own "locate-compare-select" process to save money.

TABLE 14.1	Major Types of Store Retailers

Specialty store: Narrow product line. The Limited, Forever 21.

Department store: Several product lines. JCPenney, Bloomingdale's.

Supermarket: Large, low-cost, low-margin, high-volume, self-service store designed to meet total needs for food and household products. Kroger, Safeway.

Convenience store: Small store in residential area, often open 24/7, limited line of high-turnover convenience products plus takeout. 7-Eleven, Circle K.

Drug store: Prescription and pharmacies, health and beauty aids, other personal care, small durable, miscellaneous items. CVS, Walgreens.

Discount store: Standard or specialty merchandise; low-price, low-margin, high-volume stores. Walmart, Kmart.

Extreme value or hard-discount store: A more restricted merchandise mix than discount stores but at even lower prices. Aldi, Dollar General.

Off-price retailer: Leftover goods, overruns, irregular merchandise sold at less than retail in factory outlets or independent stores. TJ Maxx, Marshalls.

Superstore: Huge selling space, routinely purchased food and household items, plus services. Category killer (deep assortment in one category) such as Staples; combination store such as Jewel-Osco; hypermarket (huge stores that combine supermarket, discount, and warehouse retailing) such as Carrefour in France.

Catalog showroom: Broad selection of high-markup, fast-moving, brand-name goods sold by catalog at a discount, with merchandise picked up at the store. Inside Edge Ski and Bike.

2. *Self-selection*—Customers find their own goods, although they can ask for assistance.

3. *Limited service*—These retailers carry more shopping goods and services such as credit and merchandise-return privileges. Customers need more information and assistance.

4. *Full service*—Salespeople are ready to assist in every phase of the "locate-compare-select" process. The high staffing cost, along with the higher proportion of specialty goods and slower-moving items and the many services, result in high-cost retailing.

Nonstore retailing has been growing much faster than store retailing. Nonstore retailing falls into four major categories: (1) *direct selling*, a multibillion-dollar industry with hundreds of companies (such as Avon) selling door-to-door or at home sales parties; (2) *direct marketing*, with roots in direct-mail and catalog marketing, also includes telemarketing and Internet selling (1-800-FLOWERS); (3) *automatic vending* used for impulse items such as soft drinks and cosmetics; and (4) *buying service*, a storeless retailer serving a specific clientele that is entitled to discounts in return for membership.

An increasing number of stores are part of a *corporate retailing* organization (see Table 14.2). Compared with independent stores, these organizations have greater economies of scale, purchasing power, and brand recognition, as well as better-trained employees.

The New Retail Environment

A number of long-term trends are evident in the new retail marketing environment. First, new retail forms are emerging to better satisfy customers' needs for convenience. One is the limited-time "pop-up" store, which allows retailers such as Target to promote their brands and create buzz for a brief period.[3] Another trend is growth in inter-type competition, with different types of stores competing for the same consumers with the same type of merchandise. In addition, store-based and nonstore based retailers are competing with each other.

Giants such as Costco have become powerful through their superior information systems, logistical systems, and buying strength, even as middle-market retailers are in decline. Another trend is higher investment in technology to improve forecasts, control inventory costs, speed ordering, and change prices quickly.[4] Also, retailers such as IKEA and UNIQLO, with unique formats and strong brand positioning, are increasingly expanding into other countries. Finally, firms are recognizing the importance of influencing shoppers at the point of purchase.[5]

TABLE 14.2   Major Types of Corporate Retail Organizations
Corporate chain store: Two or more outlets owned and controlled, employing central buying and merchandising, and selling similar lines of merchandise. Pottery Barn.
Voluntary chain: A wholesaler-sponsored group of independent retailers engaged in bulk buying and common merchandising. Independent Grocers Alliance (IGA).
Retailer cooperative: Independent retailers using a central buying organization and joint promotion efforts. ACE Hardware.
Consumer cooperative: A retail firm owned by its customers. Members contribute money to open their own store, vote on its policies, elect managers, and receive dividends. Local cooperative grocery stores can be found in many markets.
Franchise organization: Contractual association between a franchisor and franchisees, popular in a number of product and service areas. McDonald's, Jiffy Lube.
Merchandising conglomerate: A corporation that combines several retailing lines and forms under central ownership, with some integration of distribution and management. Macy's operates Macy's and Bloomingdale's department stores.

Retailer Marketing Decisions

With this new retail environment as a backdrop, we will examine retailers' marketing decisions in the areas of target market, channels, product assortment, procurement, prices, services, store atmosphere, store activities and experiences, communications, and location.

Target Market   Until it defines and profiles the target market, the retailer cannot make consistent decisions about product assortment, store decor, advertising messages and media, price, and service levels. Retailers now slice the market into ever-finer segments and introduce new lines of stores to exploit niche markets with relevant offerings, the way Gymboree launched Janie and Jack to sell apparel and gifts for babies and toddlers.

Channels   Based on a target market analysis and other considerations discussed in Chapter 13, retailers must decide which channels to employ to reach their customers. Increasingly, the answer is to integrate multiple channels, the way JCPenney ensures that its Internet, store, and catalog businesses are fully intertwined. It sells a vast variety of goods online, makes Internet access available at its 35,000 checkout counters, and allows online shoppers to pick up and return orders at stores.[6]

Product Assortment   The retailer's product assortment must match the target market's shopping expectations in *breadth* and *depth.* A restaurant can offer a narrow and shallow assortment (small lunch counters), a narrow and deep assortment (delicatessen), a broad and shallow assortment (cafeteria), or a broad and deep assortment (large restaurant). Another challenge is to develop a product-differentiation strategy by offering brands not available at competing stores, featuring mostly private-label goods, presenting distinctive merchandise events, changing merchandise frequently or offering surprise merchandise, featuring new merchandise, offering customizing services, or offering a highly targeted assortment.

Procurement   The retailer must establish merchandise sources, policies, and practices for procurement. Stores are using **direct product profitability (DPP)** to measure a product's handling costs (receiving, moving to storage, paperwork, selecting, checking, loading, and space cost) from the time it reaches the warehouse until a customer buys it in the store. They may learn that a product's gross margin bears little relation to the direct product profit. Some high-volume products may have such high handling costs that they are less profitable and deserve less shelf space than low-volume products.

Prices   Prices are a key positioning factor and must be set in relationship to the target market, product-and-service assortment mix, and competition.[7] Retailers generally fall into the *high-markup, lower-volume* group (fine specialty stores) or the *low-markup, higher-volume* group (discount stores). Most retailers will put low prices on some items to serve as traffic builders or loss leaders or to signal their pricing policies.[8]

Services   Retailers must decide on the *services mix* to offer customers. Prepurchase services include accepting telephone and mail orders, advertising, window and interior display, and fitting rooms. Postpurchase services include shipping and delivery, gift wrapping, adjustments and returns, and alterations. Ancillary services include general information, check cashing, parking, restaurants, repairs, and interior decorating.

Store Atmosphere   *Atmosphere* is another differentiation tool. Every store has a look, and a physical layout that makes it hard or easy to move around. Kohl's floor plan is modeled after a racetrack loop to convey customers past all the merchandise in the store. It includes a middle aisle that shoppers can use as a shortcut and yields higher spending levels than many competitors.[9]

Store Activities and Experiences   The growth of e-commerce has forced traditional brick-and-mortar retailers to respond. Now retailers are using the shopping experience as a strong differentiator, providing in-store activities that relate to the brand and the merchandise.[10] See "Marketing Skills: Experience Marketing" for more on this development.

Communications   Retailers use a wide range of communication tools to generate traffic and purchases, including advertising, special sales, money-saving coupons, frequent-shopper rewards, and in-store food sampling. Many work closely with suppliers to produce point-of-sale materials that reflect both the retailer's and the manufacturer's image.[11] Retailers are also using interactive and social media to convey information and create brand communities.[12]

Location   The three keys to retail success are "location, location, and location." Retailers can place their stores in the following locations:

- Central business districts. The oldest and most heavily trafficked city areas, often known as "downtown."
- Regional shopping centers. Large suburban malls containing 40 to 200 stores, a mix of smaller stores and one or two nationally known anchor stores or a combination of big-box stores.
- Community shopping centers. Smaller malls with one anchor store and 20 to 40 small stores.
- Shopping strips. A cluster of stores, usually in one long building, serving a neighborhood's needs for groceries, hardware, dry cleaning, and more.
- A location within a larger store. Concession space rented by McDonald's or another retailer within a larger operation, such as an airport or a department store.
- Stand-alone stores. Free-standing retail sites not directly connected to other stores.

Marketing Skills

EXPERIENCE MARKETING

Retailers can set themselves apart and make a strong impression by creating in-store experiences that are "entertaining, educational, aesthetic, and escapist all at once," in the words of one expert. Start with a thorough understanding of what customers value and expect, and their basic motivations. Then try to enhance the sensory experience (feel, look, sound, smell, or taste) in unique, brand-appropriate ways—the way Mattel uses Barbie's signature pink color to catch the eye in its Barbie store in Shanghai, China. In addition to putting Barbie pink on the walls, Mattel dressed the 875 dolls on display in different costumes—all in Barbie pink.

Some retailers create special themed areas to entertain shoppers and let them try before they buy. REI, which sells outdoor gear, encourages consumers to test equipment on its in-store climbing walls or try on Gore-Tex raincoats under a simulated rain shower. When Bass Pro Shops opens a new store, it might include a giant aquarium or a waterfall, an archery range, or an indoor putting green; its stores offer free classes and product demonstrations. No wonder the chain's original showroom in Missouri is the state's top tourist destination.[13]

Private Labels

A **private label brand** (also called a reseller, store, house, or distributor brand) is a brand that retailers and wholesalers develop. For many manufacturers, retailers are both collaborators and competitors. According to the Private Label Manufacturers' Association, store brands now account for one of every four items sold in U.S. supermarkets, drug chains, and mass merchandisers, up from 19 percent in 1999.[14] Although private labels are rapidly growing, some experts believe that 50 percent is the natural limit for volume of private labels to carry because consumers prefer certain national brands, and many categories are not feasible or attractive on a private label basis.[15]

Role of Private Labels

Why do intermediaries sponsor their own brands?[16] First, these brands can be more profitable. Intermediaries search for manufacturers with excess capacity to produce private label goods at low cost. Other costs, such as research and development, advertising, sales promotion, and physical distribution, are much lower, so private labels generate higher profit margins. Retailers also develop exclusive store brands to differentiate themselves from competitors. Many price-sensitive consumers prefer store brands in certain categories, which gives retailers more bargaining power with marketers of national brands.

Generics are unbranded, plainly packaged, less expensive versions of common products such as spaghetti, paper towels, and canned peaches, priced low because of low-cost labeling, minimal advertising, and sometimes lower-quality ingredients. They offer standard or lower quality at a price that may be 20 percent to 40 percent lower than nationally advertised brands and 10 percent to 20 percent lower than the retailer's private label brands.

Private Label Success Factors

In the confrontation between manufacturers' and private labels, retailers have many advantages and increasing market power.[17] Because shelf space is scarce, many supermarkets charge a *slotting fee* for accepting a new brand; retailers also charge for special in-store display space. They typically give more prominent display to their own brands and make sure they are well stocked.

Although retailers get credit for the success of private labels, the growing power of store brands has also benefited from the weakening of national brands. Many consumers have become more price sensitive, a trend reinforced by the continuous barrage of coupons and price specials that has trained a generation to buy on price. Competing manufacturers and national retailers copy and duplicate the quality and features of a category's best brands, reducing product differentiation. Moreover, by cutting communication budgets, some firms have made it harder to create any intangible differences in brand image. Yet many manufacturers or national brands are fighting back (see "Marketing Insight: Manufacturers Respond to the Private Label Threat").

Wholesaling

Wholesaling includes all the activities in selling goods or services to those who buy for resale or business use. It excludes manufacturers and farmers (because they are engaged primarily in production) and retailers. The major types of wholesalers are described in Table 14.3 on page 247.

Wholesalers (also called *distributors*) differ from retailers in several ways. First, wholesalers pay less attention to promotion, atmosphere, and location because they deal with business customers rather than final consumers. Second, wholesale transactions are usually larger than retail

Marketing   Insight

MANUFACTURERS RESPOND TO THE PRIVATE LABEL THREAT

University of North Carolina's Jan-Benedict E.M. Steenkamp and London Business School's Nirmalya Kumar offer four recommendations for manufacturers to compete against or collaborate with private labels.

- **Fight selectively** where manufacturers can win against private labels and add value, especially where the brand is a category leader or occupies a premium position. Procter & Gamble has done this, selling off brands such as Jif to focus on its 20+ brands with more than $1 billion each in sales.
- **Partner effectively** by seeking win-win relationships with retailers through strategies that complement the retailer's private labels. Estée Lauder created four brands exclusively for Kohl's, to help the retailer generate volume and to protect its more prestigious brands.
- **Innovate brilliantly** with new products to help beat private labels. Continuously launching incremental new products keeps the manufacturer brands looking fresh, but the firm must also periodically launch radical new products and protect the intellectual property of all brands.
- **Create winning value propositions** by imbuing brands with symbolic imagery as well as functional quality that beats private labels. For a winning value proposition, marketers need to monitor pricing and ensure that perceived benefits equal the price premium.

Sources: Jan-Benedict E.M. Steenkamp and Nirmalya Kumar, "Don't Be Undersold," *Harvard Business Review,* December 2009, p. 91; James A. Narus and James C. Anderson, "Contributing as a Distributor to Partnerships with Manufacturers," *Business Horizons* (September–October 1987); Nirmalya Kumar and Jan-Benedict E.M. Steenkamp, *Private Label Strategy: How to Meet the Store-Brand Challenge* (Boston: Harvard Business School Press, 2007); Nirmalya Kumar, "The Right Way to Fight for Shelf Domination," *Advertising Age,* January 22, 2007.

transactions, and wholesalers cover a larger trade area than retailers. Third, wholesalers and retailers comply with different legal regulations and taxes.

Wholesaling Functions

Why are wholesalers used at all? In general, wholesalers are more efficient in performing one or more of the following functions:

- **Selling and promoting.** Wholesalers' sales forces help manufacturers reach many small business customers at a relatively low cost.
- **Buying and assortment building.** Wholesalers can select items and build the assortments their customers need, saving them considerable work.
- **Bulk breaking.** Wholesalers achieve savings for their customers by buying large carload lots and breaking the bulk into smaller units.
- **Warehousing.** Wholesalers hold inventories, thereby reducing inventory costs and risks to suppliers and customers.
- **Transportation.** Wholesalers can often provide quicker delivery because they are closer to the buyers.

TABLE 14.3	Major Wholesaler Types

Merchant wholesalers. Independently owned businesses that take title to the merchandise they handle, including full-service and limited-service jobbers, distributors, and mill supply houses.

Full-service wholesalers. Carry stock, maintain a sales force, offer credit, make deliveries, and provide management assistance. Wholesale merchants sell primarily to retailers; industrial distributors sell to manufacturers and also provide services such as credit and delivery.

Limited-service wholesalers. *Cash and carry wholesalers* sell a limited line of fast-moving goods to small retailers for cash. *Truck wholesalers* sell and deliver a limited line of semiperishable goods to supermarkets, grocery stores, hospitals, restaurants, and hotels. *Drop shippers* serve bulk industries such as heavy equipment, assuming title and risk until the order is delivered. *Rack jobbers* serve grocery retailers in nonfood items, setting up displays, pricing goods, and tracking inventory; they retain title and bill only for goods sold. *Producers' cooperatives* assemble farm produce to sell in local markets. *Mail-order wholesalers* send catalogs to retail, industrial, and institutional customers and fill orders by mail, rail, plane, or truck.

Brokers and agents. Facilitate buying and selling, on commission; limited functions; generally specialize by product line or customer type. *Brokers* bring buyers and sellers together and assist in negotiation; they are paid the party hiring them. *Agents* represent buyers or sellers on a more permanent basis. Most agents are small businesses with a few skilled salespeople. Selling agents have contractual authority to sell a manufacturer's entire output; purchasing agents make purchases for buyers and often receive, inspect, warehouse, and ship merchandise; commission merchants negotiate sales and take physical possession of goods.

Manufacturers' and retailers' branches and offices. Wholesaling operations conducted by sellers or buyers themselves rather than through independent wholesalers. Separate branches and offices are dedicated to sales or purchasing.

Specialized wholesalers. Agricultural assemblers (buy the agricultural output of many farms), petroleum bulk plants and terminals (consolidate the output of many wells), and auction companies (auction cars, equipment, etc., to dealers and other businesses).

- Financing. Wholesalers finance customers by granting credit, and finance suppliers by ordering early and paying bills on time.
- Risk bearing. Wholesalers absorb some risk by taking title and bearing the cost of theft, damage, spoilage, and obsolescence.
- Market information. Wholesalers supply information to suppliers and customers regarding competitors' activities, new products, price developments, and so on.
- Management services and counseling. Wholesalers often help retailers improve their operations by training staff, helping with store displays, and setting up accounting and inventory-control systems.

Trends in Wholesaling

Wholesaler-distributors have felt pressure in recent years from new sources of competition, demanding customers, new technologies, and direct-buying programs by large buyers. Manufacturers say that wholesalers don't aggressively promote the manufacturer's product line and they act more like order takers; don't carry enough inventory and therefore don't fill customers' orders fast enough; don't supply the manufacturer with up-to-date market, customer, and competitive information; and charge too much.

Savvy wholesalers are adding value to the channel by adapting their services to meet their suppliers' and target customers' changing needs. They are increasing asset productivity by managing inventories and receivables better and cutting costs by investing in materials-handling technology and information systems. And they're improving strategic decisions about target markets, product assortment, services, pricing, communications, and distribution. Yet wholesaling remains vulnerable to one of the most enduring trends—fierce resistance to price increases and the winnowing out of suppliers based on cost and quality.

Market Logistics

Physical distribution starts at the factory, where managers choose warehouses and carriers that will deliver the goods to final destinations in the desired time or at the lowest total cost. Physical distribution has now been expanded into the broader concept of **supply chain management (SCM)**. Supply chain management starts before physical distribution, covering procurement of inputs (raw materials, components, and capital equipment), conversion into finished products, and product movement to final destinations. An even broader perspective looks at how the company's suppliers themselves obtain their inputs. Many firms are improving supply-chain sustainability by shrinking their carbon footprint and using recyclable packaging.

Market logistics includes planning the infrastructure to meet demand, then implementing and controlling the physical flows of materials and final goods from points of origin to points of use, to meet customer requirements at a profit. Market logistics planning has four steps:[18]

1. Deciding on the company's value proposition to its customers (What on-time delivery standard should we offer? What levels should we attain in ordering and billing accuracy?)
2. Selecting the best channel design and network strategy for reaching the customers (Should we serve customers directly or through intermediaries? How many warehouses should we have and where should we locate them?)
3. Developing operational excellence in sales forecasting, warehouse management, transportation management, and materials management.
4. Implementing the solution with the best information systems, equipment, policies, and procedures.

Integrated Logistics Systems

The market logistics task calls for **integrated logistics systems (ILS)**, which include materials management, material flow systems, and physical distribution, aided by information technology to shorten the order-cycle time, reduce errors, and improve control. Market logistics encompass several activities, starting with sales forecasting to plan distribution, production, and inventory levels. Production plans indicate the materials the purchasing department must order. These materials arrive through inbound transportation, enter the receiving area, and are stored in raw-material inventory, to be converted into finished goods. Finished-goods inventory is the link between customer orders and manufacturing activity. Customers' orders draw down the finished-goods inventory level, and manufacturing activity builds it up. Finished goods flow off the assembly line and pass through packaging, in-plant warehousing, shipping-room processing, outbound transportation, field warehousing, and customer delivery and servicing.

Companies are concerned about the total cost of market logistics, which can amount to as much as 30 percent to 40 percent of the product's cost. Lower market-logistics costs will permit lower prices, yield higher profit margins, or both. Even though the cost of market logistics can be high, a well-planned program can be a potent tool in competitive marketing.

Market-Logistics Objectives

Many companies state their market-logistics objective as "getting the right goods to the right places at the right time for the least cost." Unfortunately, no system can simultaneously maximize customer service and minimize distribution cost. Maximum customer service implies large inventories, premium transportation, and multiple warehouses, all of which raise market-logistics costs. Given that market-logistics activities require trade-offs, managers must make decisions on a total-system basis, starting with what customers require and what competitors offer. Customers want on-time delivery, responsiveness to emergency needs, careful handling of merchandise, and fast exchange of defective goods. Firms usually try to match or exceed competitors' service levels, but the objective is to maximize profits, not sales.

Given the market-logistics objectives, the company must design a system that will minimize the cost of achieving these objectives. Each possible market-logistics system will lead to the following cost:

$$M = T + FW + VW + S$$

where M = total market-logistics cost of proposed system

T = total freight cost of proposed system

FW = total fixed warehouse cost of proposed system

VW = total variable warehouse costs (including inventory) of proposed system

S = total cost of lost sales due to average delivery delay under proposed system

Choosing a market-logistics system calls for examining the total cost (M) associated with different proposed systems and selecting the system that minimizes it. If it is hard to measure S, the company should aim to minimize $T + FW + VW$ for a target level of customer service.

Market-Logistics Decisions

The firm must make four major decisions about its market logistics: (1) How should we handle orders (order processing)? (2) Where should we locate our stock (warehousing)? (3) How much stock should we hold (inventory)? and (4) How should we ship goods (transportation)?

Order Processing   Most companies want to shorten the *order-to-payment cycle*—the elapsed time between an order's receipt, delivery, and payment. This cycle has many steps, including order transmission by the salesperson, order entry and customer credit check, inventory and production scheduling, order and invoice shipment, and receipt of payment. The longer this cycle takes, the lower the customer's satisfaction and the lower the company's profits.

Warehousing   Every company must store finished goods until they are sold, because production and consumption cycles rarely match. More stocking locations mean goods can be delivered to customers more quickly, but warehousing and inventory costs are higher. To reduce these costs, the company might centralize inventory and use fast transportation to fill orders.

Some inventory is kept at or near the plant, and the rest in warehouses in other locations. The company might own private warehouses and also rent space in public warehouses. *Storage warehouses* store goods for moderate to long periods of time. *Distribution warehouses* receive goods from various company plants and suppliers and move them out as soon as possible. *Automated warehouses* employ advanced materials-handling systems under the control of a central computer and are increasingly becoming the norm.

Inventory   Salespeople would like their companies to carry enough stock to fill all customer orders immediately. However, this is not cost-effective. *Inventory cost increases at an accelerating rate as the customer-service level approaches 100 percent.* Management needs to know how much sales and profits would increase as a result of carrying larger inventories and promising faster order fulfillment times, and then make a decision.

As inventory draws down, management must know at what stock level to place a new order to avoid stock-outs. This stock level is called the *order (or reorder) point*. An order point of 20 means reordering when the stock falls to 20 units. The other decision is how much to order. The larger the quantity ordered, the less frequently an order needs to be placed. The company needs to balance order-processing costs and inventory-carrying costs. *Order-processing costs* for a manufacturer consist of *setup costs* and *running costs* (operating costs when production is running) for the item. If setup costs are low, the manufacturer can produce the item often, and the average cost per item is stable and equal to the running costs. If setup costs are high, the manufacturer can reduce the average cost per unit by producing a long run and carrying more inventory.

Order-processing costs must be compared with *inventory-carrying costs*. The larger the average stock carried, the higher the inventory-carrying costs, which include storage charges, cost of capital, taxes and insurance, and depreciation and obsolescence. Marketing managers who want their companies to carry larger inventories need to show that the incremental gross profits would exceed incremental carrying costs.

We can determine the optimal order quantity by observing how order-processing costs and inventory-carrying costs sum up at different order levels. Figure 14.1 shows that the order-processing cost per unit decreases with the number of units ordered because the order costs are spread over more units. Inventory-carrying charges per unit increase with the number of units ordered, because each unit remains longer in inventory. We sum the two cost curves vertically into a total-cost curve and project the lowest point of the total-cost curve on the horizontal axis to find the optimal order quantity Q^*.[19]

Companies are reducing their inventory costs by distinguishing between bottleneck items (high risk, low opportunity), critical items (high risk, high opportunity), commodities (low risk, high opportunity), and nuisance items (low risk, low opportunity).[20] The ultimate answer to carrying *near-zero inventory* is to build for order, not for stock.

Transportation   Transportation choices affect product pricing, on-time delivery performance, and the condition of the goods when they arrive, all of which affect customer satisfaction. In shipping goods to its warehouses, dealers, and customers, the company can choose rail, air, truck, waterway, or pipeline. Shippers consider such criteria as speed, frequency, dependability, capability, availability, traceability, and cost. For speed, air, rail, and truck are the prime contenders. If the goal is low cost, then the choice is water or pipeline.

Shippers are increasingly combining two or more transportation modes, thanks to **containerization**, putting goods in boxes or trailers that are easy to transfer between two transportation modes. *Piggyback* describes the use of rail and trucks; *fishyback,* water and trucks;

FIGURE 14.1 Determining Optimal Order Quantity

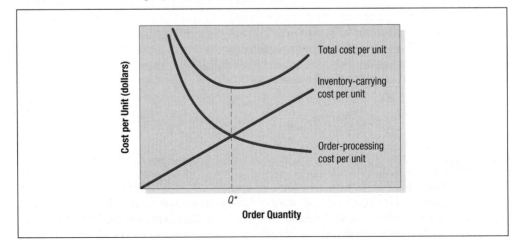

trainship, water and rail; and *airtruck,* air and trucks. Each coordinated mode offers specific advantages. For example, piggyback is cheaper than trucking alone yet provides flexibility and convenience.

Shippers can choose private, contract, or common carriers. If the shipper owns its own truck or air fleet, it becomes a *private carrier.* A *contract carrier* is an independent organization selling transportation services to others on a contract basis. A *common carrier* provides services between predetermined points on a scheduled basis and is available to all shippers at standard rates. In Europe, P&G uses a three-tier logistics system to schedule deliveries of fast- and slow-moving goods, bulky items, and small items in the most efficient way.[21]

Organizational Lessons

Market-logistics strategies must be derived from business strategies, rather than solely from cost considerations. The logistics system must be information-intensive and establish electronic links among all the significant parties. Finally, the company should set its logistics goals to match or exceed competitors' service standards and should involve members of all relevant teams in the planning process. Smart companies will adjust their logistics strategies to each major customer's requirements. The company's trade group will set up *differentiated distribution* by offering different bundled service programs for different customers.

EXECUTIVE SUMMARY

Retailing includes all the activities involved in selling goods or services directly to final consumers for personal, nonbusiness use. Retailers can be involved in store retailing, nonstore retailing, or part of a retail organization. The retail environment has changed as new retail forms have emerged, intertype and store-based versus nonstore-based competition has increased, the rise of giant retailers has been matched by the decline of middle-market retailers, investment in technology and global expansion has grown, and shopper marketing inside stores has become a priority.

Wholesaling includes all the activities in selling goods or services to those who buy for resale or business use. Wholesalers' functions include selling and promoting, buying and assortment building, bulk breaking, warehousing, transportation, financing, risk bearing, dissemination of market information, and provision of management services and consulting. Producers of physical offerings must decide on market logistics—planning the infrastructure to meet demand, then implementing and controlling the flow of materials and final goods from point of origin to point of use, to meet customer requirements at a profit. Decisions about market logistics cover order processing, warehousing, inventory, and transportation.

NOTES

1. Kimberly Palmer, "The Secrets to Zappos' Success," *U.S. News & World Report,* August 10, 2010, http://money.usnews.com/money; Helen Coster, "A Step Ahead," *Forbes,* June 2, 2008, pp. 78–80; Paula Andruss, "Delivering Wow through Service," *Marketing News,* October 15, 2008, p. 10; Jeffrey M. O'Brien, "Zappos Knows How to Kick It," *Fortune,* February 2, 2009, pp. 55–60; Brian Morrissey, "Amazon to Buy Zappos," *Adweek,* July 22, 2009;

Christopher Palmeri, "Now For Sale, the Zappos Culture," *Bloomberg BusinessWeek,* January 11, 2010, p. 57.

2. Karsten Hansen and Vishal Singh, "Market Structure across Retail Formats," *Marketing Science,* no. 28 (July–August 2009), pp. 656–73.

3. Keith Mulvihill, "Pop-Up Stores Become Popular for New York Landlords," *New York Times,* June 22, 2010, www.nytimes.com.

4. Tim Dickey, "Electronic Shelf Labels," *Retail Technology Trends*, February 26, 2010.

5. Michael C. Bellas, "Shopper Marketing's Instant Impact," *Beverage World*, November 2007, p. 18; Richard Westlund, "Bringing Brands to Life: The Power of In-Store Marketing," Special Advertising Supplement to *Adweek*, January 2010; Pierre Chandon, J. Wesley Hutchinson, Eric T. Bradlow, and Scott H. Young, "Does In-Store Marketing Work?" *Journal of Marketing Research* 73 (November 2009), pp. 1–17.

6. "JCPenney Transforms Catalog Strategy to Better Serve Customer Preferences," *BusinessWire*, November 18, 2009; Robert Berner, "JCPenney Gets the Net," *BusinessWeek*, May 7, 2007, p. 70; Robert Berner, "Penney: Back in Fashion," *BusinessWeek*, January 9, 2006, pp. 82–84.

7. Venkatesh Shankar and Ruth N. Bolton, "An Empirical Analysis of Determinants of Retailer Pricing Strategy," *Marketing Science* 23 (Winter 2004), pp. 28–49.

8. Duncan Simester, "Signaling Price Image Using Advertised Prices," *Marketing Science* 14 (Summer 1995), pp. 166–88; see also, Jiwoong Shin, "The Role of Selling Costs in Signaling Price Image," *Journal of Marketing Research* 42 (August 2005), pp. 305–12.

9. Cecile B. Corral, "Profits Pinched, Kohl's Eyes Market Share," *Home Textiles Today*, February 27, 2009; Ilaina Jones, "Kohl's Looking at Spots in Manhattan," *Reuters*, August 19, 2009; Cametta Coleman, "Kohl's Retail Racetrack," *Wall Street Journal*, March 1, 2000.

10. "Reinventing the Store," *Economist*, November 22, 2003, pp. 65–68; Moira Cotlier, "Census Releases First E-Commerce Report," *Catalog Age*, May 1, 2001; Associated Press, "Online Sales Boomed at End of 2000," *Star-Tribune of Twin Cities*, February 17, 2001; Kenneth T. Rosen and Amanda L. Howard, "E-Tail: Gold Rush or Fool's Gold?" *California Management Review* (April 1, 2000), pp. 72–100.

11. Jeff Cioletti, "Super Marketing," *Beverage World* (November 2006), pp. 60–61.

12. Ben Paynter, "Happy Hour," *Fast Company*, March 2010, p. 34; Jessi Hempel, "Social Media Meets Retailing," *Fortune*, March 22, 2010, p. 30.

13. "REI to Open New California Store, Move Another," *Puget Sound Business Journal*, August 11, 2010, www.bizjournals.com; Tim Palmer, "Sensing a Winner," *Grocer*, January 26, 2002, pp. 40+; Velitchka D. Kaltcheva and Barton Weitz, "When Should a Retailer Create an Exciting Store Environment?" *Journal of Marketing* 70 (January 2006), pp. 107–18; "Go Live with a Big Brand Experience," *Marketing*, October 26, 2000, p. 45.

14. www.plma.com, April 3, 2010.

15. Kusum Ailawadi and Bari Harlam, "An Empirical Analysis of the Determinants of Retail Margins: The Role of Store-Brand Share," *Journal of Marketing* 68 (January 2004), pp. 147–65.

16. For more on private labels, see Michael R. Hyman, Dennis A. Kopf, and Dongdae Lee, "Review of Literature—Future Research Suggestions: Private Label Brands: Benefits, Success Factors, and Future Research," *Journal of Brand Management* 17 (March 2010), pp. 368–89. See also, Kusum Ailawadi, Bari Harlam, Jacques Cesar, and David Trounce, "Retailer Promotion Profitability," *Journal of Marketing Research* 43 (November 2006), pp. 518–35; Kusum Ailawadi, Koen Pauwels, and Jan-Benedict E.M. Steenkamp, "Private Label Use and Store Loyalty," *Journal of Marketing* 72 (November 2008), pp. 19–30.

17. Michael Felding, "No Longer Plain, Simple," *Marketing News*, May 15, 2006, pp. 11–13; Rob Walker, "Shelf Improvement," *New York Times*, May 7, 2006.

18. Robert Shaw and Philip Kotler, "Rethinking the Chain: Making Marketing Leaner, Faster, and Better," *Marketing Management* (July/August 2009), pp. 18–23; William C. Copacino, *Supply Chain Management* (Boca Raton, FL: St. Lucie Press, 1997).

19. The optimal order quantity is given by the formula $Q^* = 2DS/IC$, where D = annual demand, S = cost to place one order, and I = annual carrying cost per unit. Known as the economic-order quantity formula, it assumes a constant ordering cost, a constant cost of carrying an additional unit in inventory, a known demand, and no quantity discounts.

20. William C. Copacino, *Supply Chain Management* (Boca Raton, FL: St. Lucie Press, 1997), pp. 122–23.

21. "Manufacturing Complexity," *Economist: A Survey of Logistics*, June 17, 2006, pp. 6–9.

Designing and Managing Integrated Marketing Communications

In this chapter, we will address the following questions:

1. What is the role of marketing communications?
2. What are the major steps in developing effective communications?
3. What is the communications mix, and how should it be set?
4. What is an integrated marketing communications program?

Marketing Management at Ocean Spray

Facing stiff competition and years of declining sales, Ocean Spray COO Ken Romanzi and agency Arnold Worldwide decided to "reintroduce the cranberry to America" as the "surprisingly versatile little fruit that supplies modern-day benefits." The resulting campaign, which used all facets of marketing communications, supported the firm's full range of products and leveraged the fact that the brand was born in the cranberry bogs and remained there still. Called "Straight from the Bog," the campaign reinforced two key brand benefits: Ocean Spray products taste good and are good for you.

During the campaign, miniature bogs were brought to Manhattan and featured on an NBC Today morning segment. A "Bogs across America Tour" brought the experience to Los Angeles, Chicago, London, and other cities. Television and print ads featured growers (depicted by actors) standing in a bog and talking, often humorously, about what they did. The original campaign also included a Web site, in-store displays, and events for consumers and Ocean Spray growers, supplemented by Facebook and Twitter posts in later years. Product innovation was crucial, too, with the launch of new juices and Craisins sweetened dried cranberries. Despite continued decline in the fruit juice category, this campaign helped Ocean Spray increase sales by an average of 10 percent each year from 2005 to 2009.[1]

As Ocean Spray knows, modern marketing calls for more than developing a good product, pricing it attractively, and making it accessible. Companies must also communicate with their present and potential stakeholders and the general public. The question is not *whether* to communicate but *what* to say, *how* and *when* to say it, to *whom*, and *how often*. This chapter describes how communications work, what marketing communications can do for a company, and how holistic marketers combine and integrate marketing communications. Chapter 16 examines mass (nonpersonal) communications (advertising, sales promotion, events and experiences, and public relations and publicity); Chapter 17 examines personal communications (direct and interactive marketing, word-of-mouth marketing, and personal selling).

The Role of Marketing Communications

Marketing communications are the means by which firms attempt to inform, persuade, and remind consumers—directly or indirectly—about the products and brands they sell. They represent the voice of the company and its brands and help the firm establish a dialogue and build relationships with consumers. Marketing communications show consumers how and why a product is used, by whom, where, and when; let consumers know who makes the product and what the firm and brand stand for; and offer an incentive for trial or use. They allow companies to link their brands to other people, places, events, brands, experiences, feelings, and things. They can contribute to brand equity—by establishing the brand in memory and creating a brand image—as well as strengthen customer loyalty, drive sales, and even affect shareholder value.[2]

The Changing Marketing Communications Environment

Technology and other factors have profoundly changed the way consumers process communications, and even whether they choose to process them at all. The rapid diffusion of multipurpose smart phones, broadband and wireless Internet connections, and ad-skipping digital video recorders (DVRs) have eroded the effectiveness of the mass media. Consumers not only have more choices of media, they can also decide whether and how they want to receive commercial content. "Marketing Insight: Don't Touch That Remote" describes developments in television advertising.

Commercial clutter is rampant. Marketing communications in almost every medium and form have been on the rise, and some consumers feel they are increasingly invasive. Therefore, marketers must be creative in using technology without intruding in consumers' lives.

Marketing Communications, Brand Equity, and Sales

Although advertising is often a central element of a marketing communications program, it is usually not the only one—or even the most important one—for building sales as well as increasing brand and customer equity. The **marketing communications mix** consists of eight major modes of communication:[3]

1. *Advertising*—Any paid form of nonpersonal presentation and promotion of ideas, goods, or services by an identified sponsor.
2. *Sales promotion*—A variety of short-term incentives to encourage trial or purchase of a product or service.

DON'T TOUCH THAT REMOTE

That consumers are more in charge in the marketplace is perhaps nowhere more evident than in television broadcasting, where DVRs allow viewers to skip past ads with a push of the fast-forward button. Is that all bad? Surprisingly, research shows that while focusing on an ad in order to fast-forward through it, consumers retain and recall a fair amount of information. The most successful ads in "fast-forward mode" were those consumers had already seen, that used familiar characters, and that didn't have lots of scenes. It also helped to have brand-related information in the center of the screen. Although consumers are still more likely to recall an ad the next day if they've watched it live, some brand recall occurs even after an ad has been deliberately zapped.

Nielsen, which handles television program ratings, recently began offering ratings for specific ads. Before, advertisers had to pay based on the program rating, even if as many as 5 percent to 15 percent of consumers temporarily tuned away. Now advertisers can pay based on the actual commercial audience available when their ad is shown. To increase viewership during commercial breaks, the major broadcast and cable networks are shortening breaks and delaying them until viewers are more likely to be engaged in a program.

Sources: Andrew O'Connell, "Advertisers: Learn to Love the DVR," *Harvard Business Review*, April 2010, p. 22; Erik du Plesis, "Digital Video Recorders and Inadvertent Advertising Exposure," *Journal of Advertising Research* 49 (June 2009); S. Adam Brasel and James Gips, "Breaking Through Fast-Forwarding: Brand Information and Visual Attention," *Journal of Marketing* 72 (November 2008), pp. 31–48; "Watching the Watchers," *Economist*, November 15, 2008, p. 77; Stephanie Kang, "Why DVR Viewers Recall Some TV Spots," *Wall Street Journal*, February 26, 2008; Kenneth C. Wilbur, "How Digital Video Recorder Changes Traditional Television Advertising," *Journal of Advertising* 37 (Summer 2008), pp. 143–49; Burt Helm, "Cable Takes a Ratings Hit," *BusinessWeek*, September 24, 2007.

3. *Events and experiences*—Company-sponsored activities and programs designed to create brand-related interactions.

4. *Public relations and publicity*—Programs directed internally or externally to promote or protect a company's image or its individual product communications.

5. *Direct marketing*—Use of mail, telephone, fax, e-mail, or Internet to communicate directly with or solicit response or dialogue from specific customers and prospects.

6. *Interactive marketing*—Online activities and programs to engage customers or prospects and directly or indirectly raise awareness, improve image, or elicit sales.

7. *Word-of-mouth marketing*—People-to-people oral, written, or electronic communications that relate to the merits or experiences of purchasing or using products or services.

8. *Personal selling* Face-to-face interaction with one or more prospective purchasers for the purpose of making presentations, answering questions, and procuring orders.

Company communication goes beyond the specific platforms listed in Table 15.1. The product's styling and price, the package shape and color, the salesperson's manner and dress, the store décor—all communicate something to buyers. Every *brand contact* delivers an impression that

| TABLE 15.1 | Common Communication Platforms | | | | | |

Advertising	Sales Promotion	Events and Experiences	Public Relations and Publicity	Direct and Interactive Marketing	Word-of-Mouth Marketing	Personal Selling
Print and broadcast ads	Contests, games, sweepstakes, lotteries	Sports	Press kits	Catalogs	Person-to-person	Sales presentations
Packaging–outer		Entertainment	Speeches	Mailings	Chat rooms	Sales meetings
Packaging inserts	Premiums and gifts	Festivals	Seminars	Telemarketing	Blogs	Incentive programs
Cinema	Sampling	Arts	Annual reports	Electronic shopping		Samples
Brochures and booklets	Fairs and trade shows	Causes	Charitable donations	TV shopping		Fairs and trade shows
Posters and leaflets	Exhibits	Factory tours	Publications	Fax		
Directories	Demonstrations	Company museums	Community relations	E-mail		
Reprints of ads	Coupons	Street activities	Lobbying	Voice mail		
Billboards	Rebates		Identity media	Company blogs		
Display signs	Low-interest financing		Company magazine	Web sites		
Point-of-purchase displays	Trade-in allowances					
DVDs	Continuity programs					
	Tie-ins					

can strengthen or weaken a customer's view of a company.[4] Communications contribute to brand equity and drive sales in many ways: by creating brand awareness, forging brand image in consumers' memories, eliciting positive brand judgments or feelings, and strengthening consumer loyalty. But marketing communications must be integrated to deliver a consistent message and achieve the strategic positioning.

Communications Process Models

Marketers should understand the fundamental elements of effective communications. Two models are useful: a macromodel and a micromodel. Figure 15.1 shows a macromodel with nine key factors in effective communication. Two represent the major parties—*sender* and *receiver*. Two represent the major tools—*message* and *media*. Four represent major communication functions—*encoding, decoding, response,* and *feedback*. The last element is *noise*, random and competing messages that may interfere with the intended communication.[5]

Micromodels of marketing communications concentrate on consumers' specific responses to communications. Figure 15.2 summarizes four classic *response hierarchy models*. These models assume the buyer passes through cognitive, affective, and behavioral stages, in that order. This "learn-feel-do" sequence is appropriate when the audience has high involvement with a product category perceived to have high differentiation, such as an automobile. An alternative sequence, "do-feel-learn," is relevant when the audience has high involvement but perceives

FIGURE 15.1 Elements in the Communications Process

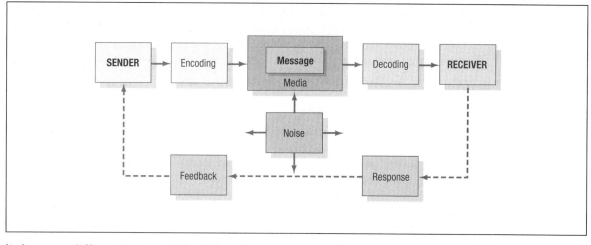

little or no differentiation within the product category, such as an airline ticket. A third sequence, "learn-do-feel," is relevant when the audience has low involvement and perceives little differentiation, such as with salt. By choosing the right sequence, the marketer can do a better job of planning communications.[6]

FIGURE 15.2 Response Hierarchy Models

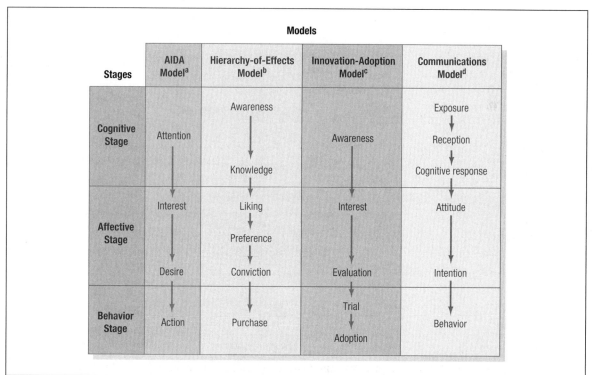

Stages	Models			
	AIDA Model[a]	Hierarchy-of-Effects Model[b]	Innovation-Adoption Model[c]	Communications Model[d]
Cognitive Stage	Attention	Awareness → Knowledge	Awareness	Exposure → Reception → Cognitive response
Affective Stage	Interest → Desire	Liking → Preference → Conviction	Interest → Evaluation	Attitude → Intention
Behavior Stage	Action	Purchase	Trial → Adoption	Behavior

Sources: [a]E. K. Strong, *The Psychology of Selling* (New York: McGraw-Hill, 1925), p. 9; [b]Robert J. Lavidge and Gary A. Steiner, "A Model for Predictive Measurements of Advertising Effectiveness," *Journal of Marketing* (October 1961), p. 61; [c]Everett M. Rogers, *Diffusion of Innovation* (New York: Free Press, 1962), pp. 79–86; [d]various sources.

Developing Effective Communications

Developing effective communications requires eight steps (see Figure 15.3). The basics are (1) identifying the target audience, (2) determining the objectives, (3) designing the communications, (4) selecting the channels, and (5) establishing the budget. The final steps, examined later in this chapter, are (6) deciding on the media mix, (7) measuring the results, and (8) managing integrated marketing communications.

Identify the Target Audience

The process must start with a clear target audience in mind: potential buyers of the company's products, current users, deciders, or influencers, and individuals, groups, particular publics, or the general public. The target audience is a critical influence on the communicator's decisions about what to say, how, when, where, and to whom.

Though we can profile the target audience in terms of any of the market segments identified in Chapter 7, it's often useful to do so in terms of usage and loyalty. Is the target new to the

FIGURE 15.3 Steps in Developing Effective Communications

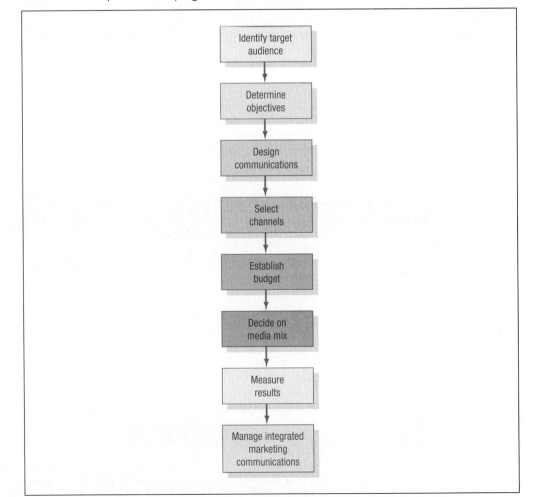

category or a current user? Is the target loyal to the brand, loyal to a competitor, or someone who switches between brands? If a brand user, is he or she a heavy or light user? Communication strategy will differ depending on the answers. We can also conduct *image analysis* by profiling the target audience in terms of brand knowledge.

Determine the Communications Objectives

John R. Rossiter and Larry Percy identify four possible objectives, as follows:[7]

1. *Category Need*—Establish a product or service category as necessary to remove or satisfy a perceived discrepancy between a current motivational state and a desired emotional state.

2. *Brand Awareness*—Foster the consumer's ability to recognize or recall the brand within the category, in sufficient detail to make a purchase. Recognition is easier to achieve than recall, but brand recall is important outside the store, whereas brand recognition is important inside the store. Brand awareness provides a foundation for brand equity.

3. *Brand Attitude*—Help consumers evaluate the brand's perceived ability to meet a currently relevant need. Relevant brand needs may be negatively oriented (problem removal, problem avoidance, incomplete satisfaction, normal depletion) or positively oriented (sensory gratification, intellectual stimulation, or social approval).

4. *Brand Purchase Intention*—Move consumers to decide to purchase the brand or take purchase-related action.

Design the Communications

Formulating the communications to achieve the desired response requires solving three problems: what to say (message strategy), how to say it (creative strategy), and who should say it (message source).

Message Strategy

In determining message strategy, management searches for appeals, themes, or ideas that will tie in to the brand positioning and help establish points-of-parity or points-of-difference. Some of these may be related directly to product or service performance (the quality, economy, or value of the brand), whereas others may relate to more extrinsic considerations (the brand as being contemporary, popular, or traditional). Researcher John C. Maloney felt buyers expected one of four types of reward from a product: rational, sensory, social, or ego satisfaction.[8] Buyers might visualize these rewards from results-of-use experience, product-in-use experience, or incidental-to-use experience.

Creative Strategy

Creative strategies are the way marketers translate their messages into a specific communication. We can classify them as either informational or transformational appeals.[9] An **informational appeal** elaborates on product or service attributes or benefits, assuming that consumers will process the communication very logically. Examples are problem solution ads (Excedrin stops the toughest headache pain), product demonstration ads (Thompson Water Seal can withstand intense weather), product comparison ads (DIRECTV offers better HD options than cable or other satellite operators), and testimonials (NBA star LeBron James pitching Nike).

The best ads with informational appeals ask questions and allow consumers to form their own conclusions.[10] If Honda had hammered away that the Element was for young people, this strong definition might have kept older drivers away. Some stimulus ambiguity can lead to a broader market definition and more spontaneous purchases. You might expect one-sided presentations that praise a product to be more effective than two-sided arguments that mention shortcomings. Yet two-sided messages may be more appropriate, especially when negative associations must be overcome.[11] Two-sided messages are more effective with more educated audiences and those who are initially opposed.[12] Finally, the order in which arguments are presented is important.[13]

A **transformational appeal** elaborates on a nonproduct-related benefit or image. It might depict what kind of person uses a brand (VW advertised to active, youthful people with its famed "Drivers Wanted" campaign) or what kind of experience results from use (Pringles advertised "Once You Pop, the Fun Don't Stop"). Transformational appeals often attempt to stir up emotions that will motivate purchase. Communicators use negative appeals such as fear, guilt, and shame to get people to do things (brush their teeth) or stop doing things (smoking). Communicators also use positive emotional appeals such as humor, love, pride, and joy. Motivational or "borrowed interest" devices—such as the presence of cute babies—attract attention and raise involvement in an ad. However, these devices may detract from comprehension, wear out their welcome fast, and overshadow the product.

Message Source   Messages delivered by attractive or popular sources can achieve higher attention and recall, which is why advertisers often use celebrities as spokespeople. Celebrities are likely to be effective when they are credible or personify a key product attribute; thus, consumers saw actress Valerie Bertinelli's ads for the Jenny Craig weight loss program as a good fit. Three factors identified as sources of credibility are expertise, trustworthiness, and likability.[14] *Expertise* is the specialized knowledge the communicator possesses to back the claim. *Trustworthiness* is how objective and honest the source is perceived to be. Friends are trusted more than strangers or salespeople, and unpaid sources are viewed as more trustworthy than paid sources.[15] *Likability* describes the source's attractiveness. Qualities such as candor, humor, and naturalness make a source more likable. The most highly credible source would score high on expertise, trustworthiness, and likability.

If a person has a positive attitude toward a source and a message, or a negative attitude toward both, a state of *congruity* is said to exist. If a consumer hears a likable celebrity praise a brand she dislikes, C. E. Osgood and P. H. Tannenbaum believe attitude change will take place in the direction of increasing the amount of congruity between the two evaluations.[16] The **principle of congruity** implies that communicators can use their good image to reduce some negative feelings toward a brand but in the process might lose some esteem with the audience.

Select the Communications Channels

Selecting an efficient means to carry the message becomes more difficult as channels of communication become more fragmented and cluttered. Communications channels may be personal and nonpersonal. Marketers must reach out carefully to consumers in all types of channel (see "Marketing Skills: Permission Marketing").

Personal Communications Channels   **Personal communications channels** let two or more persons communicate face-to-face or person-to-audience through a phone, surface mail, or e-mail. They derive their effectiveness from individualized presentation and feedback and include direct and interactive marketing, word-of-mouth marketing, and personal selling. We can draw a further distinction between advocate, expert, and social communications channels. *Advocate channels* consist of company salespeople contacting buyers in the target market. *Expert channels* consist of independent experts making statements to target buyers. *Social channels* consist of neighbors, friends, family members, and associates talking to target buyers.

PERMISSION MARKETING

Permission marketing is a targeted, cost-effective way to build relationships with customers and prospects. How do marketers develop this skill? According to Seth Godin, the first step is to assess customer lifetime value and determine a budget for customer acquisition. Next, create messages to educate targeted customers about the value of the firm's offers and get their permission to engage in ongoing dialogue. As the firm learns more about each customer, it can customize messages and provide incentives (such as discounts) for continuing the dialogue. Finally, always ask for a response, to see how customers react to the messages and to measure results.

The U.K. telecommunications firm O2, which markets cell phone services and broadband Internet access, recently used permission marketing to attract more than one million customers for its O2 More program. Customers who give permission receive brand messages via cell phone from participating firms such as Adidas and Cadbury. Because customers choose the brands they want to hear from, the messages are perceived as more relevant and of higher interest.[17]

A study by Burson-Marsteller and Roper Starch Worldwide found that one influential person's word of mouth tends to affect the buying attitudes of two other people, on average. That circle of influence jumps to eight online. Personal influence carries especially great weight (1) when products are expensive, risky, or purchased infrequently, and (2) when products suggest something about the user's status or taste. People often ask others to recommend a doctor, plumber, hotel, lawyer, accountant, insurance agent, or financial consultant.

Nonpersonal (Mass) Communications Channels   Nonpersonal channels are communications directed to more than one person and include advertising, sales promotions, events and experiences, and public relations. Companies are searching for better ways to quantify the benefits of sponsorship and demanding greater accountability from event owners and organizers. Events can create attention, although whether they have a lasting effect on brand awareness, knowledge, or preference will vary depending on the quality of the product, the event itself, and its execution.

Integration of Communications Channels   Although personal communication is often more effective than mass communication, mass media might be the major means of stimulating personal communication. Mass communications affect personal attitudes and behavior through a two-step process. Ideas often flow from radio, television, and print to opinion leaders, and from these to less media-involved population groups.

This two-step flow has several implications. First, the influence of mass media on public opinion is not as direct, powerful, and automatic as marketers have supposed. It is mediated by opinion leaders, people whose opinions others seek or who carry their opinions to others. Second, the two-step flow challenges the notion that consumption styles are primarily influenced by a "trickle-down" or "trickle-up" effect from mass media. People interact primarily within their own social groups and acquire ideas from opinion leaders in their groups. Third, two-step communication suggests that mass communicators should direct messages specifically to opinion leaders and let them carry the message to others.

Establish the Total Marketing Communications Budget

Industries and companies vary considerably in how much they spend on marketing communications. Expenditures might be 40 percent to 45 percent of sales in the cosmetics industry, but only 5 percent to 10 percent in the industrial-equipment industry, with company-to-company variations. Four common methods for deciding on a budget are:

1. *Affordable method*—setting the communication budget at what managers think the company can afford. The method ignores the role of promotion as an investment and the immediate impact of promotion on sales volume. It leads to an uncertain annual budget, which makes long-range planning difficult.

2. *Percentage-of-sales method*—setting the communication budget at a specified percentage of current or anticipated sales or of the sales price. This satisfies financial managers, who believe expenses should be closely related to the movement of corporate sales over the business cycle. It also encourages management to think of the relationship among communication cost, selling price, and profit per unit, and encourages stability when competing firms spend approximately the same percentage on communications. On the other hand, this method views sales as the determiner of communications rather than as the result. It leads to a budget set by funds availability rather than by market opportunities and it discourages experimentation with countercyclical communication or aggressive spending. This method offers no logical basis for choosing the specific percentage, nor does it allow for determining the budget each product and territory deserves.

3. *Competitive-parity method*—setting the communication budget to achieve share-of-voice parity with competitors. The idea is that competitors' expenditures represent the collective wisdom of the industry, and maintaining competitive parity prevents communication wars. Neither argument is valid. Company reputations, resources, opportunities, and objectives differ so much that communication budgets are hardly a guide. And there is no evidence that competitive parity discourages communication wars.

4. *Objective-and-task method*—developing the budget by defining specific objectives, determining the tasks that must be performed to achieve these objectives, and estimating the costs of performing them. The sum of these costs is the proposed communication budget. This method has the advantage of requiring marketers to spell out assumptions about the relationship among dollars spent, exposure levels, trial rates, and regular usage.

In theory, marketers should establish the total communications budget so the marginal profit from the last communication dollar just equals the marginal profit from the last dollar in the best noncommunication use. Implementing this principle, however, is not easy.

Deciding on the Marketing Communications Mix

Companies must allocate the marketing communications budget over the eight major modes of communication—advertising, sales promotion, public relations and publicity, events and experiences, direct marketing, interactive marketing, word-of-mouth marketing, and the sales force. Within the same industry, companies can differ considerably in their media and channel choices. Companies are always searching for ways to gain efficiency by substituting one communication tool for others. The substitutability among communication tools explains why marketing functions need to be coordinated.

Characteristics of the Marketing Communications Mix

Each communication tool has its own unique characteristics and costs. We briefly review them here and discuss them in more detail in Chapters 16 and 17.

- *Advertising* reaches geographically dispersed buyers and can build up a long-term image for a product (Coca-Cola ads) or trigger quick sales (a Macy's ad for a weekend sale). It can be pervasive, offers opportunities for dramatizing a firm and its offerings, and enables advertisers to focus on specific aspects of the brand and product.

- *Sales promotion* uses tools such as coupons, contests, premiums, and the like to draw a stronger and quicker buyer response. The three key benefits are that sales promotion draws attention to the product, provides an incentive to the customer, and invites the customer to engage in the transaction now.

- *Public relations and publicity* can be extremely effective when coordinated with other communications-mix elements. The appeal is based on three distinctive qualities: high credibility, the ability to reach hard-to-find buyers, and the ability to tell the story of the company, brand, or product.

- *Events and experiences* have the advantage of being seen as highly relevant, being more actively engaging for consumers, and being an indirect "soft sell" approach.

- *Direct and interactive marketing,* which can take many forms, share three characteristics. They are customized for the addressed individual, able to be prepared very quickly, and can be changed depending on response.

- *Word-of-mouth marketing* also takes many forms, online and offline. It can be influential, personal, and timely.

- *Personal selling* is most effective in later stages of the buying process, particularly in building up buyer preference, conviction, and action. Three notable qualities are personal interaction, the ability to cultivate relationships, and personal choices for response.

Factors in Setting the Marketing Communications Mix

Companies must consider several factors in developing their communications mix: type of product market, consumer readiness to make a purchase, and stage in the product life cycle. First, communications mix allocations vary between consumer and business markets. Consumer marketers tend to spend comparatively more on sales promotion and advertising. Although business marketers tend to spend comparatively more on personal selling, advertising still plays a role in introducing the firm and its products, explaining product features, reminding customers of the product's offerings, generating leads for sales representatives, legitimizing the firm, and reassuring customers about purchases. Personal selling can also make a strong contribution in consumer-goods marketing by helping persuade dealers to take more stock, building dealer enthusiasm, signing up more dealers, and increasing sales at existing accounts.

Second, communication tools vary in cost-effectiveness at different stages of buyer readiness (see Figure 15.4). Advertising and publicity are most important in the awareness-building stage. Customer comprehension is primarily affected by advertising and personal selling; customer conviction is influenced mostly by personal selling. Closing the sale is influenced mostly by personal selling and sales promotion. Reordering is also affected mostly by personal selling and sales promotion, and somewhat by reminder advertising and publicity.

Third, communication tools vary in cost effectiveness at different product life-cycle stages. During introduction the most cost-effective are advertising, events and experiences, and publicity,

FIGURE 15.4 Cost-Effectiveness of Three Different Communication Tools at Different Buyer-Readiness Stages

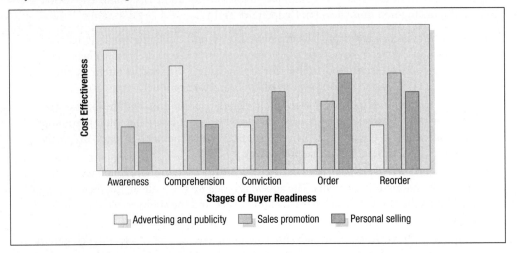

followed by personal selling to gain distribution coverage and sales promotion and direct marketing to induce trial. In the growth stage, demand has its own momentum through word of mouth and interactive marketing. Advertising, events and experiences, and personal selling become more important in the maturity stage. In the decline stage, sales promotion continues strong, other communication tools are reduced, and salespeople give the product minimal attention.

Measuring Communications Results

After implementing the communications plan, the company must measure its impact by asking members of the target audience whether they recognize or recall the message, how many times they saw it, what points they recall, how they felt about the message, and what are their previous and current attitudes toward the product and company. The communicator should also collect behavioral measures of audience response, such as how many people bought the product, liked it, and talked to others about it.

Suppose that 80 percent of the targeted customers are aware of the brand, 60 percent have tried it, and only 20 percent who tried it are satisfied. This indicates that the communications program is effective in creating awareness, but the product fails to meet consumer expectations. However, if 40 percent of the targeted customers are aware of the brand and only 30 percent have tried it—but 80 percent of them are satisfied—the communications program needs to be strengthened to take advantage of the brand's power.

Managing the Integrated Marketing Communications Process

The American Marketing Association defines **integrated marketing communications (IMC)** as "a planning process designed to assure that all brand contacts received by a customer or prospect for a product, service, or organization are relevant to that person and consistent over time." This planning process evaluates the strategic roles of a variety of communications disciplines—for example, general advertising, direct response, sales promotion, and public relations—and skillfully combines these disciplines to provide clarity, consistency, and maximum impact through the seamless integration of messages.

Coordinating Media

Media coordination can occur across and within media types, but marketers should combine personal and nonpersonal communications channels through *multiple-vehicle, multiple-stage campaigns* to achieve maximum impact and increase message reach and impact. Promotions can be more effective when combined with advertising, for example.[18] The awareness and attitudes created by advertising campaigns can increase the success of more direct sales pitches. Advertising can convey the positioning of a brand and benefit from online display advertising or search engine marketing that offers a stronger call to action.[19]

Many companies are coordinating their online and offline communications activities. Web addresses in ads (especially print ads) and on packages allow people to more fully explore a company's products, find store locations, and get more product or service information. Even if consumers don't order online, marketers can use Web sites and Facebook pages to drive buyers into stores.

Implementing IMC

Integrated marketing communications can produce stronger message consistency and help build brand equity and create greater sales impact.[20] It forces management to think about every way the customer comes in contact with the company, how the company communicates its positioning, the relative importance of each vehicle, and timing issues. It gives someone the responsibility—where none existed before—to unify brand images and messages through thousands of company activities. IMC should improve the company's ability to reach the right customers with the right messages at the right time and place.[21]

EXECUTIVE SUMMARY

The marketing communications mix consists of advertising, sales promotion, public relations and publicity, events and experiences, direct marketing, interactive marketing, word-of-mouth marketing, and personal selling. The communications process includes sender, receiver, message, media, encoding, decoding, response, feedback, and noise. Developing effective communications requires eight steps: (1) Identify the target audience, (2) determine the objectives, (3) design the communications, (4) select the communications channels, (5) establish the total communications budget, (6) decide on the communications mix, (7) measure the results, and (8) manage the integrated marketing communications process.

Communications objectives can be to create category need, brand awareness, brand attitude, or brand purchase intention. Formulating communications requires decisions about message strategy, creative strategy, and message source. Communications channels can be personal (advocate, expert, and social channels) or nonpersonal (media, atmospheres, and events). The objective-and-task method of communications budgeting is typically most effective. In choosing the communications mix, marketers must examine each tool's advantages and costs, as well as the company's market rank, type of product market, buyer readiness, and product life-cycle stage. Firms measure communications effectiveness by asking members of the target audience whether they recognize or recall the message, how many times they saw it, what they recall, how they felt about it, and what are their previous and current attitudes. Integrated marketing communications (IMC) recognizes the added value of a comprehensive plan to evaluate the strategic roles of a variety of communications disciplines, and combines these disciplines to provide clarity, consistency, and maximum impact through seamless message integration.

NOTES

1. Ken Romanzi, "Reintroducing the Cranberry to America!" Talk at the Tuck School of Business at Dartmouth, January 7, 2010; "Breakaway Brands: Ocean Spray Tells It Straight from the Bog," *MediaPost*, October 9, 2006; Francis J. Kelly III and Barry Silverstein, *The Breakaway Brand* (New York: McGraw-Hill, 2005).

2. Xueming Luo and Naveen Donthu, "Marketing's Credibility: A Longitudinal Investigation of Marketing Communication Productivity and Shareholder Value," *Journal of Marketing* 70 (October 2006), pp. 70–91.

3. Some of these definitions are adapted from Peter D. Bennett, ed., *Dictionary of Marketing Terms* (Chicago: American Marketing Association, 1995).

4. Tom Duncan and Sandra Moriarty, "How Integrated Marketing Communication's 'Touch Points' Can Operationalize the Service-Dominant Logic," Robert F. Lusch and Stephen L. Vargo, eds., *The Service-Dominant Logic of Marketing* (Armonk, NY: M.E. Sharpe, 2006); Tom Duncan, *Principles of Advertising and IMC,* 2nd ed. (New York: McGraw-Hill/Irwin, 2005).

5. For an alternate communications model developed specifically for advertising communications, see Barbara B. Stern, "A Revised Communication Model for Advertising," *Journal of Advertising* (June 1994), pp. 5–15. For additional perspectives, see Tom Duncan and Sandra E. Moriarty, "A Communication-Based Marketing Model for Managing Relationships," *Journal of Marketing* (April 1998), pp. 1–13.

6. Demetrios Vakratsas and Tim Ambler, "How Advertising Works: What Do We Really Know?" *Journal of Marketing* 63, no. 1 (January 1999), pp. 26–43.

7. This section is based on the excellent text, John R. Rossiter and Larry Percy, *Advertising and Promotion Management,* 2nd ed. (New York: McGraw-Hill, 1997).

8. James F. Engel, Roger D. Blackwell, and Paul W. Miniard, *Consumer Behavior,* 9th ed. (Fort Worth, TX: Dryden, 2001).

9. John R. Rossiter and Larry Percy, *Advertising and Promotion Management,* 2nd ed. (New York: McGraw-Hill, 1997).

10. James F. Engel, Roger D. Blackwell, and Paul W. Miniard, *Consumer Behavior,* 9th ed. (Fort Worth, TX: Dryden, 2001).

11. Ayn E. Crowley and Wayne D. Hoyer, "An Integrative Framework for Understanding Two-Sided Persuasion," *Journal of Consumer Research* (March 1994), pp. 561–74.

12. C. I. Hovland, A. A. Lumsdaine, and F. D. Sheffield, *Experiments on Mass Communication,* vol. 3 (Princeton, NJ: Princeton University Press, 1949); Crowley and Hoyer, "An Integrative Framework for Understanding Two-Sided Persuasion." For an alternative viewpoint, see George E. Belch, "The Effects of Message Modality on One- and Two-Sided Advertising Messages," Richard P. Bagozzi and Alice M. Tybout, eds., *Advances in Consumer Research* (Ann Arbor, MI: Association for Consumer Research, 1983), pp. 21–26.

13. Curtis P. Haugtvedt and Duane T. Wegener, "Message Order Effects in Persuasion: An Attitude Strength Perspective," *Journal of Consumer Research* (June 1994), pp. 205–18; H. Rao Unnava, Robert E. Burnkrant, and Sunil Erevelles, "Effects of Presentation Order and Communication Modality on Recall and Attitude," *Journal of Consumer Research* (December 1994), pp. 481–90.

14. Herbert C. Kelman and Carl I. Hovland, "Reinstatement of the Communication in Delayed Measurement of Opinion Change," *Journal of Abnormal and Social Psychology* 48 (July 1953), pp. 327–35.

15. David J. Moore, John C. Mowen, and Richard Reardon, "Multiple Sources in Advertising Appeals," *Journal of the Academy of Marketing Science* (Summer 1994), pp. 234–43.

16. C. E. Osgood and P. H. Tannenbaum, "The Principles of Congruity in the Prediction of Attitude Change," *Psychological Review* 62 (January 1955), pp. 42–55.

17. John Warrillow, "What Seth Godin Did on His Summer Vacation," *Inc.*, October 5, 2010, www.inc.com/articles/2010/10/seth-godin-on-building-a-valuable-company.html; Nicola Carpenter, "O2 Getting More People Opting in to Mobile Marketing," *Direct Marketing Association (UK),* September 20, 2010, www.dma.org.uk; James Middleton, "O2 Claims Success from Mobile Ad Unit," *Telecoms.com,* September 20, 2010, www.telecoms.com; L. Erwin, "The Secret Behind Permission-Based Marketing," *Point of Purchase,* February 2001, p. 41; John Lehmann, "Permission Marketing Personalizes the Sales Pitch," *Crain's Cleveland Business,* September 13, 2004, p. 23.

18. Scott Neslin, *Sales Promotion,* MSI Relevant Knowledge Series (Cambridge, MA: Marketing Science Institute, 2002).

19. Markus Pfeiffer and Markus Zinnbauer, "Can Old Media Enhance New Media?" *Journal of Advertising Research* (March 2010), pp. 42–49.

20. Sreedhar Madhavaram, Vishag Badrinarayanan, and Robert E. McDonald, "Integrated Marketing Communication (IMC) and Brand Identity as Critical Components of Brand Equity Strategy," *Journal of Advertising* 34 (Winter 2005), pp. 69–80; Mike Reid, Sandra Luxton, and Felix Mavondo, "The Relationship between Integrated Marketing Communication, Market Orientation, and Brand Orientation," *Journal of Advertising* 34 (Winter 2005), pp. 11–23.

21. Don E. Schultz and Heidi Schultz, *IMC, The Next Generation* (New York: McGraw-Hill, 2003); Don E. Shultz, Stanley I. Tannenbaum, and Robert F. Lauterborn, *Integrated Marketing Communications: Putting It Together and Making It Work* (Lincolnwood, IL: NTC Business Books, 1992).

chapter 16

Managing Mass Communications: Advertising, Sales Promotions, Events and Experiences, and Public Relations

In this chapter, we will address the following questions:

1. What steps are required in developing an advertising program?
2. How should sales promotion decisions be made?
3. What are the guidelines for effective brand-building events and experiences?
4. How can companies exploit the potential of public relations and publicity?

Marketing Management at Old Spice

Among the more successful commercials aired during the 2010 Super Bowl was one for Procter & Gamble's Old Spice body wash. Turning a potential negative of being an old brand into a positive of being experienced, Old Spice has made a remarkable transformation from "your father's aftershave" to a contemporary men's fragrance brand. In a new strategic move, given their important role in the purchase process, the Super Bowl spot targeted women as well as men. The tongue-in-cheek ad featured rugged ex-NFL football player Isaiah Mustafa as "The Man Your Man Could Smell Like."

In addition to the television exposure, the ad was viewed over 10 million times on YouTube and other social media sites. Old Spice's Facebook page included a Web application called "My Perpetual Love," which featured Mustafa offering men the opportunity to be "more like him" by e-mailing and tweeting their sweethearts virtual love notes. For its efforts, the ad agency behind the campaign, Wieden+Kennedy, received a Grand Prix at the Cannes International Ad Festival. A follow-up ad in June 2010 showed Mustafa in a new series of "perfect man" activities including baking birthday cakes, building a home with his own hands, and, yes, walking on water.[1]

Although Old Spice has found great success with its ad campaign, other marketers are trying to come to grips with how to best use mass media in the new—and still changing—communication environment.[2] Although there has been an enormous increase in the use of personal communications by marketers in recent years, due to the rapid penetration of the Internet and other factors, mass media still remains an important component of a modern marketing communications program. In this chapter, we examine the nature and use of four mass-communication tools—advertising, sales promotion, events and experiences, and public relations and publicity.

Developing and Managing an Advertising Program

Advertising is any paid form of nonpersonal presentation and promotion of a product by an identified sponsor. It can be a cost-effective way to disseminate messages, whether to build brand preference or to educate people. Even in today's challenging media environment, good ads can pay off, as they did for P&G's Old Spice brand.

In developing an advertising program, marketing managers must always start by identifying the target market and buyer motives. Then they can make the five major decisions, known as "the five Ms": *Mission:* What are our advertising objectives? *Money:* How much can we spend and how do we allocate our spending across media types? *Message:* What message should we send? *Media:* What media should we use? *Measurement:* How should we evaluate the results? These decisions are summarized in Figure 16.1 and described in the following sections.

FIGURE 16.1 The Five Ms of Advertising

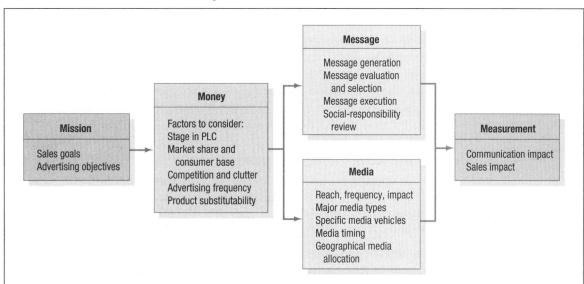

Setting the Objectives

An **advertising objective** (or advertising goal) is a specific communications task and achievement level to be accomplished with a specific audience in a specific period of time. We can classify advertising objectives according to whether their aim is to inform, persuade, remind, or reinforce. These objectives correspond to different stages in the *hierarchy-of-effects* model discussed in Chapter 15.

Informative advertising aims to create brand awareness and knowledge of new products or new features of existing products.[3] *Persuasive advertising* aims to create liking, preference, conviction, and purchase of a product or service. Some persuasive advertising uses comparative advertising, which makes an explicit comparison of the attributes of two or more brands. This works best when it elicits cognitive and affective motivations simultaneously, and when consumers are processing advertising in a detailed, analytical mode.[4] *Reminder advertising* aims to stimulate repeat purchase of products and services (Coca-Cola ads do this). *Reinforcement advertising* aims to convince current purchasers that they made the right choice. Automobile ads often depict satisfied customers enjoying special features of their new car.

The advertising objective should emerge from a thorough analysis of the current marketing situation. If the product class is mature, the company is the market leader, and brand usage is low, the objective is to stimulate more usage. If the product class is new and the company is not the market leader, but the brand is superior to the leader, then the objective is to convince the market of the brand's superiority.

Deciding on the Advertising Budget

Here are five specific factors to consider when setting the advertising budget:[5]

1. *Stage in the product life cycle*—New products typically merit large budgets to build awareness and to gain consumer trial. Established brands usually are supported with lower budgets, measured as a ratio to sales.

2. *Market share and consumer base*—High-market-share brands usually require less advertising expenditure as a percentage of sales to maintain share. To build share by increasing market size requires larger expenditures.

3. *Competition and clutter*—In a market with many competitors and high advertising spending, a brand must advertise more heavily to be heard. Even simple clutter from advertisements not directly competitive to the brand creates a need for heavier advertising.

4. *Advertising frequency*—The number of repetitions needed to put the brand's message across to consumers has an obvious impact on the advertising budget.

5. *Product substitutability*—Brands in less-differentiated or commodity-like product classes (beer, soft drinks), require heavy advertising to establish a unique image.

Developing the Advertising Campaign

In designing an ad campaign, marketers employ both art and science to develop the *message strategy* or positioning of an ad—*what* the ad attempts to convey about the brand—and its *creative strategy*—*how* the ad expresses the brand claims. Advertisers go through three steps: message generation and evaluation, creative development and execution, and social-responsibility review.

Message Generation and Evaluation   A good ad normally focuses on one or two core selling propositions. As part of refining the brand positioning, the advertiser should conduct market research to determine which appeal works best with its target audience and then prepare a *creative brief,* typically one or two pages. This is an elaboration of the *positioning statement* and includes considerations such as key message, target audience, communications objectives (to do, to know, to believe), key brand benefits, supports for the brand promise, and media. The more ad themes explored, the higher the probability of finding an excellent one. Some marketers invite consumers to serve as their creative team, a strategy sometimes called "open source" or "crowdsourcing."[6]

Creative Development and Execution   The ad's impact depends not only on what it says, but often more important, on *how* it says it. Execution can be decisive. Every advertising medium has advantages and disadvantages. For example, television, which can dramatically portray brand personality and demonstrate benefits, reaches a broad spectrum of consumers at low cost per exposure. Print ads can provide detailed product information and effectively communicate user and usage imagery. Radio, a flexible and inexpensive medium, reaches more than 90 percent of the U.S. population age 12 and older, both at home and away from home. As streaming Internet access gains ground, traditional AM/FM radio stations are feeling the pressure and account for less than half of all listening at home.[7] Two disadvantages of radio are the lack of visual images and the relatively passive nature of the consumer processing.

Legal and Social Issues   To break through clutter, some advertisers believe they have to be edgy. However, they must be sure their advertising complies with legal and regulatory guidelines and does not offend the general public, ethnic groups, racial minorities, or special-interest groups. For example, advertisers are not allowed to make false claims, such as stating that a product cures something when it does not. The challenge is telling the difference between deception and "puffery"—simple exaggerations that are not meant to be believed and that *are* permitted by law. Advertising can play a more positive broader social role. The Ad Council is a nonprofit organization that uses top-notch industry talent to produce and distribute public service announcements for nonprofits and government agencies.

Deciding on Media and Measuring Effectiveness

After choosing the message, the next task is to choose media to carry it. The steps here are deciding on desired reach, frequency, and impact; choosing among major media types; selecting specific media vehicles; deciding on media timing; and deciding on geographical media allocation. Then the marketer evaluates the results of these decisions.

Deciding on Reach, Frequency, and Impact

Media selection is finding the most cost-effective media to deliver the desired number and type of exposures to the target audience. The advertiser seeks a specified advertising objective and response from the target audience—for example, a target level of product trial—which depends on, among other things, level of brand awareness. The effect of exposures on audience awareness depends on reach, frequency, and impact:

- Reach (R). The number of different persons or households exposed to a particular media schedule at least once during a specified time period
- Frequency (F). The number of times within the specified time period that an average person or household is exposed to the message
- Impact (I). The qualitative value of an exposure through a given medium (thus a food ad will have a higher impact in *Good Housekeeping* than in *Fortune* magazine)

Although audience awareness will be greater with higher reach, frequency, and impact, there are important trade-offs here. Reach is most important when launching new products, flanker brands, extensions of well-known brands, or infrequently purchased brands; or when going after an undefined target market. Frequency is most important where there are strong competitors, a complex story to tell, high consumer resistance, or a frequent-purchase cycle.[8] A key reason for repetition is forgetting. The higher the forgetting rate associated with a brand, product category, or message, the higher the warranted level of repetition. However, advertisers should not coast on a tired ad but insist on fresh executions by their ad agency.[9]

Choosing Among Major Media Types

The media planner must know the capacity of the major advertising media types to deliver reach, frequency, and impact, along with their costs, advantages, and limitations (see Table 16.1). Media planners make their choices by considering factors such as target audience media habits, product characteristics, message requirements, and cost.

Alternate Advertising Options

In recent years, reduced effectiveness of traditional mass media has led advertisers to increase their emphasis on alternate advertising media. **Place advertising**, or out-of-home advertising, is a broad category including many creative and unexpected forms to grab consumers' attention. The rationale is that marketers are better off reaching people where they work, play, and, of course, shop. Popular options are billboards (including 3-D images), public spaces (such as movie screens and hotel elevators), product placement (in movies and television), and **point of purchase** (**P-O-P**), to

TABLE 16.1	Profiles of Major Media Types	
Medium	Advantages	Limitations
Newspapers	Flexibility; timeliness; good local market coverage; broad acceptance; high believability	Short life; poor reproduction quality; small "pass-along" audience
Television	Combines sight, sound, and motion; appealing to the senses; high attention; high reach	High absolute cost; high clutter; fleeting exposure; less audience selectivity
Direct mail	Audience selectivity; flexibility; no ad competition within the same medium; personalization	Relatively high cost; "junk mail" image
Radio	Mass use; high geographic and demographic selectivity; low cost	Audio presentation only; lower attention than television; nonstandardized rate structures; fleeting exposure
Magazines	High geographic and demographic selectivity; credibility and prestige; high-quality reproduction; long life; good pass-along readership	Long ad purchase lead time; some waste in circulation
Outdoor	Flexibility; high repeat exposure; low cost; low competition	Limited audience selectivity; creative limitations
Yellow Pages	Excellent local coverage; high believability; wide reach; low cost	High competition; long ad purchase lead time; creative limitations
Newsletters	Very high selectivity; full control; interactive opportunities; relative low costs	Costs could run away
Brochures	Flexibility; full control; can dramatize messages	Overproduction could lead to runaway costs
Telephone	Many users; opportunity to give a personal touch	Relative high cost; increasing consumer resistance
Internet	High selectivity; interactive possibilities; relatively low cost	Increasing clutter

reach consumers where buying decisions are made, usually in a retail setting (including ads on shopping carts and shelves, in-store demonstrations, and in-store radio and television).

Ads now can appear virtually anywhere consumers have a few spare minutes or even seconds to notice them. Such ads can often reach a very precise and captive audience in a cost-effective manner, if the message is simple and direct. Unique ad placements designed to break through clutter may be perceived as invasive and obtrusive, however. The challenge for nontraditional media is demonstrating its reach and effectiveness through credible, independent research.

There will always be room for creative means of placing the brand in front of consumers, as some marketers are doing through advergames (see "Marketing Insight: Playing Games with Brands").

Selecting Specific Media Vehicles

The media planner must search for the most cost-effective vehicles within each chosen media type, relying on measurement services that estimate audience size, composition, and media cost. Media planners then calculate the cost per thousand persons reached by a vehicle and rank each according to cost, favoring those with the lowest cost per thousand for reaching target consumers. Finally, they adjust the rankings for (1) audience quality, (2) the probability that the audience will pay attention to the ad, (3) the medium's editorial quality, and (4) placement policies and extra services.

Deciding on Media Timing and Allocation

In choosing media, the advertiser has both a macroscheduling and a microscheduling decision. The *macroscheduling decision* relates to seasons and the business cycle. Suppose 70 percent of a product's

Marketing Insight

PLAYING GAMES WITH BRANDS

More than half of U.S. adults age 18 and older play video games, and about one in five play every day or almost every day. Virtually all teens (97 percent) play video games. As many as 40 percent of gamers are women. Given this explosive popularity, many advertisers have decided, "if you can't beat them, join them" and are adding *advergames* to their communications mix. Advergames can be played on the sponsor's corporate homepage, on gaming portals, or even in locations such as restaurants.

Honda developed an online game that allowed players to choose a Honda and zoom around city streets plastered with Honda logos. In the first three months, 78,000 people played for an average of eight minutes each. The game's cost per thousand (CPM) of $7 compared favorably to a prime-time TV commercial's CPM of $11.65. Marketers collect valuable customer data upon registration and often seek permission to send e-mails. Mainstream marketers such as Apple, Procter & Gamble, Toyota, and Visa are all jumping on board. Research suggests that gamers accept the ad messages. One study showed that 70 percent of gamers felt dynamic in-game ads "contributed to realism," "fit the games" in which they served, and looked "cool."

Sources: "In-Game Advertising Research Proves Effectiveness for Brands across Categories and Game Titles," www.microsoft.com, June 3, 2008; Amanda Lenhart, "Video Games: Adults Are Players Too," Pew Internet & American Life Project, www.pewresearch.org, December 7, 2008; "Erika Brown, "Game On!" *Forbes,* July 24, 2006, pp. 84–86; David Radd, "Advergaming: You Got It," *BusinessWeek,* October 11, 2006; Stuart Elliott, "Madison Avenue's Full-Court Pitch to Video Gamers," *New York Times,* October 16, 2005.

sales occur between June and September. The firm can vary its advertising expenditures to follow the seasonal pattern, to oppose the seasonal pattern, or to be constant throughout the year.

The *microscheduling decision* calls for allocating advertising expenditures within a short period to obtain maximum impact. Advertising messages can be concentrated ("burst" advertising), dispersed continuously throughout the month, or dispersed intermittently. The chosen pattern should meet the communications objectives set in relationship to the nature of the product, target customers, distribution channels, and other marketing factors.

In launching a new product, the advertiser must choose among continuity, concentration, flighting, and pulsing. *Continuity* means exposures appear evenly throughout a given period; advertisers use this in expanding market situations, with frequently purchased items, and in tightly defined buyer categories. *Concentration* calls for spending all the advertising dollars in a single period, which makes sense for products with one selling season or related holiday. *Flighting* calls for advertising during a period, followed by a period with no advertising, followed by a second period of advertising activity. It is useful when funding is limited, the purchase cycle is relatively infrequent, or items are seasonal. *Pulsing* is continuous advertising at low-weight levels, reinforced periodically by waves of heavier activity, to help the audience learn the message more thoroughly and at a lower cost to the firm.

A company must decide how to allocate its advertising budget over space as well as over time. The company makes "national buys" when it places ads on national TV networks or in nationally circulated magazines. It makes "spot buys" when it buys TV time in just a few markets or in regional editions of magazines; it makes "local buys" when it advertises in local newspapers, radio, or outdoor sites.

Evaluating Advertising Effectiveness

Most advertisers try to measure the communication effect of an ad—that is, its potential impact on awareness, knowledge, or preference. They would also like to measure the ad's sales effect (for more about ads that get results during a sluggish economy, see "Marketing Skills: Advertising in Hard Times").

Marketing Skills

ADVERTISING IN HARD TIMES

Marketers who can plan effective advertising for hard times will be better able to plan ads for any kind of economic climate. When others are cutting back on advertising, firms whose messages stand out will gain an important edge. Be sure the messages offer insight into what the brand stands for; don't make decisions based solely on marketing research, because people often reject original or unconventional ideas simply for being different. Finally, target carefully to reach influential customer groups, and use creative, engaging approaches that get results.

Southwest Airlines was able to gain a full point of market share during the recent recession—a time when airlines were struggling—by making "Bags Fly Free" its main message in all media. The campaign stood out by tapping into consumers' annoyance at the many fees added by competing airlines. One humorous commercial showed four Southwest baggage handlers spelling out the word *free* with letters painted on their chests while hoisting luggage into a Southwest jet. This campaign helped Southwest target business and vacation travelers and achieve significant sales increases despite the economic downturn.[10]

Communication-effect research, called *copy testing*, seeks to determine whether an ad is communicating effectively. Marketers should perform this test both before an ad is put into media (pretesting) and after it is printed or broadcast (posttesting). Many advertisers use posttests to assess the overall impact of a completed campaign.

One way a company can find out whether it is overspending or underspending on advertising is to work with the formula shown in Figure 16.2. A company's *share of advertising expenditures* produces a *share of voice* (proportion of company advertising of that product to all advertising of that product) that earns a *share of consumers' minds and hearts* and, ultimately, a *share of market*.

Researchers try to measure the sales impact by analyzing historical or experimental data. The *historical approach* correlates past sales to past advertising expenditures using advanced statistical techniques.[11] Other researchers use an *experimental design* to measure advertising's sales impact.

Sales Promotion

Sales promotion, a key ingredient in marketing campaigns, consists of a collection of incentive tools, mostly short term, designed to stimulate quicker or greater purchase of particular products or services by consumers or the trade.[12] Whereas advertising offers a *reason* to buy, sales promotion offers an *incentive*. Sales promotion includes tools for *consumer promotion* (samples, coupons, cash refund offers, prices off, premiums, prizes, patronage rewards, free trials, warranties, tie-in promotions, cross-promotions, point-of-purchase displays, and demonstrations), *trade promotion* (prices off, advertising and display allowances, and free goods), and *business* and *sales force promotion* (trade shows and conventions, contests for sales reps, and specialty advertising).

FIGURE 16.2 Formula for Measuring Different Stages in the Sales Impact of Advertising

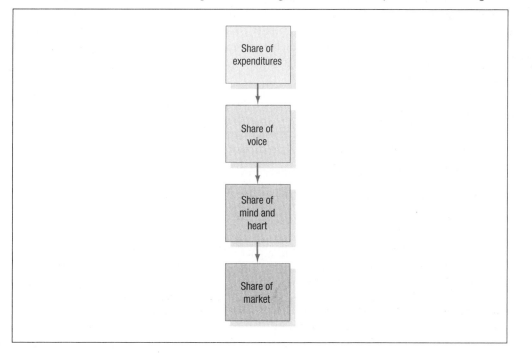

Sales Promotion Objectives

Sales promotion can be used to achieve a variety of objectives. Sellers use incentive-type promotions to attract new triers, to reward loyal customers, and to increase the repurchase rates of occasional users. Sales promotions often attract brand switchers, who are primarily looking for low price, good value, or premiums. If some of them would not have otherwise tried the brand, promotion can yield long-term increases in market share.[13] Sales promotions in markets of high brand similarity can produce a high sales response in the short run but little permanent gain in brand preference over the longer term. In markets of high brand dissimilarity, they may alter market shares permanently. In addition to brand switching, consumers may engage in stockpiling—purchasing earlier than usual (purchase acceleration) or purchasing extra quantities—although sales may then hit a postpromotion dip.[14]

Advertising versus Promotion

Several factors have contributed to the growth of sales promotion expenditures as a percentage of the overall communications budget, particularly in consumer markets. Promotion became more accepted by top management as an effective sales tool, the number of brands increased, competitors used promotions frequently, many brands were seen as similar, consumers became more price-oriented, the trade demanded more deals from manufacturers, and advertising efficiency declined.

However, the rapid growth of sales promotion has created clutter. Also, loyal brand buyers tend not to change their buying patterns as a result of competitive promotions. Advertising appears to be more effective at deepening brand loyalty, although we can distinguish added-value promotions from price promotions.[15] Price promotions may not build permanent total-category volume. One study of more than 1,000 promotions concluded that only 16 percent paid off.[16]

Small-share competitors may find it advantageous to use sales promotion, because they cannot afford to match the market leaders' large advertising budgets, nor can they obtain shelf space without offering trade allowances or stimulate consumer trial without offering incentives. Dominant brands offer deals less frequently, because most deals subsidize only current users. The upshot is that many consumer-packaged-goods companies feel forced to use more sales promotion than they wish.

Major Decisions

In using sales promotion, a company must establish its objectives, select the tools, develop the program, pretest the program, implement and control it, and evaluate the results.

Establishing Objectives   Sales promotion objectives derive from broader promotion objectives, which derive from more basic marketing objectives for the product. For consumers, objectives include encouraging purchase of larger-sized units, building trial among nonusers, and attracting switchers away from competitors' brands. Ideally, promotions with consumers would have short-run sales impact as well as long-run brand equity effects.[17] For manufacturers, objectives include persuading retailers to carry new items and higher levels of inventory, encouraging off-season buying, encouraging stocking of related items, offsetting competitive promotions, building brand loyalty, and gaining entry into new retail outlets. For the sales force, objectives include encouraging support of a new product or model, encouraging more prospecting, and stimulating off-season sales.[18]

Selecting Consumer Promotion Tools   The main consumer promotion tools are summarized in Table 16.2. *Manufacturer promotions* are, for instance in the auto industry, rebates and gifts to motivate test-drives and purchases. *Retailer promotions* include price cuts, feature advertising, retailer coupons, and retailer contests or premiums.[19]

We can also distinguish between sales promotion tools that are *consumer franchise building* and those that are not. The former impart a selling message along with the deal, such as free samples, frequency awards, and premiums when they are related to the product. Sales promotion tools that typically are *not* brand building include price-off packs, contests and sweepstakes, consumer refund offers, and trade allowances. Consumer franchise-building promotions offer the best of both worlds, building brand equity while building sales. Sampling has gained popularity in recent years—companies such as McDonald's and Starbucks have given away millions of samples of their new products—because consumers like them and they often lead to higher long-term sales for quality products.[20] Digital coupons, which can arrive by cell phone, Twitter, e-mail, or Facebook, eliminate printing costs, reduce paper waste, are easily updatable, and have higher redemption rates.[21]

TABLE 16.2   Major Consumer Promotion Tools

Samples: Offer of a free amount of a product or service delivered door-to-door, sent in the mail, picked up in a store, attached to another product, or featured in an advertising offer.

Coupons: Certificates entitling the bearer to a stated saving on the purchase of a specific product: mailed, enclosed in other products or attached to them, or inserted in print and online ads.

Cash Refund Offers (rebates): Provide a price reduction after purchase rather than at the retail shop: Consumer sends a specified "proof of purchase" to the manufacturer who "refunds" part of the purchase price by mail.

Price Packs (cents-off deals): Offers to consumers of savings off the regular price of a product, flagged on the label or package. A *reduced-price pack* is a single package sold at a reduced price (such as two for the price of one). A *banded pack* is two related products banded together (such as a toothbrush and toothpaste).

Premiums (gifts): Merchandise offered at a low cost or free as an incentive to purchase a particular product. A *with-pack premium* accompanies the product inside or on the package. A *free in-the-mail premium* is mailed to consumers who submit a proof of purchase, such as a box top or UPC code. A *self-liquidating premium* is sold below its normal retail price to consumers who request it.

Frequency Programs: Programs providing rewards related to the consumer's frequency and intensity in purchasing the company's products or services.

Prizes (contests, sweepstakes, games): *Prizes* are offers of the chance to win cash, trips, or merchandise as a result of purchasing something. A *contest* calls for consumers to submit an entry to be examined by judges who will select the best entries. A *sweepstakes* asks consumers to submit their names in a drawing. A *game* presents consumers with something every time they buy—bingo numbers, missing letters—which might help them win a prize.

Patronage Awards: Values in cash or in other forms that are proportional to patronage of a certain vendor or group of vendors.

Free Trials: Inviting prospective purchasers to try the product without cost in the hope that they will buy.

Product Warranties: Explicit or implicit promises by sellers that the product will perform as specified or that the seller will fix it or refund the customer's money during a specified period.

Tie-in Promotions: Two or more brands or companies team up on coupons, refunds, and contests to increase pulling power.

Cross-Promotions: Using one brand to advertise another noncompeting brand.

Point-of-Purchase (P-O-P) Displays and Demonstrations: Displays and demonstrations that take place at the point of purchase or sale.

Selecting Trade Promotion Tools   Manufacturers use a number of trade promotion tools (see Table 16.3).[22] Manufacturers award money to the trade (1) to persuade the retailer or wholesaler to carry the brand; (2) to persuade the retailer or wholesaler to carry more units than the normal amount; (3) to induce retailers to promote the brand by featuring, display, and price reductions; and (4) to stimulate retailers and their sales clerks to push the product. The growing power of large retailers has increased their ability to demand trade promotion at the expense of consumer promotion and advertising.[23] Trade promotion may be complex to administer and may even lead to lost revenues.

Selecting Business and Sales Force Promotion Tools   Companies spend billions of dollars on business and sales force promotion tools (see Table 16.4) to gather leads, impress and reward customers, and motivate the sales force.[24] They typically develop budgets for tools that remain fairly constant from year to year. For many new businesses that want to make a splash to a targeted audience, trade shows are an important tool, but the cost per contact is the highest of all communication options.

Developing the Program   In deciding to use a particular incentive, marketers must consider (1) the *size* of the incentive, (2) the *conditions* for participation, (3) the *duration* of the promotion, (4) the *distribution vehicle,* (5) the *timing* of promotion, and (6) the *total sales promotion budget.* The cost of a particular promotion consists of the administrative cost (printing, mailing, and promoting the deal) and the incentive cost (cost of premium or cents-off, including redemption costs), multiplied by the expected number of units sold.

Implementing and Evaluating the Program   Marketing managers must prepare implementation and control plans that cover lead time (the time necessary to prepare the program prior to launching it) and sell-in time (beginning with the promotional launch and ending when

TABLE 16.3	Major Trade Promotion Tools

Price-Off (off-invoice or off-list): A straight discount off the list price on each case purchased during a stated time period.

Allowance: An amount offered in return for the retailer's agreeing to feature the manufacturer's products in some way. An *advertising allowance* compensates retailers for advertising the manufacturer's product. A *display allowance* compensates them for carrying a special product display.

Free Goods: Offers of extra cases of merchandise to intermediaries who buy a certain quantity or who feature a certain flavor or size.

TABLE 16.4	Major Business and Sales Force Promotion Tools

Trade Shows and Conventions: Industry associations organize annual trade shows and conventions. Participating vendors expect several benefits, including generating new sales leads, maintaining customer contacts, introducing new products, meeting new customers, selling more to present customers, and educating customers with publications, videos, and other audiovisual materials.

Sales Contests: A sales contest aims at inducing the sales force or dealers to increase their sales results over a stated period, with prizes (money, trips, gifts, or points) going to those who succeed.

Specialty Advertising: Specialty advertising consists of useful, low-cost items bearing the company's name and address, and sometimes an advertising message that salespeople give to prospects and customers. Common items are ballpoint pens, calendars, key chains, flashlights, tote bags, and memo pads.

approximately 95 percent of the deal merchandise is in the hands of consumers). Manufacturers can evaluate the program using sales data, consumer surveys, and experiments. Sales (scanner) data helps analyze the types of people who took advantage of the promotion, what they bought before the promotion, and how they behaved later toward the brand and other brands. Sales promotions work best when they attract competitors' customers who then switch. Surveys can uncover how many consumers recall the promotion, what they thought of it, how many took advantage of it, and how it affected subsequent brand-choice behavior.[25]

Events and Experiences

Becoming part of a personally relevant moment in consumers' lives through events and experiences can broaden and deepen a company or brand's relationship with the target market. Daily encounters with brands may also affect consumers' brand attitudes and beliefs. *Atmospheres* are "packaged environments" that create or reinforce leanings toward product purchase. Law offices decorated with Oriental rugs and oak furniture communicate "stability" and "success."[26] A five-star hotel will use elegant chandeliers, marble columns, and other tangible signs of luxury. Many firms are creating on-site and off-site product and brand experiences, such as Everything Coca-Cola in Las Vegas and M&M's World in Times Square in New York.[27]

Events Objectives

Marketers report a number of reasons to sponsor events:

1. *To identify with a particular target market or lifestyle*—Customers can be targeted geographically, demographically, psychographically, or behaviorally according to events. Old Spice sponsors college sports and motor sports—including driver Tony Stewart's entries in the Nextel Cup and Busch Series—to highlight product relevance among its target audience of 16- to 24-year-old males.[28]

2. *To increase salience of company or product name*—Sponsorship often offers sustained exposure to a brand, a necessary condition to reinforce brand salience. Top-of-mind awareness for World Cup soccer sponsors such as Hyundai and Sony benefited from the repeated brand exposure over the one month–long tournament.

3. *To create or reinforce perceptions of key brand image associations*—Events themselves have associations that help to create or reinforce brand associations.[29] To toughen its image and appeal to America's heartland, Toyota Tundra has sponsored B.A.S.S. fishing tournaments.

4. *To enhance corporate image*—Sponsorship can improve perceptions that the company is likable and prestigious. Although Visa views its long-standing Olympic sponsorship as a means of enhancing international brand awareness and increasing usage and volume, it also engenders patriotic goodwill and taps into the emotional Olympic spirit.[30]

5. *To create experiences and evoke feelings*—The feelings engendered by an exciting or rewarding event may indirectly link to the brand, as Visa has found with its Olympic sponsorship.

6. *To express commitment to the community or on social issues*—Cause-related marketing sponsors nonprofit organizations and charities. Firms such as Timberland, Home Depot, and Stonyfield Farms have made cause-related marketing an important cornerstone of their marketing programs.

7. *To entertain key clients or reward key employees*—Many events include lavish hospitality tents and other special services or activities only for sponsors and their guests, to build

goodwill and establish valuable business contacts. BB&T Corp., a major banking and financial services firm, used its NASCAR Busch Series sponsorship to entertain business customers and its minor league baseball sponsorship to generate excitement among employees.[31]

8. *To permit merchandising or promotional opportunities*—Many marketers tie contests or sweepstakes, in-store merchandising, direct response, or other marketing activities with an event. Ford and Coca-Cola have both used their sponsorship of the hit TV show *American Idol* in this way.

Despite these potential advantages, the result of an event can still be unpredictable and beyond the sponsor's control. Although many consumers will credit sponsors for providing the financial assistance to make an event possible, some may resent the commercialization of events.

Major Sponsorship Decisions

Making sponsorships successful requires choosing the appropriate events, designing the optimal sponsorship program, and measuring the effects of sponsorship.

- Choosing event opportunities. The event must fit with the brand's marketing objectives and communication strategy, attract the desired target market, generate sufficient awareness and favorable attributions, possess the desired image, and be capable of creating the desired effects. An ideal event is also unique but not encumbered with many sponsors, lends itself to ancillary marketing activities, and reflects or enhances the sponsor's image.[32]

- Designing sponsorship programs. Many marketers believe the marketing program accompanying an event sponsorship ultimately determines its success. At least two to three times the amount of the sponsorship expenditure should be spent on related marketing activities. *Event creation* is a particularly important skill in publicizing fund-raising drives for nonprofit organizations.

- Measuring sponsorship activities. It's a challenge to measure the success of events. The *supply-side* measurement method focuses on potential exposure to the brand by assessing the extent of media coverage, and the *demand-side* method focuses on exposure reported by consumers, as well as resulting attitudes and intentions toward the sponsor. Although supply-side exposure methods provide quantifiable measures, equating media coverage with advertising exposure ignores the content of the respective communications. Media coverage and telecasts only expose the brand and don't necessarily embellish its meaning in any direct way.

Creating Experiences

A large part of local, grassroots marketing is experiential marketing, which not only communicates features and benefits but also connects a product or service with unique and interesting experiences. "The idea is not to sell something, but to demonstrate how a brand can enrich a customer's life."[33] Consumers seem to appreciate that. In one survey, four of five respondents found participating in a live event was more engaging than all other forms of communication. The vast majority also felt experiential marketing gave them more information than other forms of communication and would make them more likely to tell others about participating in the event and to be receptive to other marketing for the brand.[34]

Public Relations

Not only must the company relate constructively to customers, suppliers, and dealers, it must also relate to a large number of interested publics. A **public** is any group that has an actual or potential interest in or impact on a company's ability to achieve its objectives. **Public relations** (PR) includes a variety of programs to promote or protect a company's image or individual products.

The wise company takes concrete steps to manage successful relationships with its key publics. Most companies have a public relations department that monitors the attitudes of the organization's publics and distributes information and communications to build goodwill. The best PR departments counsel top management to adopt positive programs and eliminate questionable practices so negative publicity doesn't arise in the first place. They perform the following five functions:

1. *Press relations*—Presenting news and information about the organization in the most positive light
2. *Product publicity*—Sponsoring efforts to publicize specific products
3. *Corporate communications*—Promoting understanding of the organization through internal and external communications
4. *Lobbying*—Dealing with legislators and government officials to promote or defeat legislation and regulation
5. *Counseling*—Advising management about public issues, and company positions and image during good times and bad

Marketing Public Relations

Many companies are turning to **marketing public relations** (MPR) to support corporate or product promotion and image making. MPR, like financial PR and community PR, serves a special constituency, the marketing department. The old name for MPR was **publicity**, the task of securing editorial space—as opposed to paid space—in print and broadcast media to promote or "hype" a product, service, idea, place, person, or organization. MPR goes beyond simple publicity and plays an important role in the following tasks:

- **Launching new products.** The amazing commercial success of toys such as a recent kids' craze, Silly Bandz, owes much to strong publicity.
- **Repositioning a mature product.** In a classic PR case study, New York City had bad press in the 1970s until the "I Love New York" campaign.
- **Building interest in a product category.** Companies and trade associations have used MPR to rebuild interest in declining commodities such as eggs, milk, and potatoes and to expand consumption of such products as tea and orange juice.
- **Influencing specific target groups.** McDonald's sponsors special neighborhood events in Latino and African American communities to build goodwill.
- **Defending products that have encountered public problems.** PR professionals must be adept at managing crises, such as those weathered by such well-established brands as Tylenol, Toyota, and BP in 2010.
- **Building the corporate image in a way that reflects favorably on its products.** Steve Jobs's heavily anticipated Macworld keynote speeches have helped to create an innovative, iconoclastic image for Apple.

As the power of mass advertising weakens, marketing managers are turning to MPR to build awareness and brand knowledge for both new and established products. MPR is also effective in

TABLE 16.5	Major Tools in Marketing PR

Publications: Companies rely extensively on published materials (printed and online) to reach and influence their target markets. These include annual reports, brochures, articles, company newsletters and magazines, and audiovisual materials.

Events: Companies can draw attention to new products or other activities by arranging and publicizing special events such as news conferences, outings, trade shows, contests and competitions, and celebrations that will reach the target publics.

Sponsorships: Companies can promote their brands and corporate name by sponsoring and publicizing sports and cultural events and highly regarded causes.

News: One of the major tasks of PR professionals is to find or create favorable news about the company, its products, and its people.

Speeches: Increasingly, company executives must field questions from the media or give talks at trade associations or sales meetings, and these appearances can build the company's image.

Public Service Activities: Companies can build goodwill by contributing money and time to good causes.

Identity Media: Companies need a visual identity that the public immediately recognizes. The visual identity is carried by company logos, stationery, brochures, signs, business cards, buildings, uniforms, and dress codes.

blanketing local communities and reaching specific groups and can be more cost-effective than advertising. Nevertheless, it must be planned jointly with advertising.[35]

Major Decisions in Marketing PR

In considering when and how to use MPR, management must establish the marketing objectives, choose the PR messages and vehicles, implement the plan carefully, and evaluate the results. The main tools of MPR are described in Table 16.5.

In setting objectives for MPR, companies can seek to build *awareness* by placing stories in the media to bring attention to a product, service, person, organization, or idea. They can also use MPR to build *credibility* by communicating the message in an editorial context and to boost sales force and dealer *enthusiasm* with stories about a new product before it is launched. MPR can hold down *promotion cost* because MPR costs less than direct-mail and media advertising.

Next, the MPR practitioner must develop or identify interesting stories about the product or brand. If there are no interesting stories, the MPR practitioner should propose newsworthy events to sponsor as a way of stimulating media coverage. After implementing the plan, the company will want to evaluate it. However, MPR's contribution to the bottom line is difficult to measure, because it is used along with other promotional tools. The easiest measure of MPR effectiveness is the number of *exposures* carried by the media. A better measure is the *change in product awareness, comprehension, or attitude* resulting from the MPR campaign (after allowing for the effect of other promotional tools).

EXECUTIVE SUMMARY

Advertising is any paid form of nonpersonal presentation and promotion of ideas, goods, or services by an identified sponsor. Developing an advertising program is a five-step process: (1) Set advertising objectives, (2) establish a budget, (3) choose the advertising message and creative strategy, (4) decide on the media, and (5) evaluate communication and sales effects.

Sales promotion consists of mostly short-term incentive tools, designed to stimulate quicker or greater purchase of particular products or services by consumers or the trade. Sales promotion can also be used to gather leads, reward business customers, and motivate sales representatives. Events and experiences are a means to become part of special and more personally relevant moments in consumers' lives. If managed properly, these can broaden and deepen the sponsor's relationship with its target market. Public relations (PR) includes a variety of programs to promote or protect a company's image or its individual products. Marketing public relations (MPR), which support the marketing department in corporate or product promotion and image making, can affect public awareness at a fraction of the cost of advertising and is often much more credible.

NOTES

1. Jessica Shambora, "The Adman Behind Old Spice's New Life," *Fortune,* October 18, 2010, p. 39; Dan Sewall, "Old Spice Rolls Out New Ads," *Associated Press*, July 1, 2010; Adam Tschorn, "Old Spice Ad Connects Women to Male Brand with a Wink," *Los Angeles Times*, March 6, 2010; Mary Elizabeth Williams, "Take That, Super Bowl," *Salon.com*, www.salon.com, February 22, 2010.

2. Paul F. Nunes and Jeffrey Merrihue, "The Continuing Power of Mass Advertising," *Sloan Management Review* (Winter 2007), pp. 63–69.

3. Wilfred Amaldoss and Chuan He, "Product Variety, Informative Advertising, and Price Competition," *Journal of Marketing Research* 47 (February 2010), pp. 146–56.

4. "Responses to Comparative Advertising," *Journal of Consumer Research* 32 (March 2006), pp. 530–40; Dhruv Grewal, Sukumar Kavanoor, and James Barnes, "Comparative versus Noncomparative Advertising: A Meta-Analysis," *Journal of Marketing* (October 1997), pp. 1–15; Randall L. Rose, Paul W. Miniard, Michael J. Barone, Kenneth C. Manning, and Brian D. Till, "When Persuasion Goes Undetected: The Case of Comparative Advertising," *Journal of Marketing Research* (August 1993), pp. 315–30.

5. Rajesh Chandy, Gerard J. Tellis, Debbie MacInnis, and Pattana Thaivanich, "What to Say When: Advertising Appeals in Evolving Markets," *Journal of Marketing Research* 38, no. 4 (November 2001); Gerard J. Tellis, Rajesh Chandy, and Pattana Thaivanich, "Decomposing the Effects of Direct Advertising," *Journal of Marketing Research* 37 (February 2000), pp. 32–46; Peter J. Danaher, André Bonfrer, and Sanjay Dhar, "The Effect of Competitive Advertising," *Journal of Marketing Research*, 45 (April 2008), pp. 211–25; Donald E. Schultz, Dennis Martin, and William P. Brown, *Strategic Advertising Campaigns* (Chicago: Crain Books, 1984), pp. 192–97.

6. Eric Pfanner, "When Consumers Help, Ads Are Free," *New York Times*, June 22, 2009, p. B6; Elisabeth Sullivan, "H. J. Heinz: Consumers Sit in the Director's Chair for Viral Effort," *Marketing News*, February 10, 2008, p. 10; Louise Story, "The High Price of Creating Free Ads," *New York Times*, May 26, 2007; Laura Petrecca, "Madison Avenue Wants You! (or at Least Your Videos)," *USA Today*, June 21, 2007; Eric Pfanner, "Leave It to the Professionals? Hey, Let Consumers Make Their Own Ads," *New York Times*, August 4, 2006.

7. "The Infinite Dial 2009," *Arbitron*, April 2009.

8. Schultz et al., *Strategic Advertising Campaigns* (Chicago: NTC/Contemporary Publishing Company, September 1994), p. 340.

9. Prashant Malaviya, "The Moderating Influence of Advertising Context on Ad Repetition Effects," *Journal of Consumer Research* 34 (June 2007), pp. 32–40.

10. Rich Thomaselli, "Marketing of the Year Runner-Up: Southwest," *Advertising Age,* October 18, 2010, www.adage.com; Cheryl Hall, "For Southwest Airlines, 'Bags Fly Free' Is Paying Off," *Seattle Times,* April 26, 2010, http://seattletimes.nwsource.com/html/travel/2011708848_websouthwest26.html?syndication=rss.

11. David B. Montgomery and Alvin J. Silk, "Estimating Dynamic Effects of Market Communications Expenditures," *Management Science* (June 1972), pp. 485–501; Kristian S. Palda, *The Measurement of Cumulative Advertising Effect* (Upper Saddle River, NJ: Prentice Hall, 1964), p. 87.

12. From Robert C. Blattberg and Scott A. Neslin, *Sales Promotion: Concepts, Methods, and Strategies* (Upper Saddle River, NJ: Prentice Hall, 1990). A comprehensive review of academic work on sales promotions can be found in Scott Neslin, "Sales Promotion," Bart Weitz and Robin Wensley, eds., *Handbook of Marketing* (London: Sage, 2002), pp. 310–38.

13. Kusum Ailawadi, Karen Gedenk, and Scott A. Neslin, "Heterogeneity and Purchase Event Feedback in Choice Models," *International Journal of Research in Marketing* 16 (September 1999), pp. 177–98. See also, Kusum L. Ailawadi, Karen Gedenk, Christian Lutzky, and Scott A. Neslin, "Decomposition of the Sales Impact of Promotion-Induced Stockpiling," *Journal of Marketing Research* 44 (August 2007); Eric T. Anderson and Duncan Simester, "The Long-Run Effects of Promotion

Depth on New versus Established Customers," *Marketing Science* 23, no. 1 (Winter 2004), pp. 4–20; Luc Wathieu, A. V. Muthukrishnan, and Bart J. Bronnenberg, "The Asymmetric Effect of Discount Retraction on Subsequent Choice," *Journal of Consumer Research* 31 (December 2004), pp. 652–65; Praveen Kopalle, Carl F. Mela, and Lawrence Marsh, "The Dynamic Effect of Discounting on Sales," *Marketing Science* 18 (Summer 1999), pp. 317–32.

14. Harald J. Van Heerde, Sachin Gupta, and Dick Wittink, "Is 75% of the Sales Promotion Bump Due to Brand Switching?" *Journal of Marketing Research* 40 (November 2003), pp. 481–91; Harald J. Van Heerde, Peter S. H. Leeflang, and Dick R. Wittink, "The Estimation of Pre- and Postpromotion Dips with Store-Level Scanner Data," *Journal of Marketing Research* 37, no. 3 (August 2000), pp. 383–95.

15. Robert George Brown, "Sales Response to Promotions and Advertising," *Journal of Advertising Research* (August 1974), pp. 36–37. See also, Kamel Jedidi, Carl F. Mela, and Sunil Gupta, "Managing Advertising and Promotion for Long-run Profitability," *Marketing Science* 18, no. 1 (Winter 1999), pp. 1–22; Carl F. Mela, Sunil Gupta, and Donald R. Lehmann, "The Long-term Impact of Promotion and Advertising on Consumer Brand Choice," *Journal of Marketing Research* (May 1997), pp. 248–61; Purushottam Papatla and Lakshman Krishnamurti, "Measuring the Dynamic Effects of Promotions on Brand Choice," *Journal of Marketing Research* (February 1996), pp. 20–35.

16. Magid M. Abraham and Leonard M. Lodish, "Getting the Most Out of Advertising and Promotion," *Harvard Business Review,* May–June 1990, pp. 50–60. See also, Shuba Srinivasan, Koen Pauwels, Dominique Hanssens, and Marnik Dekimpe, "Do Promotions Benefit Manufacturers, Retailers, or Both?" *Management Science* 50, no. 5 (May 2004), pp. 617–29.

17. Rebecca J. Slotegraaf and Koen Pauwels, "The Impact of Brand Equity Innovation on the Long-Term Effectiveness of Promotions," *Journal of Marketing Research* 45 (June 2008), pp. 293–306.

18. For a model for setting sales promotions objectives, see David B. Jones, "Setting Promotional Goals: A Communications Relationship Model," *Journal of Consumer Marketing* 11, no. 1 (1994), pp. 38–49.

19. Kusum L. Ailawadi, Bari A. Harlam, Jacques Cesar, and David Trounce, "Promotion Profitability for a Retailer," *Journal of Marketing Research* 43 (November 2006), pp. 518–36.

20. Emily Bryson York and Natalie Zmuda, "Sampling: The New Mass Media," *Advertising Age*, May 12, 2008, pp. 3, 56.

21. Sarah Skidmore, "Coupons Evolve for the Digital Age," *Associated Press*, August 30, 2009; "20 Most Popular Comparison Shopping Websites," *eBizMBA,* www.ebizmba.com, June 2010.

22. Miguel Gomez, Vithala Rao, and Edward McLaughlin, "Empirical Analysis of Budget and Allocation of Trade Promotions in the U.S. Supermarket Industry," *Journal of Marketing Research* 44 (August 2007); Norris Bruce, Preyas S. Desai, and Richard Staelin, "The Better They Are, the More They Give: Trade Promotions of Consumer Durables," *Journal of Marketing Research* 42 (February 2005), pp. 54–66.

23. Kusum L. Ailawadi and Bari Harlam, "An Empirical Analysis of the Determinants of Retail Margins," *Journal of Marketing* 68 (January 2004), pp. 147–66; Kusum L. Ailawadi, "The Retail Power-Performance Conundrum: What Have We Learned?" *Journal of Retailing* 77, no. 3 (Fall 2001), pp. 299–318; Paul W. Farris and Kusum L. Ailawadi, "Retail Power: Monster or Mouse?" *Journal of Retailing* (Winter 1992), pp. 351–69; Koen Pauwels, "How Retailer and Competitor Decisions Drive the Long-term Effectiveness of Manufacturer Promotions," *Journal of Retailing* 83, no. 3, (2007), pp. 364–90.

24. IBIS World USA, www.ibisworld.com; Noah Lim, Michael J. Ahearne, and Sung H. Ham, "Designing Sales Contests: Does the Prize Structure Matter?" *Journal of Marketing Research* 46 (June 2009), pp. 356–71.

25. Joe A. Dodson, Alice M. Tybout, and Brian Sternthal, "Impact of Deals and Deal Retraction on Brand Switching," *Journal of Marketing Research* (February 1978), pp. 72–81.

26. Philip Kotler, "Atmospherics as a Marketing Tool," *Journal of Retailing* (Winter 1973–1974), pp. 48–64.

27. Kathleen Kerwin, "When the Factory Is a Theme Park," *BusinessWeek,* May 3, 2004, p. 94; Vanessa O'Connell, "'You-Are-There' Advertising," *Wall Street Journal,* August 5, 2002.

28. "Personal Care Marketers: Who Does What," *IEG Sponsorship Report*, April 16, 2007, p. 4.

29. Bettina Cornwell, Michael S. Humphreys, Angela M. Maguire, Clinton S. Weeks, and Cassandra Tellegen, "Sponsorship-Linked Marketing: The Role of Articulation in Memory," *Journal of Consumer Research* 33 (December 2006), pp. 312–21.

30. Hilary Cassidy, "So You Want to Be an Olympic Sponsor?" *Brandweek*, November 7, 2005, pp. 24–28.

31. "BB&T Continues Sponsorship with Clint Bowyer, Richard Childress Racing," *SceneDaily*, January 14, 2010; "BB&T Puts Name on New Winston-Salem Ballpark," *Winston-Salem Journal*, February 24, 2010; "Bank's New Department, Deals Reflect Elevated

Sponsorship Status," *IEG Sponsorship Report*, April 16, 2007, pp. 1, 8.

32. T. Bettina Cornwell, Clinton S. Weeks, and Donald P. Roy, "Sponsorship-Linked Marketing," *Journal of Advertising* 34 (Summer 2005).

33. B. Joseph Pine and James H. Gilmore, *The Experience Economy* (Cambridge, MA: Harvard University Press, 1999).

34. "2006 Experiential Marketing Study," *Jack Morton*, www.jackmorton.com.

35. "Do We Have a Story for You!" *Economist*, January 21, 2006, pp. 57–58; Al Ries and Laura Ries, *The Fall of Advertising and the Rise of PR* (New York: HarperCollins, 2002).

chapter 17

Managing Personal Communications: Direct and Interactive Marketing, Word of Mouth, and Personal Selling

In this chapter, we will address the following questions:

1. How can companies conduct direct marketing and interactive marketing for competitive advantage?
2. How does word of mouth affect marketing success?
3. What decisions do companies face in designing and managing a sales force?
4. How can salespeople improve their selling, negotiating, and relationship marketing skills?

Marketing Management at PepsiCo

PepsiCo tried something new in 2010 when it chose not to advertise any of its soft drink brands during the biggest U.S. media event, the Super Bowl. Instead, it launched its ambitious Pepsi Refresh Project. With a tagline "Every Pepsi Refreshes the World," Pepsi earmarked $20 million to fund projects from local organizations and causes that "make the world a better place" in six areas: health, arts and culture, food and shelter, the planet, neighborhoods, and education. Pepsi invited ideas at *www.refresheverything.com and consumers voted online to select the winners. The program included a significant presence on Facebook, Twitter, and other social networks.*

The first grants funded such projects as building a community playground, buying computers for schools, providing care packages for wounded troops recovering at home, and conducting financial literacy sessions for teens. Since then, Pepsi has allocated more money to communities in the Gulf of Mexico region affected by the catastrophic oil spill. The campaign has helped Pepsi engage consumers in every state while polishing its reputation for social responsibility.[1]

Marketing communications today increasingly occur as a dialogue between the company and its customers. Companies must ask not only "How should we reach our customers?" but also "How should our customers reach us?" and "How can our customers reach each other?" New technologies have encouraged companies to move from mass communication to more targeted, personalized two-way communications. In this chapter, we consider direct and interactive marketing, word-of-mouth marketing, and personal selling and the sales force.

Direct Marketing

Direct marketing is the use of consumer-direct (CD) channels to reach and deliver goods and services to customers without using marketing middlemen. These channels include direct mail, catalog marketing, telemarketing, interactive TV, kiosks, Web sites, and mobile devices. Direct marketers often seek a measurable response, typically a customer order, through **direct-order marketing**. Direct marketing has been outpacing U.S. retail sales. It accounted for almost 53 percent of total advertising spending in 2009, and companies spent more than $149 billion on direct marketing per year, accounting for 8.3 percent of GDP.[2]

The Benefits of Direct Marketing

Consumers short of time and tired of traffic and parking headaches appreciate toll-free phone numbers, always-open Web sites, next-day delivery, and direct marketers' commitment to customer service. In addition, many chain stores have dropped slower-moving specialty items, creating an opportunity for direct marketers to promote these to interested buyers instead. Direct marketers benefit as well: They can buy mailing lists for almost any group (left-handed people, millionaires), customize and personalize messages to build customer relationships, reach interested prospects at the right moment, easily test alternative media and messages, and measure responses to determine profitability.

Direct Mail

Direct-mail marketing means sending an offer, announcement, reminder, or other item to an individual consumer. Using highly selective mailing lists, direct marketers send out millions of mail pieces each year—letters, flyers, DVDs, and other "salespeople with wings." Direct mail is popular because it permits target market selectivity, can be personalized, is flexible, and allows early testing and response measurement. Although the cost per thousand is higher than for mass media, the people reached are much better prospects.

In constructing an effective direct-mail campaign, direct marketers must choose their objectives, target markets and prospects, and offer elements; provide a means of testing the campaign; and measure campaign success.

- **Objectives.** Marketers judge a campaign's success by the response rate. An order-response rate of 2 percent to 4 percent is normally considered good, depending on the product category, offering, and price.[3] Other objectives may include generating leads, strengthening customer relationships, informing and educating customers, reminding customers of offers, and reinforcing purchase decisions.

- Target markets and prospects. Direct marketers apply the RFM (*recency, frequency, monetary amount*) formula to select customers according to how much time has passed since their last purchase, how many times they have purchased, and how much they have spent since becoming a customer. Marketers also identify prospects on the basis of age, sex, income, education, previous mail-order purchases, occasion, and lifestyle. In B2B direct marketing, the prospect is often a group or committee of both decision makers and decision influencers.

- Offer elements. The offer strategy has five elements—the *product*, the *offer*, the *medium*, the *distribution method*, and the *creative strategy*—all of which can be tested.[4] The direct-mail marketer also must choose five components of the mailing itself: the outside envelope, sales letter, circular, reply form, and reply envelope. Often direct mail is followed up by e-mail.

- Testing elements. One of direct marketing's great advantages is the ability to test, under real marketplace conditions, elements such as products and features, copy platform, mailer type, envelope, prices, or mailing lists. Response rates typically understate a campaign's long-term impact. This is why some firms measure direct marketing's effect on awareness, intention to buy, and word of mouth.

- Measuring success: lifetime value. By adding up the planned costs, the direct marketer can determine the needed break-even response rate (net of returned merchandise and bad debts). A campaign may fail to break even in the short run yet still be profitable in the long run if customer lifetime value is factored in. Calculate the average customer longevity, average customer annual expenditure, and average gross margin, minus the average cost of customer acquisition and maintenance (discounted for the opportunity cost of money).[5]

Catalog Marketing

In catalog marketing, companies may send full-line merchandise catalogs, specialty consumer catalogs, and business catalogs, usually in print form but also as DVDs or online. Many direct marketers find combining catalogs and Web sites an effective way to sell, especially internationally. Catalogs are a huge business—the Internet and catalog retailing industry includes 16,000 companies with combined annual revenue of $235 billion.[6]

The success of a catalog business depends on managing customer lists carefully to avoid duplication or bad debts, controlling inventory, offering good-quality merchandise so returns are low, and projecting a distinctive image. Some companies add literary or information features, send swatches of materials, operate an online chat function or a telephone hotline to answer questions, send gifts to their best customers, and donate a percentage of profits to good causes.

Telemarketing

Telemarketing is the use of the telephone and call centers to attract prospects, sell to existing customers, and provide service by taking orders and answering questions. Companies use call centers for *inbound telemarketing*—receiving calls from customers—and *outbound telemarketing*—initiating calls to prospects and customers. Although outbound telemarketing was traditionally a major direct marketing tool, its potentially intrusive nature led the Federal Trade Commission to establish a

National Do Not Call Registry in 2003. Because only political organizations, charities, telephone surveyors, or companies with existing relationships with consumers are exempt, consumer telemarketing has now lost much of its effectiveness.[7] Business-to-business telemarketing is increasing, however.

Other Media for Direct-Response Marketing

Direct marketers use all the major media. Newspapers and magazines carry ads offering books, clothing, appliances, vacations, and other goods and services that individuals can order via toll-free numbers. Radio ads present offers 24 hours a day. Some companies use 30- and 60-minute *infomercials* to combine the sell of television commercials with the draw of information and entertainment. At-home shopping channels are dedicated to selling goods and services via a toll-free number or the Web for speedy delivery.

Public and Ethical Issues in Direct Marketing

Direct marketers and their customers usually enjoy mutually rewarding relationships. Occasionally, however, a darker side emerges. Many people don't like hard-sell, direct marketing solicitations. Some direct marketers take advantage of impulsive or less sophisticated buyers or prey on the vulnerable, especially the elderly.[8] Some direct marketers design mailers and write copy intended to mislead; the Federal Trade Commission receives thousands of complaints each year about fraudulent investment scams and phony charities. Critics worry that marketers may know too much about consumers' lives, and that they may use this knowledge to take unfair advantage. Most direct marketers, however, want what consumers want: honest and well-designed offers targeted only to those who appreciate hearing about them.

Interactive Marketing

The fastest-growing channels for communicating with and selling directly to customers are electronic; today, few campaigns are considered complete without an online component. The Internet provides marketers and consumers with opportunities for much greater *interaction* and *individualization*. Another advantage is the availability of *contextual placement*, buying ads on sites related to the marketer's offerings. Marketers can also reach people when they've actually started the buying process and firms can track campaign results in detail.[9] Moreover, firms can build or tap into online communities, inviting consumer participation and creating a long-term marketing asset in the process.

One disadvantage, however, is that consumers can screen out most online messages. Advertisers also lose some control over their online messages, which can be hacked or vandalized. Finally, marketers may think their ads are more effective than they are if bogus clicks are generated by software-powered Web sites.[10]

Some of the main categories of interactive marketing are:

- Web sites. Web sites should embody or express the firm's purpose, history, products, and vision; be attractive on first viewing; and encourage repeat visits.[11] **Microsites**, individual Web pages or page clusters that supplement a primary site, are particularly relevant for selling low-interest products. Jeffrey Rayport and Bernard Jaworski propose that effective sites feature seven design elements (see Table 17.1).[12] Visitors will judge site performance on ease of use (quick downloads, first page easy to understand, easy navigation) and physical attractiveness (pages clean and not crammed, text readable,

TABLE 17.1	Effective Web Design
Design Element	**Description**
Context	Layout and design.
Content	Text, pictures, sound, and video on the site.
Community	How the site enables user-to-user communication.
Customization	Site's ability to tailor itself to different users or allow users to personalize the site.
Communication	How the site enables site-to-user, user-to-site, or two-way communication.
Connection	Degree to which the site is linked to other sites.
Commerce	Site's capabilities to enable commercial transactions.

Source: Jeffrey F. Rayport and Bernard J. Jaworski, *e-Commerce* (New York: McGraw-Hill, 2001), p. 116.

good use of color and sound). Companies must also be sensitive to online security and privacy-protection issues.[13]

- Search ads. A hot growth area in interactive marketing is **paid search** or **pay-per-click ads**, which account for roughly half of all online ad spending.[14] In paid search, marketers bid on search terms that serve as a proxy for the consumer's product or consumption interests. When a consumer searches for those words using Google, Yahoo!, or Bing, the marketer's ad will appear on the results page, the placement depending on how much the company bids and on the ad's relevance to the search.[15] Advertisers pay only if people click on the links. *Search engine optimization* has become a crucial part of marketing and a number of guidelines have been suggested for more effective search ads.[16]

- Display ads. **Display ads** or **banner ads** are small, rectangular boxes containing text and perhaps an image that firms pay to place on relevant Web sites.[17] The larger the audience, the higher the cost. Given that Internet users spend only 5 percent of their time online actually searching for information, display ads still hold great promise compared to popular search ads. But ads need to be more attention-getting and influential, better targeted, and more closely tracked.[18] **Interstitials** are advertisements, often with video or animation, which pop up between changes on a Web site. Because consumers found pop-up ads intrusive and distracting, many used software to block them.

- E-mail. E-mail allows marketers to communicate at a fraction of the cost of direct mail. Consumers are besieged by e-mails, though, and many employ spam filters. Some firms are asking consumers to say whether and when they would like to receive e-mails. FTD, the flower retailer, allows customers to choose whether to receive e-mail reminders to send flowers for virtually any holiday or occasion.[19]

- Mobile marketing. As noted in Chapter 13, mobile marketing is growing. Cell phones represent a major opportunity for advertisers to reach consumers on the "third screen" (TV and the computer are first and second). In addition to text messages and ads, much interest has been generated in mobile apps—"bite-sized" software programs that can be loaded onto smart phones. Smart phones also allow loyalty programs with which customers can track their visits and purchases at a merchant and receive rewards.[20] By monitoring the location of customers who opt in to receive communications, retailers can send them location-specific promotions (including digital coupons) when they are near shops or outlets. Marketers should design simple, clear, and "clean" sites for mobile marketing, paying careful attention to user experience and navigation.[21]

Word of Mouth

Consumers use *word of mouth* to talk about dozens of brands each day, from media and entertainment products such as movies, TV shows, and publications to food products, travel services, and retail stores.[22] Positive word of mouth may be generated organically with little advertising, but it can also be managed and facilitated.[23] *Paid media* results from press coverage of company-generated advertising or other promotional efforts. *Earned media*—sometimes called *free media*—is all the PR benefits a firm receives without having directly paid for anything—all the news stories, blogs, and social network conversations that deal with a brand. Earned media isn't literally free—the company has to invest in products, services, and marketing to get people to pay attention and write and talk about them, but the expenses are not devoted to eliciting a media response.

We first consider how social media promotes the flow of word of mouth before delving into more detail on how word of mouth is formed and travels.

Social Media

Social media are a means for consumers to share text, images, audio, and video information with each other and with companies and vice versa, encouraging brand engagement at a deeper and broader level than ever before. Marketers can use social media to establish a public voice and presence on the Web and to reinforce other communication activities. But as useful as they may be, social media can never become the sole source of marketing communications. And embracing social media, harnessing word of mouth, and creating buzz requires companies to take the good with the bad.

The three main platforms for social media are online communities and forums, blogs, and social networks.

Online Communities and Forums   Many online communities and forums are created by consumers or groups of consumers with no commercial interests or company affiliations. Others are sponsored by firms whose members communicate with the sponsor and with each other through postings, instant messaging, and chat discussions about special interests related to the company's products and brands. Information flow in online communities and forums is two-way and can provide companies with useful, hard-to-get customer insights.

Blogs   *Blogs*, regularly updated online journals or diaries, have become an important outlet for word of mouth. One obvious appeal of blogs is bringing together people with common interests. Blog networks such as Gawker Media offer marketers a portfolio of choices. Corporations are also creating their own blogs and carefully monitoring those of others. Because many consumers examine product information and reviews contained in blogs, the Federal Trade Commission now requires bloggers to disclose any relationship with marketers whose products they endorse.

Social Networks   Social networks such as Facebook, LinkedIn, and Twitter have become an important force in both business-to-consumer and business-to-business marketing.[24] Marketers are still learning how to best tap into social networks and their huge, well-defined audiences. Given networks' noncommercial nature—users are generally there looking to connect with others—attracting attention and persuading are more challenging. Also, given that users generate their own content, ads may appear beside inappropriate or even offensive content.[25] Having a Facebook page has become a virtual prerequisite for many companies, and Twitter can benefit even the smallest firm.

Buzz and Viral Marketing

Some marketers highlight two particular forms of word of mouth—buzz and viral marketing.[26] *Buzz marketing* generates excitement, creates publicity, and conveys new, relevant, brand-related information through unexpected or even outrageous means.[27] *Viral marketing* is another form of word of mouth, or "word of mouse," that encourages consumers to pass along company-developed products and services or audio, video, or written information to others online.[28] Buzz and viral marketing both try to create a splash in the marketplace to showcase a brand and its noteworthy features. Ultimately, the success of any viral or buzz campaign depends on the willingness of consumers to talk to other consumers.[29] See "Marketing Skills: How to Start a Buzz Fire" for more about how to generate buzz.

Opinion Leaders

Communication researchers propose a social-structure view of interpersonal communication.[30] They see society as consisting of *cliques,* small groups whose members interact frequently. Clique members are similar, and their closeness facilitates effective communication but also insulates the clique from new ideas. The challenge is to create more openness so cliques exchange information with others in society. This openness is helped along by people who function as liaisons and connect two or more cliques without belonging to either, and by *bridges,* people who belong to one clique and are linked to a person in another.

Marketing Skills

HOW TO START A BUZZ FIRE

Although many word-of-mouth effects are beyond marketers' control, certain steps improve the likelihood of starting a positive buzz. First, identify influential individuals and companies and devote extra energy to them. Also cultivate community influentials such as local disk jockeys, class presidents, and heads of local groups. Next, supply these key contacts with product samples to encourage word of mouth. Systematically develop word of mouth referral channels to build business. Finally, provide compelling information that people want to pass along.

For example, Ford's prelaunch "Fiesta Movement" U.S. campaign invited 100 handpicked young adults or "millennials" to live with the Fiesta car for six months. People were chosen based on their blogging experience, social network, and a video they submitted about their desire for adventure. After six months, the campaign had millions of YouTube and Twitter impressions, over 500,000 Flickr views, and 50,000 potential customers, 97 percent of whom didn't already own a Ford. The buzz was so successful that Ford used many of the same techniques for its Ford Focus launch.[31, 32]

Best-selling author Malcolm Gladwell says three factors work to ignite public interest in an idea.[33] The first is reaching the three types of people who can spread an idea like an epidemic: *mavens,* knowledgeable people; *connectors,* people who know and communicate with many others; and *salesmen,* who possess natural persuasive power. The second factor is "stickiness," expressing an idea so that it motivates people to act. The third factor, "the power of context," controls whether those spreading an idea are able to organize groups and communities around it. Not everyone agrees with Gladwell's ideas, however.[34]

Measuring the Effects of Word of Mouth[35]

Research and consulting firm Keller Fay notes that although 80 percent of word of mouth occurs offline, many marketers concentrate on online effects, given the ease of tracking them through advertising, PR, or digital agencies.[36] Through demographic information or proxies and cookies, firms can monitor when customers blog, comment, post, share, link, upload, friend, stream, write on a wall, or update a profile. With these tracking tools it is possible, for example, to sell movie advertisers "1 million American women between the ages of 14 and 24 who had uploaded, blogged, rated, shared, or commented on entertainment in the previous 24 hours."[37] Another way to understand online word of mouth is to evaluate blogs according to relevance, sentiment, and authority.[38]

Personal Selling and the Sales Force

The original and oldest form of direct marketing is the field sales call. To locate prospects, develop them into customers, and grow the business, most industrial companies rely heavily on a professional sales force or hire manufacturers' representatives and agents. Many consumer companies, including Allstate and Mary Kay, also use a direct-selling force. Not surprisingly, companies are trying to increase sales force productivity through better selection, training, supervision, motivation, and compensation.[39]

Types of Sales Representatives

The term *sales representative* covers six positions, ranging from the least to the most creative types of selling:[40]

1. *Deliverer*—A salesperson whose major task is the delivery of a product (water, fuel).
2. *Order taker*—An inside order taker (behind the counter) or outside order taker (calling on store managers).
3. *Missionary*—A salesperson not permitted to take an order but expected rather to build goodwill or educate the user (the medical "detailer" representing a pharmaceutical firm).
4. *Technician*—A salesperson with a high level of technical knowledge (the engineering salesperson who is primarily a consultant to client companies).
5. *Demand creator*—A salesperson who relies on creative methods for selling tangible products (vacuum cleaners) or intangibles (advertising services).
6. *Solution vendor*—A salesperson whose expertise is solving a customer's problem, often with a system of the company's products and services (for example, computer systems).

Personal Selling and Relationship Marketing

Effective salespeople require more than instinct; they must be trained in methods of analysis and customer management so they become active order getters, not passive order takers. The six major steps in any effective sales process are shown in Table 17.2.[41]

The principles of personal selling and negotiation are largely transaction-oriented because their purpose is to close a specific sale. But in many cases the company seeks not an immediate sale but rather a long-term supplier–customer relationship. Today's customers prefer suppliers who can sell and deliver a coordinated set of products and services to many locations, who can quickly solve problems in different locations, and who can work closely with customer teams to improve products and processes. They should monitor key accounts, know customers' problems, and be ready to serve them in a number of ways, adapting and responding to different customer needs or situations.[42]

Relationship marketing is not effective in all situations. But when it is the right strategy and is properly implemented, the organization will focus as much on managing its customers as on managing its products.

Designing the Sales Force

Salespeople are the company's personal link to its customers. In designing the sales force, the company must develop sales force objectives, strategy, structure, size, and compensation (see Figure 17.1). These steps are discussed next.

TABLE 17.2	Major Steps in Effective Selling
Sales Step	**Application in Industrial Selling**
Prospecting and qualifying	Firms generate leads and qualify them by mail or phone to assess their level of interest and financial capacity. "Hot" prospects are turned over to the field sales force; "warm" prospects receive telemarketing follow-up.
Preapproach	The sales rep researches what the prospect needs, how the buying process operates, who is involved in buying, and the buyers' personal characteristics and buying styles. The rep also sets call objectives to qualify the prospect, gather information, or make an immediate sale; decides whether to visit, call, or write; plans the timing of the approach; and sets an overall sales strategy.
Presentation and demonstration	The salesperson tells the product "story" to the buyer, using a features, advantages, benefits, and value approach. Reps should avoid spending too much time on product features (product orientation) and not enough on benefits and value (customer orientation).
Overcoming objections	Salespeople must handle objections posed by buyers during the presentation or when asking for the order. Here, the rep must maintain a positive approach, ask for clarification, ask questions that lead buyers to answer their own objections, deny the validity of the objection, or turn an objection into a reason for buying.
Closing	To close the sale, the rep can ask for the order, recapitulate points of agreement, emphasize the value of the offer, help to write up the order, ask whether the buyer wants A or B, get the buyer to make minor choices such as color or size, or show what the buyer will lose by not ordering now. The rep might offer an inducement to close, such as additional service or a token gift.
Follow-up and maintenance	To ensure customer satisfaction and repeat business, the rep should confirm details such as delivery time and purchase terms immediately after closing. Also, the rep should schedule a follow-up call to check on proper installation and training after delivery. This helps detect problems, shows interest, and reduces any cognitive dissonance. Each account needs a maintenance and growth plan, as well.

FIGURE 17.1 Designing a Sales Force

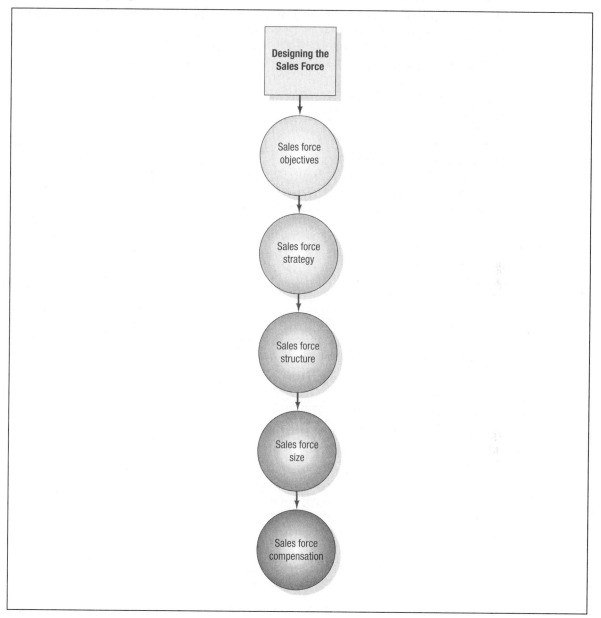

Sales Force Objectives and Strategy

Companies need to define specific sales force objectives. For example, a company might want its sales representatives to spend 80 percent of their time with current customers and 20 percent with prospects, and 85 percent of their time on established products and 15 percent on new products. Today's sales representatives act as "account managers," arranging fruitful contact between people in the buying and selling organizations. Increasingly, effective selling calls for teamwork and the support of others, such as top management, especially when national accounts or major sales are at stake; technical people, who supply information and service before, during, and after the purchase; customer service representatives, who provide installation, maintenance, and other services; and an office staff of sales analysts, order expediters, and assistants.[43]

Once the company chooses its strategy, it can use a direct or a contractual sales force. A **direct (company) sales force** consists of paid employees who work exclusively for the company. Inside sales personnel conduct business from the office using the telephone and receive visits from prospective buyers, and field sales personnel travel and visit customers. A **contractual sales force** consists of manufacturers' reps, sales agents, and brokers, who earn a commission based on sales.

Sales Force Structure

The sales force strategy has implications for its structure. A company that sells one product line to one end-using industry with customers in many locations would use a territorial structure. A company that sells many products to many types of customers might need a product or market structure, or an even more complex structure. "Marketing Insight: Major Account Management" discusses a specialized form of sales force structure.

Sales Force Size

Once the company establishes the number of customers it wants to reach, it can use a *workload approach* to establish sales force size, following five steps: (1) group customers into size classes according to sales volume; (2) establish call frequencies (number of calls on an account per year); (3) multiply the number of accounts in each size class by the call frequency to arrive at the total workload, in sales calls per year; (4) determine the average number of calls a sales rep can make per year; (5) divide the total annual calls (calculated in step 3) by the average annual calls made by a rep (calculated in step 4) to see how many reps are needed.

Marketing Insight

MAJOR ACCOUNT MANAGEMENT

Marketers typically single out for attention major accounts (also called key accounts, national accounts, global accounts, or house accounts). These are important customers with multiple divisions in many locations who use uniform pricing and coordinated service for all divisions. A major account manager (MAM) usually reports to the national sales manager and supervises field reps calling on customer plants within their territories.

Procter & Gamble has a strategic account management team of 300 staffers to work with Walmart in its U.S. headquarters, with more personnel stationed at Walmart offices in Europe, Asia, and Latin America. Major account managers such as those from P&G act as the single point of contact, develop and grow customer business, understand customer decision processes, identify added-value opportunities, provide competitive intelligence, negotiate sales, and orchestrate customer service.

Sources: Noel Capon, Dave Potter, and Fred Schindler, *Managing Global Accounts: Nine Critical Factors for a World-Class Program*, 2nd ed. (Bronxville, NY: Wessex Press, 2008); Peter Cheverton, *Global Account Management: A Complete Action Kit of Tools and Techniques for Managing Key Global Customers* (London, UK: Kogan Page, 2008); Malcolm McDonald and Diana Woodburn, *Key Account Management: The Definitive Guide*, 2nd ed. (Oxford, UK: Butterworth-Heinemann, 2007); Jack Neff, "Bentonville or Bust," *Advertising Age*, February 24, 2003.

Suppose the company estimates it has 1,000 A accounts and 2,000 B accounts. A accounts require 36 calls a year, and B accounts require 12, so the company needs a sales force that can make 60,000 sales calls (36,000 + 24,000) a year. If the average full-time rep can make 1,000 calls a year, the company needs 60 reps.

Sales Force Compensation

To attract top-quality reps, the company needs an attractive compensation package. The company must quantify four components of sales force compensation. The *fixed amount*, a salary, satisfies the need for income stability. The *variable amount*, whether commissions, bonus, or profit sharing, serves to stimulate and reward effort. *Expense allowances* enable sales reps to meet the expenses of travel and entertaining. *Benefits*, such as paid vacations, provide security and job satisfaction.

Fixed compensation is common in jobs with a high ratio of nonselling to selling duties, and jobs where the selling task is technically complex and requires teamwork. This approach, easy for the firm to administer, encourages reps to complete nonselling tasks and reduces the incentive to overstock customers. Variable compensation works best where sales are cyclical or depend on individual initiative. These plans attract high performers, provide more motivation, require less supervision, and control selling costs, although they emphasize getting the sale over building the relationship.

Combination plans feature the benefits of both plans while limiting their disadvantages. One current trend deemphasizes sales volume in favor of gross profitability, customer satisfaction, and customer retention. Other companies reward reps partly on sales team or even company-wide performance, motivating them to work together for the common good.

Managing the Sales Force

Various policies and procedures guide the firm in recruiting, selecting, training, supervising, motivating, and evaluating representatives to manage its sales force (see Figure 17.2).

Recruiting and Selecting Representatives

At the heart of any successful sales force is a means of selecting effective representatives. One survey revealed that the top 25 percent of the sales force brought in over 52 percent of the sales. It's a great waste to hire the wrong people. The average annual turnover rate of sales reps for all industries is almost 20 percent. Sales force turnover leads to lost sales, the expense of finding and training replacements, and often pressure on existing salespeople to pick up the slack.[44]

After management develops its selection criteria, it must recruit by soliciting names from current sales representatives, using employment agencies, placing job ads, and contacting college students. Selection procedures can vary from a single informal interview to prolonged testing and interviewing.

Studies have shown little relationship between sales performance on one hand, and background and experience variables, current status, lifestyle, attitude, personality, and skills on the other. Although scores from formal tests are only one element in a set that includes personal characteristics, references, past employment history, and interviewer reactions, they have been weighted quite heavily by some firms. Gillette says tests have reduced turnover and scores correlated well with the progress of new reps.

Training and Supervising Sales Representatives

Today's customers expect salespeople to have deep product knowledge, add ideas to improve operations, and be efficient and reliable. This requires companies to make a much greater investment in sales training. New reps may spend a few weeks to several months in training. The median training period

FIGURE 17.2 Managing the Sales Force

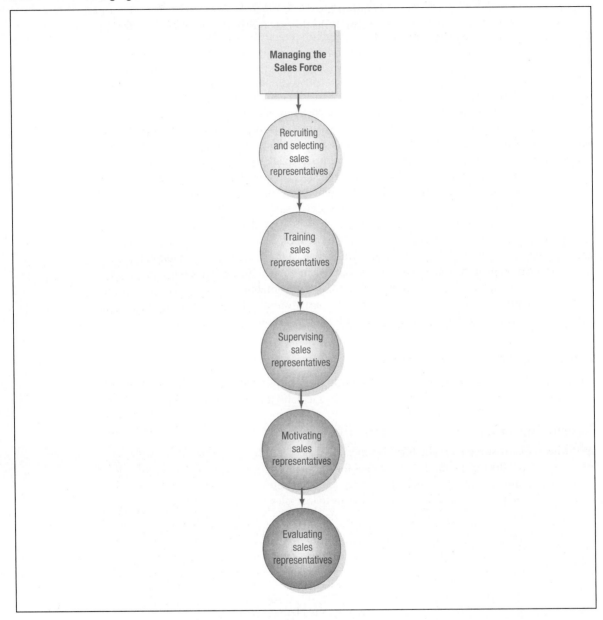

is 28 weeks in industrial-products companies, 12 in service companies, and 4 in consumer-products companies. Training time varies with the complexity of the selling task and the type of recruit.

Sales Rep Productivity

How many calls should a company make on a particular account each year? Some research suggests today's sales reps spend too much time selling to smaller, less profitable accounts instead of focusing on larger, more profitable accounts.[45]

Firms therefore often specify how much time reps should spend prospecting for new accounts, and some rely on a missionary sales force to open new accounts.

The best sales reps manage their time efficiently. *Time-and-duty analysis* helps reps understand how they spend their time and how they might increase their productivity. In the course of a day, sales reps spend time planning, traveling, waiting, selling, and doing administrative tasks (writing reports, billing, attending sales meetings, and talking to others in the company about production, delivery, billing, and sales performance). It's no wonder face-to-face selling accounts for as little as 29 percent of total working time![46]

To cut costs, reduce time demands on the outside sales force, and leverage computer and telecommunications innovations, many firms have expanded their inside sales force. Inside salespeople are of three types: *Technical support people* provide technical information and answers to customers' questions. *Sales assistants* provide clerical backup for outside salespersons by confirming appointments, running credit checks, following up on deliveries, and answering customers' questions. *Telemarketers* find new leads, qualify them, and sell to them.

Today's salesperson has truly gone electronic. Not only is sales and inventory information transferred much faster, but specific computer-based decision support systems have been created for sales managers and sales representatives. Using laptops or smart phones, salespeople can access valuable product and customer information. The company Web site is also a valuable tool for reps, especially for prospecting. Web sites can help define the firm's relationships with individual accounts and identify those whose business warrants a personal sales call. They provide an introduction to self-identified potential customers and might even receive the initial order. For more complex transactions, the site provides a way for the buyer to contact the seller.

Motivating Sales Representatives

The majority of sales representatives require encouragement and special incentives, especially those in field selling.[47] Most marketers believe that the higher the salesperson's motivation, the greater the effort and the resulting performance, rewards, and satisfaction—all of which increase motivation. Marketers reinforce intrinsic and extrinsic rewards of all types. One study found the reward with the highest value was pay, followed by promotion, personal growth, and sense of accomplishment.[48] Least valued were liking and respect, security, and recognition. In other words, salespeople are highly motivated by pay and the chance to get ahead and satisfy their intrinsic needs, and less motivated by compliments and security.

Many companies set annual sales quotas, based on the annual marketing plan, for dollar sales, unit volume, margin, selling effort or activity, or product type. Compensation is often tied to degree of quota fulfillment. The company first prepares a sales forecast that becomes the basis for planning production, workforce size, and financial requirements. Then it establishes quotas for regions and territories, which typically add up to more than the sales forecast to encourage managers and salespeople to perform at their best. If they fail to make their quotas, the firm may still reach its sales forecast.

Each area sales manager divides the area's quota among its reps. Sometimes a rep's quotas are set high, to spur extra effort, or more modestly, to build confidence. One general view is that a salesperson's quota should be at least equal to last year's sales, plus some fraction of the difference between territory sales potential and last year's sales. The more favorably the salesperson reacts to pressure, the higher the fraction should be.

Evaluating Sales Representatives

We have been describing the *feed-forward* aspects of sales supervision—how management communicates what the sales reps should be doing and motivates them to do it. But good feed-forward requires good *feedback,* which means getting regular information from reps to evaluate performance. Information about reps can come from sales reports and self-reports, personal observation, customer comments, customer surveys, and conversations with other reps.

Many firms require reps to create an annual territory-marketing plan for developing new accounts and increasing business from existing accounts. Sales reps write up completed activities on *call reports* and also submit expense reports, new-business reports, lost-business reports, and reports on business and economic conditions. Reports provide raw data from which sales managers can extract key indicators of sales performance: (1) average number of sales calls per rep per day, (2) average sales call time per contact, (3) average revenue per sales call, (4) average cost per sales call, (5) entertainment cost per sales call, (6) percentage of orders per hundred sales calls, (7) number of new customers per period, (8) number of lost customers per period, and (9) sales force cost as a percentage of total sales.

Even a rep who is effective in producing sales may not rate high with customers. Success may come because competitors' salespeople are inferior, the rep's product is better, or new customers are always found to replace those who dislike the rep. Sales performance might also be related to internal factors (effort, ability, and strategy) and/or external factors (task and luck).[49]

EXECUTIVE SUMMARY

Direct marketing is an interactive marketing system that uses one or more media to effect a measurable response or transaction. Direct marketers plan campaigns by deciding on objectives, target markets and prospects, offers, and prices. Next, they test and establish measures to determine the campaign's success. Major direct marketing channels include face-to-face selling, direct mail, catalog marketing, telemarketing, interactive TV, kiosks, Web sites, and mobile devices. Interactive marketing provides marketers with opportunities for greater interaction and individualization through Web sites, search ads, display ads, and e-mails. Mobile marketing, a growing form of interactive marketing, relies on text messages, software apps, and ads. Word-of-mouth marketing finds ways to engage customers so they talk with others about products, services, and brands. Increasingly, word of mouth is being driven by social media such as online communities and forums, blogs, and social networks.

Designing the sales force requires choosing objectives, strategy, structure, size, and compensation. There are five steps in managing the sales force: (1) recruiting and selecting representatives; (2) training reps in sales techniques and in the company's products, policies, and customer-satisfaction orientation; (3) supervising the sales force and helping reps to use their time efficiently; (4) motivating the sales force and balancing quotas, monetary rewards, and supplementary motivators; (5) evaluating individual and group sales performance. Personal selling is a six-step process: prospecting and qualifying customers, preapproach, presentation and demonstration, overcoming objections, closing, and follow-up and maintenance.

NOTES

1. Elaine Wong, "Pepsi's Refresh Project Drives Social Buzz," *Brandweek,* June 9, 2010; Stuart Elliott, "Pepsi Invites the Public to Do Good," *New York Times,* February 1, 2010; Suzanne Vranica, "Pepsi Benches Its Drinks," *Wall Street Journal,* December 17, 2009.
2. www.the-dma.org, home page of Direct Marketing Association.
3. "DMA Releases 2010 Response Rate Trend Report," *Direct Marketing Association,* June 15, 2010, www.the-dma.org.
4. Edward L. Nash, *Direct Marketing: Strategy, Planning, Execution,* 4th ed. (New York: McGraw-Hill, 2000).
5. The *average customer longevity* (N) is related to the *customer retention rate* (CR). If the company retains

80 percent of its customers each year, the average customer longevity is given by: N = 1/(1 – CR) = 1/.2 = 5 years.

6. "Industry Overview: Internet and Catalog Retailers," *Hoovers*, www.hoovers.com, accessed August 22, 2010.

7. "Biennial Report to Congress: Pursuant to the Do Not Call Registry Fee Extension Act of 2007," *Federal Trade Commission*, www.ftc.gov, December 2009.

8. Charles Duhigg, "Telemarketing Thieves Sharpen Their Focus on the Elderly," *New York Times*, May 20, 2007.

9. For example, see André Bonfrer and Xavier Drèze, "Real-Time Evaluation of E-mail Campaign Performance," *Marketing Science* 28 (March–April 2009), pp. 251–63.

10. Kenneth C. Wilbur and Yi Zhu, "Click Fraud," *Marketing Science* 28 (March–April 2009), pp. 293–308.

11. John R. Hauser, Glen L. Urban, Guilherme Liberali, and Michael Braun, "Website Morphing," *Marketing Science* 28 (March–April 2009), pp. 202–23; Peter J. Danaher, Guy W. Mullarkey, and Skander Essegaier, "Factors Affecting Web Site Visit Duration," *Journal of Marketing Research* 43 (May 2006), pp. 182–94; Philip Kotler, *According to Kotler* (New York: American Management Association, 2005).

12. Jeffrey F. Rayport and Bernard J. Jaworski, *e-Commerce* (New York: McGraw-Hill, 2001), p. 116.

13. Julia Angwin and Tom McGinty, "Sites Feed Personal Details to New Tracking Industry," *Wall Street Journal*, July 31, 2010.

14. *eMarketer*, www.emarketer.com, May 2010.

15. Emily Steel, "Marketers Take Search Ads beyond Search Engines," *Wall Street Journal*, January 19, 2009.

16. Paula Andruss, "How to Win the Bidding Wars," *Marketing News*, April 1, 2008, p. 28; "Jefferson Graham, "To Drive Traffic to Your Site, You Need to Give Good Directions," *USA Today*, June 23, 2008.

17. Peter J. Danaher, Janghyuk Lee, and Laoucine Kerbache, "Optimal Internet Media Selection," *Marketing Science* 29 (March–April 2010), pp. 336–47; Puneet Manchanda, Jean-Pierre Dubé, Khim Yong Goh, and Pradeep K. Chintagunta, "The Effects of Banner Advertising on Internet Purchasing," *Journal of Marketing Research* 43 (February 2006), pp. 98–108.

18. Brian Morrissey, "Big Money Bet on Display Ad Tech," *Adweek*, August 1, 2010; Brian Morrissey, "Beefing Up Banner Ads," *Adweek NEXT*, February 15, 2010, pp. 10–11; Robert D. Hof, "The Squeeze on Online Ads," *BusinessWeek*, March 2, 2009, pp. 48–49; Emily Steel, "Web Sites Debate Best Values for Advertising Dollars," *Wall Street Journal*, August 13, 2009, p. B7.

19. Natalie Zmuda, "How E-Mail Became a Direct-Marketing Rock Star in Recession," *Advertising Age*, May 11, 2009, p. 27.

20. Peter DaSilva, "Cellphone in New Role: Loyalty Card," *New York Times*, May 31, 2010.

21. Piet Levy, "Set Your Sites on Mobile," *Marketing News*, April 30, 2010, p. 6; Tom Lowry, "Pandora: Unleashing Mobile-Phone Ads," *BusinessWeek*, June 1, 2009, pp. 52–53.

22. Louise Story, "What We Talk About When We Talk About Brands," *New York Times*, November 24, 2006.

23. Robert V. Kozinets, Kristine de Valck, Andrea C. Wojnicki, and Sarah J. S. Wilner, "Networked Narratives: Understanding Word-of-Mouth Marketing in Online Communities," *Journal of Marketing* 74 (March 2010), pp. 71–89; David Godes and Dina Mayzlin, "Firm-Created Word-of-Mouth Communication: Evidence from a Field Test," *Marketing Science* 28 (July–August 2009), pp. 721–39.

24. For a review of relevant academic literature, see Christophe Van Den Bulte and Stefan Wuyts, *Social Networks and Marketing* (Marketing Science Institute Relevant Knowledge Series, Cambridge, MA, 2007); for some practical considerations, see "A World of Connections: A Special Report on Social Networking," *Economist*, January 30, 2010.

25. "Profiting from Friendship," *Economist*, January 30, 2010, pp. 9–12.

26. Ralf van der Lans, Gerrit van Bruggen, Jehoshua Eliashberg, and Berend Wierenga, "A Viral Branching Model for Predicting the Spread of Electronic Word of Mouth," *Marketing Science*, 29 (March–April 2010), pp. 348–65; Dave Balter and John Butman, "Clutter Cutter," *Marketing Management* (July–August 2006), pp. 49–50.

27. Emanuel Rosen, *The Anatomy of Buzz* (New York: Currency, 2000).

28. George Silverman, *The Secrets of Word-of-Mouth Marketing* (New York: AMACOM, 2001); Emanuel Rosen, *The Anatomy of Buzz* (New York: Currency, 2000), chapter 12; "Viral Marketing," *Sales & Marketing Automation* (November 1999), pp. 12–14.

29. Amar Cheema and Andrew M. Kaikati, "The Effect of Need for Uniqueness on Word of Mouth," *Journal of Marketing Research* 47 (June 2010), pp. 553–63.

30. Jacqueline Johnson Brown, Peter M. Reingen, and Everett M. Rogers, *Diffusion of Innovations*, 4th ed. (New York: Free Press, 1995); J. Johnson Brown and Peter Reingen, "Social Ties and Word-of-Mouth Referral Behavior," *Journal of Consumer Research* 14, no. 3 (December 1987), pp. 350–62; Peter H. Riengen and

Jerome B. Kernan, "Analysis of Referral Networks in Marketing," *Journal of Marketing Research* 23, no. 4 (November 1986), pp. 37–78.

31. Keith Barry, "Fiesta Stars in Night of the Living Social Media Campaign," *Wired*, May 21, 2010; Matthew Dolan, "Ford Takes Online Gamble with New Fiesta," *Wall Street Journal*, April 8, 2009.

32. Guy Bird, "Creating a New Roadmap for One Ford's Marketing," *Marketing Week*, October 28, 2010, www.marketingweek.co.uk/in-depth-analysis/features/creating-a-new-roadmap-for-one-ford%E2%80%99s-marketing/3019775.article; Matthew Dolan, "Ford Takes Online Gamble with New Fiesta," *Wall Street Journal*, April 8, 2009; John Batelle, "The Net of Influence," *Business 2.0* (March 2004): 70; Ann Meyer, "Word-of-Mouth Marketing Speaks Well for Small Business," *Chicago Tribune*, July 28, 2003; Malcolm Macalister Hall, "Selling by Stealth," *Business Life* (November 2001), pp. 51–55.

33. Malcolm Gladwell, *The Tipping Point* (Boston: Little, Brown & Company, 2000).

34. Terry McDermott, "Criticism of Gladwell Reaches Tipping Point," *Columbia Journalism Review*, November 17, 2009; Clive Thompson, "Is the Tipping Point Toast?" *Fast Company*, February 1, 2008; Duncan Watts, *Six Degrees: The Science of a Connected Age* (New York: W.W. Norton, 2003).

35. This section is based in part on: "Is There a Reliable Way to Measure Word-of-Mouth Marketing?" *Marketing NPV* 3, no. 3 (2006), pp. 3–9, available at www.marketingnpv.com.

36. Suzanne Vranica, "Social Media Draws a Crowd," *Wall Street Journal*, July 19, 2010; Jessi Hempel, "He Measures the Web," *Fortune*, November 9, 2009, pp. 94–98.

37. Adam L. Penenberg, "How Much Are You Worth to Facebook?" *Fast Company*, October 1, 2009.

38. Rick Lawrence, Prem Melville, Claudia Perlich, Vikas Sindhwani, Steve Meliksetian, Pei-Yun Hsueh, and Yan Liu, "Social Media Analytics," *OR/MS Today*, February 2010, pp. 26–30.

39. Shrihari Sridhar, Murali K. Mantrala, and Sönke Albers, "Personal Selling Elasticities: A Meta-Analysis," *Journal of Marketing Research* (October 2010).

40. Adapted from Robert N. McMurry, "The Mystique of Super-Salesmanship," *Harvard Business Review*, March–April 1961, p. 114. See also, William C. Moncrief III, "Selling Activity and Sales Position Taxonomies for Industrial Sales Forces," *Journal of Marketing Research* 23, no. 3 (August 1986), pp. 261–70.

41. Some of the following discussion is based on a classic analysis in W. J. E. Crissy, William H. Cunningham, and

Isabella C. M. Cunningham, *Selling: The Personal Force in Marketing* (New York: Wiley, 1977), pp. 119–29. For some contemporary tips, see Jia Lynn Yang, "How to Sell in a Lousy Economy," *Fortune*, September 29, 2008, pp. 101–6.

42. V. Kumar, Rajkumar Venkatesan, and Werner Reinartz, "Performance Implications of Adopting a Customer-Focused Sales Campaign," *Journal of Marketing* 72 (September 2008), pp. 50–68; George R. Franke and Jeong-Eun Park, "Salesperson Adaptive Selling Behavior and Customer Orientation," *Journal of Marketing Research* 43 (November 2006), pp. 693–702; Richard G. McFarland, Goutam N. Challagalla, and Tasadduq A. Shervani, "Influence Tactics for Effective Adaptive Selling," *Journal of Marketing* 70 (October 2006), pp. 103–17.

43. Michael Ahearne, Scott B. MacKenzie, Philip M. Podsakoff, John E. Mathieu, and Son K. Lam, "The Role of Consensus in Sales Team Performance," *Journal of Marketing Research* 47 (June 2010), pp. 458–69.

44. Tony Ritigliano and Benson Smith, *Discover Your Sales Strengths* (New York: Random House Business Books, 2004).

45. Michael R. W. Bommer, Brian F. O'Neil, and Beheruz N. Sethna, "A Methodology for Optimizing Selling Time of Salespersons," *Journal of Marketing Theory and Practice* (Spring 1994), pp. 61–75. See also, Lissan Joseph, "On the Optimality of Delegating Pricing Authority to the Sales Force," *Journal of Marketing* 65 (January 2001), pp. 62–70.

46. Dartnell Corporation, *30th Sales-Force Compensation Survey* (Chicago: Dartnell Corp., 1999). Other breakdowns show that 12.7 percent is spent in service calls, 16 percent in administrative tasks, 25.1 percent in telephone selling, and 17.4 percent in waiting/traveling. For analysis of this database, see Sanjog Misra, Anne T. Coughlan, and Chakravarthi Narasimhan, "Salesforce Compensation: An Analytical and Empirical Examination of the Agency Theoretic Approach," *Quantitative Marketing and Economics* 3 (March 2005), pp. 5–39.

47. Willem Verbeke and Richard P. Bagozzi, "Sales-Call Anxiety: Exploring What It Means When Fear Rules a Sales Encounter," *Journal of Marketing* 64 (July 2000), pp. 88–101. See also, Douglas E. Hughes and Michael Ahearne, "Energizing the Reseller's Sales Force: The Power of Brand Identification," *Journal of Marketing* 74 (July 2010), pp. 81–96.

48. Gilbert A. Churchill Jr., Neil M. Ford, Orville C. Walker Jr., Mark W. Johnston, and Greg W. Marshall, *Sales-Force Management,* 9th ed. (New York: McGraw-Hill/Irwin, 2009). See also, Eric G. Harris, John C. Mowen, and Tom J. Brown, "Reexamining

Salesperson Goal Orientations: Personality Influencers, Customer Orientation, and Work Satisfaction," *Journal of the Academy of Marketing Science* 33, no. 1 (Winter 2005), pp. 19–35; Manfred Krafft, "An Empirical Investigation of the Antecedents of Sales-Force Control Systems," *Journal of Marketing* 63 (July 1999), pp. 120–34; Wujin Chu, Eitan Gerstner, and James D. Hess, "Costs and Benefits of Hard Sell," *Journal of Marketing Research* 32, no. 1 (February 1995), pp. 97–102.

49. Philip M. Posdakoff and Scott B. MacKenzie, "Organizational Citizenship Behaviors and Sales-Unit Effectiveness," *Journal of Marketing Research* 31, no. 3 (August 1994), pp. 351–63. See also, Andrea L. Dixon, Rosann L. Spiro, and Magbul Jamil, "Successful and Unsuccessful Sales Calls: Measuring Salesperson Attributions and Behavioral Intentions," *Journal of Marketing* 65 (July 2001), pp. 64–78; Willem Verbeke and Richard P. Bagozzi, "Sales-Call Anxiety," *Journal of Marketing* 64 (July 2000), pp. 88–101.

Managing Marketing in the Global Economy

In this chapter, we will address the following questions:

1. What factors should a company review before deciding to market internationally?
2. What are the major ways of entering foreign markets?
3. What are the keys to effective internal marketing?
4. How can companies be responsible social marketers?
5. What tools can companies use to monitor and improve their marketing activities?

Marketing Management at Timberland

Timberland, the maker of rugged boots, shoes, clothing, and gear, has a passion for the great outdoors. The company targets individuals who live, work, and play outdoors, so it only makes sense that it wants to do whatever it takes to protect the environment. Over the years, Timberland's commitment and actions have blazed trails for green companies around the world. Its revolutionary initiatives include giving its shoes a "nutrition label" that measures their "greenness"—how much energy was used in making them, what transportation and labor costs were incurred, and what portion is renewable.

Timberland also introduced a line of shoes called Earthkeepers, made of organic cotton, recycled PET, and recycled tires (for the soles). The shoes are designed to be taken apart and over 50 percent of the parts can be recycled. Timberland has attracted an online community for Earthkeepers by offering tips and information about events focused on preserving the environment. Its business accomplishments prove that socially and environmentally responsible companies can be successful. Sales topped $1.2 billion in 2009, and Timberland has won numerous awards, including a steady spot on Fortune's 100 Best Companies to Work For.[1]

To support healthy, long-term brand growth, holistic marketers such as Timberland must engage in a host of carefully planned, interconnected marketing activities and satisfy an increasingly broader set of constituents and objectives. They must also consider the global marketplace, corporate social responsibility, and sustainability when making marketing decisions. In this chapter, we explore how companies expand into global markets, how they organize their marketing efforts, and how they manage, control, and evaluate marketing implementation in a context heightened by social responsibility.

Competing on a Global Basis

Many companies have been global marketers for decades—firms like Shell, Bayer, and Toshiba have sold goods around the world for years. But global competition is intensifying in more product categories as new firms make their mark on the international stage.[2] In a **global industry**, competitors' strategic positions in major geographic or national markets are affected by their overall global positions.[3] A **global firm** operates in more than one country and captures R&D, production, logistical, marketing, and financial advantages not available to purely domestic competitors.

Global firms plan, operate, and coordinate their activities on a worldwide basis. Many successful global U.S. brands have tapped into universal consumer values and needs—such as Nike with athletic performance. Global marketing extends beyond products. Services represent the fastest-growing sector of the global economy and account for two-thirds of global output, one-third of global employment, and nearly 20 percent of global trade. For a company of any size or any type to go global, it must make a series of decisions (see Figure 18.1, on the next page).

Deciding Whether to Go Abroad

Several factors draw companies into the international arena. Some international markets present better profit opportunities than the domestic market. A firm may need a larger customer base to achieve economies of scale, or it may want to reduce dependence on any one market. Sometimes a firm decides to counterattack global competitors in their home markets, or it sees its customers going abroad and requiring international service.

Before making a decision to go abroad, the company must also weigh several risks. First, the firm might not understand foreign preferences and could fail to offer a competitively attractive product. Second, it might not understand the foreign country's business culture or know how to deal effectively with foreign regulations. Third, it might lack managers with international experience. Finally, the other country might change its commercial laws, devalue its currency, or undergo a political revolution and expropriate foreign property.

Deciding Which Markets to Enter

In deciding to go abroad, the company needs to define its marketing objectives and policies. What proportion of international to total sales will it seek? Most companies start small when they venture abroad. Some plan to stay small; others have bigger plans. Typical entry strategies are the *waterfall* approach, gradually entering countries in sequence, and the *sprinkler* approach, entering many countries simultaneously. Increasingly, firms—especially technology-intensive firms—are *born global* and market to the entire world from the outset.

The company must also choose the countries to consider, based on the product and on geography, income and population, and political climate. Developed nations account for about 20 percent of the world's population. Can marketers serve the other 80 percent, which has much less purchasing power and living conditions ranging from mild deprivation to severe deficiency?

FIGURE 18.1 Major Decisions in International Marketing

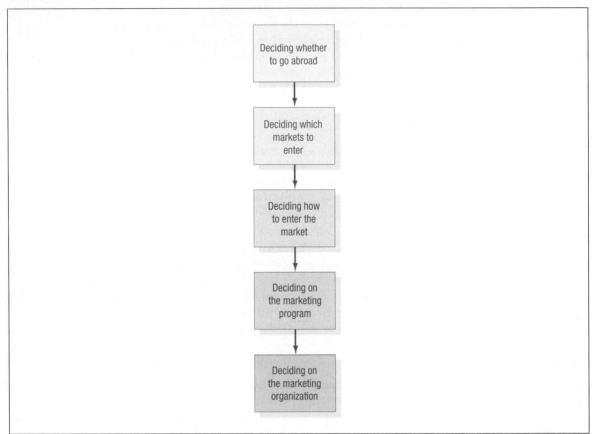

Economic and cultural differences abound, a marketing infrastructure may barely exist, and local competition can be surprisingly stiff.[4] However, marketing success is possible when firms plan carefully. Nestlé, the world's largest food company, gets about a third of its revenue from emerging countries and has set a goal of increasing that to 45 percent within a decade.[5] Many firms are using lessons gleaned from marketing in developing markets to better compete in their developed markets. The challenge is to think creatively about how marketing can fulfill the dreams of most of the world's population for a better standard of living.[6]

Deciding How to Enter the Market

Next, the firm must determine the best mode of entry. As shown in Figure 18.2, each succeeding strategy entails more commitment, risk, control, and profit potential.

- **Indirect and direct export.** Companies typically start with indirect export, working through independent intermediaries, and may move into direct export later. Indirect exporting requires less investment and entails less risk. Because international marketing intermediaries bring know-how and services to the relationship, the seller will make fewer mistakes. A company can also use the Internet to attract new customers overseas, support existing customers located abroad, source from international suppliers, and build global brand awareness. Successful companies adapt their Web sites to provide country-specific

FIGURE 18.2 Five Modes of Entry into Foreign Markets

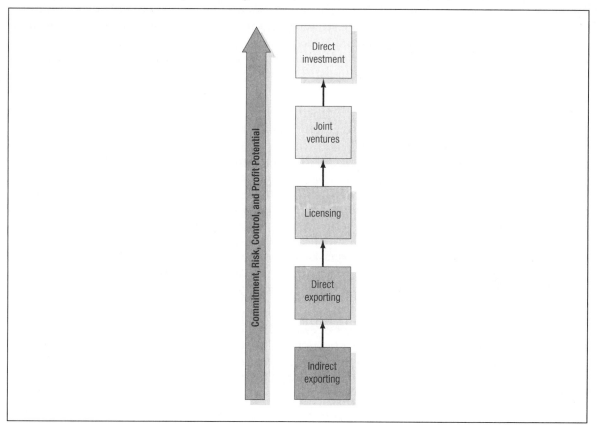

content and services to their highest-potential international markets, ideally in the local language.

- Licensing. The licensor issues a license to a foreign company to use a manufacturing process, trademark, patent, or other item of value for a fee or royalty. The licensor gains entry at little risk; the licensee gains production expertise or a well-known product or brand name. The licensor, however, has less control over the licensee than over its own production and sales facilities. If the licensee is very successful, the firm has given up profits; if and when the contract ends, the firm might find it has created a competitor.

- Joint ventures. Foreign investors may join local investors in a **joint venture** company in which they share ownership and control, sometimes desirable for political or economic reasons. However, the partners might disagree over investment, marketing, or other policies. One might want to reinvest earnings for growth while the other wants to declare more dividends. Joint ownership can also prevent a multinational company from carrying out specific manufacturing and marketing policies on a worldwide basis.

- Direct investment. The ultimate form of foreign involvement is direct ownership: the foreign company can buy part or full interest in a local company or build its own manufacturing or service facilities. If the market is large enough, direct investment offers distinct advantages. First, the firm secures cost economies through cheaper labor or raw materials, government incentives, and freight savings. Second, the firm strengthens its image in the host country because it creates jobs. Third, the firm deepens its relationship with government, customers, local suppliers, and distributors. Fourth, the firm retains full control over its investment and can implement policies that serve its long-term international objectives. Fifth, the firm assures itself of access to the market in case the host country insists locally purchased goods have domestic content. The main disadvantage is exposure to risks such as blocked or devalued currencies, worsening markets, or expropriation.

Deciding on the Marketing Program

Companies must decide how much to adapt their marketing strategy to local conditions when entering foreign markets.[7] At one extreme is a *standardized marketing program* worldwide, which promises the lowest costs; Table 18.1 summarizes some pros and cons. At the other extreme is an *adapted marketing program* in which the company, consistent with the marketing concept, believes consumer needs vary and tailors marketing to each target group.

The best global brands are consistent in theme but reflect significant differences in consumer behavior, brand development, competitive forces, and the legal or political environment. Some products cross borders without adaptation better than others. Culture and wealth factors influence how quickly a new product takes off in a country, although adoption and diffusion rates are becoming more alike across countries over time.[8] Warren Keegan has distinguished five product and communications adaptation strategies (see Figure 18.3).[9]

Product **Straight extension** introduces the product in the foreign market without any change, a successful strategy for cameras, consumer electronics, and many machine tools. **Product adaptation** alters the product to meet local conditions or preferences, developing a *regional version* of its product, a *country version*, a *city version*, or different *retailer versions*. **Product invention** creates something new. It can take two forms: *backward invention* (reintroducing

---

TABLE 18.1	Globally Standardized Marketing Pros and Cons

Advantages

Economies of scale in production and distribution

Lower marketing costs

Power and scope

Consistency in brand image

Ability to leverage good ideas quickly and efficiently

Uniformity of marketing practices

Disadvantages

Ignores differences in consumer needs, wants, and usage patterns for products

Ignores differences in consumer response to marketing programs and activities

Ignores differences in brand and product development and the competitive environment

Ignores differences in the legal environment

Ignores differences in marketing institutions

Ignores differences in administrative procedures

FIGURE 18.3 Five International Product and Communications Strategies

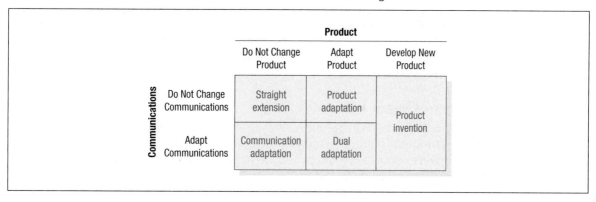

earlier product forms well adapted to a foreign country's needs) or *forward invention* (creating a new product to meet a need in another country). When they launch products and services globally, marketers may need to change certain brand elements.[10]

Communications   Changing marketing communications for each local market is a process called **communication adaptation**. If it adapts both the product and the communications, the company engages in **dual adaptation**. Consider the message. The company can use one message everywhere, varying only the language, name, and perhaps colors to avoid taboos in some countries. Or it might use the same message and creative theme globally but adapt the execution. Another approach, which Coca-Cola and Goodyear have used, consists of developing a global pool of ads from which each country marketing manager selects the most appropriate. Finally, some companies allow their country managers to create country-specific ads, subject to certain guidelines. Personal selling tactics may need to change too.

Price   Multinational manufacturers selling abroad must contend with *price escalation,* having to raise the price to cover the added cost of transportation, tariffs, importer margin, wholesaler margin, and retailer margin, as well as the risk of currency fluctuation, so it can earn the same profit. Pricing choices include setting a uniform price in all markets, a market-based price in each market, or a cost-based price in each market. When companies sell over the Internet, price becomes transparent and price differentiation between countries declines.

Many multinationals are plagued by the **gray market**, which diverts branded products from authorized distribution channels either in-country or across international borders. Dealers in the low-price country sell some products in higher-price countries, thus earning more. Companies fight back by policing the distributors, raising their prices to lower-cost distributors, or altering product characteristics or service warranties for different countries.[11] Fakes and imitations are another costly concern for multinational brand marketers. Online, firms are using technology to search for counterfeit storefronts and sales by detecting domain names similar to legitimate brands and unauthorized Web sites that plaster brand trademarks and logos on their home pages.

Distribution   Companies must consider how to get products to other nations as well as how the product moves within the foreign country, taking a whole-channel view of distributing products to final users. Distribution channels within countries vary considerably, as do the size and character of retail units. Large-scale retail chains dominate the U.S. scene, but much foreign retailing is in the hands of small, independent retailers. Markups are high, but the real price comes down through haggling. Incomes are low, and people shop daily for whatever they can carry home on foot or bicycle. Breaking bulk remains an important function and helps perpetuate long channels of distribution, a major obstacle to the expansion of large-scale retailing in developing countries. On the other hand, large retailers are increasingly moving into new global markets, offering firms the opportunity to sell in more countries and creating a challenge to local distributors and retailers.[12] Clearly, the multinational must choose the right distributors, invest in them, and set up performance goals to which they can agree.[13]

Country-of-Origin Effects

Country-of-origin perceptions are the mental associations and beliefs triggered by a country. Government officials want to strengthen their country's image to help domestic marketers who export, and to attract foreign firms and investors. Marketers want to use positive country-of-origin perceptions to sell their products and services. Global marketers know that buyers hold distinct attitudes and beliefs about brands or products from different countries.[14] The mere fact that a brand is perceived as successful on a global stage—whether it sends a quality signal, taps into cultural myths, or reinforces a sense of social responsibility—may lend credibility and respect.[15]

Marketers must look at country-of-origin perceptions from both a domestic and a foreign perspective. In the domestic market, these perceptions may stir consumers' patriotic notions or remind them of their past. As international trade grows, consumers may view certain brands as symbolically important in their own cultural heritage and identity. Many small businesses tap into community pride to emphasize their local roots. To be successful, these need to be clearly local and offer appealing product and service offerings.[16]

Internal Marketing

In a networked enterprise, *every* functional area can interact directly with customers. Marketing no longer has sole ownership of customer interactions; rather, it now must integrate all the customer-facing processes so customers see a single face and hear a single voice when they interact with the firm.[17] *Internal marketing* requires that everyone in the organization accept marketing concepts and goals and engage in choosing, providing, and communicating customer value. Only when *all* employees realize their job is to create, serve, and satisfy customers does the company become an effective marketer.[18] Let's look at how marketing departments are organized and how they can work effectively with other departments.

Organizing the Marketing Department

Modern marketing departments can be organized in a number of different, sometimes overlapping ways: functionally, geographically, by product or brand, by market, or in a matrix.

Functional Organization   In the most common form of marketing organization, functional specialists (such as the sales manager and marketing research manager) report to a marketing vice president who coordinates their activities. The main advantage is administrative simplicity, although it can be a challenge for the department to develop smooth working relationships. This form also can result in inadequate planning as the number of products and markets increases and each functional group vies for budget and status. The marketing vice president constantly weighs competing claims and faces a difficult coordination problem.

Geographic Organization   A company selling in a national market often organizes its sales force (and sometimes marketing) along geographic lines.[19] Some companies are adding *area market specialists* (regional or local marketing managers) to support sales efforts in high-volume markets. Because geography alters their brand development so much, some companies develop different marketing programs in different parts of the country.

Product- or Brand-Management Organization

Companies producing a variety of products and brands often establish a product- (or brand-) management organization, not to replace the functional organization but as another layer of management. A group product manager supervises product category managers, who in turn supervise specific product and brand managers. This type of organization makes sense if the company's products are quite different or there are more than a functional organization can handle.

The product-management organization lets the product manager concentrate on developing a cost-effective marketing program and react more quickly to new products in the marketplace; it also gives the company's smaller brands a product advocate. However, product managers may lack authority to carry out their responsibilities or be experts in their product without achieving functional expertise. Appointing product managers for major and even minor products can be costly. Brand managers may manage a brand for a short time, leading to short-term thinking instead of taking a long-term view. The fragmentation of markets makes it harder to develop a national strategy. Finally, product and brand managers often focus the company on building market share rather than customer relationships.

A second alternative is *product teams*. Some firms assign each major brand to a *brand-asset management team (BAMT)* consisting of representatives from functions that affect the brand's performance. These BAMT report to a BAMT directors committee, which itself reports to a chief branding officer. A third alternative is to eliminate product manager positions for minor products and assign two or more products to each remaining manager. This is feasible where two or more products appeal to a similar set of needs.

A fourth alternative is to introduce *category management*, focusing on product categories to manage the firm's brands. Procter & Gamble, a pioneer of the brand-management system, and other top packaged-goods firms have made a major shift to category management, as have firms outside the grocery channel.[20] By fostering internal competition among brand managers, the traditional brand-management system created strong incentives to excel, but also internal competition for resources and a lack of coordination. The new scheme was designed to ensure adequate resources for all categories. In some packaged-goods firms, category management has evolved into aisle management and encompasses multiple related categories typically found in the same sections of supermarkets and grocery stores.

Market-Management Organization

When customers fall into different user groups with distinct buying preferences and practices, a *market-management organization* is desirable. Market managers supervise several market-development managers, market specialists, or industry specialists and draw on functional services as needed. Market managers are staff (not line) people, with duties like those of product managers. Because this system organizes marketing activity to meet the needs of distinct customer groups, it shares many advantages and disadvantages of product-management systems. Many companies are reorganizing along market lines and becoming *market-centered organizations*. In a *customer-management organization*, firms organize to deal with individual customers rather than the mass market or market segments.[21]

Matrix-Management Organization

Companies that produce many products for many markets may adopt a *matrix organization* employing both product and market managers. However, this is costly and often creates conflicts as well as questions about authority and responsibility. Some corporate marketing groups assist top management with overall opportunity evaluation, provide divisions with consulting assistance on request, help divisions that have little or no marketing, and promote the marketing concept throughout the company.

Relationships with Other Departments

Under the marketing concept, all departments need to "think customer" and work together to satisfy customer needs and expectations. The top marketing executive must usually work through persuasion rather than through authority to (1) coordinate the company's internal marketing activities and (2) coordinate marketing with finance, operations, and other company functions to serve the customer. To help marketing and other functions jointly determine what is in the company's best interests, firms can provide joint seminars, joint committees and liaison employees, employee exchange programs, and analytical methods to determine the most profitable course of action.

Many companies now focus on key processes rather than departments, because departmental organization can be a barrier to smooth performance. They appoint process leaders, who manage cross-disciplinary teams that include marketing and sales people. Marketers thus may have a solid-line responsibility to their teams and a dotted-line responsibility to the marketing department.

Although it's *necessary* to be customer oriented, it's not *enough*. The organization must also be creative. Companies today copy each others' advantages and strategies with increasing speed, making differentiation harder to achieve and lowering margins as firms become more alike. The only answer is to build a capability in strategic innovation and imagination. This capability comes from assembling tools, processes, skills, and measures that let the firm generate more and better new ideas than its competitors.[22]

Socially Responsible Marketing

Effective internal marketing must be matched by a strong sense of ethics, values, and social responsibility.[23] A number of forces are driving companies to practice a higher level of corporate social responsibility, such as rising customer expectations, evolving employee goals and ambitions, tighter government legislation and pressure, investor interest in social criteria, media scrutiny, and changing business procurement practices.[24]

Virtually all firms have decided to take a more active, strategic role in corporate social responsibility, carefully scrutinizing what they believe in and how they should treat their customers, employees, competitors, community, and the environment. Taking this broader stakeholder view is believed to also benefit another important constituency—shareholders. Although some critics worry that important business investment in areas such as R&D could suffer as a result of a focus on social responsibility, these critics are in a tiny minority.[25]

Many now believe that satisfying customers, employees, and other stakeholders and achieving business success are closely tied to the adoption and implementation of high standards of business and marketing conduct. A further benefit of being seen as socially responsible is the ability to attract employees who want to work for companies they feel good about. The world's most admired—and most successful—companies abide by a code of serving people's interests, not only their own. Procter & Gamble's CEO has made "brand purpose" a key component of the company's marketing strategies. Raising the level of socially responsible marketing calls for a three-pronged attack that relies on proper legal, ethical, and social responsibility behavior. Sustainability is also being addressed through marketing.

Legal and Ethical Behavior

Organizations must ensure every employee knows and observes relevant laws.[26] Certain business practices are clearly unethical or illegal: bribery, theft of trade secrets, false and deceptive advertising, exclusive dealing and tying agreements, quality or safety defects, false warranties, inaccurate labeling, price-fixing, and predatory competition. Companies must adopt and disseminate a written code of ethics, build a company tradition of ethical behavior, and hold their people fully responsible for observing ethical and legal guidelines.[27] The general distrust of companies among U.S. consumers is evident in research showing the percentage who view corporations unfavorably has reached 26 percent.[28]

Social Responsibility Behavior

Individual marketers must exercise their social conscience in specific dealings with customers and stakeholders. Increasingly, people check a company's record on social and environmental responsibility to help them decide which companies to buy from, invest in, and work for.[29] Communicating corporate social responsibility can be a challenge. Once a firm touts an environmental initiative, it can become a target for criticism. Many well-intentioned product or marketing initiatives can have unforeseen or unavoidable negative consequences.

Often, the more committed a company is to sustainability and environmental protection, the more dilemmas that can arise. Corporate philanthropy also can pose dilemmas. Merck, DuPont, Walmart, and Bank of America have each donated $100 million or more to charities in a year. Yet good deeds can be overlooked—even resented—if the company is seen as exploitive or fails to live up to a "good guys" image.

Sustainability

Sustainability—the ability to meet humanity's needs without harming future generations—now tops many corporate agendas. Major corporations outline in great detail how they are trying to improve the long-term impact of their actions on communities and the environment. As one sustainability consultant put it, "There is a triple bottom line—people, planet, and profit—and the people part of the equation must come first. Sustainability means more than being eco-friendly, it also means you are in it for the long haul."[30] Some feel companies that score well on sustainability typically exhibit high-quality management in that "they tend to be more strategically nimble and better equipped to compete in the complex, high-velocity, global environment."[31] Consumer interest in sustainability is also creating market opportunities (see "Marketing Insight: The Rise of Organic Products").

Heightened interest in sustainability has also unfortunately resulted in *greenwashing*, which gives products the appearance of being environmentally friendly without living up to that promise. Because of insincere firms jumping on the green bandwagon, consumers bring a healthy skepticism to environmental claims, but they are also unwilling to sacrifice product performance and quality.[32] Many firms are rising to the challenge and are using the need for sustainability to fuel innovation. Sales of products emphasizing sustainability remained strong through the recent economic recession.[33]

Cause-Related Marketing

Many firms blend corporate social responsibility initiatives with marketing activities.[34] **Cause-related marketing** links the firm's contributions to a designated cause to customers' engaging directly or indirectly in revenue-producing transactions with the firm.[35] Cause marketing is part

THE RISE OF ORGANIC PRODUCTS

Organic and natural products have become a strong presence in many categories today. Chipotle Mexican Grill's mission statement, "Food with Integrity," reflects its focus on good food with a socially responsible message. One of the first fast-casual restaurant chains, Chipotle uses natural and organic ingredients and serves more naturally raised meat than any other restaurant. As another example, Caster & Pollux's success with organic and natural pet foods led to its distribution in major specialty retail chains such as PETCO.

Many companies beyond the food industry are embracing organic offerings that avoid chemicals and pesticides to stress ecological preservation. Organic nonfood items make up 7 percent of the $26.6 billion organic products industry—which translates into $1.8 billion in annual sales. Just one example: Organic cotton grown by farmers who fight boll weevils with ladybugs, weed crops by hand, and use manure for fertilizer has become a hot product at retail.

Sources: "Industry Statistics and Projected Growth," Organic Trade Association, June 2010; Victor Reklaitis, "Chipotle's Steve Ells Fine-Tunes Fast Food," *Investor's Business Daily*, November 2, 2010, www.investors.com; Kenneth Hein, "The World on a Platter," *Brandweek*, April 23, 2007, pp. 27–28; Megan Johnston, "Hard Sell for a Soft Fabric," *Forbes*, October 30, 2006, pp. 73–80.

of *corporate societal marketing (CSM)*, which Minette Drumwright and Patrick Murphy define as marketing efforts "that have at least one noneconomic objective related to social welfare and use the resources of the company and/or of its partners."[36]

A successful cause-marketing program can improve social welfare, create differentiated brand positioning, build strong consumer bonds, enhance the company's public image, create a reservoir of goodwill, boost internal morale and galvanize employees, drive sales, and increase the firm's market value.[37] Specifically, from a branding point of view, cause marketing can (1) build brand awareness, (2) enhance brand image, (3) establish brand credibility, (4) evoke brand feelings, (5) create a sense of brand community, and (6) elicit brand engagement.[38]

Some critics worry that cause marketing or "consumption philanthropy" may replace virtuous actions with less-thoughtful buying, reduce emphasis on real solutions, or deflect attention from the fact that markets may create many social problems to begin with.[39] Also, cause-related marketing may backfire if consumers question the link between the product and the cause or see the firm as self-serving and exploitive.[40] (See "Marketing Skills: Cause-Related Marketing" for more on how to plan such activities.)

Marketing Implementation and Control

Marketing implementation is the process that turns marketing plans into action assignments and ensures they accomplish the plan's stated objectives.[41] A brilliant strategic marketing plan counts for little if not implemented properly. Strategy addresses the *what* and *why* of marketing activities; implementation addresses the *who, where, when,* and *how.* They are closely related: One layer of strategy implies certain tactical implementation assignments at a lower level. For example, top management's strategic decision to "harvest" a product must be translated into specific actions and assignments. Companies today are striving to make their marketing operations more efficient and their return on marketing investment more measurable. Marketers need better

CAUSE-RELATED MARKETING

To develop cause-related marketing skills, marketers first learn to choose the cause(s) to support. Most firms choose causes that fit their corporate or brand image and matter to their employees and stakeholders. Next, prepare to brand the program, perhaps with a new self-branded organization associated with the cause, such as the Ronald McDonald House charities. A second approach is to co-brand the program as sponsor or supporter, which complements the brand's image with associations "borrowed" or "transferred" from the cause. A third option is to partner with a cause and brand the program linked with the cause. Finally, plan and manage cause-related marketing as carefully as all other marketing programs.

Procter & Gamble's Dawn, the leading U.S. dishwashing liquid, has long highlighted its unusual side benefit—it can clean birds caught in oil spills. A report by the U.S. Fish and Wildlife Service called Dawn "the only bird-cleaning agent that is recommended because it removes oil from feathers; is non-toxic; and does not leave a residue." After the catastrophic BP oil spill in 2010, P&G donated thousands of bottles as well as placing a code on bottles and donating $1 to Gulf wildlife causes for each code customers activated online, eventually raising more than $500,000. The brand also drew massive publicity and visits to its Facebook page, which outlined the environmental cleanup and relief effort.[42]

templates for marketing processes, better management of marketing assets, and better allocation of marketing resources.

Marketing Control and Metrics

Marketing control is the process by which firms assess the effects of their marketing activities and programs and make necessary changes and adjustments. Table 18.2 lists four types of needed marketing control: annual-plan control, profitability control, efficiency control, and strategic control.

Annual-plan control ensures the company achieves the sales, profits, and other goals established in its annual plan. Management sets monthly or quarterly goals, monitors performance in the marketplace, determines the causes of serious performance deviations, and takes corrective action to close gaps between goals and performance (see Figure 18.4).

Marketers today have better marketing metrics for measuring the performance of marketing plans (see Table 18.3 for some samples).[43] Four tools for evaluating performance are sales analysis, market share analysis, marketing expense-to-sales analysis, and financial analysis. Suppose a profitability analysis reveals the company is earning poor profits in certain products, territories, or markets. Are there more efficient ways to manage the sales force, advertising, sales promotion, and distribution?

Some companies have established a *marketing controller* position to improve marketing efficiency. At companies such as Johnson & Johnson, marketing controllers perform a sophisticated financial analysis of marketing expenditures and results, examining adherence to profit plans, helping prepare brand managers' budgets, measuring promotion efficiency, analyzing media production costs, evaluating customer and geographic profitability, and educating marketing staff on the financial implications of their decisions.[44]

TABLE 18.2	Types of Marketing Control		
Type of Control	Prime Responsibility	Purpose of Control	Approaches
I. Annual-plan control	Top management Middle management	To examine whether the planned results are being achieved	• Sales analysis • Market share analysis • Sales-to-expense ratios • Financial analysis • Market-based scorecard analysis
II. Profitability control	Marketing controller	To examine where the company is making and losing money	Profitability by: • product • territory • customer • segment • trade channel • order size
III. Efficiency control	Line and staff management Marketing controller	To evaluate and improve the spending efficiency and impact of marketing expenditures	Efficiency of: • sales force • advertising • sales promotion • distribution
IV. Strategic control	Top management Marketing auditor	To examine whether the company is pursuing its best opportunities with respect to markets, products, and channels	• Marketing effectiveness rating instrument • Marketing audit • Marketing excellence review • Company ethical and social responsibility review

The Marketing Audit

The average U.S. corporation loses half its customers in five years, half its employees in four years, and half its investors in less than one year. Clearly, this points to some weaknesses. Companies that discover weaknesses should undertake a marketing audit.[45] A **marketing audit** is a comprehensive, systematic, independent, and periodic examination of a company's or business unit's marketing environment, objectives, strategies, and activities, with a view to determining problem areas and opportunities and recommending a plan to improve the company's marketing performance.

FIGURE 18.4 The Control Process

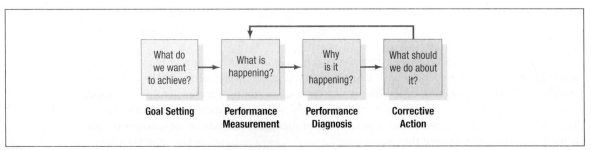

TABLE 18.3	Marketing Metrics

Sales Metrics	**Distribution Metrics**
• Sales growth	• Number of outlets
• Market share	• Share in shops handling
• Sales from new products	• Weighted distribution
Customer Readiness to Buy Metrics	• Distribution gains
• Awareness	• Average stocks volume (value)
• Preference	• Stocks cover in days
• Purchase intention	• Out of stock frequency
• Trial rate	• Share of shelf
• Repurchase rate	• Average sales per point of sale
Customer Metrics	**Communication Metrics**
• Customer complaints	• Spontaneous (unaided) brand awareness
• Customer satisfaction	• Top of mind brand awareness
• Ratio of promoters to detractors	• Prompted (aided) brand awareness
• Customer acquisition costs	• Spontaneous (unaided) advertising awareness
• New-customer gains	• Prompted (aided) advertising awareness
• Customer losses	• Effective reach
• Customer churn	• Effective frequency
• Retention rate	• Gross rating points (GRP)
• Customer lifetime value	• Response rate
• Customer equity	
• Customer profitability	
• Return on customer	

A marketing audit should cover the macro- and micromarketing environments, marketing objectives and strategies, marketing systems, and specific activities, identifying the most-needed improvements and incorporating them into a corrective-action plan with short- and long-run steps. Usually independent consultants will bring the necessary objectivity, experience, time, and attention to carry out a thorough audit. A periodic marketing audit can benefit companies in good health as well as those in trouble.

The Future of Marketing

Top management recognizes that marketing entails more accountability than in the past. To succeed in the future, marketing must be more holistic and less departmental. Marketers must achieve larger influence in the company, continuously create new ideas, and strive for customer insight by treating customers differently but appropriately. They must build their brands more through performance than promotion. They must go electronic and win through building superior information and communication systems. To accomplish these changes and become truly holistic, marketers need a new set of skills and competencies in customer relationship management, partner relationship management, database marketing and data mining, contact center management and telemarketing, public relations marketing, brand-building and brand-asset management, experiential marketing, integrated marketing communications, and profitability analysis.

Looking ahead, emerging markets such as India and China will offer enormous new sources of demand—but often only for certain types of products and at certain price points. Across all markets, marketing plans and programs will grow more localized and culturally sensitive, while strong brands that are well differentiated and continually improved will remain fundamental to marketing success. Businesses will continue to use social media more and traditional media less. The Web allows unprecedented depth and breadth in communications and distribution, and its transparency requires companies to be honest and authentic.

Marketers also face ethical dilemmas and perplexing trade-offs. Consumers may value convenience, but how to justify disposable products or elaborate packaging in a world trying to minimize waste? Increasing material aspirations can defy the need for sustainability. Given increasing consumer sensitivity and government regulation, smart companies are creatively designing with energy efficiency, carbon footprints, toxicity, and disposability in mind. Some are choosing local suppliers over distant ones. Therefore, marketers will have to use creative win-win solutions to balance conflicting demands and develop fully integrated marketing programs for meaningful relationships with a range of constituents.

EXECUTIVE SUMMARY

In deciding to enter international markets, a firm must examine its goals and objectives, weigh the risks, decide which and how many countries to enter, and determine the mode of entry (indirect and direct exporting, licensing, joint ventures, or direct investment). Firms going global have to decide how much to adapt their marketing strategy to local conditions. Country-of-origin effects can affect consumers and businesses alike. Companies can organize marketing by function, geography, product and brand, market segment, or as a matrix organization. All departments need to work together to satisfy customer needs and expectations.

Effective internal marketing must be matched by a strong sense of ethics, values, and social responsibility, as well as an eye toward sustainability. Cause marketing can be a means for companies to productively link social responsibility to consumer marketing programs. Effective implementation is needed to ensure that marketing plans are translated into activities that accomplish the objectives. The marketing department must monitor and control marketing activities continuously to assess the outcome of marketing actions and make necessary changes and adjustments. To uncover marketing weaknesses and areas for improvement, firms should apply a systematic, comprehensive marketing audit. Achieving marketing excellence in the future will require a new set of skills and competencies.

NOTES

1. Aman Singh, "Timberland's Smoking Ban: Good Corporate Citizenship or Overkill?" *Forbes,* June 3, 2010; Mark Borden and Anya Kamentz, "The Prophet CEO," *Fast Company*, September 2008, pp. 126–29; Tara Weiss, "Special Report: Going Green," *Forbes.com,* July 3, 2007; Matthew Grimm, "Progressive Business," *Brandweek*, November 28, 2005, pp. 16–26; Kate Galbraith, "Timberland's New Footprint: Recycled Tires," *New York Times,* April 3, 2009; Amy Cortese, "Products; Friend of Nature? Let's See Those Shoes," *New York Times,* March 6, 2007; Timberland, www.timberland.com.

2. Michael Elliott, "The New Global Opportunity, *Fortune,* July 5, 2010, pp. 96–102.

3. Michael E. Porter, *Competitive Strategy* (New York: Free Press, 1980), p. 275.

4. Bart J. Bronnenberg, Jean-Pierre Dubé, and Sanjay Dhar, "Consumer Packaged Goods in the United States," *Journal of Marketing Research* 44 (February 2007), pp. 4–13; Bart J. Bronnenberg, Jean-Pierre Dubé, and Sanjay Dhar, "National Brands, Local Branding: Conclusions and Future Research Opportunities," *Journal of Marketing Research* 44 (February 2007), pp. 26–28; Bart J. Bronnenberg, Sanjay K. Dhar, and Jean-Pierre Dubé, "Brand History, Geography, and the Persistence of CPG Brand Shares," *Journal of Political Economy* 117 (February 2009), pp. 87–115.

5. Tom Mulier and Shin Pei, "Nestle's $28.1 Billion Payday Gives Google-Size Cash," *Bloomberg BusinessWeek*, June 30, 2010.

6. Peter J. Williamson and Ming Zeng, "Value for Money Strategies for Recessionary Times," *Harvard Business Review*, March 2009, pp. 66–74; Vikram Skula, "Business Basics at the Base of the Pyramid," *Harvard Business Review*, June 2008, pp. 53–57.

7. "Burgers and Fries a la Francaise," *Economist*, April 17, 2004, pp. 60–61; Johny K. Johansson, "Global Marketing: Research on Foreign Entry, Local Marketing, Global Management," Bart Weitz and Robin Wensley, eds., *Handbook of Marketing* (London: Sage, 2002), pp. 457–83; Shaoming Zou and S. Tamer Cavusgil, "The GMS: A Broad Conceptualization of Global Marketing Strategy and Its Effect on Firm Performance," *Journal of Marketing* 66 (October 2002), pp. 40–56; David M. Szymanski, Sundar G. Bharadwaj, and P. Rajan Varadarajan, "Standardization versus Adaptation of International Marketing Strategy," *Journal of Marketing* 57, no. 4 (October 1993), pp. 1–17; Theodore Levitt, "The Globalization of Markets," *Harvard Business Review,* May–June 1983, pp. 92–102.

8. Deepa Chandrasekaran and Gerard J. Tellis, "Global Takeoff of New Products: Culture, Wealth, or Vanishing Differences?" *Marketing Science* 5 (September–October 2008), pp. 844–60.

9. Walter J. Keegan and Mark C. Green, *Global Marketing*, 4th ed. (Upper Saddle River, NJ: Prentice Hall, 2005); Warren J. Keegan, *Global Marketing Management,* 7th ed. (Upper Saddle River, NJ: Prentice Hall, 2002).

10. Ralf van der Lans, Joseph A. Cote, Catherine A. Cole, Siew Meng Leong, Ale Smidts, Pamela W. Henderson, Christian Bluemelhuber, Paul A. Bottomley, John R. Doyle, Alexander Fedorikhin, Janakiraman Moorthy, B. Ramaseshan, and Bernd H. Schmitt, "Cross-National Logo Evaluation Analysis: An Individual-Level Approach," *Marketing Science* 28 (September–October 2000), pp. 968–85.

11. David Blanchard, "Just in Time—How to Fix a Leaky Supply Chain," *IndustryWeek,* May 1, 2007.

12. Katrijn Gielens, Linda M. Van De Gucht, Jan-Benedict E. M. Steenkamp, and Marnik G. Dekimpe, "Dancing with a Giant: The Effect of Wal-Mart's Entry into the United Kingdom on the Performance of European Retailers," *Journal of Marketing Research* 45 (October 2008), pp. 519–34.

13. David Arnold, "Seven Rules of International Distribution," *Harvard Business Review,* November–December 2000, pp. 131–37.

14. Zeynep Gurhan-Canli and Durairaj Maheswaran, "Cultural Variations in Country-of-Origin Effects," *Journal of Marketing Research* 37 (August 2000), pp. 309–17. For some different related issues, see also, Lily Dong and Kelly Tian, "The Use of Western Brands in Asserting Chinese National Identity," *Journal of Consumer Research* 36 (October 2009), pp. 504–23; Yinlong Zhang and Adwait Khare, "The Impact of Accessible Identities on the Evaluation of Global versus Local Products," *Journal of Consumer Research* 36 (October 2009), pp. 524–37; Rohit Varman and Russell W. Belk, "Nationalism and Ideology in an Anticonsumption Movement," *Journal of Consumer Research* 36 (December 2009), pp. 686–700.

15. Douglas B. Holt, John A. Quelch, and Earl L. Taylor, "How Global Brands Compete," *Harvard Business Review* 82 (September 2004), pp. 68–75; Jan-Benedict E. M. Steenkamp, Rajeev Batra, and Dana L. Alden, "How Perceived Brand Globalness Creates Brand Value," *Journal of International Business Studies* 34, no. 1 (January 2003), pp. 53–65.

16. Kimberly Weisul, "Why More Are Buying into 'Buy Local,'" *Bloomberg BusinessWeek*, March 1, 2010, pp. 57–60.

17. Frederick E. Webster Jr., "Expanding Your Network," *Marketing Management* (Fall 2010), pp. 16–23; Frederick E. Webster Jr., Alan J. Malter, and Shankar Ganesan, "Can Marketing Regain Its Seat at the Table?" *Marketing Science Institute Report No. 03-113* (Cambridge, MA: Marketing Science Institute, 2003); Frederick E. Webster Jr., "The Role of Marketing and the Firm," Barton A. Weitz and Robin Wensley, eds., *Handbook of Marketing* (London: Sage, 2002), pp. 39–65.

18. Jan Wieseke, Michael Ahearne, Son K. Lam, and Rolf van Dick, "The Role of Leaders in Internal Marketing," *Journal of Marketing* 73 (March 2009), pp. 123–45; Hamish Pringle and William Gordon, *Beyond Manners: How to Create the Self-Confident Organisation to Live the Brand* (West Sussex, England: Wiley, 2001); John P. Workman Jr., Christian Homburg, and Kjell Gruner,

"Marketing Organization: An Integrative Framework of Dimensions and Determinants," *Journal of Marketing* 62 (July 1998), pp. 21–41.

19. Todd Guild, "Think Regionally, Act Locally: Four Steps to Reaching the Asian Consumer," *McKinsey Quarterly* 4 (September 2009), pp. 22–30.

20. "Category Management Goes beyond Grocery," *Cannondale Associates White Paper,* www.cannondaleassoc.com, February 13, 2007; Laurie Freeman, "P&G Widens Power Base: Adds Category Managers," *Advertising Age*; Michael J. Zenor, "The Profit Benefits of Category Management," *Journal of Marketing Research* 31 (May 1994), pp. 202–13; Gerry Khermouch, "Brands Overboard," *Brandweek,* August 22, 1994, pp. 25–39; Zachary Schiller, "The Marketing Revolution at Procter & Gamble," *BusinessWeek,* July 25, 1988, pp. 72–76.

21. Larry Selden and Geoffrey Colvin, *Angel Customers & Demon Customers* (New York: Portfolio [Penguin], 2003).

22. Gary Hamel, *Leading the Revolution* (Boston: Harvard Business School Press, 2000).

23. William L. Wilkie and Elizabeth S. Moore, "Marketing's Relationship to Society," Barton A. Weitz and Robin Wensley, eds., *Handbook of Marketing* (London: Sage, 2002), pp. 1–38.

24. "Special Report: Corporate Social Responsibility," *Economist,* January 17, 2008. For a broader academic perspective, see Michael E. Porter and Mark R. Kramer, "Strategy & Society," *Harvard Business Review,* December 2006, 78–82; Clayton M. Christensen, Heiner Baumann, Rudy Ruggles, and Thomas M. Stadtler, "Disruption Innovation for Social Change," *Harvard Business Review,* December 2006, 94–101.

25. Brian Grow, "The Debate over Doing Good," *BusinessWeek,* August 15, 2005.

26. Elisabeth Sullivan, "Play by the New Rules," *Marketing News,* November 30, 2009, pp. 5–9.

27. Shelby D. Hunt and Scott Vitell, "The General Theory of Marketing Ethics," John Quelch and Craig Smith, eds., *Ethics in Marketing* (Chicago: Irwin, 1992).

28. "Distrust, Discontent, Anger and Partisan Rancor," *The Pew Research for the People & the Press,* April 18, 2010.

29. Mary Jo Hatch and Majken Schultz, *Taking Brand Initiative* (San Francisco: Jossey-Bass, 2008); Majken Schultz, Yun Mi Antorini, and Fabian F. Csaba, *Corporate Branding* (Køge, Denmark: Copenhagen Business School Press, 2005); Ronald J. Alsop, *The 18 Immutable Laws of Corporate Reputation* (New York: Free Press, 2004); Marc Gunther, "Tree Huggers, Soy Lovers, and Profits," *Fortune,* June 23, 2003, pp. 98–104;

Ronald J. Alsop, "Perils of Corporate Philanthropy," *Wall Street Journal,* January 16, 2002.

30. Sandra O'Loughlin, "The Wearin' o' the Green," *Brandweek,* April 23, 2007, pp. 26–27. For a critical response, see also, John R. Ehrenfield, "Feeding the Beast," *Fast Company,* December 2006–January 2007, pp. 42–43.

31. Pete Engardio, "Beyond the Green Corporation," *BusinessWeek,* January 29, 2007, pp. 50–64.

32. Mark Dolliver, "Thumbs Down on Corporate Green Efforts," *Adweek,* August 31, 2010; Betsy Cummings, "A Green Backlash Gains Momentum," *Brandweek,* March 3, 2008, p. 6; Michael Hopkins, "What the 'Green' Consumer Wants," *MIT Sloan Management Review* (Summer 2009), pp. 87–89. For some related consumer research, see also, Julie R. Irwin and Rebecca Walker Naylor, "Ethical Decisions and Response Mode Compatibility," *Journal of Marketing Research* 46 (April 2009), pp. 234–46.

33. Jack Neff, "Green-Marketing Revolution Defies Economic Downturn," *Advertising Age,* April 20, 2009, pp. 1, 23; Ram Nidumolu, C. K. Prahalad, and M. R. Rangaswami, "Why Sustainability Is Now the Key Driver of Innovation," *Harvard Business Review,* September 2009, p. 57.

34. Larry Chiagouris and Ipshita Ray, "Saving the World with Cause-Related Marketing," *Marketing Management* 16, no. 4 (July–August 2007), pp. 48–51; Hamish Pringle and Marjorie Thompson, *Brand Spirit: How Cause-Related Marketing Builds Brands* (New York: Wiley, 1999); Sue Adkins, *Cause-Related Marketing* (Oxford, England: Butterworth-Heinemann, 1999); "Marketing, Corporate Social Initiatives, and the Bottom Line," *Marketing Science Institute Conference Summary, MSI Report No. 01-106,* 2001.

35. Rajan Varadarajan and Anil Menon, "Cause-Related Marketing: A Co-Alignment of Marketing Strategy and Corporate Philanthropy," *Journal of Marketing* 52 (July 1988), pp. 58–74.

36. Minette Drumwright and Patrick E. Murphy, "Corporate Societal Marketing," Paul N. Bloom and Gregory T. Gundlach, eds., *Handbook of Marketing and Society* (Thousand Oaks, CA: Sage, 2001), pp. 162–83. See also, Minette Drumwright, "Company Advertising with a Social Dimension," *Journal of Marketing* 60 (October 1996), pp. 71–87.

37. C. B. Bhattacharya, Sankar Sen, and Daniel Korschun, "Using Corporate Social Responsibility to Win the War for Talent," *MIT Sloan Management Review* 49 (January 2008), pp. 37–44; Xueming Luo and C. B. Bhattacharya, "Corporate Social Responsibility, Customer

Satisfaction, and Market Value," *Journal of Marketing* 70 (October 2006), pp. 1–18; Pat Auger, Paul Burke, Timothy Devinney, and Jordan J. Louviere, "What Will Consumers Pay for Social Product Features?" *Journal of Business Ethics* 42 (February 2003), pp. 281–304; Dennis B. Arnett, Steve D. German, and Shelby D. Hunt, "The Identity Salience Model of Relationship Marketing Success," *Journal of Marketing* 67 (April 2003), pp. 89–105; C. B. Bhattacharya and Sankar Sen, "Consumer-Company Identification: A Framework for Understanding Consumers' Relationships with Companies," *Journal of Marketing* 67 (April 2003), pp. 76–88; Sankar Sen and C. B. Bhattacharya, "Does Doing Good Always Lead to Doing Better? Consumer Reactions to Corporate Social Responsibility," *Journal of Marketing Research* 38, no. 2 (May 2001), pp. 225–44.

38. Paul N. Bloom, Steve Hoeffler, Kevin Lane Keller, and Carlos E. Basurto, "How Social-Cause Marketing Affects Consumer Perceptions," *MIT Sloan Management Review* (Winter 2006), pp. 49–55; Carolyn J. Simmons and Karen L. Becker-Olsen, "Achieving Marketing Objectives through Social Sponsorships," *Journal of Marketing* 70 (October 2006), pp. 154–69; Guido Berens, Cees B. M. van Riel, and Gerrit H. van Bruggen, "Corporate Associations and Consumer Product Responses," *Journal of Marketing* 69 (July 2005), pp. 35–48; Donald R. Lichtenstein, Minette E. Drumwright, and Bridgette M. Braig, "The Effect of Social Responsibility on Customer Donations to Corporate-Supported Nonprofits," *Journal of Marketing* 68 (October 2004), pp. 16–32; Stephen Hoeffler and Kevin Lane Keller, "Building Brand Equity through Corporate Societal Marketing," *Journal of Public Policy and Marketing* 21, no. 1 (Spring 2002), pp. 78–89. See also, Special Issue: Corporate Responsibility, *Journal of Brand Management* 10, nos. 4–5 (May 2003).

39. Angela M. Eikenberry, "The Hidden Cost of Cause Marketing," *Stanford Social Innovation Review* (Summer 2009); Aneel Karnani, "The Case against Corporate Social Responsibility," *Wall Street Journal*, August 23, 2010.

40. Mark R. Forehand and Sonya Grier, "When Is Honesty the Best Policy? The Effect of Stated Company Intent on Consumer Skepticism," *Journal of Consumer Psychology* 13, no. 3 (2003), pp. 349–56; Dwane Hal Dean, "Associating the Corporation with a Charitable Event through Sponsorship," *Journal of Advertising* 31, no. 4 (Winter 2002), pp. 77–87.

41. For more on developing and implementing marketing plans, see H. W. Goetsch, *Developing, Implementing, and Managing an Effective Marketing Plan* (Chicago: NTC Business Books, 1993). See also, Thomas V. Bonoma, *The Marketing Edge: Making Strategies Work* (New York: Free Press, 1985). Much of this section is based on Bonoma's work.

42. "Cone to Corporate America: 'Cause Marketing Is Dead (as We Know It),'" *USA Today*, November 4, 2010, www.usatoday.com; Melissa Bell, "Dawn Dishwashing Detergent Saves Wildlife," *Washington Post*, June 17, 2010, www.washingtonpost.com.

43. For other examples, see Paul W. Farris, Neil T. Bendle, Phillip E. Pfeifer, and David J. Reibstein, *Marketing Metrics: 50+ Metrics Every Executive Should Master* (Upper Saddle River, NJ: Wharton School Publishing, 2006); John Davis, *Measuring Marketing: 103 Key Metrics Every Marketer Needs* (Hoboken, NJ: Wiley, 2006).

44. Sam R. Goodman, *Increasing Corporate Profitability* (New York: Ronald Press, 1982), chapter 1. See also, Bernard J. Jaworski, Vlasis Stathakopoulos, and H. Shanker Krishnan, "Control Combinations in Marketing: Conceptual Framework and Empirical Evidence," *Journal of Marketing* 57, no. 1 (January 1993), pp. 57–69.

45. Philip Kotler, William Gregor, and William Rodgers, "The Marketing Audit Comes of Age," *Sloan Management Review* 30, no. 2 (Winter 1989), pp. 49–62; Frederick Reichheld, *The Loyalty Effect* (Boston: Harvard Business School Press, 1996) discusses attrition of the figures.

Glossary

A

adoption   an individual's decision to become a regular user of a product.

advertising   any paid form of nonpersonal presentation and promotion of a product by an identified sponsor.

advertising objective   a specific communications task and achievement level to be accomplished with a specific audience in a specific period of time.

aspirational groups   groups a person hopes to join.

associative network memory model   conceptual representation that views memory as consisting of nodes and interconnecting links, where nodes represent stored information or concepts and links represent strength of association between information or concepts.

attitudes   a person's enduring favorable or unfavorable evaluations, emotional feelings, and action tendencies toward some object or idea.

available market   the set of consumers who have interest, income, and access to a particular offer.

average cost   the cost per unit at a given level of production; it equals total costs divided by production.

B

belief   a descriptive thought that a person holds about something.

brand   a name, term, sign, symbol, or design, or a combination of these, intended to identify the offering of one seller or seller group and differentiate it from competing offers.

brand associations   all brand-related thoughts, feelings, perceptions, images, experiences, beliefs, attitudes, and so on that become linked to the brand node.

brand audit   a consumer-focused series of procedures to assess the health of the brand, uncover its sources of brand equity, and suggest ways to improve and leverage its equity.

brand community   a specialized community of consumers and employees whose identification and activities focus around the brand.

brand contact   any information-bearing experience that a customer or prospect has with the brand, its product category, or its market.

brand dilution   when consumers no longer associate a brand with a specific product or highly similar set of products and start thinking less of the brand.

brand elements   trademarkable devices that identify and differentiate the brand.

brand equity   the added value a brand endows on products and services.

brand extension   using an established brand to launch a new product.

brand knowledge   all the thoughts, feelings, images, experiences, and beliefs associated with the brand.

brand line   all the products (including line and category extensions) sold under a particular brand.

brand mix   the set of all brand lines that a particular seller offers.

brand personality   the specific mix of human traits attributed to a particular brand.

brand portfolio   the set of all brands and brand lines a particular firm offers in a particular category or market segment.

brand promise   the marketer's vision of what the brand must be and do for consumers.

brand valuation   estimating the brand's total financial value.

branded variants   specific brand lines supplied to specific retailers or distribution.

branding   endowing products and services with the power of a brand.

branding strategy   the number and nature of both common and distinctive brand elements applied to the firm's offerings.

brick-and-click   existing companies that have added an online site for information or e-commerce.

business market   all the organizations that acquire goods and services used in the production of other products or services that are sold, rented, or supplied to others.

C

capital items   long-lasting business goods that facilitate developing or managing the finished product.

category extension   using a parent brand to enter a different category from the one it currently serves.

category membership   the products or sets of products with which a brand competes and which function as close substitutes.

cause-related marketing   marketing that links a firm's contributions to a designated cause to customers' engaging directly or indirectly in revenue-producing transactions with the firm.

channel conflict   when one channel member's actions prevent another member from achieving its goal.

channel coordination   when channel members are brought together to advance the goals of the channel.

channel power   the ability to alter channel members' behavior so they take actions they would not have taken otherwise.

co-branding   also called dual branding or brand bundling, combining two or more well-known brands into a joint product or marketing them together in some fashion.

communication adaptation   changing marketing communications programs for each local market.

communication-effect research   determining whether an ad is communicating effectively.

company demand   company's estimated share of market demand at alternative levels of company marketing effort in a given period.

company sales forecast   expected level of company sales based on a chosen marketing plan and an assumed marketing environment.

competitive advantage   a company's ability to perform in one or more ways that competitors cannot or will not match.

competitive frame of reference   defining which other brands a brand competes with and which should be the focus of competitive analysis.

conformance quality   the degree to which all produced units are identical and meet promised specifications.

consumer behavior   the study of how individuals, groups, and organizations select, buy, use, and dispose of goods, services, ideas, or experiences to satisfy needs and wants.

containerization   putting goods in boxes or trailers that are easy to transfer between two transportation modes.

contractual sales force   manufacturers' reps, sales agents, and brokers, who are paid a commission based on sales.

convenience goods   consumer goods that are purchased frequently, immediately, and with minimal effort.

core competency   attribute that is a source of competitive advantage by contributing to perceived customer benefits, has applications in a wide variety of markets, and is difficult for competitors to imitate.

core values   the belief systems that underlie attitudes and behaviors and determine people's long-term choices and desires.

corporate culture   the shared experiences, stories, beliefs, and norms that characterize an organization.

countertrade   when buyers offer items instead of cash as payment for a purchase.

cues   minor stimuli that determine when, where, and how a person responds.

culture   the fundamental determinant of a person's wants and behavior.

customer churn   rate of customer defection.

customer lifetime value (CLV)   the net present value of the stream of future profits expected over the customer's lifetime purchases.

customer-perceived value (CPV)   the difference between the prospective customer's value of all the benefits and all the costs of an offering and the perceived alternatives.

customer relationship management (CRM)   process of managing detailed information about individual customers and all customer touch points to maximize loyalty.

customer-value hierarchy   five product levels that must be addressed by marketers in planning an offering.

customerization   combination of operationally driven mass customization with customized marketing that empowers consumers to design the offering of their choice.

D

data mining   use of statistical and mathematical techniques to extract useful information about individuals, trends, and segments.

data warehouse   collection of data drawn from company contact with customers that marketers can analyze to draw inferences about an individual customer's needs and responses.

database marketing   the process of building, maintaining, and using databases to contact, transact with, and build relationships with customers.

demand chain planning   the process of designing the supply chain based on adopting a target market perspective and working backward.

design   the totality of features that affect how a product looks, feels, and functions to a consumer.

direct (company) sales force   full- or part-time paid employees who work exclusively for the company.

direct marketing   the use of consumer-direct (CD) channels to reach and deliver goods and services to the customer without using marketing middlemen.

direct marketing channel   channel arrangement in which the manufacturer sells directly to final customers; also known as a zero-level channel.

direct-order marketing   marketing in which direct marketers see a measureable response, typically a customer order.

direct product profitability (DPP)   a way of measuring a product's handling costs from the time it reaches the warehouse until a customer buys it in the store.

display ads (or **banner ads**) small, rectangular boxes containing text and perhaps an image that firms pay to place on relevant Web sites.

dissociative groups   groups whose values or behavior an individual rejects.

drive   a strong internal stimulus impelling action.

dual adaptation   adapting both the product and the communications to the local market.

E

e-commerce   using a Web site to transact or facilitate the sale of goods and services online.

environmental threat   challenge posed by an unfavorable trend or development that, in the absence of defensive marketing action, would lead to lower sales or profit.

everyday low pricing (EDLP)   charging a constant low price with little or no price promotions and special sales.

exclusive distribution   channel strategy in which a producer severely limits the number of intermediaries to maintain control over resellers' service level and outputs.

expectancy-value model   consumers evaluate products and services by combining their brand beliefs—the positives and negatives—according to importance.

experience curve   decline in the average cost that occurs with accumulated production experience; also known as the *learning curve*.

F

fad a craze that is unpredictable, of brief duration, and without long-term significance.

family brand *see* master brand.

family of orientation parents and siblings.

family of procreation spouse and children.

features characteristics that supplement a product's basic function.

fixed costs also known as *overhead*, costs that do not vary with production level or sales revenue.

forecasting the art of anticipating what buyers are likely to do under a given set of conditions.

form the product's size, shape, or physical structure.

frequency programs (FPs) programs to reward customers who buy frequently and in substantial amounts.

G

generics unbranded, plainly packaged, less expensive versions of common products.

global firm a firm that operates in more than one country and captures R&D, production, logistical, marketing, and financial advantages in its costs and reputation that are not available to purely domestic competitors.

global industry an industry in which the strategic positions of competitors in major geographic or national markets are fundamentally affected by their overall global positions.

going-rate pricing prices based largely on competitors' prices.

gray market branded products diverted from authorized distribution channels in the country of product origin or across international borders.

H

heuristics rules of thumb in the decision process.

high-low pricing in retailing, charging higher-than-EDLP prices on an everyday basis with frequent promotions that temporarily lower prices.

holistic marketing concept based on the development, design, and implementation of marketing programs, processes, and activities that recognize their breadth and interdependencies.

horizontal marketing system channel arrangement in which two or more unrelated firms put together resources or programs to exploit a marketing opportunity.

hybrid channels the use of two or more marketing channels to reach customer segments; also known as multichannel marketing.

I

industry group of firms offering a product or class of products that are close substitutes for one another.

informational appeal elaborates on product or service attributes or benefits, assuming that consumers will process the communication very logically.

ingredient branding   a special case of co-branding that creates brand equity for materials, components, or parts contained in a branded product.

innovation   any good, service, or idea that someone *perceives* as new, no matter how long its history.

innovation diffusion process   the spread of a new idea from its source of invention or creation to its ultimate users or adopters.

integrated logistics systems (ILS)   materials management, material flow systems, and physical distribution, aided by information technology.

integrated marketing   mixing and matching marketing activities to maximize their individual and collective effects.

integrated marketing channel system   marketing channel in which the strategies and tactics of selling through one channel reflect the strategies and tactics of selling through one or more other channels.

integrated marketing communications (IMC)   a planning process designed to assure that all brand contacts received by a customer or prospect for a product, service, or organization are relevant to that person and consistent over time.

intensive distribution   channel strategy in which producer places its offerings in as many outlets as possible.

internal marketing   element of holistic marketing that involves hiring, training, and motivating able employees who want to serve customers well.

interstitials   advertisements, often with video or animation, which pop up between changes on a Web site.

J

joint venture   a company in which multiple investors share ownership and control.

L

learning   changes in consumer behavior arising from experience.

licensed product   using the brand name licensed from one firm on a product made by another firm.

life-cycle cost   the product's purchase cost plus the discounted cost of maintenance and repair less the discounted salvage value.

life stage   a person's major concern, such as going through a divorce, taking care of an older parent, or deciding to buy a new home.

lifestyle   a person's pattern of living in the world as expressed in activities, interests, and opinions.

line extension   using a parent brand on a new product within a category it currently serves.

line stretching   when a company lengthens its product line beyond the current range.

loyalty   a deeply held commitment to rebuy a market offering in the future despite situational influences and marketing efforts that might cause switching behavior.

M

market   groupings of customers.

market demand   the total volume that would be bought by a defined customer group in a defined geographical area in a defined time period in a defined marketing environment under a defined marketing program.

market forecast   the market demand corresponding to the level of industry marketing expenditure.

market logistics   planning the infrastructure to meet demand, then implementing and controlling the physical flows of materials and final goods from points of origin to points of use, to meet customer requirements at a profit.

market-penetration pricing   pricing strategy where firms set the lowest price, assuming the market is price sensitive, to drive higher sales volume.

market potential   the limit approached by market demand as industry marketing expenditures approach infinity for a given marketing environment.

market share   level of selective demand for a company's product.

market-skimming pricing   pricing strategy where prices start high and slowly drop over time to maximize profits from less price-sensitive customers.

marketer   someone who seeks a response from another party (the prospect).

marketing   identifying and meeting human and social needs; the activity, set of institutions, and processes for creating, communicating, delivering, and exchanging offerings that have value for customers, clients, partners, and society at large.

marketing audit   a comprehensive, systematic, independent, and periodic examination of a company's or business unit's marketing environment, objectives, strategies, and activities.

marketing channel system   the particular set of marketing channels a firm employs.

marketing channels   sets of interdependent organizations participating in the process of making a product or service available for use or consumption; also called trade channels or distribution channels.

marketing communications   means by which firms attempt to inform, persuade, and remind consumers—directly or indirectly—about the products and brands they sell.

marketing communications mix   advertising, sales promotion, events and experiences, public relations and publicity, direct marketing, interactive marketing, word of mouth, and personal selling.

marketing funnel   tool used to identify the percentage of the potential target market at each stage in the decision process.

marketing implementation   the process that turns marketing plans into action assignments and ensures they accomplish the plan's stated objectives.

marketing information system (MIS)   the people, equipment, and procedures to gather, sort, analyze, evaluate, and distribute needed, timely, and accurate information to marketing decision makers.

marketing intelligence system   set of procedures and sources that managers use to obtain everyday information about developments in the marketing environment.

marketing management   the art and science of choosing target markets and getting, keeping, and growing customers through creating, delivering, and communicating superior customer value.

marketing metrics   the set of measures organizations use to quantify, compare, and interpret marketing performance.

marketing network   the company and its supporting stakeholders, with whom it has built mutually profitable business relationships.

marketing opportunity   area of buyer need and interest that a company can profitably satisfy.

marketing plan   the central instrument for directing and coordinating the marketing effort; a written document that summarizes what the firm knows about the marketplace, how it will reach its marketing objectives, and how it will direct and coordinate its marketing.

marketing public relations (MPR)   publicity and other activities that build corporate or product image to facilitate marketing goals.

marketing research   the systematic design, collection, analysis, and reporting of data and findings relevant to a specific marketing situation facing the company.

markup   pricing an item by adding a standard increase to the product's cost.

mass customization   how a company meets each customer's requirements, on a mass basis, by individually designing products, services, programs, and communications.

master (family) brand   a parent brand that is associated with multiple brand extensions.

media selection   finding the most cost-effective media to deliver the desired number and type of exposures to a target audience.

membership groups   groups having a direct influence on consumer behavior.

microsite   a limited area on the Web managed and paid for by an external advertiser/company.

mission statement   statement of what the organization exists to accomplish, which provides employees with a shared sense of purpose, direction, and opportunity.

motive   a need that is aroused to a sufficient level of intensity to drive someone to take action.

multichannel marketing   *see* hybrid channels.

O

opinion leader   person who offers informal advice or information about a specific product or product category.

organizational buying   the decision-making process by which organizations establish the need for purchases and identify, evaluate, and choose among alternative brands and suppliers.

P

packaging   all the activities of designing and producing a product's container.

paid search (or **pay-per-click ads**)   marketers bid on search terms; when a consumer searches for those words using Google, Yahoo!, or Bing, the marketer's ad will appear on the results page, and advertisers pay only if people click on links.

parent brand   an existing brand that gives birth to a brand extension or sub-brand.

partner relationship management (PRM)   forming and managing mutually satisfying, long-term relations with key partners such as suppliers and distributors.

penetrated market   the set of consumers who are buying the company's product.

perception   process by which people select, organize, and interpret information inputs to create a meaningful picture of the world.

performance marketing   part of holistic marketing that involves understanding the financial and nonfinancial returns to business and society from marketing activities and programs.

performance quality   the level at which the product's primary characteristics operate.

personal communications channel   two or more persons communicating face-to-face or person-to-audience through a phone, surface mail, or e-mail.

personal influence   the effect one person has on another's attitude or purchase probability.

personality   distinguishing human psychological traits that lead to relatively consistent and enduring responses to environmental stimuli.

place advertising (also known as **out-of-home advertising**)   a broad category including many creative and unexpected forms to grab consumers' attention.

point of purchase (P-O-P)   the location where a purchase is made, typically thought of in terms of a retail setting.

points-of-difference (PODs)   attributes or benefits that consumers associate with a brand, positively evaluate, and believe they could not find with a competitive brand.

points-of-parity (POPs)   attribute or benefit associations that are not necessarily unique to the brand but may be shared with other brands.

positioning   designing a company's offering and image to occupy a distinctive place in the minds of the target market.

potential market   the set of consumers with a sufficient level of interest in a market offer.

price discrimination   pricing approach in which a firm sells an offering at two or more prices that do not reflect a proportional difference in costs.

principle of congruity   communicators can use their good image to reduce some negative feeling toward a brand but in the process might lose some esteem with the audience.

private label brand   a brand that retailers and wholesalers develop; also called a reseller, store, house, or distributor brand.

product   anything that can be offered to a market to satisfy a want or need.

product adaption   altering the product to meet local conditions or preferences.

product assortment   *see* product mix.

product invention   creating something new.

product line   products within a product class that are closely related because they perform similar functions, are sold to the same customer groups, are marketed through the same channels, or fall within given price ranges.

product mix   also called a *product assortment,* the set of all products and items a particular seller offers for sale.

product-mix pricing   the firm plans a set of prices that maximizes profits on the total product mix.

product system   a group of diverse but related items that function in a compatible manner.

profitable customer　a person, household, or company that over time yields a revenue stream exceeding by an acceptable amount the company's costs for attracting, selling, and serving that customer.

prospect　an individual or group from whom a marketer seeks a response such as a purchase, a vote, or a donation.

psychographics　the science of using psychology and demographics to better understand consumers.

public　any group that has an actual or potential interest in or impact on a company's ability to achieve its objectives.

public relations (PR)　a variety of programs designed to promote or protect a company's image or its individual products.

publicity　the task of securing editorial space—as opposed to paid space—in print and broadcast media to promote something.

pull strategy　channel strategy in which the producer uses communications to persuade consumers to demand the product from intermediaries, inducing the intermediaries to order it.

pure-click　companies that have launched a Web site without any previous existence as a firm.

push strategy　channel strategy in which a producer uses its sales force or other means to induce intermediaries to carry, promote, and sell the product to end users.

Q

quality　the totality of features and characteristics of a product or service that bear on its ability to satisfy stated or implied needs.

R

reference groups　all the groups that have a direct or indirect influence on a customer's attitudes or behavior.

reference price　internal or external price against which a customer compares an observed price.

relationship marketing　building mutually satisfying long-term relationships with key parties to earn and retain their business.

retailer　any business enterprise whose sales volume comes primarily from retailing.

retailing　all the activities in selling goods or services directly to final consumers for personal, nonbusiness use.

role　the activities a person is expected to perform.

S

sales budget　conservative estimate of the expected volume of sales, primarily for making current purchasing, production, and cash flow decisions.

sales promotion　a collection of incentive tools, mostly short term, designed to stimulate quicker or greater purchases of particular products or services by consumers or the trade.

sales quota　sales goal set for a product line, company division, or sales representative.

satisfaction   a person's feelings of pleasure or disappointment that result from comparing a product's perceived performance to expectations.

scenario analysis   developing plausible representations of a firm's possible future using assumptions about forces driving the market and different uncertainties.

selective attention   mental process of screening out some stimuli while noticing others.

selective distribution   channel strategy in which a manufacturer relies on only some of the intermediaries willing to carry a particular product.

service   any act or performance one party can offer to another that is essentially intangible and does not result in the ownership of anything.

shopping goods   goods that consumers compare on the basis of suitability, quality, price, and style.

social classes   homogeneous and enduring divisions in a society, hierarchically ordered and with members who share similar values, interests, and behavior.

specialty goods   consumer goods with unique characteristics or brand identification for which enough buyers are willing to make a special purchasing effort.

status   one's position within a group or society.

straight extension   introducing a product in a foreign market without any change in the product.

strategic business unit (SBU)   a business that can be planned separately from the rest of the company, with its own set of competitors and a manager responsible for strategic planning and profit performance.

strategic marketing plan   plan that lays out the firm's target markets and value proposition, based on an analysis of the best market opportunities.

strategy   firm's game plan for achieving its goals.

sub-brand   combining a new brand with an existing brand.

subcultures   groups with shared values, beliefs, preferences, and behaviors emerging from their special life experiences or circumstances.

supersegment   a set of market segments sharing some exploitable similarity.

supply chain   the partnerships a firm forges with suppliers and distributors to deliver value to customers; also known as a value delivery network.

supply chain management (SCM)   managing the supply chain from procurement of inputs through efficient conversion into finished products and then the movement of products to final destinations.

T

tactical marketing plan   plan that specifies the firm's marketing tactics, including product features, promotion, merchandising, pricing, sales channels, and service.

target costing   determining the cost that must be achieved to sell a new product at the price consumers are willing to pay, given its appeal and competitors' prices.

target market   the part of the qualified available market the company decides to pursue.

target-return pricing   determining the price that will yield the firm's target rate of return on investment.

telemarketing   the use of telephone and call centers to attract prospects, sell to existing customers, and provide service by taking orders and answering questions.

total costs   the sum of the fixed and variable costs for a given level of production.

total customer benefit   the perceived monetary value of the bundle of economic, functional, and psychological benefits customers expect from a market offering.

total customer cost   the perceived monetary value of the bundle of costs customers expect to incur in evaluating, obtaining, using, and disposing of the market offering.

transformational appeal   elaborates on a nonproduct-related benefit or image.

trend   a direction or sequence of events with momentum and durability.

U

unsought goods   goods that the consumer does not know about or normally think of buying.

V

value chain   a tool for identifying ways to create more customer value; nine strategically relevant activities that create value and cost in a specific business.

value delivery network   *see* supply chain.

value delivery system   all the experiences the customer will have in obtaining and using the offering.

value network   a system of partnerships and alliances that a firm creates to source, augment, and deliver its offerings.

value pricing   pricing method in which the firm wins loyal customers by charging a fairly low price for a high-quality offering.

value proposition   set of benefits that a marketer proposes to deliver to satisfy customers' needs.

variable costs   costs that vary directly with the level of production.

vertical marketing system (VMS)   a channel arrangement in which the producer, wholesaler(s), and retailer(s) act as a unified system.

W

warranties   formal statements of expected product performance by the manufacturer, legally enforceable.

wholesaling   all the activities in selling goods or services to those who buy for resale or business use.

Z

zero-level channel   *see* direct marketing channel.

Brand, Company, and Name Index

Subject Index